THE ESCHATOLOGICAL ECONOMY

THE ESCHATOLOGICAL ECONOMY

Time and the Hospitality of God

Douglas H. Knight

WILLIAM B. EERDMANS PUBLISHING COMPANY
GRAND RAPIDS, MICHIGAN / CAMBRIDGE, U.K.

Wm. B. Eerdmans Publishing Co.
255 Jefferson Ave. S.E., Grand Rapids, Michigan 49503 /
P.O. Box 163, Cambridge CB3 9PU U.K.

Printed in the United States of America

11 10 09 08 07 06   7 6 5 4 3 2 1

Library of Congress Cataloging-in-Publication Data

Knight, Douglas H.
The eschatological economy: time and the hospitality of God /
Douglas H. Knight.
p.   cm.
ISBN-10: 0-8028-6315-9   ISBN-13: 978-0-8028-6315-7 (pbk.: alk. paper)
1. Theology, Doctrinal. 2. Church history. 3. Spiritual formation.
4. Time — Religious aspects — Christianity. 5. History —
Religious aspects — Christianity.   I. Title.

BT75.3.K55   2006

230 — dc22

2006004256

www.eerdmans.com

Contents

Preface   viii

Introduction   xiii

1. **Persons**   1

   1.1 Theology   1

   1.2 Persons   5

   1.3 Persons and Time   18

   1.4 God   27

   1.5 The Holy Spirit   30

2. **Paideia**   35

   2.1 Two Analogies for Learning   36

   2.2 The Child as Learner   40

   2.3 Mind as Mode of Embodiment   43

   2.4 The Limits of Representation   46

   2.5 Place   50

   2.6 Time   52

   2.7 Plurality   54

3. **God, His Servant, and Their Work**   61

   3.1 God and His Servant   62

   3.2 Israel as Son   75

   3.3 Israel and Its King   85

   3.4 Who Can Tell the Story of the Son?   88

   3.5 The Work of God   95

   3.6 The Work of the Servant   105

   3.7 Sacrifice and Law   110

4. **The Medium of God's Work**   125

   4.1 Accounting for Cost   125

   4.2 The Indivisibility of God's Time   138

   4.3 Sacrifice: Creation Theology as Action   142

   4.4 The Temple   149

   4.5 Israel Scattered   159

   4.6 Seeing and Being Brought into Being   162

   4.7 Biblical Scholarship on Israel's Cultic Action 168

5. **Mediation and History**   173

   5.1 Paideia   173

   5.2 Enlightenment as Immediacy   181

   5.3 The Collapse of Mediation   188

   5.4 Law and Accommodation   194

   5.5 Inside and Outside   200

   5.6 Metaphysics as Theological Task   204

6. **The Economy of the One God**   211

   6.1 Scripture in the Economy of God   211

   6.2 Immediacy or Formation?   217

   6.3 The Protological Ontology   222

Contents

6.4 Christianity as Discipline   231

6.5 The King and His People   242

6.6 The Two Economies   248

6.7 The Responsibility of Theology   254

Bibliography   259

Index   282

Preface

This is a book of Christian theology. Theology is what the church does when it checks that it is fully expressing and passing on the word it receives from God. This book relates our understanding of time and history to Christian theology, to conform our understanding of ourselves to the theological truth that God is changing us. "Sanctification" is the term the Christian tradition uses for the process of our transformation. In this book I connect the concept of paideia, our formation, with the doctrine of sanctification. It is a very old theme in Christian theology, associated with Irenaeus, that God always intended to come to humankind and stay with them, and that in the course of this coming humankind would grow up — a process delayed, but not halted, by sin and rebellion. This book discusses the ways in which Christian doctrine and biblical studies tackle this issue of the education or formation of humanity, and in particular the role of the people of Israel in this process. It explores the relationship of sacrifice, along with other models of the work of Christ, to sanctification, and it re-examines the connections between Israel, Jesus Christ, time, history, and Scripture, by closely linking them to the Christian doctrine of God.

This book compares the Christian view of who we are with other modern views. It suggests that modern thought, ever ready to take things apart but unable to put them together again, creates intellectual divisions that give us a series of partial, and thus defective, understandings of who we are. In this book I suggest that the trinitarian doctrine of God alters the way we understand secularization and the world of modernity and avoids the tunnel vision that characterizes modern existence. To do this, this book makes some proposals about the relation of theology to the world:

1. Christian thought is political. It contradicts other systems of ideas and creates a real encounter and contest of worldviews. Modernity is a religion, a deeply conservative one. It is contested by Christianity. Only Christianity can consistently point to a future. Modernity and Christianity are both forms of enlightenment, but modernity is the counterfeit version, Christianity the real one.

2. Christian thought is not just about ideas but also about life, practice, and action. It is not only about action but also about the church, the community in which the future of the world, and with it all plurality and diversity, is inaugurated by God.

3. This book gives a new account of human relations that shows that we owe one another all the being we have. God gives us the life and the being that we are to supply to one another. Our failure to provide this being for one another means that we deny others the goods and recognition that God considers due to them, so they suffer a deficiency, for which the theological term is "sin." We make other people sinful, and God will hold their deficiencies against us.

4. This more ontological treatment of the doctrine of sin puts the fall into a properly Christian framework, which determines that we live in the context of God's ambitions for us and of our redemption from sin.

5. This book sets out a new understanding of the work, and the death, of Christ. It shows the cross and atonement, not as a metaphorical description of the human predicament or a kind of mechanism, but as the labor of God.

6. This book offers a Christian teaching that listens to the Scriptures. It suggests that Christian doctrine represents centuries of Christian listening to Scripture and that contemporary theology and biblical scholarship can be in conversation with, and under the discipline of, the whole tradition of Christian reception of Scripture.

7. This book gives an account that unites theology and modern political economy. Our talk about sin, guilt, and morality has been separated from our talk about our material and financial interaction and exchange. This split of religious thought from economic thought means that we cannot see how our own public and economic behavior can have a devastating impact on people beyond our field of view, which isolates us from the consequences of our (economic) actions. Religion has been turned into inoffensive metaphorical talk — about our own inner spiritual or emotional states — that has no impact on the world.

We have divided the theological confession of sin to create two parallel worlds, one in which the language of guilt describes some private state of our own, the other in which the language of credit and debit describes the external world but is not thought to impact on our own inner being. This book attempts to reconnect these two worlds of thought.

None of these proposals is completely new. Everything on offer here comes from the huge resources of the church, in particular the early church. These resources are discounted in modern theology and unknown to parts of the contemporary church. Much contemporary theology, gullible enough to believe that it has discovered issues that really are new, does not imagine that the Christian tradition has the resources to respond and provide answers. Effective theological solutions have been forgotten, but they can also be remembered again. Only the Christian theological tradition can set an issue in the context in which its resolution can emerge.

So, for example, the world is not increasingly secular. It is always secular, by definition, and the church is here for the sake of this world. But it is not that society is secular while Christians are religious, but rather the other way around. All members of this secular society are propelled by unnameable forces and defer to authorities that are the creations of fear and superstition. They are in denial about this and unable to name these forces, and it is precisely this that makes these so effectively their religions. Christianity is a secular movement in that it frees us from submission to such phenomena. The gospel frees us from the gods of this world.

In this book I make some suggestions about how Christianity is to respond to modern and postmodern thought. The church must not take society's claims and description of itself with too much seriousness. When a social or religious movement is described as new, or when society is described as postmodern, the church must point out that these phenomena are the return of some very old patterns. The society that does not cultivate its intellectual traditions, which are the resources of its memory, will always be proclaiming its own novelty and originality. The Christian community is here to remind our society of its intellectual parentage and to express a healthy skepticism of its claim to be self-made. Though the current intellectual environment has little idea of what it is, the Christian gospel is the most exhilarating thing in the marketplace. But, for the sake of the world, the church must always be concerned first about its own obedience to God and concerned with the discipline that keeps it refreshed by God's word and thankful for it.

Colin Gunton introduced me to many of the ideas explored in this book. Over many years of teaching at King's College London, Professor Gunton set the agenda for me, and much of this work has been thought through in conversation with him, or by listening to his colleagues Christoph Schwöbel, Francis Watson, Douglas Farrow, and Alan Torrance. Professor Gunton presided hospitably and incisively over the weekly seminar of the Research Institute in Systematic Theology at King's College London, and he was always professing to learn from his students.

Colin Gunton introduced me to two other thinkers who have taught me much of what you will find in this book. The first of these is John Zizioulas. Professor Zizioulas, a visiting professor at King's, represents the most profound and yet approachable expression of the resources of the early and Eastern church. He is also inconveniently modest and elusive. He gave a number of papers at King's that remain unpublished or inaccessible, in English at least, which partly explains why the Roman Catholic and Protestant worlds have not yet begun seriously to learn from him. Perhaps when more of his work is published it will be easier to see that Zizioulas is at least as significant as the familiar names of early-twentieth-century Continental philosophy to which he is compared, perhaps more so.

Colin Gunton also introduced me to Professor Robert Jenson. Because Jenson is a student of Luther, he is able to avoid the Reformed tendency to dualism. This makes Jenson a good find for theologians in Britain, where Luther's extremely dynamic ontology, erratically derived from a theology of the Word, is not well known. This has allowed Jenson to identify modern ontology as the redundant old ontology in new guise and to cut it out in swathes, in its place putting a more scriptural account of God's dealings with us. Professor Jenson has given me encouragement and warning, interceded for me, and led by example with the deftest scholarship and the driest humor.

I am grateful to all members of the Research Institute seminar at King's for their responses to the many papers they have heard from me, and to many others on other occasions and at other conferences. Many thanks to my students at Birkbeck FCE, Richmond; the South East Institute for Theological Education; and Ealing Benedictine Study and Arts Centre, who listened while I learned how to say things simply.

I am also very grateful to George Ille for conversations on the logic and responsibilities of God-talk, to Dan Bailey for explaining the state of play in German biblical scholarship, and to Jeremy Thomson for asking what sort of church is presupposed in any theological approach. Many friends have either commented on drafts or kept me going with their interest and encouragement; among these are Brian Brock, Chris and Hannah Roberts, Murray Rae, Luke Bretherton, Marion Gray, Mihail Neamțu, and Lincoln Harvey.

To Ann Knight, Silke Diener, and Rebecca Diener Knight I am more grateful than I can say. They could have made me give this book up. But they didn't, so here it is.

Introduction

This book invites you to hear what Christian theology has to say to the contemporary world. Christian theology is the creature of the church, and the church is the creature of God. When the church lives out of the tradition it has received and passes on the good things of that tradition, it has something to say about the world. It speaks theologically when it offers coherent and public talk about God and humankind. The church has a more generous definition of the world than our contemporary world has of itself. Theology has a more sophisticated idea of time than does the surrounding world. It talks about time because this is the way to say that the world is not yet settled and will not be settled until it is established in relationship with God. We raise the subject of time to draw our attention to the way things come and go, and to remind us to be realistic in estimating what we know about them. "Eschatology" is the church's term for this form of self-control.

To show what theology has to say to the world I will compare two communities and their respective ways of being. I will contrast the eschatological economy, to which the church points, with what I shall call the economy of modernity. Modernity is nebulous and not easy to define, but these two communities must nevertheless be compared. The community brought into being by the speech of God must be contrasted with the many speeches and claims of the world, to show that the world and its speech has a place in the speech of God and that it is now being ushered into that place.

The two central chapters of this book are about the Scriptures and the teaching of the Christian community that arises from them. They are followed by chapters that deal first with the way we talk about modernity, and then with how Scripture and modernity relate. I argue that modern discourse fits into scriptural discourse, not the other way around. The Bible contains the world: the world does not absorb the Bible. But more than that, the Scriptures invite the world to grow. I hope to show that Christians must live out of the whole Bible, as much out of the Old Testament as out of the New. To this end I talk at some length about the whole people of God and suggest some of the links that must be made between the people of Israel and the church and its present practices. I give an account of the action of Jesus Christ that depends on a social account of human action, and I suggest that this means that we can avoid religious language and discussions of its justification. I link the work of Jesus Christ to a number of Old Testament discussions and indicate what difference a more coherent account of Christian doctrine might make to some established readings of Scripture. The doctrine will be more coherent because it will be more informed by hope, that Christian attitude to which eschatology refers.

This book offers a reading of the Christian tradition in confrontation with the central trends of political philosophy. It suggests that this conversation and confrontation are required by any properly theological discussion of modernity. Much current theology is content with an anthropology in which humankind is already all it ever will be. This makes it sub-Christian. A distinctively Christian theology will say that the individual is a work in progress, not yet a finished product. The individual does not yet have a single mind or will, so modern anthropology is impatient and premature. A theological anthropology must sustain a sense of struggle, the outcome of which is not yet known. Will humankind appear finally at the end of the story, or will other logics and entities prevail over humanity? Our discussion will include an account of resistance to the gospel that the Christian tradition has variously termed the "bondage of the will," the "hardening of hearts," or the rule of the principalities and powers. What existence this individual mind and will may have is not yet known by the world. It is merely confessed by the church. It offers an account in which human beings grow into their agency, and into a mature mind, and it uses the doctrines of Jesus Christ and the Holy Spirit to do so.

Talk about the one economy of the God who is God for humankind and will in his own time be God with humankind requires two complementary ways of talking about the way things are. We can call these two "economies," one of being and one of time. We always need these two parallel accounts, one describing what there is, and the other describing the changes to what there is. This second economy shows that the world has not always been, and will not always be, the way it is now. The question of what duration it has and whether it can sustain itself must always be put to whatever state of affairs we find. It is the task of the Christian community to question every would-be definitive statement about the world.

I discuss the world of modernity under both terms, "being" and "becoming." The claim of the world of modernity is that it is not threatened by change. It has already arrived and is sure of itself. It presents itself as the two economies of nature and freedom that make up a single economy of being. I will argue that the merging of these two economies is not the implementation of its unity that modernity takes it to be. Rather, these two economies just collapse into one economy of nature that cannot support persons, sociality, or freedom. The ostensibly public world of political speech and encounter is really just a matter of many private wills, none of which is ready to hear any others. Our expression of our will does not derive from public discourse and does not promote our public life. The economy of modernity claims to have been brought together by history but to be no longer subject to change. Individuals do not concede that they are impacted on by other people, because they believe that this admission would threaten their independence. I argue that this economy cannot secure itself against the change imposed on it by God. The Word of God identifies Western being as a failure of action and of relatedness, and thus as a failure of *being*. We may not yet know whether the outcome of our history will be the emergence of humankind. The outcome is unknown other than as theological knowledge of the resurrection and the arrival of one man, Jesus Christ, with God.

The first chapter of this book sets out a theory of persons in constitutive relationship. Neither *things* nor *being* are fundamental. *Persons* are fundamental. I set out two accounts of the person. One of these is natural, in that we understand persons on the analogy with things. The second I shall call doxological. It is in this second account that persons are fundamental, so we cannot understand them as sorts of things. The concept of person prevents the reduction of the person to being accounted for by nature, or by power, or by will.

Being and doing are one and the same thing. The *work* of each creature is the *being* of all other creatures. Their work is not only the *well-being* of all other creatures, but their very *being*. But there is more at issue even than this. It is not only the *being* but the *freedom* of other creatures that is our purpose. The freedom of all creatures is the *task* of all other creatures, and it is sustained only by live relationship with all other creatures. This nexus of relationship that sustains the freedom of each is itself sustained by the ongoing relationship of the Creator with the creation that he has made and now maintains. Our Creator intends not that we merely *are,* but that we *live,* that we become animate and vocal and able to respond to one another. He intends that we participate in one another's formation and do so freely and willingly. An account of humankind must therefore include an account of the place and work into which persons are to grow, and so of the ongoing co-labor of creation. The perfection of creation is dependent on the finished and perfected freedom and personhood of humanity. Human beings do not yet have freedom. Their freedom depends on God's determination not to cease from his work until humanity has grown into that freedom. The freedom of humankind is the task of God, and very subordinately it is the task into which God introduces human beings. Under God, we bring one another into being. This participative ontology is a philosophical breakthrough. Perhaps we should say that it would be a breakthrough, if it was taken up by what now passes for philosophy. Why should contemporary philosophy continue to insist that it can accept only an individualist monist ontology, rather than a pluralist — or better, a triune — one?

The second chapter offers an account of how a holy community comes into being. It sets out on what will at first seem a new tack. Instead of talking directly about holiness, it deals in quite general terms with how we change and grow. The discussion is not in terms of familiar religious language of sanctification but in a new, ostensibly quite secular, vocabulary. This allows us to confess that we are not the sole agent of our own being. We are not self-made. Though to some extent we help *each other* to grow, we do not make *ourselves* grow up. This discussion of our formation shows what resources are available for talking about ourselves when we do not consider ourselves the sole agent of our being. This will allow us to talk about becoming holy in terms of a growth of competence — in the life that God shares with us. The rest of this book depends on what we say in this chapter about our formation and upbringing, which I refer to by the traditional term "paideia."

This account of change is framed in terms of learning. Learning accounts for the relationship between Israel's *elect being* and *holy becoming*. It relates the doctrine of sanctification to training, law, and various other intermediary forms that change through time in response to the requirements of the learning community. It shows that the secular concept of history intends to open a gap between God and his action, to take God's action out of his hands to form a secular history. The people of Israel, however, keep narrative in conversation with law, each disciplining the other, which allows Israel to refuse this foreign secular history along with all such concepts of nature and fate. God fashions for himself a people. This fashioning includes his own commentary on this intrinsically linguistic work, and this commentary he also shares with that people. The Christian community now has that commentary in the form of Scripture. I argue that we need to make explicit the schemas and cosmology of modernity; each schema should be under the control of all the others, so none is allowed to predominate. They must not be collapsed into a simple contrast of interiority and exteriority, or mind and world. Such a contrast has resulted in the predominance of epistemology over issues of performance and formation. We exist in a complex relationship of voluntary and involuntary action that we enforce on others and oblige others to enforce on us, which always puts our particularity and our social life under threat.

The third chapter argues that the doctrine of the Trinity does not allow us to separate God from his work — either from his activity or from its result. This grammar of God's work is not the function of some outside logic, so God is not called to account for his work in terms not of his own making. God's choice of a people is his opening move in his action toward humankind. God chooses a new exemplum to determine what humankind is to be. He supplies this new people with all that they need, so that they do not lack anything, and this people does represent the intentions of God for a new humanity. God is speaker and listener, commander and obeyer, judge and among those judged. He is also the means of this speaking and listening, commanding and obeying, and the language spoken, the medium shared, and the judgment made. The chapter relates the doctrines of creation and reconciliation and anthropology to an account of the worship of Israel as the work that forms a holy people who obediently receive the world from God. For Israel-theology and creation-theology to support each other would involve a recovery of the insights of an earlier theology in which the creature and creation become subordinate actors in their own making.

A trinitarian and Irenaean view of Israel's anthropology puts human beings in touch with the creation of which they are members. Humankind is hosted by God and brought up by him into the practice of God's hospitality. Humanity is made mediator and high-point of this creation. This relationship of humanity to the world is made visible by the act of sacrifice in which human beings are set over creation. This event does not rely on any mechanism but is the outworking of the relationship of God to humankind. The elect and baptized community learns this relationship by being brought up in the conceptuality of *relationship,* and of *missing* relationship, known to the Bible respectively as righteousness and sin. In its political cosmology, Israel understands that it is mandated by God to rule his creation with him. Adam is set over creation as its lord; Israel is Adam-in-waiting. By its action Israel transforms what we do from our estimation of it to God's estimation of it. Israel undoes the stalled rival work of old Adam and rebinds it into the living and lasting creation of God. Israel deconstructs the myth of the single agent in combat with his fate. That the Father and Son share a single action means that the Son is able to face and oppose the world, to copy and imitate it, and so, in gathering it up and replaying it, to transform and redeem the world. A discussion of Old Testament themes of seed, blood, and sonship demonstrates that biology is one proper idiom of God's spiritual generosity toward his people. We see that there is no need to treat the spiritual and material as though they were opposites. Instead, we can say that materiality is derived from the Spirit, and that, properly located and employed by the Spirit, it functions spiritually without being any the less created materiality. It is good to be a creature.

The fourth chapter argues that the creation is the place and medium by which we are made holy. This medium is the Holy Spirit, in whom we are presented to the Son and, in him, are made present to each other. We are being integrated into the person of the Son. As we learn his character and action, we become members of his body. We have a place and a role. The Holy Spirit adopts all creation as the medium within which he gives us the being of the Son. The event of the cross, in which God and humanity meet, is our baptism into this new medium. In it the Spirit acts on us, without trespassing against our integrity as creatures, to produce that transforming switch-work by which the greater freedom-reproducing capability of the Spirit is settled upon the people of the Son. The Holy Spirit supplies the biological and material modalities by which he will establish us as members of the Son and bring us to the Father. The Spirit creates our increased embodiment, not disembodiment. I review a selection of biblical and systematic scholarship in search of a conceptuality in which to say that this nation becomes holy. In conversation with it, I sketch an Adam-theology in which human beings have a task and a place, and, in them, freedom.

The fifth chapter points to the responsibilities of theology and so to the range of audiences and conversations that theology should engage. It asks what is at stake in accounts of secularization. We must decide how to assess the disappearance of theological accounts of mediation, the secularization of the West, and the arrival of modernity. I suggest that these are narratives of the fall, the separation of humankind from God, but that unless they are related to some theological concepts, such as paideia, they are no more than stories. I attempt to arbitrate between accounts of secularization. I examine accounts of the changing ontology and epistemology that made God one being among others and that removed the need for the scriptural and liturgical mediation of theological knowledge and the training of the community that could acquire it. I consider accounts of the seventeenth-century divorce of nature and culture and of body and action, along with the changing concept of religion, the cultivation of interiority, and the modern story of the rationalization and disenchantment of the world. I suggest that theological discourse must include an account of the medium in which the theological account is rendered and that under a number of definitions the public and political world must be that medium. For much of the theological tradition, Aristotle provided the complex conceptuality for this account. From the seventeenth century on, this gave way to a simpler conceptuality that made discussion of humankind as creature nested in nature, or as work in progress, more difficult. Nevertheless, we must provide such a complex account, and there are always resources for doing so.

All intellectual effort is in the service of life. It is therefore about comparing different definitions of life. Since we have to compare ways of life, it is important that we say how different these are. We really are engaged in saying that one way of being human is very considerably better than other ways. This does entail that they can be compared. The best way to compare them is to maximize, not minimize, the differences between them. We can compare life with God to life without God.

In Chapters 5 and 6 I examine a central myth of the modern West. The myth is that the West was once religious but now is secular, and that it is now difficult to talk about God. These assertions must be contradicted. It is not that the world is becoming secular, but that the world is always secular by definition. The world always resists hearing the gospel, but no more so now than before. The gospel encounters and confronts other claims and messages. We should call these other claims "pagan," for we can then see that there is a real contest of ideas and of ways of life, and this makes intellectual debate worthwhile.

Most theological discussion is concerned with the problem of religious language. This is because it has not tackled modern ontology critically enough. Christian theological language is fully able to deconstruct the language moderns regard as secular and use to describe themselves, chiefly the language of modern anthropology and psychology. Only theology that cares for its own conceptual resources can show that this belief in secularity is dramatically mistaken.

The central claim of secularization is that religion is trying to tell us that there are two worlds, and that secularity knows that there is only this world. This is entirely untrue. The case is almost the reverse. Secular modernity is itself two worlds: one of nature, and one of human action. But these two worlds are defined in opposition (as though set for a fight to the death), and so they are never established. These two worlds are defined and created by the world of human action, which consists in dividing one world into two, but then not admitting that it is simultaneously combining these two worlds into one — itself. It understands only that it divides and separates, not that it unites them, as it is itself united. It does not acknowledge that what it divides always merges together again, that it cannot make any separation or distinction stay where it is put. It cannot establish its action. Nothing it holds apart stays apart. Rather, it comes together, and it comes together as to make that very separating creature, the human being. Human beings prefer to keep these not only separate actions, but also separate economies that know nothing of each other. Human beings are in denial, preferring not to acknowledge not only that they divide and create, but that they are divided and created.

We can sum up three of the themes of this book thus:

1. Christian theology is not only about ideas, but also about life, practice, and action. Ideas serve to improve our practice. Christian doctrine is not therefore a merely internal discussion.
2. Christian theology is about the establishment of plurality and com-

munity. This starts with the Christian community, which is the beginning of plurality established on earth. Plurality, which inaugurates church, is the act of God.

3. Christian theology shows that there is a contest between two ways of life. One of these ways of life is witnessed to by Christians and represented by Christian doctrine. The other is that way of life actually lived by our contemporaries. It is only very tenuously represented by any contemporary system of ideas, because our contemporaries do not have any means of their own by which to establish who they are. Nonetheless, they have Christians to point to what they can be.

CHAPTER 1

Persons

1.1. Theology

Theology is a junior partner in a conversation brought into being by God. This conversation creates and sustains a community. By speaking gently to it, God brings the world up to be his creature and a partner in conversation with him. He intends to make the world competent to participate freely in the speech and conversation that brings it into being. The church is the event in which God is heard, and the first community brought into being by this conversation. It is a foretaste of the life and freedom that God intends for the world as a whole. The church engages the world in conversation, to tell it that it is created by God and addressed by him. Theology is the church's work of hearing and following God's word, and of passing on what it has heard. It is the effort by which the word of the church is checked and kept responsible to the word of God. This means that theology has a number of audiences and responsibilities. It must contrast the speech of God with the speech of the world, to show that the world is brought into an obedient and subordinate position under God. It must show that humankind is not yet able to hear the word of God, or to refuse it and dispense with it, for it is God, not humanity, who first hears and receives God.

This first chapter attempts to show that humankind is not yet the finished article that it will be. Human beings are not yet themselves, not yet mature or free. Christian doctrine insists that we consider this possibility that humanity is made for freedom but does not yet have it. It teaches that human beings may become free by growing and being eased into their role as creatures of God. God creates and forms an agency and freedom for human beings that they will exercise with God together, and God also provides the medium within which human beings may come into that agency and that freedom. It really is for us to take. Yet, despite our desire to be free, we also prevent one another from becoming free. We get in one another's way. We are not yet of one mind. We do not have a stable set of desires and purposes, and we are unable to sustain our own agency. There is one single exception to this. A settled human identity and mind does already exist in one person, Jesus Christ, the Son made man. His being is made available to us by the Spirit. He is given to us, not as the object of our knowledge, but as the agent of our formation. He is now at work forming us, making us participants in our own formation; so while we are the objects of his work, we are being made agents too. This process of the arrival of humankind is available only as theological knowledge.

Theology is not just a jousting about ideas. It is a way of talking about life and the world we live in. We need a name for the way we are and for what we say about ourselves. To refer to "the way we are and what we say about ourselves" I will use the term "the economy of modernity." I have chosen "economy" to indicate the whole reach of human being that is defined by our place in and relationship with the world. We are not talking just about contemporary society, or about the state of being human, either as a given of nature or as a problem of self-realization. Humanity is not made more secure when it is made everything. The word "economy" indicates that humanity has a place in an arrangement. We must be demoted a little so that we can find our place in the arrangement that is made for us, but that is also more than we are. The "economy of modernity," however, denies that humanity is set in any such arrangement: it is an arrangement that denies that it is an arrangement. This modern economy in which we find ourselves asserts that God has left the scene, leaving us to create and sustain ourselves, and that we should do this by refusing every arrangement or given. We cannot *take* our place; we must *make* it, and assert it against any claim that it is already there for us. Theological knowledge is able to challenge what the economy of modernity asserts by insisting that we do not make our place; we receive it. Theology sets out to replace the logic of the economy of modernity with a less desperate way of being human.

A theological account will show that the world is addressed, challenged, and transformed by God. From this challenge, the world will receive a new being, and humankind will receive a new work. I will argue that an account of God's action requires an account not only in which God speaks but also in which God is the first hearer of his word and is the means of this speaking and this answering. God intends that we become the second hearer and respondent of his word and that our speech comes to participate in his. God's address to the world transforms it into his new creation and creature. But this speaking and transformation are not without resistance. Another entity attempts to intercept the speech of God, to take it from God and employ it to other ends. An account of the address of God to humanity must include an account of the resistance this address receives, and simultaneously of the overcoming of that resistance.

The economy of modernity intends to make itself the replacement of the word of God, its usurper and opponent. It claims that the word of God has been superseded by the many words of the world. So it claims that, in Western history, theological speech has given way to secular speech. We must assess the truth of this claim. To do so, I will offer an account of the resistance to the gospel, and of the word of God's overcoming of that resistance. The world, in the person of Christ and the community he gathers, gives the answering word that the Father recognizes as his own word coming back to him. This will contrast the modern understanding of being as that which underlies and causes all that is with an eschatology that will show that this modern ontology does not succeed in holding out against the word of God, but is itself transformed and established by the action of this word.

In the course of its talk about God, theology must talk about the world and modernity. It must refer what it says about them to talk about God. Theology must also say something about the reality and time of the world. This is not simply a matter of saying what the world *is*. The world is not a settled thing but many contesting words and counter-words. Theology does not have to accept the world's own claims but can contradict them and tell the world what it is and what it may become. By contrasting the action of God with the action of modernity, we establish that one has a coming reality and the other a fading reality. The second is already made powerless by the first, but it will also be given new being and employment by that coming reality. I will talk about the world as varieties of action, some of which are self-defeating and so represent a failure of action. "Economy" is the term I shall use for a field of action; this will allow us to see that it is not simply the case that we are, and then we do things. We also have to say that various amorphous forms of action, themselves bigger than us, make us who we are. Not only do we make actions but actions also make us.

An account of the oneness of the work of God requires two accounts of his work. One of these will be an account of God's election of a people, and the other of the processes of the training and sanctification of that people — an account of *being,* and an account of *becoming.* The Western philosophical tradition understands modern society to be the function of a single time and movement toward unity. I will suggest that theology can refute this protological claim by showing that the freedom of humankind is not the *presupposition* of its being, but the outcome of its history with God. Humankind *becomes* free. Human beings are brought up into their place and task by the action of God who, by denying reinforcement to options that do not lead to this outcome, draws them into a full and active freedom. God sets out for humanity an agency that human beings will exercise with God together, and God provides the medium in which this may happen. God has chosen a people to be that medium: the people of Israel. Their worship of God points to the freedom God intends for the world and now brings to it.

All talk of what we are and do takes place in the active voice. It implies that we are only ever agents, never the passive objects of the agency of others. Yet we are always the recipients of the generosity of God, so we are passive, and yet in that passivity and reception we may be active and willing. This first passivity by which we receive a place from God is the condition for all our activity and agency. I hope to convince you that an action is always a product of what two people do in the company of a third party. It is therefore not meaningful to talk about the action of an individual as though he or she were alone in the world. We do not have to be individuals, individuating ourselves and making ourselves up out of resources, the extrinsic provenance of which we cannot admit to.

Talk of what is, and of *being,* must be accompanied by talk not only of what *time* this being takes but also of what time it *generates.* It must say what sociality created it and is created by it. We are brought into being by the action of others. Human actions do not create something that is alien to us, but they create the capabilities, character, and practices of which humans consist. Though we may make and shape many things, principally we shape one another.

The work of each creature is to establish the life and freedom of all other creatures. The work of each creature is the result of an active and ongoing relationship of the Creator with his creature. An account of humankind must therefore include an account of the place and work into which human beings are to grow, and thus an account of the co-labor of human creation. This chapter therefore sets out a theory of persons in constitutive relationship. The concept of person prevents the reduction of the person to *being*, to *nature*, or to *substance*. It stops us thinking about persons as though they were things, inert and inanimate, and helps us to think about them as persons, which is what they really will be.

1.2. Persons

We have to find a new way of thinking about being. We have to think of being as *personal*. What is needed is a new and much fuller account of what it is to be personal, and this is what this chapter will try to provide. An ontology is an account of what is — that is, of something called "being." But as we have said, there is not only this stuff curiously called "being." There is also that "stuff" which we call movement, or change, and so of all that has no settled being.

We therefore have two domains. One covers what is motionless, the other all that is in motion — respectively *being* and *becoming*. Can we find a single term to cover them both? I shall use the term "doxological ontology," because this suggests that *being* is the result of *doing*. The environment we live in, for example, is the product of centuries of human building. A doxological ontology is one that recognizes that human culture is entirely a function of what people *do* and *say*. *Being* is a product of *doing*, and doing is a function of how people give and take from one another. A doxological ontology also allows the idea that we are what we make of each other. We receive from other people the accounts of the world they give us. This world is shaped by what persons understand to be true, and so by the consensus (also, *doxa*). Though appearances need interpretation, they do not systematically deceive us and so do not need to be rejected and overcome. Appearances are what really is, and both appearances and being are part of a constant process of give and take. Being *(ousia)* is the sum of appearances *(doxa)*.

The Western ontology of personhood assumes that each of us is already a person. Each of us is a discrete integer, already identifiably separate from all others. But this is only a half-truth. We need two accounts: one in which we are already persons, and the other in which we are not yet persons. We need to be able to say that we are deeply tangled up within one another in a single undifferentiated lump. How can I be differentiated from the rest of the lump of human being? And we must also say that my being comes to me from outside me. It is the work of others, many others. It is not a finite quantity of something already existing, but rather it is the work of many persons, who extend my identity to me in time as they are ready. They own and possess me. Whatever they do, or fail to do, determines the being I have; to some degree my being rises or falls, quite apart from what I do. The whole economy of being is a matter of what is given and taken, and all this exchange means that the being of every one of us is in gentle flux. Our being is not static, and our ontology must be able to reflect this.

Yet Western ontology has divorced being from participation in one another and so from the idea that we host, or share in, one another. It has lost any sense that being is related to action on the one hand and owner-ship, possession, and mutual coinherence on the other. It believes that in-dividuals give and receive nothing in their encounters with their peers; in-dividuals do not suffer either gain of being or loss of being from others. The result of denying ourselves the conceptuality of ontological credit and debt is that we are unable to say that what we *do* changes what we *are*. The Western tradition does not give us the wherewithal to relate our doing to our being, or to explain where our being comes from. It sees a gap between doing and being, and between being active and being passive. This gap has had huge consequences. It does not allow for the fact that we are bringing one another into being or preventing one another from coming into being. And it does not show that we are brought into being, that we suffer the do-ing of others, that we are *done*. We suffer and are passive in our own con-stitution; our being is put upon us. The economy of modernity sees that there are bodies (being as *substance*) and there is action (being as *doing*), but it does not recognize that each determines the other. It keeps them in two separate domains, represented by two quite different metaphysics.

A doxological ontology will not split the world into appearances and reality. It understands that there is just the single reality of a constant bliz-zard of views and surfaces. Things have no being, apart from the world of persons to whom they are given and by whom they are identified and brought into being. A Christian doctrine of creation, however, says that our environment precedes us — that is, that the creation has being given it, and approved for it, by the persons of the Trinity.

6

1.2.1. Persons and Action

We must link who we are to what we do, our being *(ontology)* to our action *(praxeology)*. This is not merely a matter of what we do as individuals but also of what all others do, to us and for us. We do not simply make ourselves. Others make us who we are. What being we have is given by what they render us, by the recognition and esteem they give us, and by the opportunities and resources they let us have.

We need an account of the world as the sum of human action and interaction. The Western philosophical tradition and the modern political tradition have found it difficult to show what action and work are available for the person to do. What do they have to be engaged in? The West puts the individual before the social, the interior world before the exterior. This means that the individual appears to have no stake in others, in the world; and this leaves the individual with no reason to be involved.

In the Christian tradition, however, the work and its reward are sociality, life lived with other persons. In the patristic and Eastern Christian traditions in particular, the doctrine of humankind and its salvation is linked to the doctrines of the creation and redemption of the world. Creation and redemption are parts of a single drama. We are intended to exercise the generosity of God, to host and supply one another as he gives us the means to do so, and so we are to be instrumental in bringing one another into being. We have work to do in giving to others the recognition and resources that God determines for them. This means that we have a stake in the world and work to do in it.

To make sense of this talk of work we have to show that *being* is constituted by the whole economy of action in which we give and receive our identities. We demand of others that they give us something of themselves, and that that something should be an account of themselves, and an account in which we feature. They have to sketch out for us the relationship they have with us. Those who do not acknowledge their fellows, and offer some account of themselves among them, leave themselves without anyone to return their own name to them. The accounts we make of each other, and offer to each other, constitute the whole currency and medium of human interaction.

If being is both the *action* of recognition-giving and the *fabric* that is created by it, it can be damaged by infringement or lack. When praise and reputation are not given, there is a deficit of being, both as fabric and as action. Praise and recognition are due to God as the issuer of this economy, and therefore also to every creaturely member of this economy. What is due to the Creator is also due to his creatures, just because the Creator insists that it is also due to them. Each has to receive his or her specific praise — respectively as creature and as Creator.

In what I have said so far, I have contrasted two ways of considering human being. I have argued that there is no plateau of clear or stable human identity. We are not yet free and mature agents. The finalized, individual self has nowhere been reached. Modern anthropology, of course, believes that there is already such a complete individual, who knows and can make others the object of his knowing. Kant, for instance, supposed that we are already individuals, and so are already able to hear and weigh every claim freely. But this is to insist on a premature unity and uniformity, which prevents the emergence of the human being and anthropology that it describes.

Trinitarian theology must meet this modern anthropology with an account that says that the world must first be released from the compulsion to create this illusory individual. This being must be addressed both as not-yet-one and as not-yet-many. To this end trinitarian theology provides its eschatological account of anthropology.

The influential Greek Orthodox theologian John Zizioulas offers the most sophisticated account of the challenge Christian theology represents to the way in which the Western philosophical tradition understands personhood. Zizioulas does this by showing the impact of theology on the history of the term "being." An analysis of this term can reveal some of the history of the Western tradition's attempt to understand humanity, without the relationship God has with humankind.

Zizioulas distinguishes between the individual and the person.[1] The individual is defined in abstraction from the whole sum of the relationships by which he or she was constituted. As such the individual is a tragic being, even a demonic being. A person, on the other hand, is an intrinsically plural being, who sums up and makes present the whole world of relationship. The identity of a particular person is not to be found somewhere deep inside him or her; there is no self, center, soul, or other form of

---

1. John D. Zizioulas, *Being as Communion: Studies in Personhood and the Church* (London: Darton, Longman & Todd, 1985); Zizioulas, "Human Capacity and Incapacity: A Theological Exploration of Personhood," *Scottish Journal of Theology* 28 (1975).

private existence prior to his or her entry to the world of relationship. The identity of each person is spread across the whole nexus of human personhood. It is not hidden in a single interior place; it is constituted and sustained everywhere and by everyone. A person is not the function of *some* other persons. Then the question would be, Which persons and which community? Rather, each person is the function of all persons. All the persons in the whole history of the world, future as much as past, will be constitutive of the being of each and every person in the world.

Certainly all the fallen creatures of the world together are not sufficient to sustain the being of a single creature. They do not manage to bring even one of their number to perfection. So the logic of this doxological ontology must be eschatological. But this world has no other logic than as the creation of God, and its Creator is free to be present to his creatures in it, one economy with them. The persons of the Trinity must therefore be included among the persons who constitute the world. Father, Son, and Holy Spirit bring into being all other persons. The persons of the Trinity are therefore the full and sufficient condition of human persons; the conditions of personhood for all are met. The whole nexus of humanity contributes to the identity of each one of us. The sum of humanity is not of itself sufficient to do this, but the identity of humanity, and with it the particularity of every one of us, is really given and secured by the Father, Son, and Holy Spirit. Neither humanity as a whole nor individuals can diminish or add to it. God is already society, and "human" society is not — yet — society. Our personhood is the work of the divine persons. Now, in the church, the whole personhood of Adam's race becomes a work we can take part in.

Zizioulas thinks of bodies, and other persons, as events of God's generosity. Aristotle understood that bodies are finite and sustain their own limits. A complex mixture of Aristotle's and the ancient atomist account has come to determine how we see things. We believe that things are just neutrally and inertly there before us, before we set them into relationships. Zizioulas does not believe that we can accept this account, which sees bodies in terms of nature and then starts to think about what relationships we may set them in. Things are intrinsically related in that they are products of the graciousness of God toward us. Our account of the mercy and action of God must be in full effect in our account of what is, and therefore fully determinative of the metaphysic through which we talk about bodies. God gives things their limits and definition. Things do not have or create or sustain their own boundaries. The boundaries are not already there.

9

They are given to us as gifts. God widens our boundaries for us as we are ready, and reduces them as we need closer support. He does this in response to our ability to receive what he gives. Yet modern theology continues to employ an account of bodies that says that we already know what bodies are, and what they can do, quite apart from what God intends. This account employs a concept of nature that declares that, underneath, things are constant, regardless of purposes or relationships, and that persons are one of the products of this nature that underlies all that is.

Aristotle is often regarded as the philosopher of substance. But Aristotle did not make any final and definitive statement about what is. He understood that we ask a series of questions (categories) about any entity, and that each question receives an answer, but that we can always go on asking questions. Even when we have run out of questions there may be something that we have not discovered; a remainder is perhaps left unaccounted for. The etymology of the Greek *hypo-stasis,* and the Latin *substantia,* refer to what remains below the reach of our questions. Aristotle understood that our categories do not account for everything without remainder; his ontology was aporetic, which means that it was prepared to admit that there are still things we do not know, and so we should be properly cautious about the claims we make.[2] But in subsequent centuries, the Platonic and Aristotelian tradition, particularly after Avicenna, produced a cruder and more totalitarian ontology. It considers this notional remainder an actual substrate out of which everything was made. Every entity belongs to one economy, of nature; all "nature" is of one kind — it is "natural." Everything may be known by this one fundamental category. Everything can be an object, something known without reserve. The resulting Western tradition asserts that there is first *being,* and only subsequently *action.* So it understands that there is first world and, secondly and

---

2. Donald MacKinnon, "'Substance' in Christology — A Crossbench View," in *Christ, Faith and History: Cambridge Studies in Christology,* ed. S. W. Sykes and J. P. Clayton (London: Cambridge University Press, 1972), p. 287: "Aristotle alternates between characterising the subject-matter of metaphysics as substance or being qua being. What he sees the metaphysician as concerned with are aspects of the world that are at once totally familiar and everyday, and at the same time highly elusive and even mysterious in the paradoxical character that they immediately disclose to more minute inspection. For this same reason he seems to tend in his own metaphysical practice between the most strenuous abstraction, testing to the utmost the reader's power to follow his argument or to see what he is getting at, and an attention to the ordinary and concrete."

more problematically, relationship with it and knowledge of it. This ontology and epistemology was once represented by Plato. But, something over two centuries ago, it was given a re-launch and is now best represented by Kant. The *separation* of being and doing, and of being and knowing, and the *act* that produces this separation and this dualist cosmology, I shall refer to as the economy of modernity.

Without persons, there is no being. Being is not a substrate that underlies persons or acts as a basis of them. The persons of the Trinity are persons to one another and are fully able to correspond to each other. Their being and doing does not require the supply of any being-stuff, nor is there any remainder of being-stuff behind it.[3] Persons are already entirely plural; particularity and diversity are both safeguarded by the conceptuality of personhood, which does not allow one to be secured at the cost of the other. The fundamental assumption of modern sociological, political, and ethical debate is that the one must always and inevitably assert himself or herself against the many. But we do not have to assume that the particular thing and the universal, the one and the many, are irreconcilable. The concept of persons in constitutive relation allows us to avoid setting the one person in opposition to the many of the community. This opposition of one and many, created by the dualism of being and action, has established the modern definition of humanity and sociality. It has been systematized in modern social science, and it is still assumed by much modern theological anthropology. The conceptuality of persons in constitutive relation, and a doxological ontology, however, do not place oneness first and manyness subsequent to it. They do not place being first and action second, or substance first and diversity second. They make oneness and manyness co-equal and co-fundamental. Trinitarian theology has the conceptual resources to replace this protological ontology of the economy of modernity and replace it by an eschatological ontology that establishes humankind and God as free.[4]

1.2.2. The Human Being as Created Being

God's intention is to come to human beings and be with them. God's coming to humankind was not initiated by the fall, though the fall now dictates

3. Zizioulas, *Being as Communion*, pp. 40-41.
4. Zizioulas, *Being as Communion*, pp. 39-40.

that salvation must be the idiom of this coming. The fall does not make sin constitutive. We talk properly about sin only by going on to say that it is dissolved by salvation. Zizioulas argues that though only sin is possible for bodies determined by death, death also sets the limits to what sin can do.[5] Sin cannot speak a defining word or become terminal. It is contained and sealed off in the damage-limitation exercise of the biological hypostasis, which is the term Zizioulas uses for the world and those bodies, human and other, of which the world consists. Considered on its own terms this body is also tragic.[6] By its bounds this body of ours is made for communion with others and is driven by its desire to meet and be with others. But these very same bounds also deny it communion, because they separate it from other bodies.[7] Sin individualizes being; it isolates and dissolves it. However, this is not a problem for which a new, extrinsic solution has to be sought, for it is already part of a solution. God has, from the first, kept human beings safe within the biological hypostasis of the world, held where they cannot do any serious damage to themselves. God does not have to cross alien ground to reach humankind, nor to recover human beings from some state that they have achieved and sustained for themselves from their own resources. There is no stable human *nature,* nor have we accomplished for ourselves something we could call *fallen nature.* The tragic form taken by our biology is a function not merely of our fallenness but of God's arrangement to nullify and redeem our fallenness. This will be completed when the resurrection turns the biological body into a meta-biological body, the eschatological body of humankind in relationship with God.[8]

Human identity must not be too simply linked to human fallenness. It has too often been linked to an identity humankind is supposed to have achieved by some primal act of disobedience. This was the move that Kant made.[9] But because human identity is not in humanity's own possession, human fallenness will not finally succeed in constituting humankind. Freedom is not the cause of a problem. God intends no less than perfect freedom for humanity, so it is because human beings were not able to exercise the priesthood for which they were made that humankind fell, not be-

---

5. Zizioulas, *Being as Communion,* pp. 50-53, 102.

6. Zizioulas, *Being as Communion,* pp. 51-53.

7. Zizioulas, *Being as Communion,* p. 47.

8. Zizioulas, *Being as Communion,* p. 53.

9. Immanuel Kant, "Speculative Beginning of Human History," in *Perpetual Peace and Other Essays,* ed. T. Humphrey (Indianapolis: Hackett, 1983), p. 51.

cause they demanded freedom in the first place. Human beings must be free.[10] Without humankind to make it free, creation cannot achieve its *telos* and, apart from it, has become so disordered that nothing acquires its proper form and everything can result only in sin.

In the Augustinian theological tradition it has been supposed that there was no death before the arrival of man and woman in creation. According to this tradition, death came as a punishment for Adam's disobedience, and God himself introduced this evil, which he then had to remove through his Son. Zizioulas responds with an account that relies instead on Irenaeus. Things are given their own proper demarcation and boundaries by God; as they have beginnings, they have ends, so mortality is intrinsic to the world. Boundaries, and with them mortality, are necessary to allow the organism to move through stages on its way to freedom and duration. "Nothing was created perfect from the beginning. Everything, including especially the human being, was meant to grow into perfection."[11] Isolated from the *eschaton,* the organism remains stalled in each early form of life. The whole adds up only to mortality, and mortality results in sin. But we may not talk about sin apart from eschatology, for there cannot be a concept of sin apart from the concept of freedom as the end toward which everything is orientated. Sin is not deviation from an original state, but from what *will be.*

The hope of creation is dependent on humanity's hope of absolute freedom.[12] If humankind is not free, the creation cannot reach its own proper order and loses its hope for survival. It is better that Adam retained his claim to absolute freedom, and fell, than that he renounced this claim to freedom, and so lost hope of it. And yet, as it is viewed from what it will be, it is the actual condition of the world on its own terms — sin — that makes it impossible for the creation to raise itself from these boundaries and make itself free.

Right at the beginning of our theological account we have to decide on the order of our two accounts of humankind. We need to make Irenaeus's

10. John D. Zizioulas, "Preserving God's Creation: Three Lectures on Theology and Ecology," *King's Theological Review* 12-13 (1989-90): third lecture, p. 3.

11. John D. Zizioulas, "Towards an Eschatological Ontology," paper given at King's College, London, 1999, p. 6.

12. Zizioulas, "Preserving God's Creation," third lecture, p. 3: "If Adam ought not to exercise an absolute freedom, why did God give him the drive towards it? . . . it was not a question of exceeding the limits of freedom. . . . If man gave up his claim to absolute freedom, the whole creation would automatically lose its hope for survival."

account of the growth of Adam the main story and to tell Augustine's account of the fall of Adam only as its subplot. The subplot must not replace the main story. The story is that God brings humankind into being; it is not that humankind defeats God's intention. As John Behr puts it, "As God is the One who fashions man, and the source of his life, the more man remains in subjection to God, the greater will be his freedom as a living human being."[13] The project of humankind will not be brought to an end by human beings' attempts to turn in on themselves or to separate themselves from God. "Irenaeus is not interested in such interiority. Rather when speaking of growth, Irenaeus, more simply and more realistically, focuses on the fashioning of the handiwork of God into a full human being."[14] According to Irenaeus himself,

> It was first necessary for man to be created;
> and having been created, to increase;
> and having increased, to become an adult;
> and having become an adult, to multiply;
> and having multiplied, to strengthen;
> and having strengthened, to be glorified;
> and having been glorified, to see his Master.[15]

The history of Adam is a double movement that reflects God coming to humanity and humanity brought God-wards by God's calling. One movement leads *toward* the end for which the world was created, and the other leads outward *from* that end. Though the world consists of all movement in all directions, the movement from the eschaton grasps this movement and makes it correspond to itself, to the end. It is the outward movement of the eschaton that makes all other movement, movement toward the eschaton. Movement that does not correspond to this is mere deviation, without telos or being. Evil is not, as Origen and Augustine believed, a deviation from the beginning, but from the end. It is an irrational movement toward things other than the end.[16] The creation is held up by this evil, and

---

13. John Behr, *Asceticism and Anthropology in Irenaeus and Clement* (Oxford: Oxford University Press, 2000), p. 122.

14. Behr, *Asceticism and Anthropology in Irenaeus and Clement*, p. 124.

15. Irenaeus, *Against Heresies* 4.38.3, quoted by Behr, *Asceticism and Anthropology in Irenaeus and Clement*, p. 124.

16. Zizioulas, "Towards an Eschatological Ontology," p. 6.

those processes which should have been ongoing are instead brought to a halt by non-being. But sin *has* no being: it is failure of being. Since the end decides finally about the truth of history, only those events leading to the end will be shown to possess true being, being as such. The historical events of revelation, therefore, are true and real because they lead to the end from which they came into being. Not even the cross has a meaning of its own; it is the resurrection that makes the cross the event it is. Though everything may be said to end in death, only one death, that of Jesus Christ, was taken up by the movement of the end and made to correspond to itself. By this event of encounter with the eschaton, this death has been made the saving death, the death that gathers in death and brings it to nothing. It is the movement from the end that makes the movement to the end. "It is the eschaton that gives being to history."[17]

1.2.3. Priesthood

According to Zizioulas, creation is in a state of mortality because it had a beginning. It awaits the arrival of the being determined not by a beginning but by the end — humankind, the perfecter of creation.

> A personal approach to creation would thus elevate the material to the level of man's existence. The material creation would in this way be liberated from its own limitations and by being placed in the hands of man, it would itself acquire a personal dimension; it would be humanised.[18]

Had Adam acted as priest of creation, within the freedom of the end, rather than the constraint of his origin, he would have overcome the mortality inherent in these beginnings and ends, and so freed all creation for the life of the creature of God. Adam's fall represented his reluctance to overcome the mortality inherent in creation. Being dependent on a creature, who had not yet learned his freedom and grown into it, creation was not liberated from its mortality.

But it is the end that is determinative, not the beginning. The end re-determines the beginning.[19] The beginning is reckoned from him who is at

---

17. Zizioulas, "Towards an Eschatological Ontology," p. 10.

18. Zizioulas, "Preserving God's Creation," third lecture, p. 4.

19. Zizioulas, "Towards an Eschatological Ontology," p. 9: "If we take Irenaeus and Maximus again as our guides, we have to think of history as a movement consisting of two

the end, and who is that end. All beginnings and ends take their orientation from him. By taking the world into his hands and creatively integrating it and referring it to God, the new Adam liberates creation from the failed priesthood of Adam the individual. The future is determined by the Adam who is with God, the creature who is with his Creator. By his resurrection, Jesus Christ is revealed and empowered to the determinative definition of Adam, the head of creation and telos of all biology.

God is free, and he will make his creation share his freedom. As the Father and the Son are free for each other in the Spirit, so they are free to be for this creation and for us. The Father is Father because the Son, who answers him, gives him this name. Since, in the Spirit, the Father is free to be Father to the Son, the creation is not a necessary outcome of their being. Since God is not dependent on his creation, it may really rely on him and receive its freedom from him. Zizioulas has been challenged on the issue of the *monarchia* of the Father and his use of the term *aitia*, usually translated "cause," for the Father. But these terms are essential to an eschatological ontology.[20] *Aitia* is not a synonym for *archē* (source). It would be better translated "agency" so that we can confess the Father as agent, the starter because the finisher. The Father initiates, and the Son takes that initiative as the cue for his own action. The Father's initiative is really the proper beginning because the Son takes it as such. It prompts his corresponding action. The Father receives and approves the action of the Son and recognizes it as the action that proceeded from his beginning. The Father is not cause *by necessity* but as person, freely, because his actions are freely received and returned as God's acts by the Son and the Spirit. Zizioulas refuses to allow that the Father's agency or monarchy *emanates* from him as from a monad or individual, so the monarchy is not being *explained* in terms of some deeper origin or nature.[21] It is freely

---

kinds of directions: one is the direction toward the end for which the world was created; the other is away from this end. Since the end decides finally about the truth of history only those events leading to the end will be shown to possess true being or being tout court. The historical events of revelation, therefore, are true and real only because they lead to the end from which they came into being, not in themselves."

20. For discussions of Zizioulas on the *monarchia* of the Father see Alan J. Torrance, *Persons in Communion: Trinitarian Description and Human Participation* (Edinburgh: T&T Clark, 1996), pp. 288-91; and Thomas G. Weinandy, *The Father's Spirit of Sonship* (Edinburgh: T&T Clark, 1995), pp. 61-64.

21. Zizioulas, "The Father as Cause: A Response to Alan Torrance," paper given at King's College, London, 1998.

exercised by the Father and freely taken by the Son. Similarly, the Son's agency is not his alone; he does not work as an individual. It is the Father's work he is about, and what he does, he does with the Father; and because he is not alone, his agency is valid. This is to say that this agency is both plural, "of the Son" because "of the Father," and that it is the single agency of the One God, thus not divisible. This rules against the further and inappropriate use of cause or agency language. That there is one God is our liberation. It means that necessity is not intrinsic to our createdness. This "monotheism" and "monarchia" are our freedom from the other gods, forces, and guises of necessity.

Zizioulas places considerable emphasis on the community of the church as the work of God. Simply put, God is plurality and community. He has already inaugurated plurality and community on earth, for this is what the church is. Is this to attribute too much to the church? Should we not say that there is real sociality apart from the church? One expression of this concern comes from Alan Torrance. He asks how the "trans-subjectivity" of the church is the foundation and cause of human relationships on what he calls a "wider scale."[22] Of the church and the world, which represents a wider, and which a narrower, space? It is the church which is wider than the world. The world has a vanishing duration, while the church, and the new creation inaugurated in it, has an expanding duration. The church is an eschatological being, not a special case of relationships, the possibility of which is established elsewhere.[23] The church is the visible tip of the not yet visible company of heaven. This company is held together by God, and made visible by him to us on earth. The church understood on this eschatological definition, holds together what would otherwise drift apart. The church sustains the world, which has no unity of its own, and so the church represents that future in which the world will be spacious and free. In raising Jesus Christ, and calling out the church, God has elected the human race. He has made the church to be the body that embodies and guarantees both plurality and unity for the world. As the church is itself the work of the Spirit, it works this priestly task of making the world one, and no part of the world is able to secure itself in

---

22. Torrance, *Persons in Communion*, p. 358.

23. John D. Zizioulas *Eucharist, Bishop, Church: The Unity of the Church in the Divine Eucharist and the Bishop during the First Three Centuries* (Brookline, MA: Holy Cross Orthodox Press, 2001), pp. 117-20.

unfreedom, against this end. The doctrine of creation is an eschatological doctrine that sets out the future of man as the priest of creation, a future in which he is freely with God.

1.3. Persons and Time

It is persons who make persons present to each other. Persons suffer one another. The triune persons of Father, Son, and Holy Spirit create the possibility of all other persons. If we do not obediently, together with God, constitute one another, much of each of us remains missing and never comes to be. We are all equally in debt, and *each other* is precisely what we owe each other. If much of what any person can be is not in fact brought into place by those related to him or her, all parties are stalled. It is the real task of each of us to come up with the whole of the rest of us, a whole that is coincident with the end that God works. Each of us owes all others this future, and it is to this end that we are determined and from which we are measured. The future is not an aspect of time, but time is the future's work-in-progress.

What we owe one another is measured from what God intends that we become. We owe each other, and God, this relationship and this being. Western theology termed this relationship "righteousness." Anselm argued that, even if people could pay God all God was due, they would have no excess. If they once failed to worship God, they would have no means of catching up on the praise owed to him. The lost time could never be made up.[24] The very strong reality he attributes to evil makes Kant believe, like Anselm, that no human being can ever pay his or her own debt of being, much less anyone else's. Relationship cannot be swapped between persons, because it is not transferable. It is impossible to catch up on unpaid relationship, and the debt of being that we do pay is of no avail anyway if it does not come from the good disposition of the individual.[25] But Kant believes that we should really ask whether one person can supply what another person lacks at all. Human beings cannot stand in for one another, so

---

24. Anselm *Cur Deus Homo* Book 1, chapters 12 & 13, Book 2, chapters 19-24.

25. Immanuel Kant, *Religion within the Boundaries of Mere Reason,* trans. and ed. Alan Wood and George di Giovanni (Cambridge: Cambridge University Press, 1998), 6.72: "This original debt . . . cannot be erased by somebody else."

no one can be justified by anyone else. "It can further be asked whether this deduction of the idea of a justification of a human being who is indeed guilty but has passed into a disposition well-pleasing to God has any practical use at all."[26] There is something that does not ring true about the forensic exposition in which God holds his Son to account for our sin.

But behind this doubt, there is an even wider question. Whom can we hold responsible for the juridical idiom of Western ontology? It is not entirely fair for Kant to make Augustine, Anselm, or Luther responsible for it. Kant himself is at least as committed to it for his Stoic program of moral paideia as they are for their account of the gospel of Christ. Ours is the Roman tradition, and the Roman thought-world is expressed in terms of masters and servants, of property, default, and penalty. In this conceptuality, there is always a master who is angry and a servant who is at fault; the servant can never escape the guilt that expresses this unequal relationship. Kant did not identify or refute the one-sided relationship made timeless by this metaphysic or allow his doctrine of guilt to be defined in terms of our failure to bring one another up into the full status of persons in constitutive relationship. He decided that humankind was guilty, and human disposition marred by nature, but insisted that each individual was alone with this problem. There is no rationality for the substitution of one by another, or of sacrifice, and talk of substitution and sacrifice is offensive to the dignity of the individual. Can a more sophisticated and more social ontology help us here?

The West takes a courtroom model for our public action. It is not Christian theology, but the Western ontology, derived from Roman jurisprudence, that understands us in these terms. But the courtroom account is inadequate. It describes our interaction in terms of unspecified guilt, rather than of action and of being. But the Western metaphysics, which understands everything in terms of our being declared in default by a court, does not reveal one important consideration. This court is the court of public opinion in which we are all present. It is we who call each other here to witness the claim we make. But more than that, we also summon one another as the accused, in a case in which we are the defendant, and perhaps also the prosecutor. We build one another up as supporters of our case, and knock one another down as those who have not paid us what we are owed. In this we still act as masters, enraged by the deficient performance of servants. We are enraged because we are threatened, for we as

---

26. Kant, *Religion within the Boundaries of Mere Reason* 6.76.

masters are dependent on our servants for our very being. The courtroom idiom of the West hides from us that it is our very being that we give to, or withhold from, one another. A doxological ontology, of persons in constitutive relation, is the conceptual means of showing that we do really derive our being from others.

The ontology of personhood demands that we give an account of time. But time cannot be examined with the conceptuality we use to discuss substance. Time is to be understood as an economy of action and passion. Within this economy we can ask who suffers the impact of whom, who is timed and measured by whom. Here we must relate the concept of time to the determination of God to be for humanity. God gives being and recognition to us, and as a result we are able to return recognition to him and to give being and recognition to each other. In the same way we can say that God makes time for us. We are in the time he makes for us, not he in the time we concede him. But though we give him no time, he takes our time and is more at home in it than we are. He takes it from us and returns it to us, redeemed. Time does not relate to one, but to two and more, and so to persons. It is the mode and expression of their relationship. The question of time is a question about God's condescension to suffer and bear us, take our weight, be measured and timed by us, and so bring us to him.

According to the idea of progress, we move forward, as though to meet someone. But, as Zizioulas suggests, our movement can be said to be forward only if it corresponds to something other than itself. It is really God who moves toward us. God moves to find us and meet us, and our movement can be described as such only retrospectively, inasmuch as God takes it to correspond to his movement to us. Only in this way can we speak of a unity of direction, and so of a single unified time.

The economy of modernity believes that time steadily increases our distance from past events. The modern invention of "the past" as distance grounds the illusion that we increasingly leave behind the event of Jesus Christ, by necessity, because time passes. And it is now asserted that time also puts distance between ourselves and the church, just as the church once put distance between itself and the people of Israel. Of course, this may not be simply a matter of the passing of time, for it is not simply *by nature* that time passes. We actively disassociate ourselves from the people of Israel, thereby insisting that, while we are present and active in this time of ours, they are no longer present in it or significant to us. We have a growing being and presence, they an almost vanished being and presence.

But there are powerful reasons for resisting such an understanding. Robert Jenson, for instance, insists that Israel is not back there somewhere in the past, but right here: the actual presence of the Jewish people is a vital theological given. The survival of Israel is the evidence of God's faithfulness, and the guarantee of the redefinition of this time as the joint time of Israel and God, into which we are also called and gathered.[27] If we refuse to acknowledge this people as the elect people we cannot make a coherent claim on the concept of time. Then the very idea of historical progress would represent the reduction of the people of Israel, first to a mere idea about election, and then to the turning of this idea against Israel.

But Israel is not being drawn by nature away from us, into the past. Rather, it is we moderns who set out to make Israel of no significance, to put distance between Israel and ourselves until Israel is beyond retrieval. God is offering the mediation of this people to us, but we disdain to receive it. By not receiving this specific mediation that God provides, we are rendering ourselves less and less able to take anything else that is given. Since our whole action has come to deny the being and significance of this people, we are less able to receive or acknowledge the being and otherness of any people. Without the aid God provides, we become more enfeebled and less able to perceive and receive otherness in any form. Our own being dwindles away. The economy that cuts itself off from the generosity of God has a merely fading being.

How can we relate these two discussions, of time and of persons? How can the future affect "the past"?[28] A recursive and eschatological account of human being provides such a linkage. What is present to one is not present to another, so there is no canonical version of the present. Any time or present has only a local presence within a conversation. The divine conversation is eternal: nothing interrupts it. It generates for us a world full of openings for conversation. These openings constitute the time we are given for each other. Our time is then one product of the hospitality of God. Time and eternity are not opposites, so eternity is not timelessness. But Augustine, failing to link time and history to the generosity of God, set

27. Robert W. Jenson, *Systematic Theology* (New York: Oxford University Press, 1999), vol. 2, p. 336: "Thus until the Last Judgement and our resurrection, Christ has *not* yet come in the way that fully consummates Israel's history."

28. In Chapter 2 we will find cognitive science arguing that there is no single version of the present, no single point at which it is settled, but that the present is a matter of contending movements and directions.

time and eternity in opposition.[29] This gave the impression that being in time is an unfortunate state, from which spiritual beings have to be rescued. Pannenberg believes that Kant repeated the mistake, making time a function of the individual subject. But time and plurality are not unfortunate deviations. Time is rather a function of a continuum made up of many agents, themselves hosted by the triune persons. We could call this continuum the eschatological economy, or simply the generosity of God who makes time for us.

We should rethink the dichotomy of presence and appearance formalized by Kant that makes us prisoners of a specious present. Kant saved talk about *being* and about *cause* by locking them into a closed economy of nature, where all is object of pure knowing. I will argue that we hold them apart as different discourses. On the one hand is our material *presence*, as bodies in the presence of other bodies, and on the other is the *action* of these bodies in *presenting* ourselves, as persons in the presence of other persons. By our action we make ourselves presentable, get ourselves noticed, and so win ourselves presence. We sustain a dichotomy of ontology of substance and an ontology of action. The conceptuality of persons-in-constitutive-relation understands that we are what we do. I will argue later that we dress one another in bodily being as surely as we dress ourselves in clothes. The dressing and formation of bodies merely takes place over a longer cycle.

The ontology of social science prefers the conceptuality of center-and-periphery, rather than of social roles, with the result that the person is first individual, and only subsequently social.[30] The whole claim of philosophy of reflection is that thought *re-presents*, that is, that it does not *make* our acts, but merely makes them *again*, gesturing to what is always already there before us. On the basis of representation, everything we do refers only to what already is, and so to an origin, the status of which cannot itself be established. All action of ours is merely mimesis.[31] What is really

29. See Wolfhart Pannenberg, *Metaphysics and the Idea of God* (Edinburgh: T&T Clark, 1990), p. 97; and his *Systematic Theology* (Edinburgh: T&T Clark, 1994), vol. 2, pp. 89-95.

30. An example is provided by the discussion in M. Carrithers, S. Collins, and S. Lukes, *The Category of the Person: Anthropology, Philosophy, History* (Cambridge: Cambridge University Press, 1985). Pannenberg, *Anthropology in Theological Perspective* (Edinburgh: T&T Clark, 1985), pp. 170-79, discusses "antagonism between self and society."

31. Cornelius Castoriades, *The Imaginary Institution of Society* (Cambridge: Polity, 1987), pp. 189-98, protests against this mimetic ontology, which he attributes to Plato, because it does not allow that we can bring anything new into being.

there we cannot change. It is not a matter of presence, but of our *presencing*, bringing into prominence and making conspicuous.[32] Perhaps we should attempt to use "being" as a transitive verb. The being and reputation (not merely *doxa* but *ousia*) of each of us is in the hands of our peers, constituted by what takes place publicly between them, and is only subsidiarily also a function of our own action.

So far I have suggested that being is constituted by the whole economy of action in which we give and receive our identities. Now we must say that appearances add up to create beings. What we come to be is really a matter of the accounts that other people render of us. We demand that others speak and tell us who they are. We want them to spell out for us the relationship they have with us, and that they want with us, and what we have to gain from them. Their accounts either give or withhold our being from us. We must connect the discourses of guilt and debt to the discourse of being by linking the forensic and economic discourses of Western metaphysics to a doxological ontology of persons. We must relate the ontology of personhood and the Western idiom of the courtroom to the question of who provides the medium of all our account-rendering and sustains this medium in the face of the deficiency of these accounts. This economy of account-rendering is not autonomous. We prosper within it to the extent that we are able to say this.

God is our host. He honors us with the hospitality by which we may be with one another and admit to knowing and approving of one another. God provides the wherewithal for us to come together. He has even made himself known to us as our host so that we can be confident in this possibility. Praise and recognition are due to God as the provider of this generosity, and they are also due to every member of the economy of God.[33] Anselm is the chief exponent of the language of the courtroom. "God is the one to whom certain obligations are due: 'to sin is the same thing as

---

32. L. Hemming, "Nihilism," in *Radical Orthodoxy: A New Theology*, ed. John Milbank et al. (London: Routledge, 1999), p. 101, protests that *being* has become substance, instead of a project, *conatus*, and "being present" has entirely taken over "becoming present." He points out that substance cannot be the basis of discursivity.

33. Such a doxological theology appears in D. W. Hardy and D. F. Ford, *Jubilate: Theology in Praise* (London: Darton, Longman & Todd, 1984), p. 157: "If life is the process of self-refinement which occurs in praise, and if the condition for this occurs when the excellent-in-itself is present, it can be said that the praise of God actually constitutes the life which we live."

not to render his due to God.'"[34] It is God to whom these obligations are due; but we must spell out a little further the fact that, because they are due to God the Creator, they are due also to his creatures. This is not because these creatures have a right, but because it is the will of their Creator that these creatures grow up into the estate he intends for them. The courtroom metaphor that dominates the Western tradition makes explicit that there is always a crisis of being, caused by the failure of creatures to pass on to one another all that each of them has received. According to Colin Gunton, "Anselm's argument depends upon a particular conception of justice. He holds that God cannot simply overlook breaches of the universal law."[35] Gunton argues that the "'plausibility structure' supporting Anselm's work is the belief in a divine universal order in which God, man and the creation are to be in harmonious relation."[36] Such breaches are missing person-fabric that God *fore-gives*. God does not forgive by announcing that the past is of no account; rather, God makes up what is missing from it. Penalties cannot be remitted without making all relationships impossible.[37] God does not simply make the past of no account, for merely to erase whatever has happened would be to destroy the continuity of those relationships. Rather, he notices the missing fabric and makes it public. There are judgment and wrath. Those who have withheld being from others are brought to court and charged. The event of justice makes

34. Colin E. Gunton, *The Actuality of Atonement: A Study of Metaphor, Rationality and the Christian Tradition* (Edinburgh: T&T Clark, 1988), p. 89, quoting Anselm, *Cur Deus Homo* 1.9.

35. See Anselm, *Cur Deus Homo* 1.12-15; 2.18.221-93. Gunton, *The Actuality of Atonement*, p. 89: "It is sometimes dismissively observed that Anselm takes his view of legality from the medieval feudal order, and the suggestion is that this is to liken the deity to an arbitrary or oppressive ruler. The fact is, however, that the opposite is the case. It was the duty of the feudal ruler to maintain the order of rights and obligations without which society would collapse." We return to this issue in Chapter 4 (§ 4.4).

36. Gunton, in a review of Steindl, *Genugtuung: Biblisches Versöhnungsdenken — eine Quelle für Anselms Satisfaktionstheorie? Journal of Theological Studies* 43 (1992): 284. See Richard W. Southern, *Saint Anselm: A Portrait in a Landscape* (Cambridge: Cambridge University Press, 1990), p. 226: "God's honour is the complex of service and worship which the whole Creation, animate and inanimate, in Heaven and earth, owes to the Creator, and which preserves everything in its due place . . . another word for the ordering of the universe in its due relationship to God. In withholding his service, a man is guilty of attempting to put himself in the place of the Creator."

37. Colin Gunton, *Theology through the Theologians* (Edinburgh: T&T Clark, 1996), p. 177.

their offense public and they are made to feel the lack that they have caused. He himself supplies what is missing. What was hidden may not remain hidden, so the account and being not given is now given with extra emphasis. His account will restore the account that has been given so that the whole economy of relationship is secured. This embraces Kant's insistence that one cannot substitute for another, and it meets the claim of justice, because the poor are supplied with what has been withheld from them. What God does is evident only within the medium he supplies. We may not say that God gave us his Son, or talk about what goes on in the temple of the God of Israel under the rubric of sacrifice and loss, without also giving an account of the medium shared by God and humankind in which this account is meaningful. We can talk about gain and loss, exchange and transaction only when we are dealing in a common currency. It is precisely the establishment of this medium that is at issue. This common currency must be founded in the doctrine of God. To say that God provides the medium is to confess this world as the economy of his creation. He provides the currency and economy in which persons may meet and find each other, and exchange accounts of each other, and in this account-giving confess God. The action of God opens three and more dimensions to us, but this action must be represented in the two-dimensional terms of exchange. We must talk about the action of God in the terms of a finite economy in which a gain here is a loss there. We must be able to say that the work of God involves cost.

Our own medium is taken away from us. It is replaced — or rather, repositioned — by another, larger, and more adequate medium. The price for which you were redeemed is *the whole currency* and medium in which you related and existed. We believe that each of us is his or her own work, but by the act of God the whole fabric of this false belief is removed. We are paid not in the currency that we ourselves have issued, but by the reception of a new medium. This medium opens a world and new forms of action to us and makes us for the first time compatible with others.

Talk of being refers to an end. The terms "debt" and "credit" denominate the movement to that end, the becoming of that being. But being is the function of an economy not just of talk, but of social intercourse and turn-taking on the widest definition.[38] I have said that theology must

---

38. Some social science, the science of *social* being, has adopted discursivity to describe its turn to performance. Being is account-rendering. The next chapter will show the argu-

identify modern and Kantian anthropology as premature, an anthropology that may represent a person who has as yet no being. Anthropology has become the new ontology. Foucault's dismay at this anthropology is summarized by Quentin Skinner:

> Kant is precisely the one who fell into this anthropological sleep with his Copernican revolution in philosophy which put "man" at the centre of things, and thus condemns the post-Kantian tradition to an unfortunate anthropologism, or idealism, or humanism.[39]

The conceptuality of giving recognition and giving accounts of one another — doxology — will extricate us from an economy in which being means only substance on the one hand and the interior life of the individual on the other. A doxological ontology describes an economy in which men and women are public beings, members of one economy by virtue of what we do and what is done to us. This public or honor economy is the antidote to the turn to interiority. This turn has allowed the West to believe that our real being is somehow not where we are committed to each other in the public square, that the public square represents a threat to our self.[40] But ours is no less an honor economy than was that of the ancients. We may equally denominate our relations with one another in terms of the recognition, respect, and regard in which we hold one another. The concept of honor allows us to avoid this protological ontology. I will argue that two accounts are always required. One says that together we co-constitute the world, that all our acts alter the world and give it its being. The second says that *showing* is all

ment for seeing discursive agents in constitutive relation, and the array of public and interpersonal linguistic and practical acts as the primary reality.

39. Quentin Skinner, *The Return of Grand Theory in the Human Sciences* (Cambridge: Cambridge University Press, 1985), p. 46. In the words of Foucault himself, *The Order of Things: The Archaeology of the Human Sciences* (London: Tavistock, 1970), pp. 341-42: "What is man? This question, as we have seen, runs through thought from the early nineteenth century: this is because it produces surreptitiously and in advance, the confusion of the empirical and transcendental.... We find philosophy falling asleep once more in the hollow of this Fold; this time not the sleep of Dogmatism, but that of Anthropology."

40. Immanuel Kant, *Groundwork of the Metaphysic of Morals*, ed. M. Gregor (Cambridge: Cambridge University Press, 1997), 4.4.32, pp. 40-41, believes that "It was seen that the human being is bound to laws by his duty, but it never occurred to them that he is subject *only to laws given by himself but still universal* and that he is bound only to act in conformity with his own will.... I will call this basic principle the principle of the autonomy of the will in contrast with each other, which I accordingly count as heteronomy" (Kant's emphasis).

that is required to establish the being of what we do. All making present is *re-presentation,* all *ousia* is *doxa,* a showing and showing off until everybody accepts your claim; nevertheless, it is really *being* that results.

This chapter has so far indicated some of the links we may make between being, on the one hand, and action and its public reception and recognition on the other. Subsequent chapters will show what all this relational conceptuality can do for us. Now, however, we must take steps to show that we are not trying merely to exchange one metaphysic for another, but to talk about God.

1.4. God

Talk of persons is theological and eschatological talk. We are preceded by a conversation, the conversation of Father, Son, and Holy Spirit. We must set out some of the logic of that conversation and narrative. The logic does not precede the narration of the gospel, but it corresponds to it. Word and logic are constituted together, so the narrative, and the justification of each account of it, must be kept together. This will allow me to say that a word is really word not when it is spoken but when it is finally heard and an event is created by its hearing.[41] Everything that is, is because it is derived from this divine conversation. The conversation creates an assembly and communion, the church, and then brings into being a world that sustains, and is sustained by, that assembly and communion. There is nothing more basic or irreducible than words, specifically the words spoken by the Son and the Father, who hear and respond to one another, and whose words are therefore acts. We are becoming part of the conversation of the Son and the Father. We will become the words they use. We have no being outside their conversation; when they cease to employ us as the words with which they respond to one another, we are gone.

Unless the Son and the Father utter us, there is no us. But they do utter us, and they hear and receive us from one another. They make us speakers whom the Spirit will animate so that we will learn to utter one another.

---

41. "Logos" means, and requires that we articulate, all of the following: Word, the "second" person of the Trinity, words, speech, an event of speech (an announcement, for example), language, grammar/logic/order, narrative, and hearing and reception (and thus a competent audience).

Each of us is commissioned to speak others into being. Our existence is entirely a matter of what others say in reply to the Son and in gratitude to the Son. They, along with all the rest of the company of heaven and the communion of saints, are the medium made and employed by the Spirit to bring us into being, which they do by bringing us into the assembly of those whom God has made holy.

The three persons of God have distinct works, yet they make one single work. Relations within the Trinity are not just about origins — *begetting, proceeding, sending* — but also about the reception of and response to these actions. That is to say that everything demands an audience, and nothing is what it is until it has been confirmed by the right audience. The constitutive audience is the Father, but at one point in the account we must be the proper audience of the Son, too. The Son does not act alone but is accompanied and driven in all he does by the Spirit. The Spirit distinguishes the Son and the Father from one another. The Spirit not only holds them together but makes them distinct and free in their proper mutual relationship. But the Father, not the Spirit, is finally the perfecter and consummator: the Spirit is this subordinately. A theology of God's word requires a Spirit Christology, and both require an account of the Father as initiator and proper audience.

God comes to us. God is articulate and vocal, generous and forthcoming. His speech is not a front for something beyond speech. The Father speaks. The Son is what the Father says; he is the speech of the Father. This is the first part-statement that we must make about God. It needs three further moments of theo-logic. The next is that the Son hears the Father. The speech of the Father does not disappear into emptiness but finds its hearer. The Son receives the speech of the Father, so it comes to its proper place and is vindicated. In the Son, the Father's word finds its proper audience and home. He is the event of the Father's word's arrival and reception. The third is that the Son does what the Father says; the Son carries out the instruction of the Father. The Son answers the Father — with his act. The Son is the act of obedience that hears and does the Father's word, so that it is not just word but *act,* word-act. The fourth moment is that the Father receives the Son; his is the voice the Father wants to hear and the answer the Father is looking for. Everything the Son says is acceptable to the Father.

The Father sends and the Son receives. The Son sends and the Father receives back. They do this in themselves; it is their joint act of conversation and communion. By one free act within this conversation they bring creation into being. The Father gives the Son the world, and the Son receives it and gives thanks for it. He takes the world and cares for it, and having brought it to completion, he brings the world to the Father. The Father approves the Son's custodial and parental work and receives the world back from him. In this return act of conversation, creation is perfected, which means that it is initiated as a living, conversational being. Their act of conversation makes this an act of institution, reception, and finally presentation to the Father again. The world is the product of these various actions, and the single vindicated act of creation is one item of the conversation of the Son with the Father.

We can also put this the other way around. The Father gives the Son to the world. God presents the world with this gift of himself in the person of the Son. Then, when many ages have passed, the perfected world presents the Son to the Father, by the Spirit. The Son will present the world, in the form of us, to the Father, to receive his inspection and approval. But the Son also continually presents the first installments of the future world, the perfected creation, to the Father. The *future* world is entirely present to the Father in the Son. It is created by that conversation and continuously opened by the Spirit who sustains their conversation. The future and completed world is continually given to the *present* world by the Spirit in the church, which is itself the body of the Son for world. The Spirit stands in for the future act of the world. Where the world is going to be one day established in its own free and joyful activity, there the Spirit is now, representing it and preparing it for this future. The someday competent world will accompany the Spirit; it will take the action the Spirit gives it and, in the company of the Spirit, it will take what is the Spirit's and return it via the Son to the Father. In that joint act of Spirit and world, the world will become living, active, and free.

The Father tells the world about his Son. He tells that particular form of the world chosen for this purpose, the church, about his Son. It is in God's telling the world about his Son that the church is brought into being. The church is brought into being by the Father's joy in his Son and the Son's joy in the world that he brings to the Father. The Son is telling about his Father to those he wants to present to the Father. God is telling us about himself in the third person. This narration of God is not something outside God, but is itself a third person. The story and speech of God is himself the person of God, the Holy Spirit. We are told the story by being drawn into the story and becoming characters in it. God draws and assembles us into his narration, so the story of God's action is both the *story* of our being brought into being within his action and the *event* of our being

29

brought into being within his action. The action of God in telling, hearing, and receiving constitutes the whole economy in which we receive our being. The call and response of Father and Son create a conversation, and this conversation is a work they share between them.

The Holy Spirit is the mediator of the persons of the Trinity. All the movement of the Son to the Father is the work of the Spirit, who calls, sends, trains, and makes him obedient, and who raises him and seats him on the right hand from where he now works. God is both enthroned and at rest, and God is in action for us now, working a creation for us. God has a time that is now perfect and complete. This perfect time now extends to us a time in which we are being worked to perfection and completeness — two times, and two discourses. God is at work because there is work still to be done. The Son is with us by the Spirit, such that we are visible to him, but he is not visible to us. He extends being to us with the purpose that we become able to receive it from him and return it to him. We receive our being from him as we learn to return what he gives and to receive from him again in an economy of action. It is God's intention that humankind should be with him as a free and finished creature; it is God's determination for this end that will bring it about.

1.5. The Holy Spirit

The Holy Spirit is the medium of God for humankind. He makes a real and material place for us and supplies the whole resource of our creaturely life with God. The Father and the Son speak the Spirit. The Spirit is the language they speak. But the Spirit can speak and be many languages, without being less the language of the Son and Father. The Spirit extends their speech to create a new language, which the Father and the Son are content to speak. They speak humanity. Humanity is one of the modes in which they speak divinity to each other. Humanity does not give divinity something that it did not have before; it is not a reduction of, or addition to, their divinity. The Son is the first speaker and the native speaker. He speaks humanity perfectly and is at home in the flesh; and in the flesh of humanity he is perfectly at home with the Father. He is not impeded by or disguised by the flesh, for it is brought into existence by the speaking of the Son and the Father. The human entity and mode of being are spoken by that enfleshing word and utterance. Having spoken us into being, they also speak *through* us: the Son replies to the Father in the flesh. They make us speakers. Then they speak *to* us and so make hearers of us. They speak to us with the intention that we hear and receive one another. They speak to us *one another,* giving us in this speech one another as words and gifts from God. We are to learn to speak to one another and receive one another from them, with thanksgiving.

This humanity the Son receives from the Father, by the Spirit. The Spirit takes from the materiality of the Father and gives it to us, making himself material to us (incarnation) and us to him (creation). The fleshly materiality of Jesus of Nazareth derives from, and is supplied by, the consummated materiality of the Spirit. As yet we speak humanity very badly. It is a language and a life we are scarcely acquainted with, so like any foreigner we mangle this language, not because we are native speakers of some other language but just because we are scarcely able to speak. But our bad performance of flesh does not make flesh problematic for God. The Father and Son speak the language of flesh perfectly; this language is sustained by their use of it, and they will enable us to be at home in it to them.

This account of humanity and materiality has avoided a simple contrast between material and spiritual. The Spirit extends to us some of the materiality of the relation of the Son to the Father. "More spiritual" therefore means more real, more solid, more material, more lasting. Under such a theological definition, "spiritual" and "material" are two terms for the single continuum of the complex act of God. There may be many gradations in this act and continuum, as many degrees of differentiation as are required to move us up, one at a time, one lesson after another, from level to level, from bottom to top, to the full measure of Christ. The Spirit intends to coax us up from the bottom of the gradient to the top, from no materiality or reality, through the very sketchy and provisional reality we have now, on to a full creaturely participation in the being of the Son, who is Reality. We must not decide, therefore, that Christ has *either* a spiritual body *or* a physical body, or attribute some actions to a divine nature and others to a human nature. We must say that Christ is fully present to the Father — fully embodied to him — by the Spirit. The Spirit makes the Son embodied and present to us, so the Son always has a spiritual body and is dressed, escorted, and presented by the Spirit.[42]

---

42. According to Robert W. Jenson, "You Wonder Where the Body Went," in *Essays in the Theology of Culture* (Grand Rapids: Eerdmans, 1995), p. 221: "What bodies really are, is *availabilities* that enable *freedom.*"

But we are not yet mature and substantial enough to receive such a direct embodiment. Since we have as yet so little reality, we have nothing to receive the Son's reality with. Because we are not spiritual — not yet proficient at the life of the Son — this spiritual body in which the Son meets us must have the specific form that we do share. It must be a body in the partial and serial sense in which we are embodied and present to one another.[43] He must dress down for us and be much more diffidently present, under-embodied, or serially embodied. The Son is dressed by the Spirit in a body constituted by all the presences (bodies) of the people of Israel who have looked forward to him. He is present to us as all the faithful of Israel, the body of witnesses that constitute the Old Testament. The Old Testament is the Son dressed down in the form of many bodies, for us.

Yet even that is too much for us. This host is too overwhelming for us to receive. So he is present as this host embodied in a single body of the man from Nazareth. He is present in this way only to a single generation of Israel by the one physical-and-spiritual body of Jesus Christ. Now, because this generation saw the Son and because we have believed their reports, we may also start to receive him. We receive him first in the form of all the physical bodies of those saints who presently surround us in this generation, and through them in the form of his officers, the apostles, and through the apostolic witness of the Scriptures, and all this through baptism in the Spirit. All these witnesses are held together by the Spirit to serve us as the single body of the Son to us.[44] The Spirit wraps them up to make them the whole Christ *(totus Christus)* to us.[45]

A truly theological pneumatology prevents us from setting spiritual and material in opposition. The Spirit is not less material but more mate-

43. The creature is constituted in installments, delivered one after another and each integrated into the previous, to make the whole person, the new Adam. First comes the natural (partial) then the spiritual (whole). "The spiritual did not come first, but the natural, and after that the spiritual" (1 Cor. 15:47).

44. Augustine, *City of God,* Book 17, chapter 4: "Certainly we can apply the name 'anointed' (*christus*) to all who have been anointed with his chrism; and yet it is the whole body, with its head, which is the one Christ." This does not entail that the Son is absorbed into the church. The Spirit has distinguished him from us and gives him his particular body, by which he is one identifiable human at the right hand of God.

45. The parts must be clothed by the whole. "For the perishable must clothe itself with the imperishable and the mortal with immortality" (1 Cor. 15:53). So we have two accounts of one act, in one of which the parts are covered by the whole (= the Head), in the other of which the many parts are integrated to make that whole (= body).

rial, more real, so when the Spirit integrates us into the whole body, the resurrection body, we will be real at last. But, if we do not continually take steps against it, these two concepts always settle back to become opposites. The reigning metaphysic of our society reverts all such theological statements to what it regards as the norm, its default setting.

It is not the case that the Son is available to us in terms of dualism, in just one of these two modes, either spiritual or physical. We must move the discussion out of our naturalistic default ontology and find an alternative ontological paradigm. Language serves as an alternative paradigm, because language is simultaneously one and many, discrete and open; it is both one language and very many utterances. So now we can say that the Son is available to us in the many modes, and many dosages, that he decides are required for us to learn to receive him. He can give himself to us faster or more slowly and gently, adjusting himself to our pace. He wears the body that we can catch hold of.[46] He is present to us in the slower and more considered way that one of us would use in talking to a young child, with those pauses for checking, reinforcement, and reassurance. He can supply us with, and build us up into, that real materiality that he intends for us, which is his and which he intends to share with us.

In the final chapter I will argue that the world is already commandeered and reemployed to bring us to God. We think that the world is closed against God, but in fact God encloses us in this world and uses it to prepare us for closer relationship with him and with one another. The closed world is a function of the action of God, which opens us and our world up to greater and greater freedom of action. God provides the boundaries and structures, and he commandeers the structures and discourses of the world to be this medium to us. He moves back the boundaries as the sanctified community becomes ready for a larger world. Each economy is a local economy of cause, but it is driven by an economy of participation that derives from the faithful continuity of God's action for

---

46. Otherwise we would be, as Gregory Nazianzen puts it in *Fifth Oration on the Holy Spirit* 26, "like men loaded with food beyond their strength and presenting eyes yet too weak to bear even the sun's light, risk[ing] the loss of that which was within the reach of their powers; . . . that by gradual additions . . . the light of the Trinity might shine upon the more illuminated. For this reason it was I think that he gradually came to dwell in the disciples, measuring himself out to them according to their capacity to receive him, at the beginning of the gospel, after the passion, after the ascension, making perfect their powers, being breathed upon them and appearing in fiery tongues."

us. The triune God releases us from all rival powers and from the closed system that we know as the unified economy of Western time. The Trinity is not only a doctrine about God but a rule about how to talk about the God who, in the course of addressing himself and corresponding to himself, addresses the world, defeats his rivals, and gives the world his own speech. It is a rule for talk about ourselves that corresponds to our future as his creatures, as those who can talk about him because they have been not only addressed by him but won by him and taught by him. The doctrine of the Trinity is our means of talking about the One and the Many, and oneness and plurality as such, without putting one before the other. It requires the giving of two forms of account at once: one in terms of being, an eschatological account; and the other in terms of becoming, an account of the work of this eschatological being. It is the grammar that corresponds to what God does and in our time has still to do, a practice that must be learned, and it is the practice of the particular community to which he gives it.

Accounting for newness requires, as we shall see, a concept of plural agency. A trinitarian eschatology is the grammar of plurality. By it, persons — and within the relationships of persons, the world of things — may come into being, so that there is not merely a repetition and representation of what was, but a new thing. We cannot lay out such a grammar of plural agency before us to see it all at once, for it is not the function of our action alone but also the means by which we are acted on and changed from a simpler to a more complex grammar of action. It is not therefore our time that lays out this grammar but rather this grammar of the action of God that lays time out for us. It is plural in that it allows for and opens the freedom of two parties, God and humankind, humankind and God. By the trinitarian conceptuality of eschatology, freedom is described not as an anomalous local breakdown of necessity but as incremental under the rule of God. It is not as if the gods may be willful and free, and humanity unfreely subject to them, or that human beings may work out the period of their tutelage to the powers, slowly freeing themselves and harnessing them. It is that God and humankind may be together free, both free, and that this is the work of God who does something new. There is a process of transformation. We must therefore see what resources we can find for talking about transformations.

34

CHAPTER 2

Paideia

God has chosen to make a people holy. From him this people receives a new form of life. In communion with God, Israel learns and practices the life God gives. What constitutes life with God is in process of settlement by God and Israel together. This work of formation takes place in the course of Israel's worship of God. Knowledge of Israel's relationship with God, or the status of this people's performance of this worship, is not available to the world of the gentiles. The progress of Israel is measured by the time of God, not by the time of the gentiles. Israel is the recapitulation and transformation of the world of the gentiles into the creation and economy of God, where theology must show that the nature of humanity is not yet settled. A fixed and stable human nature that cannot be changed by relationship with God cannot know God. We need an account of how humankind may *become* humankind, by being brought into relationship with God. This requires a conceptuality in which we can say that humankind is *not yet* humankind.

This chapter sets out to show how change takes place. It will link our body, community, mind, and institutions to the process of our formation, a process I will call "paideia." To demonstrate how we must speak of humankind as coming into being, I will sketch a paideutic and dynamic conception of the creaturely being that God intends for us. Being brought up involves teaching and learning. These are social processes directed toward ends, which depend on anticipation. The learner is educated into a new language and a new and larger way of being in the world and with other people. The Scripture of Israel describes the form of the sociality that Israel is being taught, and it provides the supportive framework by which Israel may grow into that sociality.

2.1. Two Analogies for Learning

We have to show how learning takes place in freedom. Such freedom allows the coming into being of a subsidiary and second agency. At the beginning of the process there is one agent; at the end of it there are two or more. The subject of learning will be introduced in this chapter first by analogy. Our aim will be to link action to talk about action, then to link talk and thought, and then to see that these three — thought, talk, and action — are complexly related. None precedes the others.

First, let us imagine an action. Let us imagine a sport, and a sportsman introducing a beginner to the game. Let us say, for example, that you are teaching me to play tennis. It may be that I want to learn tennis only in order to enjoy your company. Perhaps we both know that the point of any sport is conviviality, no higher goal than just spending time together, and that in this way sport is just like life as a whole. For whatever reason, you are prepared to spend time with me. We start a game of tennis. You quickly discover that I need to work on my stroke, then that my whole posture needs attention. Perhaps you see that my whole mental attitude is wrong. But you don't give up playing tennis with me. I am only going to improve by playing. You play with me, and so you play against me. I would be losing badly were it not that you keep making concessions. By reducing your game, not playing at your real level, you allow me to score a point against you. Scoring is also part of the game of tennis, and it must be taught in the course of playing. By scoring, you, the instructor, teach me, the beginner, how to assess my game, so I can recognize that I am winning or losing and that one game has gone better than another. You will also teach me how to assess my stroke, by analyzing which muscles to employ or relax at each point in each stroke. I will learn with your help to become aware of my own action. We will talk through how to name the sensations involved in each movement and, by breaking them into units and working on each, you will help me to discover a better action. You, the teacher, will teach the articulation of each movement in order to give me, the learner, the means to assess and improve my performance. Talk, and thought, serves action. As long as we are playing, you comment on our strokes and on the state of the game. Because you are a good teacher, you will not let your commentary be a monologue but will also allow me to offer my commentary. That way I will not only learn to play, but I will also learn to talk the talk, and I will gain a mind for the game. Tennis is not just a game; it is also a talk and a mind-set. As I get better I acquire the mind of a tennis player.

The point of commentary and articulation is performance of the game. Articulation is not itself the whole game. Our use of our intellects and rationality serves to provide commentary on the action, in the service of better action. We bring our powers of reasoning to the game and develop a local game-related reason. Our use of reason serves the formation of our sociality. The ongoing exertion of playing the game serves this sociality, and of course it also serves to develop the physique required by that game. We get fitter by continuing to play. The game will produce the material wherewithal for the game, represented by the physical body of the player. Tennis will produce a tennis player's physique. It will also produce the clubby and social attitude and the social world in which people relate via this game, its clubs and institutions. It builds up both the interior apparatus and the exterior environment.

Talk about what is wrong with my game serves to improve my performance. It allows me to become aware of my own mistakes, so I develop the skill of identifying mistakes and a feel for the bodily shapes of which the game is comprised. Talk of what is missing or wrong — and talk of *sin* therefore — refers to a teleology. Because my teacher is ambitious for me, he corrects me. It is only inasmuch as someone looks forward to the day when you are a good player, and insists that you should too, that it makes sense to talk about your present performance as not yet good. Talk about the game accompanies the play and is intrinsic to it. Giving an account of what is yet to be learned, an account in terms of lack and fault, is part of the game. The instructor teaches us a new vocabulary and teaches us the conceptuality of winning and losing, in order that we can discover for ourselves how to improve on the movements we make. We have to learn the zero-sum language of winning and losing as the means of growing up into the more complex language and many-dimensional space of the proficient or virtuoso action. Only after a lifetime of experimenting and learning individual cases do we become expert enough to improvise, to create new law and modes of instruction. To anticipate our argument a little, we could refer to these as three-dimensions and then *n*-dimensions, or as closed and open economies. The closed we might call the paideutic or orthopedic economy; the open we could also call the eschatological economy. Then we could say that the closed (orthopedic) economy is created to bring us into the open (eschatological) economy, and that the eschatological economy creates and powers the orthopedic economy to this end.

Instructors offer commentary on the performance of students until the students are ready to provide their own commentary. Performance and commentary inform and improve each other. In the case of the people of Israel, Scripture is commentary on the action of the ritual. Ritual is intended to teach this people the holy action of their God. Ritual is commentary on Scripture and on Israel's current experience; it enlarges Israel's reading of Scripture and redescription of life. Israel is taught self-criticism. The words of the prophets directed against Israel, which include promises of assured condemnation, must be understood as the words of a coach to a team, not intended to be heard by outsiders. Israel is not in any real sense losing, for Israel is not yet good enough to lose against God. Gradually, over time, there does grow an implied integrity of action between Israel and God. Israel makes progress and takes on the character of God, because she spends time in no company other than that of her instructor. Since he is at her side, her failure is not allowed to develop any momentum of its own. Israel's mis-shots are identified as such, repented of, and not allowed to remain constitutive of her performance.

The concepts of deficiency and failure are both termed *sin* in Israel's vocabulary. They have a function only within the process of learning, in which good shots are recognized as such and reinforced, and bad shots are recognized as such and count for nothing. It is her poor use of her body that accounts for her poor performance, and all her poor performance can be traced back to a body not yet mature. Yet it is not the case that Israel must wait until she is perfect before she may begin her proper action. It is relentless reinforcement of the right pattern that makes bad patterns more difficult to repeat, and which finally replaces them. Israel will find it difficult to remember how to play badly, will find it easier to make a good move than a bad one. The specific form of life of Israel does not exist prior to her relationship and interaction ("game") with God. It is not only that God invents the hoops that Israel then has to leap through. Rather, Israel's mind is formed by the set of events and references experienced and articulated by Israel and God together. Israel constitutes with God together the record and rules of their relationship.

The doctrine of creation requires two accounts, in one of which creation is a single finished event, and in the other of which creation and its vindication are a process that continues. In this second account God sustains his creation in the face of the resistance represented by other incompatible goals and creations. A second analogy may help establish the complexity of the link between the doctrines of creation and reconciliation. We need to show that God makes the world new by picking up and reusing what is to hand, without this being any the less entirely his own work. This second analogy is about building a house and a society. Building a house is a relatively unproblematic business. It involves the accurate measurement and assembly of inanimate pieces at right angles to each other. But let us imagine that at the same time it was our task to bring up a group of children, to build both a house and a society. Imagine that this group of children includes a mixture of the very young, the disturbed, and the delinquent. The learning environment for some could be constrained or threatened by the behavior of others, and their learning outcomes may be very different. To build a house in order *to live in it together* would be straightforward. But to build that house together as the *means of bringing up* a gang of delinquent children to adulthood would be more of a challenge. For the children this would be not only the first time building anything, but the first time for any social behavior. Whatever the children built or destroyed in the course of a day, the builder would have to integrate into the construction of a house. The builder must make good a building that does not suffer from the deficiencies of the efforts of children, or even the willful deconstruction caused by disaffected delinquents. It is not that the upbringing and education of the children is an interim goal, and the building of the house an ultimate goal. Neither goal can be subordinated to the other. The house must have the objective reality of a building; it must become the place in which they can live. It must also, however, be the wherewithal by which they grow to be adults and are provided with support that increases and decreases at every stage as appropriate to each learner.

We are always tempted to determine that one thing is more fundamental than another. What comes first — the physical environment that makes the social formation possible, or the social formation that is the whole purpose of the physical environment? Which is most important — the attitudes and mind-set, or the physical and institutional framework? Is the interior and mental prior to the exterior, political, and material? Over the long run, one is not more fundamental than the other. The world (the house) is not more important than the development of humanity (the children), and equally humanity is not more important than the world. We cannot have one without the other. So we cannot have humanity without a world and without all those practices by which people are able to receive and interact constructively with the world they receive.

I will argue in a later chapter that the temple is that model house that prepares Israel for life in the household of God. It is not enough to say that creation is analogous to building a house, and bringing up the children is analogous to the work of reconciliation. Creation is equally about bringing up humankind from childhood to maturity. Neither children nor house is prior: they refer to each and together point away from themselves to God. The doctrines of creation and reconciliation require the doctrine of consummation.

2.2. The Child as Learner

For a second approach to paideia let us consider again the case of bringing up a child. Augustine produced a celebrated account of this process. It has often been said that Augustine understood learning to be a form of passively accepting labels, as it were from the things themselves.[1] He believed infants learn to talk, matching word for thing, in the same way that adults learn a second language, matching a word in the new language to a word in their first language. It has been an influential theory. But it is also wrong.[2] We do not learn the language for a world we already know, a word for each thing. We do not match an item in the world to a label inside our head. We learn packets of relationships, comprised of things, their uses, and the utterances that relate to them. We do not learn language alone, but learn language, body, sociality, and world all at once. We learn all these together from the communities that bring us up.

It is the mother's attribution of intentionality to her child that brings about the learning of the child. It was not the infant Augustine who strained to grasp and name, but his mother who named his inchoate movements as reaching and grasping, and the noises he made as the attempt to pronounce whatever she decided that he was reaching for. She re-

---

1. See Brian Stock, *Augustine the Reader: Meditation, Self-Knowledge and the Ethics of Interpretation* (Cambridge: Harvard University Press, 1996), pp. 23-25.

2. P. M. S. Hacker, *Insight and Illusion: Themes in the Philosophy of Wittgenstein* (Oxford: Clarendon, 1986), pp. 130-31; see also Fergus Kerr, *Theology after Wittgenstein* (London: SPCK, 1997), pp. 38-44.

warded his movements by the stimulus of smile and conversation, which he learned to solicit by producing the behavior she was looking for.[3] He responded to her stimuli. We learn as a result of effort, of anticipation afforded not by us but by someone else who has hopes of us. The infant knows of no object-world for which to reach out, because it is not obvious to a newborn that there are a world, and bodies, and objects. This has to be taught, and it is a social business. Because his mother is a social animal, she interprets his movements proleptically, and so they come to be. World and body and mind all arrive simultaneously with our first language. There is no set of dualities — of body and mind, or world and thought, or world and language about it — that is fundamental. Such dualities are not givens of the world. They are heuristics. We articulate our world by identifying such distinctions because this helps us to learn and grow.

It is not only language that we are learning. We learn to be with each other. We pick up a way of being in our bodies that orients us to other bodies. By a particular idiom of being bodily we become available to each other in the world. It is not merely that we must learn words that we do not know in order to refer to the things that exist in the world. The utterly unformed chaotic movements of the infant body must be ordered into complex arrangements that we can refer to as intentionality and as action. The exercises taught by a sports instructor lay down specific pathways in the body of the learner, to form a new ergonomic grammar. The pathways *are* this body. Were the pathways to be taken away, no body would remain. Moreover, the pathways are also the mind. They are located in the brain (they are what the brain is), but they also stretch out from the brain all over the body. Pathways create both our mind and our body. But, more than that, pathways *are* mind *and* body. Our analogy from sports suggests that physical being is linguistic, and that language is somatic. Bodies are informed by a bodily grammar, and language is an additional idiom of bodily being. We use language to be more efficiently bodily in this or that particular respect. The conventional, and thus language, is always characterized by the analogue, the actual rude movement of bodies. The conven-

3. Augustine, *Confessions* 1.8.13: "By groans and various sounds and various movements of parts of my body I would endeavour to express the intentions of my heart. . . . My grasp made use of memory: when people gave a name to an object and when, following the sound, they moved their body towards that object, I would see and retain the fact that that object received from them this sound . . . their intentionality was evident from the gestures which are, as it were, the natural vocabulary of all races."

tional or linguistic is an emergent feature of the analogue. What is socially constructed is always just a particular idiom of bodily movement. There is no gap between semantics and syntax, or between language and bodies in the world.

So far we have very briefly outlined a way of avoiding a dualism of body and mind. If we can find resources to fill in this outline perhaps we can hope to make some progress beyond the dichotomy of material and spiritual that informs much modern theology and that prevents theology from constructive relation to the world.[4] The argument of this section will form the hermeneutics employed in the discussion of the political and cosmological theology of Israel in which there is no prior gap between language and peoples in the world.

What Augustine attributed to the innate power of his infant mind belonged to the labor of his mother. She formatted the infant into the complex space of the body-and-*habitus* she determined for him. Language is an extrapolation of the prosody of the movement of the bodies of our parents.[5] Our posture and our place in the social world are functions of their verbal correction of our posture and bodily performance. Our body is not merely the envelope of flesh, but the habits, regularities, and institutions in which we are present with others. Persons are available to each other only within the set of rules. They learn the rules, and so they learn the relationships. Over the longer term the relationships and the rules evolve. Consequent on the relationships, we learn rules by which to abstract rules from relationships and use them to build new relationships. We use the idiosyncratic way in which we are in our own body, and in our nearest relationships, as the foundation for learning the reductive, and therefore shareable, symbol systems and rules of behavior that make us members of groups and by which we interact with our environment. Because we learned to be precisely ourselves, we could increasingly easily learn to adopt the sketchier but also more uniform "selves" of these institutions.[6] The world is

4. In Chapter 5 I will argue that theology must also employ and respond to a non-dualist metaphysic that does not contrast body and mind, material and spiritual.

5. This is the argument of Terence Deacon, *The Symbolic Species: The Co-evolution of Language and the Human Brain* (Harmondsworth: Penguin, 1997), p. 364; and Horst Hendriks-Jansen, *Catching Ourselves in the Act: Situated Activity, Interactive Emergence, Evolution and Human Thought* (Cambridge: MIT, 1996), p. 289.

6. It is others who make us available to themselves. We are able to inform their performance and co-determine our availability. The multiple drafts theory of Daniel C. Dennett,

"bodies" of behavior that exist in shifting perichoretic hierarchies and ethologies. It is others who clothe and dress us in our bodies. We owe our mind, and our way of being in the world, in large part to them. We receive our location within these large and shifting sets of ways of being human.

Introducing these points here by analogies from sports and child development has allowed them to be made without interruption. They are crucial to the argument against the autonomy of reason and the mind. They will help us discover that there is no necessary separation of mind from bodiliness, sociality, and the extended "body" of a tradition. Next we must establish them again in conversation with the literature of cognitive science, where the connections between play, iteration, emulation, and freedom will be made more explicit. We must provide a third term so the distinctions of body and *habitus,* letter and spirit, presence and absence do not become first dichotomies and then separate economies. This will prepare us to understand that one task of theology is to confront our dualizing of mind and world.

2.3. Mind as Mode of Embodiment

Language is an idiom of animal behavior. The elements of language that are most easily taken up by infant language-learners are the elements that become its most stable features. These evolve from being items of vocabulary to elements of grammar and then the categories in which we think. Each element of a language competes to secure its place in our linguistic stock by making itself indispensable to our communicating, by allowing us to do so with less effort.[7] Speech is the more efficient way of moving your own and other bodies, and writing is a further way of economizing the effort of embodiment. This much is familiar to popular cognitive science. It attributes language to agency, because it understands language to be the product of previous generations of agents and understands that agents are always also the patients and products of agency that is not their own.

The world is to a large degree already shaped for us. Julius Kovesi ar-

---

Consciousness Explained (Harmondsworth: Penguin, 1991), pp. 101-37, suggests that our "self" is a moment of mediation between competing sets of others, and that our present is a provisional version made from many competing versions of time, each intending to make itself definitive by referring its claim to an origin. I will call this the protological economy.

7. Deacon, *The Symbolic Species,* pp. 125-26, 302.

gues that in this sense there is no important distinction to be made between, say, a piece of furniture and any other much more obviously intentional event, like an act of murder. We do not need to say that murder is wrong, because wrongness is part of the concept. It is called murder for this reason. The "sittingdownableness" of a chair is intrinsic to the concept. If it is called a chair, it is because it conforms to a convention of what constitutes "sittingdownableness." The chair is an article of sculptured intention.[8] The world is full of facts that are already structured and laden with significance and value. In part at least this is the result of human action. Though these facts do not constitute all facts of the world, they do co-determine the world.

Herbert McCabe expands on Kovesi's argument.[9] The animal vitalizes and endows its world with significance. The world is the extension and clothing of the animal's body. The simple moral certainties of the pre-human animal world, the clear inhibitions, the fixed social structures of the animal have broken down, and the human animal is faced with a much more complex world. Everything human beings share with other animals is transfigured by being that part of animality that issues in language.[10] The linguistic animal creates its own modes of response to the environment, of constituting a world, so it is not the prisoner of its environment. The signal codes of animals are not something distinct from the rest of their bodily behavior. It is simply that communication by bodily behavior reaches a new intensity in human beings when it becomes language. Language is the free structuring of structure that is already there. McCabe ar-

---

8. Julius Kovesi, *Moral Notions* (London: Routledge & Kegan Paul, 1967). Burrell, *Aquinas: God and Action* (London: Routledge & Kegan Paul, 1979), p. 128, asks: "How can we conceive actions for what they are: the acts of persons? . . . In Aquinas's analysis it is not any decision that makes this the act of a person, but it is by a much more prosaic process whereby acts accumulate into stable principles of action . . . principles generically called habitus (or dispositions) and specifically named virtues. . . . Aquinas identifies a feedback process whereby actions not only accomplish the deed intended, but also develop a facility in the agent for acting likewise in the future."

9. Herbert McCabe, *Law, Love and Language* (London: Sheed & Ward, 1979), pp. 71-91. See also Wolfhart Pannenberg, *Anthropology in Theological Perspective* (Edinburgh: T&T Clark, 1985), pp. 27-79, who reviews the literature that attempts to identify what is specifically human and relate it to the *imago Dei* and the vitalist tradition represented by Herder; this is discussed also by John H. Zammito, *The Genesis of Kant's Critique of Judgement* (Chicago: University of Chicago Press, 1992), pp. 181-82, 198-206.

10. McCabe, *Law, Love and Language*, pp. 68-78.

gues that the relation of action and ethical judgment is a question of modalities, and therefore an aesthetic question. Kovesi and McCabe have given us ways to see the interaction between us and our environment, between our freedom and the givenness of the world. They have done so by not understanding us simply as minds, and by not understanding minds as unchanging and timeless, prior to any events in the world. They have pointed to the regularities of our behavior and have used "mind" to refer to the unity of these. They have introduced us to a more Aristotelian notion of human being.[11]

Aristotle's account has another champion in Martha Nussbaum. She is impressed by Aristotle's conceptuality of animal being because it is able to deal with the change and constancy of our behavior. Aristotle used the concept of impulse *(orexis)* to describe all the lunging and seizing of which animal life is made up.[12]

> The intention of *orexis* accomplishes several purposes directly. First it makes us focus on the intentionality of animal movement: both its object-directedness and its responsiveness, not to the world *simpliciter,* but to the animal's own view of it. Second it demystifies rational action by asking us to see it as similar to other animal motions.[13]

Animals are complexes of movement and of desires and appetites that combine to create complex self-motivating units of motives and emotion. *Orexis* is usually translated "appetite" or "desire," but Aristotle has more in mind than this. Animals are animate because they have *anima, viva vis,* propulsive force. Each is comprised not only of a drive, but a drive in a specific direction with a determinate effect. It is an algorithm that does something specific. It impacts on an environment, itself composed of other thrusts or algorithms, combining with them or catalyzing them. "Algorithm" translates what in the seventeenth century were called (animal) spirits.[14] Aristotle offers accounts of animal motion in terms both of appe-

---

11. We will return to this Aristotelian notion of the virtuosity of public human being in Chapter 6.

12. Martha C. Nussbaum, *The Fragility of Goodness* (Cambridge: Cambridge University Press, 1986), pp. 265, 273.

13. Nussbaum, *The Fragility of Goodness,* p. 276.

14. See John Sutton, *Philosophy and Memory Traces: Descartes to Connectionism* (Cambridge: Cambridge University Press, 1998).

tite and intention and of muscles and sinews, keeping together what animals are accustomed to do with what they therefore can do. Over the long term the one co-determines the other, so *doing* determines *being*, behavior determines species.[15] We do not therefore have a world composed simply of bodies and forces, of vehicles and extrinsic movement that temporarily animates them. Aristotle showed that rational and intellective action is similar to other sorts of animal motion. It is responsiveness not to the world as such, but to the animal's own view of it, the species-specific world of the animal. Kovesi, McCabe, and Nussbaum suggest that language is structure, continuous with the structure of both the moral and animal and therefore "natural" world, and this structure opens a particular local world. "Meaning" is a moving and shifting within the whole space of humankind's intrinsic animality and the process of its redefinition.[16] With language humankind is not doing anything non-animal, but more reflexively animal. Animality consists in taking advantage of existing complexes of action, navigating (and redefining) pathways, powered by physical consumption of the resources of its environment. As every animal looks for a less effortful way to be itself, we also compete to do what others do, in a single economy of emulation and competition, and find better ways of doing it.

2.4. The Limits of Representation

I have said that an account of persons requires an account of the world as the place of persons. A philosophy of representation, which is what the dominant intellectual tradition amounts to, will assume a world that does not change and therefore is not changed by our relationship to it. We need to find the means to show that the world is not changeless, that its changing is to some degree determined by our action, and that includes our ac-

15. Action results in the development of skills and faculties; or, in Dennett's terms, the software becomes the hardware over the longer term. There is a dialectic between action and character, and our accounting for either must be an accounting for both, an accounting in two periodicies.

16. Elaine Scarry, *The Body in Pain: The Making and Unmaking of the World* (Oxford: Oxford University Press, 1985), p. 253: "Thus the hand is not only the organ of labour, it is the product of labour. The hand is also an artefact, gradually altered by its own activity of altering the world."

tion of knowing this world. The philosophy of representation conceives of our knowledge as solely a reflection of what is out there. It has an input-output model that assumes the priority of mind (inside) over world (outside).[17] The dominant philosophical tradition has relied on the conceptuality of inputs and outputs and the internal representations between them.[18] It has assumed that an explanation of the underlying mechanisms of behavior must take a Cartesian view of "inside" and "outside." Rom Harré, however, argues that a theory that understands everything as turn-taking, conversation, and discursivity removes the need for a concept of mind that opposes a mental, inside world to a material, outside world. He argues that we should study discourse, actions, interpersonal networks, and historical developments. These are linked by norms and purposes, not by mechanisms.[19] We cannot explain intentional acts in terms of nature and causality. Human beings are simultaneously involved in two modalities: the purposeful and expressive modality of performative acts, and the causal modality of their natural environment.[20] Cognition is conversational in character, so mental states and processes are not the products of some mind-stuff, nor the properties of individual brains. Our actions are what we say they are only because our group of language users decides that they fit relevant norms and conventions. We cannot say what actions are without there being a normative understanding of what they are supposed to be. Cognition is not a matter of computation but of social action that aims at agreement.

---

17. The philosophy of representation is attacked by Richard Rorty in *Philosophy and the Mirror of Nature* (Princeton: Princeton University Press, 1979), pp. 7-10, and by Antonio R. Damasio in *Descartes's Error: Emotion, Reason and the Human Brain* (London: Macmillan, 1996), pp. 243-51.

18. The input-output model is not redundant. I will suggest that we need both a discourse of inside and a discourse of outside, and then a number of other schemas altogether.

19. Rom Harré, "Berkeleyan Arguments," in *The Future of the Cognitive Revolution*, ed. David M. Johnson and Christina E. Erneling (New York: Oxford University Press, 1997), pp. 36-50. In her "Afterword" to *The Future of the Cognitive Revolution* (p. 377) Erneling suggests that once Descartes, Locke, and Hume had made mind into a separate area of study, it was easy for Kant to separate mind from epistemology, making psychology a separate field of study from philosophy, with the pure rules of understanding and rational structures on one hand, and humans' bodies and psychological functions that can be studied empirically on the other.

20. See Stanley J. Tambiah, *Culture, Thought and Social Action: An Anthropological Perspective* (Cambridge: Harvard University Press, 1985), p. 2.

Cognitive science is founded on hierarchies of interpersonal relational structures. Their units are acts. A hierarchy of personal skills supports these relational structures.[21] Meanings are immanent in networks, and mental models are immanent in hierarchies of personal skills. The primary cognitive reality is therefore the array of public and interpersonal linguistic and practical acts. Our job is to describe these arrays of nested acts and the hierarchies of skills by which persons perform acts and tasks.[22] Though people have to learn the majority of these skills, this is not behaviorism. Skill is a normative concept, which requires a semi-permanent state of the body of the skilled person and some meta-personal system of norms. Skills are located in persons, not in their brains.

We learn within the body of a tradition of knowledge. This insight has often been associated with Michael Polanyi.[23] The research project of pragmatics is built on it. Mark Johnson has argued for the conceptuality of body schemas, or orientation schemas, to replace the too simple modern account of the relationship of the subject to the world the subject knows. There is no direct transition from light into our eyes to the view we receive. There is no "depiction" or immediacy. Imagination orders mental representations into unified, coherent, meaningful wholes.[24] We understand our progress by mapping states onto physical locations. Prepositions such as "in," "out," "near," and "under" have meaning only because we have an embodied notion of containment.

> From the beginning we experience constant physical containment in our surroundings (those things that envelop us). We move in and out of rooms, clothes, vehicles and numerous kinds of bounded spaces. We manipulate objects, placing them in containers (cups, boxes, cans, bags,

21. See Harré, "Berkeleyan Arguments," p. 337, and Hendriks-Jansen, *Catching Ourselves in the Act,* p. 319, for a similar argument.

22. Harré, "Berkeleyan Arguments," argues that since "discursive acts do not cause each other, a hidden realm of linguistic acts cannot be supposed to cause the elements that appear in the overt world of discursive acts" (p. 347). "Mental models cannot exist as mental entities behind or transcendent to the cognitive and material practices to which they are relevant, together with the open sets of rules, conventions and customs that define the necessary skills" (p. 350).

23. Michael Polanyi, *Personal Knowledge: Towards a Post-critical Philosophy* (London: Routledge and Kegan Paul, 1958), pp. 53-56.

24. Mark Johnson, *The Body in the Mind: The Bodily Basis of Meaning, Imagination, and Reason* (Chicago: University of Chicago Press, 1987), pp. 101-38.

etc). In each of these cases there are repeatable spatial and temporal organizations. In other words, there are typical schemata for physical containment.[25]

Johnson argues that metaphorical projections are not arbitrary. It is not the case that anything can be mapped onto anything else. Words, images, and spaces belong to codes that are learned. The concept of affordance has been used by cognitive science to describe this tradition-embodied teleological aspect of perception.[26] J. J. Gibson argued that opportunities (affordances), not things, are our first objects of perception.[27] Our behavior is best understood in terms of our alertness to opportunities for action. What we see are openings and advantages. Animals move in response to the affordances of their species-world. Different animals show different degrees of complexity in their appreciation of multiplicities of affordances available in particular parts of the surrounding environment. Worlds (in the plural) of objects and events are carved out of the world (in the singular). All animals perceive affordances, and the human animal is better able than others to create and communicate subtle multiplicities of affordances in his or her environments.[28] To touch any part of this tensed environment is to release a force that opens and closes various sets of options. These affordances are not causally related to the different behavioral capacities of different organisms but are another way of expressing these different ca-

25. Johnson, *The Body in the Mind*, p. 21.

26. This discussion of affordance will be taken up again in discussion of practical philosophy, the situatedness of knowledge, and the process of deliverance and purification required for knowledge of the world as God's creation that will contribute to my argument for mediation in Chapter 5.

27. J. J. Gibson, *The Ecological Approach to Visual Perception* (Boston: Houghton Mifflin, 1986). Gibson's position is summarized by John T. Sanders, "Affordances: An Ecological Approach to First Philosophy," in *Perspectives on Embodiment: The Intersections of Nature and Culture,* ed. G. Weiss and H. F. Haber (London: Routledge, 1999).

28. Frederick A. Olafson, *What Is a Human Being? A Heideggerian View* (Cambridge: Cambridge University Press, 1995), pp. 166-67, gives a more sophisticated version of the account offered by McCabe and Nussbaum. According to Pannenberg, *Anthropology in Theological Perspective,* p. 43, Johann Gottfried von Herder's starting point in discussion of the origin of language is that humankind is peculiarly deficient, naked, and unarmed, and that this accounts for the origin of the human mind. Frederick C. Beiser, *The Fate of Reason: German Philosophy from Kant to Fichte* (Cambridge: Harvard University Press, 1997), p. 146, argues that for Herder "the mind and body are not distinct types of substance but different degrees of organisation and development of a single living power."

pacities. This ecological psychology makes no strong contrast between the organism and its environment, because environments are organism-indexed parts of the world.

I have drawn your attention to the deep patterns that order our life and our thought about it. The conceptuality of body- and orientation-schemas introduced in this section may help us to conceive the way we are located in the world. These schemas form the platform on which the world presents itself to us and allows us to move through it. Such schemas are often referred to as metaphors. Underneath all that we can be scientific about, there is a deep set of things that are fundamentally controversial and unsupported. Beneath all that we are able to rationalize, there is a level of story-like interpretations. We can call these metaphors, as long as we realize that they are the inherited matrices of our very own action. Together they make up our metaphysic or ontology, and that constitutes the deep structure that informs and determines the life and thought of our society, our own as much as any other. We think we may "use" metaphors as we may use tools — that is, that we may use them or not, as we like. But this is not quite right, for two reasons. The first is that we do always employ tools and cannot not do so. We do not interact with the world raw. We are able only to some small degree to choose which tools. The second point is that the world itself is not raw surface, but is itself nothing but an assemblage of tools that compete to put themselves into our hands and to hold on to us. Each tool or metaphor intends not only that we should use it but also that it should become our dominant schema. It tends to expand to become our only schema and our whole world. The world is a slowly shifting accretion of metaphors that act as templates for our action and perception. Any metaphor not controlled and balanced by others serves only to reduce the moral space we think is available to us. The world is not a blank sheet but a palimpsest. As we act, we create marks on the surface made up of all previous things. By all that we do, we rearrange things, partially effacing them, sometimes bringing back earlier things beneath them, in a ceaseless process of cannibalization and reutilization.

2.5. Place

Whose world and whose economy is this? Some account of our location in a world is required by any account of persons coming into being. It is the action of God that causes human beings to grow and helps them ease into their place and task. The human realm is the economy and work of God for us. God does not have to gain permission from humanity before he can enter the human realm. The human city does not succeed in holding out against the divine city, nor does earthly and human history succeed in establishing any definition of humanity against God's definition of humanity. Robert Jenson and Wolfhart Pannenberg treat space in terms of God's action, and thus in moral terms.[29] They understand that the human city and history have a merely provisional and propaideutic status that is the function of the work of the divine city and history.[30] God employs the earthly city for a double function. In it he keeps us in some measure secured in and by our self-deceit, so our own self-destructive ends are prevented. And God uses the earthly city, despite us, to bring us to his own end, the full freedom of the creature. In Chapter 4 I shall argue that, for Israel, the temple is the model of the earth, and earth a model of the larger eschatological economy of heaven-and-earth. By practicing on this model, Israel will pick up the skills of householding for God and his creation. This people has been entrusted with a little, so that they may come to be entrusted with much.

But we cannot yet give God his place. We are placed by, and contained within, the world of God's working, and by the same working this world is broken open. In this world God places us before him, placed and closed by the crucifixion, and placed and opened by the resurrection. As Jenson points out, the church gathered around the sacraments is the location of heaven, and of Jesus, for us.[31] The God-man at the right hand of the Father is the source of the integrity and unity of the church in the place and time the Spirit now supplies to it and supplies to the world through it. Wannenwetsch and Hütter discuss the advantages of the discourse of *out-*

---

29. For more discussion see my essay "Jenson on Time," in *Trinity, Time and Church: A Response to the Theology of Robert W. Jenson*, ed. Colin E. Gunton (Grand Rapids: Eerdmans, 2000). Edward S. Casey, *The Fate of Place: A Philosophical History* (Berkeley: University of California Press, 1997), offers a fuller historical account of the concept of space.

30. Robert W. Jenson, *Systematic Theology* (New York: Oxford University Press, 1999), vol. 2, pp. 76-81, 204-6. Wolfhart Pannenberg, *Systematic Theology* (Edinburgh: T&T Clark, 1994), vol. 2, p. 81, and Amos Funkenstein, *Theology and the Scientific Imagination from the Middle Ages to the Seventeenth Century* (Princeton: Princeton University Press, 1986), p. 193, suggest that the concept of space is derived from that of spirit.

31. Jenson, *Systematic Theology,* vol. 1, p. 205.

side, church as *polis,* and show that the inner "natural" world of individual bodily needs becomes, in the church, the open public world of equal citizens.[32] The closed mechanistic economy is a falsehood we inflict on one another. But it has also been imposed on us by God. He subjects us to the working of this economy that, by enclosing and containing us, prepares us for life in a single open economy with God. We should consider space under the concepts of action and work, and thus as a moral concept, and relate it to the action of bodies together. We must restate the claim of the public, the outside, the marketplace and public arena, over the claims of interiority given priority in the Cartesian and Kantian tradition. We may not reject the discourse of inside, or of input and output, but we must also find another discourse that does not merely contrast outside and inside, but that understands the world as a function of alternation, conversation, and linguisticality. Space is not a uniform, regular, empty field that is unaffected by what happens in it. Next we must turn to an approach that gives action a role to play in the definition of place.

2.6. Time

Time is a register. There are many registers, and thus many times.[33] The economy of modernity does not succeed in acting as a meta-time, which orders the registers sequentially into one time. We do not stand outside time. Whatever we moderns know, we are not able to order everything into one sequential account and thus know it utterly. We are subject to time, and so we are not its arbitrator. Time does not flow up to us, stop before us, and deposit all things obediently at our feet. Time is recursive. It has no center apparent to us. It is the coming and going of time-schemas, a continuum of registers and their units. It is not simply a forward flow but has

32. See Reinhard Hütter, *Suffering Divine Things: Theology as Church Practice* (Grand Rapids: Eerdmans, 1999), pp. 158-71, and Bernd Wannenwetsch, "The Political Worship of the Church," *Modern Theology* 12 (1996).

33. Ingolf Dalferth, *Gedeutete Gegenwart: Zur Wahrnehmung Gottes in den Erfahrungen der Zeit* (Tübingen: Mohr Siebeck, 1997), p. 239: "There is no single time, only a plurality of times." For discussion of time as many registers, see Alfred Gell, *The Anthropology of Time: Cultural Constructions of Temporal Maps and Images* (Oxford: Berg, 1992), and John Bender and David E. Wellbery, *Chronotypes: The Construction of Time* (Stanford: Stanford University Press, 1991).

"undercurrents, tributaries and reversals, floods and islands."[34] There are many possible things happening all at once, only some of which will prove to be canonical, to have lasting being. The "multiple drafts" model of perception introduced by Dennett reflects this, as does the "scenario-spinning" model of consciousness, in which there are, at any point in time, multiple drafts of narrative fragments at various overlapping stages of editing, not in one place but at all places in the brain.[35]

We do not start thinking about what has happened when it is all over. There is no obvious moment at which we can decide that it is over and that we may now start to consider what any chain of events amounted to. We think ceaselessly about what is going on, and there is no definitive point at which we can look back to find a single uncontroversial account of what has happened. Kontopoulos sees the process of accounting "not as an activity that occurs after the completion of interaction — a recollective gathering of the meanings produced — but a constitutive process of the very interaction itself and of the meanings deployed in it."[36] All judgment and knowledge are not only interim but actually determine events that must then also be judged.

If all consciousness is consciousness of something, all time is the time *of* something, or time *for* something. Time is, of course, not *thing*, but affordance. It is an opportunity for a happening, which involves more than the individual. Two agents make time for each other. Time may be said to be generated by their meeting and acting together. Discursivity and diffuse intentionality are required to understand agency as plural, the work of more than one person.[37] Discursivity describes the turn-taking, or alternation, that characterizes conversation and human relating in general. Diffuse intentionality relates to the expert audience of commentators, whose participation gives mere movement the significance of the action of persons.

Now we have found support from a range of contemporary academic

34. Shaun Gallagher, *The Inordinance of Time* (Evanston: Northwestern University Press, 1998), p. 200.

35. Dennett, *Consciousness Explained*, pp. 126-34.

36. Kyriakos M. Kontopoulos, *The Logics of Social Structure* (Cambridge: Cambridge University Press, 1993), p. 99.

37. Simon Glendinning, *On Being with Others: Heidegger, Derrida, Wittgenstein* (London: Routledge, 1998), makes the philosophical case for discursivity and diffuse intentionality; Bradd Shore, *Culture in Mind: Cognition, Culture and the Problem of Meaning* (New York: Oxford University Press, 1996), makes the case in the terms employed by social anthropology.

disciplines for the idea that what is basic is conversation. I introduced this idea at the end of the last chapter, where I said that the conversation of Father and Son is basic, and that one freely chosen idiom of their conversation is humanity. Their speech brings us into being, and we have being inasmuch as we respond to that speech and participate in it. This response is made for us and also frees and animates us, so that it becomes really our own speech. We have found a body of scholarship for which such coming to be within conversation is not a new idea. Being is not prior to talk, for being and talk are equally basic. Here we have found another tool with which to identify and resist the protological trend of the ontology of modernity.

2.7. Plurality

I have been arguing for a plural, trinitarian concept of agency that will allow for the pneumatology that I will develop in subsequent chapters. Our action is action only when it is the work of two, and it is the work of two only when an appropriate audience is convinced by this work; so in any account of action, a third party constituted by an expert audience is required. Speech-acts are acts of agreeing and contracting that make up the whole action that constitutes the world.

2.7.1. The Expert Audience

I suggested that we demand an account of each other. We give each other accounts of the world. We live in complex covenants of reciprocal account-giving; narrative is the whole idiom in which we relate with one another. We could even say that all our being is a matter of telling one another stories. Our stories are to be entertaining and hospitable. They have to be gripping. We demand to be enraptured by whatever story the other has to tell us. By them we hold one another captive. All action involves convincing an appropriate audience of your action, by established routines of demonstration, until this audience signals its acknowledgment.[38] Such exchange and acknowledgment of accounts are the means whereby we enter contracts and create business relationships.

---

38. Pierre Bourdieu, *Language and Symbolic Power* (Oxford: Polity, 1991), p. 77: "Utterances receive their value (and their sense) only in relation to a market."

The event of a binding relationship, a contract, depends on the creation of a narrative. That narrative will be recorded, and it will be reinforced by symbols that are abbreviated forms of those records and that narrative. But symbols, formalities, and ritual are not secondary.[39] Making a public contract involves the manipulation of symbols and the formal, even ritual, employment of a number of tokens. Records on paper — or, in the ancient world, blood — not only make an occasion memorable but also make a relationship binding and contractual. The minutiae of terms set down on paper are a public demonstration by the two parties to the witnessing and sponsoring community of the earnestness of their intent. The gesturing with these various props and tokens is intended to create a narrative that will win an audience, which will ensure that the contract is subsequently honored. The audience bound by this narrative is the guarantor of the contract. The paperwork and other ritual of the contract are the means by which this community is gathered and the contract is written. We might say that the contract is written in the memory of the community that witnesses and judges it binding. The action of the courtroom is casuistry, the discussion of case histories. In court the two sides offer analogies from previous cases: when these are accepted as analogies by the court, they argue from them. Argument *(logic)* follows analogy (*analogic,* narrative).

The domination of the philosophy of reflection has resulted in our failure to understand ourselves within skeins of expectation and involvement. This is in part because philosophy and theology have not remained in conversation with the law faculty, which does understand that we make things happen by contracting and making oaths. The result is that philosophy and theology, along with social science, have had to look for other ways to show that formal and ritual public action is not simply incomprehensible and irrational. The interest in speech acts, and the concept of

---

39. Contracts in the ancient world created the sense of occasion by the employment of animals and their blood. Sacrifice was in the ancient world the mode of making contracts. Such ritual for ancient sacrifices is documented by Walter Burkert, *Greek Religion: Archaic and Classical* (Oxford: Blackwell, 1985). Victor Turner, *Dramas, Fields and Metaphors: Symbolic Action in Human Society* (Ithaca: Cornell University Press, 1974), pioneered anthropological literature on performance and ritual. Mary Carruthers, *The Book of Memory: A Study of Memory in Medieval Culture* (Cambridge: Cambridge University Press, 1990), and Paul Connerton, *How Societies Remember* (Cambridge: Cambridge University Press, 1989), summarize the literature on the arts and technology of pre-modern memory.

perlocution, is an attempt to show how on certain occasions words are binding and create valid contracts and acceptable sacrifices, while on other occasions identical words are not.[40] What to nineteenth-century scholarship of religion looked like primitive and superstitious attempts to manipulate the world or its gods should instead be seen in the much more mundane terms of commercial interaction.[41] The sacrificing of ancient societies was speech-act by which they performed the very same public acts of economic and institutional construction we do. The concept of speech-act serves to represent the binding and contracting effect of all public performance, which creates all public relationships.[42]

We have seen that language is not first representation (reflection) and only secondarily and more problematically performance and (speech-) act. We are situated in a single, though complex, social fabric of attachment, connectedness, and contract. We are implicated in one another and held together by this fabric. Language is in itself sets of regularities and rules. Law and reason are what language is. This fabric of connectedness is composed of sets of rules. Law is the medium of the life of a community and consequently of its formation and instruction. The discussion by hermeneutics of speech-acts betrays at least an ignorance of the legal and commercial discourse of oaths and trust, and much more of the participative ontology that supports it. It is of a piece with the failure of modern theology to conceptualize the plurality and therefore the situatedness of human interaction, as a

40. See John R. Searle, *Expression and Meaning: Studies in the Theory of Speech Acts* (Cambridge: Cambridge University Press, 1979), pp. 1-29.

41. See the discussion of Frank Cioffi, *Wittgenstein on Freud and Frazer* (Cambridge: Cambridge University Press, 1998), pp. 80-92.

42. Tim W. Murphy, *The Oldest Social Science? Configurations of Law and Modernity* (Oxford: Clarendon, 1997), p. 106, describes this involuntary mutual involvement or "implicature" in terms of trust. This has had to be laboriously established by Austin and Searle by appeal to Wittgenstein. Peter Ochs, "Rabbinic Pragmatism," in *Theology in Dialogue: Essays in Conversation with George Lindbeck,* ed. Bruce Marshall (Notre Dame: University of Notre Dame Press, 1990), establishes the link between Scripture and law. Anthony C. Thiselton, *Interpreting God and the Postmodern Self on Meaning, Manipulation and Promise* (Edinburgh: T&T Clark, 1995); Sue Patterson, *Realist Christian Theology in a Postmodern Age* (Cambridge: Cambridge University Press, 1999); and Kevin Vanhoozer, *Is There a Meaning in This Text? The Bible, the Reader and the Morality of Literary Knowledge* (Leicester: Apollos, 1998), along with that majority of theological discussion of hermeneutics that does not connect speech-acts and law, represent the failure of biblical-theological hermeneutics to understand itself also as political-theological hermeneutics, a failure I discuss in Chapters 5 and 6.

result of which it has resorted to metaphor and the special logic of religious language to fill the gap. There is no gap, if we concede that conversation, account-giving, narrative, and law are fundamental.

2.7.2. The Turn to Performance

We need to find a more action-oriented ontology. We could perhaps call this a praxeology, or a dramaturgy. We have said that the world is a courtroom. Now we can say it is also a stage, on which all of us are acting for an audience. Our audience knows this, and we know that they know this. Actor and audience indicate that they receive one another's cues and make their appropriate responses. The actor on stage shows the audience its own action, and the audience recognizes itself in the actor's performance.[43] The actor shows the audience its action, complete with its result, and demonstrates that it never manages to complete an action without interrupting it with another. The unforeseen continually interrupts our action. Our action consists of adopting, and discarding again, a succession of behavioral patterns, with the result that all our action comes to nothing.[44] We claim that our action is exclusively our own. But actors' performances show that they can repeat what we do, and since we cannot show that we succeed in outdoing them by doing what they cannot do, our claim that our action is ours exclusively fails. All drama is parody of life. The point of all drama is to wrench its audience into new realization of the limits of their own action.

---

43. The actor has license to look to imitate, parody, and frighten us. See James W. Fernandez, *Persuasions and Performances: The Play of Tropes in Culture* (Bloomington: Indiana University Press, 1986), and Erving Goffman, *Interaction Ritual: Essays on Face-to-Face Behaviour* (New York: Doubleday, Anchor Books, 1967) and *The Presentation of Self in Everyday Life* (New York: Doubleday, Anchor Books, 1959), for discussion of the use of the conceptuality of actor, audience, and dramaturgy in daily life.

44. Charles L. Griswold, *Adam Smith and the Virtues of Enlightenment* (Cambridge: Cambridge University Press, 1999), p. 109, argues that "without a mask we cannot be actors either to ourselves or to others, and do not exist as human or moral selves. In this sense human life is fundamentally theatrical. It is not simply that we cannot be known as we really are; it is that we are not unless we are known by the spectator." Support for Griswold's case can be found in Michael Billig, *Arguing and Thinking: A Rhetorical Approach to Social Psychology* (Cambridge: Cambridge University Press, 1987), pp. 49-53; Christopher P. Smith, *The Hermeneutics of Original Argument: Demonstration, Dialectic, Rhetoric* (Evanston: Northwestern University Press, 1998), pp. 97, 236-42; and Alfred Gell, *Art and Agency: An Anthropological Theory* (Oxford: Clarendon, 1998), pp. 14-23, 99-104.

We will see in the next chapter that what members of Israel did in the temple can be understood as the mode of the formation of the house of Israel; and in Chapter 4 we will see that, on the cross, one member of Israel performed this to the satisfaction of God.[45] By God's better performance toward us in the single dramaturgical economy he sustains for us, we are shamed into leaving behind our inept action and participating in and imitating his virtuoso action. God out-acts us, and so draws us into his more convincing performance, so that it becomes truly our own.

Practical knowledge is the medium of knowledge, and the aesthetic is the mode of practical knowledge. We are driven to seek a mode that will allow greater economy of effort. In knowledge, too, we are driven to find an easier way. Theological and philosophical enquiry that insists on looking for a new and specific telos for each action does not allow for the frivolity and indifference of the greater part of our doing. Most of our activity has no particular rationale, but only the general rationale of all performance — that it feels good and looks good. We should ask not only *why,* for what specific reason, but also *how?* How well is it done? With what success? The question of *how* holds good for the whole effort of the formation and education of the body, and thus for the sphere of public interaction and politics. Good politics, in the form of new opportunities for the formation of the body, arise in the medium of emulation and competition, in which all our mundane contracting together takes place. We must resist the impulse to examine every move only under the twin concepts of truth and good; instead we must also employ the aesthetic as the category of work, efficiency, and purposes.[46] This will allow us to make a comparison and contrast between the Christian and the pagan forms of life in our final chapter.

All the forms of action, by which we hold ourselves together and negotiate our way through moral space, were formed by the social body into which we have grown. Those body-schemas which the community ceases to name come to determine that community. They devolve into the dichotomies of inner and outer, and higher and lower, that derive from the priority given to the one over the many in the protological ontology. The Christian community has to bring such body-schemas back into public

45. We will discuss narrative and enthrallment along with the issue of who may read the Scriptures and who has access to the liturgy and sacrificial office of Israel.

46. The concepts of the aesthetic and efficiency relate to the discussion of fit, bodily effort, and the single continuum of emulation.

thought, keep them in use, and continually reintegrate them into the social body. I will use the resources sketched in this chapter to argue that the forms of action of the economy of modernity have given all our movements a crampedness that God does not intend for his creature. God calls us into a larger territory. This allows us to say that we resist being moved beyond the familiar bounds of nature and necessity into the larger place of God. Apart from this commandeering by God, all our pathways and orientations become cosmologies and paganisms, forms of the recalcitrant and merely animal life. In the next two chapters I will argue that under God's direction, and with his enabling, Israel obediently builds the house where God's people may be with him. In building this model Israel learns God's action. Israel learns to pull down rival constructions, redeeming the earth from other claimants, to make it the creature and creation of the one God. This destruction and building are a single act. Israel's address to the gentiles is always a commandeering and abuse of their conceptuality, but by sketching the new creation over the old Israel points to its redemption and looks forward to a new being.

CHAPTER 3

God, His Servant, and Their Work

God has determined us for life with him. He has started the work of making a holy people, and it is now under way. This is the account that this chapter will offer. It will relate the oneness of God to God's determination to make us one with himself. Making one is an action of God that has the double form of distinguishing and reconciling, separating and bringing together. My account of this atonement will rely on a doxological and eschatological ontology. It will not therefore tackle the issue of models of atonement in a separate discussion, which would then require a further and separate discussion of metaphor and religious language, and so refer to a sphere of distinctly religious concerns. Instead my account will relate hermeneutical issues to the doctrine of God. It will refer the question of what Scripture says to the question of which community is addressed by Scripture because addressed by God. I will argue that only the doctrines of God and of creation secure for us a world that is one, and in which therefore we can know, and be known by, one another. I do this here in terms of the Jewish and Christian claims to knowledge of the one God, and thus through discussion of the issue of supersession and salvation history. I recount the history of Israel and the church as the one ongoing work of God, and I relate this single salvation history to the modern concept of time. This will take the form of an examination, not of the Scriptures themselves, but of the range of resources that biblical studies are able to provide for theological questions.

Israel is the work of God on the world of his creation and also the medium of that work, apart from which there is no knowledge of God. Israel is the election of humanity by God to the office of steward of creation and leadership of the peoples of the world. The nations have no means to know the identity of Israel and Israel's God other than through the people God has chosen for this purpose.

3.1. God and His Servant

We turn to the issues of God and his servant and God and his work. The freedom of the creature is the purpose of God. The concepts of person and creature allow us to talk about this purpose. The creature is in relationship with God; creatureliness therefore represents a high status, not a low one. But we do not yet have the full status of creature. The question of the identity of God's creature and agent must be referred to God, not the agent. To answer it by referring to the agent would be to divide God from his messenger and to turn the messenger back on the grounds that he is not God himself. But God allows no identification of himself apart from the one race of people he has chosen. Inasmuch as they are his property and have his name, they are the agent of God for us. It would be wrong to say that they *are* he if that is all we said, but with the Trinity we have the conceptuality to provide two distinct but simultaneous accounts of God's action that allow that God remains free in them.

Is God still Yahweh, the God of Israel? Have Yahweh and his servant been engaged from the beginning in a work that has never ceased to be successful? Or should we say, in more supersessionist mode, that the time of the many generations recorded in the Old Testament was just the passing of so many generations that have now vanished? Though this time might have been productive, it turned out not to be because, though God always expected Israel finally to spring into life, Israel never did. Is this the story of the Old Testament, one of delay and finally of failure? This is how it may seem if time is understood as a stuff that, at least in dealing with humanity, God has to endure. But God does not endure time as something that sprang from some other and rival source, but rather himself makes time and gives it its telos. Indeed, it is not properly time until it is united with its telos. In this case we can say both that the Old Testament was the real time of God and Israel together and that it is their continuing time. It is not past; rather, it is the ongoing time in which Israel is borne to adulthood and to the full office of creature and servant.

Some scholarship identifies the Trinity as the concept that separates

Christians from Jews. It assumes that the way to Jewish-Christian dialogue is to emphasize monotheism and play down the doctrine of the Trinity. James Dunn tells us that "Christianity is only Christianity when it is monotheistic. Only so can Christians remain true to their roots, to their heritage within the religion of Israel."[1] Francis Watson counters,

> If "monotheism" here refers to a view on which Jews and Christians agree, over against classical Christian trinitarianism, these statements would have to be reversed. Christianity is only Christianity when it is trinitarian. Only so can Christians remain true to their Jewish roots and to the Jewish Scriptures within their canon. A "Christian" unitarianism is not a Christian faithfulness to Jewish roots and Scripture.[2]

I will argue with Watson that the Trinity is the doctrine that keeps Christians in relationship with Jews.

There were many Judaisms. Some of them were inherited by Judaism, some by Christianity.[3] It was only with regard to what it called Christianity that Judaism insisted that it was one Judaism and not many. Likewise Christianity insisted it was one only with regard to what it called Judaism. Considered apart, they make two. But apart from Israel, the church may not confess itself one. The unity of each community is the function of the indivisible work of God. Each side played up the differences and claimed that the other party had moved away from its origin. In actuality neither side took anything away from the other or made it impossible for the other to make proper use of the Scriptures. What in the apologists' period be-

1. James D. G. Dunn, *The Parting of the Ways between Christianity and Judaism and Their Significance for the Character of Christianity* (London: SCM, 1991), p. 247. The "Parting of the Ways" debate identifies supersessionism as an error but continues to rely on the concepts the error has created. It is an inverse supersessionism, in which some anachronistically defined, temporally static community (Christianity) is guilty of causing the break of which it is the product.

2. Francis Watson, *Text and Truth: Redefining Biblical Theology* (Edinburgh: T&T Clark, 1997), p. 329 n. 18.

3. Jacob Neusner, "Judaism and Christianity in the First Century," in *Essays on Jewish and Christian Literature and History*, ed. Philip R. Davies and Richard T. White (Sheffield: JSOT Press, 1990), p. 254. The analogies of quarreling siblings or failed marriage rely on the prior existence of more than one entity. It seems much safer to start with Neusner from the point that what we have too casually called Judaism was always a coalition of parties — Judaisms — gathering round competing readings of the Scriptures, readings that could not be reduced to a single canonical version.

came Christian theology was not a fixed quantity but competition for the resources of Scripture. Patristic and conciliar theology did not arise as part of a growing away from Jewish resources, or living from its "own" resources, but as a continual process of the rising to expression of Israel's Scriptures as address to the world.

3.1.1. Election

The doctrine of the election of Israel, and thus of the Jewish people, returned to the center of dogmatics in the twentieth century.[4] This was in large part due to Karl Barth.[5] Barth insisted that God is faithful and worthy of trust to the extent that he keeps his promise to this people. Barth's recovery of typology, in the form of the pairs election-rejection, man-woman, and Jew-Gentile, made possible the recovery of the whole Old Testament for Christology. But Barth contrasted the pairs of types he identified in the Old Testament, one of which stands for election, the other for rejection. What will prevent these becoming static and creating two opposing sorts of people? Only the Spirit, God himself, can make one people out of two. So Jesus Christ is the rejected and the elected man. But the power of Jesus Christ is an abstraction if it is not bound to the act of a particular community. Barth avoids an abstraction from Christ, Rogers believes, but he abstracts from the Spirit. Though God has a particular relationship with Israel, Barth cannot say what that is, because he does not show that God's relationship to the Jewish people is ongoing. The "Old Testament in abstracto" for Barth, is the "passing" form of the human being. Then the people of Israel, the Jewish people, is just a shadow that gives way to the

---

4. Eugene Rogers, "Supplementing Barth on Jews and Gender," *Modern Theology* 14 (1998): 61, believes Barth is the "father of many late twentieth century doctrines of Israel that improve on him." Wolfgang Kraus, *Das Volk Gottes. Zur Grundung des Ekklesiologie bei Paulus,* Wissenschaftliche Untersuchungen zum Neuen Testament 85 (Tübingen: Mohr-Siebeck, 1996), p. 356, agrees: "Paul's notion of the people of God at work within his doctrine of justification — seen at work in Rome — is the only conception in the New Testament that solves the problem of Israel and the pagans in such a way that the people of God are secured, while both sides are vindicated. It justifies the Christian self-understanding as the final people of God, while supporting the continuing election of Israel to whom God has indissolubly bound himself."

5. Barth, *Church Dogmatics,* ed. T. F. Torrance and G. W. Bromiley (Edinburgh: T. & T. Clark, 1956-75), IV/3, p. 878: "Thus it [the Church] still owes everything to those [the Jews] to whom it is indebted for everything."

coming community, a different community. Rogers argues that Barth has allowed us to believe that the people of Israel are no longer led by the Spirit of God; the synagogue is what human beings need to be saved from. Barth has reestablished the centrality of the election of the people of Israel, while also seeming to suggest that Israel is replaced by the Christian community.

Robert Jenson offers a solution to the problem. He proposes that to Barth's phrase "Jesus Christ is the electing God" we add that "the Holy Spirit is the electing God."[6] Rogers agrees that we must supplement each of Barth's contrasted types with the Spirit as their third term. It is not individuals that correspond to types, but community, this specific community, that is elect.[7] We should then identify God by focusing, not on Jesus Christ as *individual*, but on Jesus *and the community the Holy Spirit gives to him.* "To identify God by the Holy Spirit is to refuse to abstract from God's concrete self-determination to be for Israel."[8] Israel does not need salvation, but only vindication, for this people has the unalterable promise of the faithful God. Consummation, not redemption, is the proper model for understanding Israel's relationship with God. Attempts to ask about Israel's salvation submit Israel to an inappropriate logic, one in which an unredeemed community is replaced by a redeemed community. This is the logic of supersessionism.

Kendall Soulen identifies three forms of supersessionism. Economic supersessionism is the idea that from the beginning God's purpose for carnal Israel in the economy of salvation was destined to be fulfilled and completed by Christ's coming, after which its place was to be taken by the church. Punitive supersessionism is the idea that God has abrogated the covenant with Israel in anger because of Israel's rejection of the gospel. Structural supersessionism refers to the classical history of salvation *(ordo salutis),* which takes the form "creation-fall-redemption-consummation," which is present whenever the Old Testament does not determine Christology.[9]

---

6. Robert W. Jenson, "You Wonder Where the Spirit Went," *Pro Ecclesia* 2, no. 3 (1993).

7. Rogers, "Supplementing Barth on Jews and Gender," p. 70: Barth's I-Thou categories "hide the presence of third parties and the mediation of disciples, crowds and friends. Christ promises to be with human beings not each individually but when *two or three* are *already* gathered in his name."

8. Rogers, "Supplementing Barth on Jews and Gender," p. 62, argues that "for Gentiles redemption is the plot, consummation, the denouement; for Jews consummation is the main plot, redemption the subplot, the outcome of which is never in real doubt."

9. Kendall Soulen, "Karl Barth and the Future of the God of Israel," *Pro Ecclesia* 6, no. 4 (1997).

Barth repudiated structural and punitive supersessionism and made God's election of Israel central to God's faithfulness. But he is not quite free of the Augustinian tendency to understand salvation as redemption from the people constituted by God's actual, historical interaction, the people of Israel, and so to think of redemption in terms of deliverance from history. Soulen wants to see "the classical account of trinitarian relations originating from the Father . . . supplemented by relations originating from the eschatological dominion of the Holy Spirit."[10] He points out that the name Jesus (Yēshua') means "YHWH saves" and that this has been interpreted since Irenaeus in a trinitarian sense.[11] Soulen concludes that "The name Jesus Christ may thus not unreasonably be said to contain internal reference to the name YHWH and to the triune shape of the evangelical history as this history is packed into the title Christ."[12] The resurrection is the resurrection not of an individual, but of Israel, and by it Israel is vindicated and established. Soulen sets us two questions: Can Christians concede that God's election of Israel, and the consequent distinction between Israel and the nations, is as permanently relevant to God's consummation of the world — past, present, future — as, for instance, the distinction between Creator and creature? Can Christians see the two Scriptures without claiming that the Old Testament is "exhausted by or even primarily located in its reference to Jesus"?[13]

Robert Jenson also argues that there is for us no knowledge of God that does not come in the form of this people. Israel is central for our confession of God. God is himself a participant in Israel's history. "What the Lord does to Israel he does to himself, in that the shekinah shares Israel's lot and the Lord's being."[14] The angel to Abraham, for example, "is a messenger 'of' God who nevertheless refers to God in the first person. He is

10. Kendall Soulen, "YHWH the Triune God," *Modern Theology* 15 (1999): 44.

11. Basil, *On the Holy Spirit*, quoted by Soulen, "YHWH the Triune God," p. 46, agrees: "To address [Jesus as the Christ] is a complete confession of faith, because it clearly reveals that God anoints the Son (the Anointed One) with the unction of the Spirit."

12. Soulen, "YHWH the Triune God," pp. 44-45; see also Christopher Seitz, *Word without End: The Old Testament as Abiding Theological Witness* (Grand Rapids: Eerdmans, 1998), p. 234.

13. Soulen, "Karl Barth and the Future of the God of Israel," p. 427.

14. Robert W. Jenson, *Systematic Theology* (New York: Oxford University Press, 1997-99), vol. 1, p. 76: "With the phrase 'the Shekinah', the rabbis gathered a whole range of biblical discourse that speaks of God as 'settled' to and within Israel while not ceasing to stand over Israel."

God himself as a participant within Israel's story, who is nevertheless related to God as the one who sends him and who determines Israel's story."[15] Jenson's approach prevents the Old Testament being reduced to the New Testament by a promise-and-fulfillment pattern. "Until the Last Judgement and our resurrection," says Jenson, "Christ has not yet come in the way that fully consummates Israel's history."[16] The New Testament can be understood not only as a reading of the Old Testament but also as the reading made by the One who may open the scroll. But this Reader is not here, so the New Testament is that reading in which God has left us to go elsewhere, there to prepare a place for us. This argument is supported by Douglas Farrow. He insists that the ascension, and thus the withdrawal of Jesus, is the major teaching of the New Testament. Jesus is not here — he is ascended. "Worse than the world's ignorance of Jesus's absence . . . is the Church's failure to proclaim the absence clearly, to witness in its every act of worship that it really is 'looking for his coming again with power and great glory.'" Jesus is seated at the right hand of the Father, from where he has released to us his Spirit, and by him sends his own spiritual flesh to clothe us.[17]

To ask about the "pre-existence" of the Son, the time before he was Jesus, is to ask about a time before God made time for us. But time is the very medium we have for talking about God's determination to be for us. There is no way for us to see behind God's determination to come to us and be with us; there is no further thing behind it. So rather than provide a concept of existence, an ontology, at this point, we must talk about communion, in the specific, twofold form of the communion of God with humankind in the people of Israel and of the church of the gentiles added to them. They are the existence of the Son that climaxes in Jesus Christ, and all those he brings with him. Some biblical scholarship has responded to the issue of the relationship of church and Israel by downplaying the doctrines of election and atonement. As we shall see, some of the discussion that stresses the centrality of the people of Israel also tends to minimize Israel's worship, or not to allow discussion of this worship to meet dogmatic talk of representation and substitution or of Israel's ongoing action and office.

15. Jenson, *Systematic Theology*, vol. 1, p. 76.
16. Jenson, *Systematic Theology*, vol. 2, p. 336.
17. Douglas Farrow, *Ascension and Ecclesia* (Edinburgh: T&T Clark, 1999), p. 272.

3.1.2. The Trinity as the Concept of God,
His Servant, and His Work

The Torah is the native language of Israel. But for the gentiles brought by baptism into Christ, it is a language they have to learn. Because it was not their first language, they had to discover its grammar for themselves. In making the Torah explicit to themselves, the Christians realized that the grammar of the dealings of God with Israel is plural and open. Because the Torah concerns God's lordship and the future he has for us, it is not determined simply by what is past. Since Israel did not have to learn the grammar of their language the hard way, they did not make explicit to themselves that God is speaker and listener, commander and obeyer. In each case he is also the means of this speaking and listening, commanding and obeying, that is, the language spoken, the medium shared and inhabited. This logic may be called trinitarian.

The doctrine of God the Creator is a doctrine about God who is with his creature. The Trinity is the conceptuality by which we can express this.[18] Barth proposed that the covenant of election is the internal basis of the covenant of creation to this end.[19] On the basis of natural theology, creation is a synonym for *existence:* on such a natural basis we believe that we already know, prior to the gospel, what a creature is and that God cannot be a creature. But creation is a doctrine taught and confessed by the church. It is not a statement merely about what *is,* or about what is *visible,* but about what will be the case about the world.[20] The doctrine of creation states that the world is someone's piece of property. The question is not, therefore, What is the nature of this piece of property? but whose property is it? What is the character of its owner?

This allows us to say that Israel is the only people holy enough to recognize the mediator between humankind and God. It takes the Son (Israel) to know the Father. The Father has been everywhere at work, but to know him and recognize him requires co-familiarity with him. By the

18. There is no *prior* difference between God *with* his creature and God who *is* that creature whom God is with. The difference between *with*-creature *(relation)* and *is*-creature *(being)* is a difference that is established by *God's creating action,* not one prior to creation. I argued for such a relational ontology in Chapter 1.

19. Barth, *Church Dogmatics,* III/1 § 41.

20. This is argued by Ingolf Dalferth, "Creation: Style of the World," *International Journal for Systematic Theology* 1 (1999).

Spirit the Son gets the practice, and acquires the skill, correctly and obediently to return to God that recognition. Israel hides from its office of lord. Yet the church must confess that this hiding is an option that Israel finally turns from. Each generation of Israel has produced those who watched for the coming of the bridegroom. In their priestly performance they have obediently witnessed to him, learned the name to call him by, and prayed for his return to Israel. In many priestly and prophetic forms, the Son has always been at work, laboring and serving the Father. God is a member of Israel.[21] As this member, God is responsible, and of course also solely responsible, for Israel's faithfulness. So we can say that God is always with, and among, Israel. The Spirit is always at work to make Israel holy and to make good Israel's election. In Jesus, the Spirit succeeded in making one single instance of Israel, one man who is with God. By making copies of this obedient Son, the Spirit will succeed in making many sons for Abraham. This is the outcome of reading the Old and New Testaments as the single testament of the triune God.

In order to show more adequately the plural aspect of the electing action of God, we must let the concept of Israel contribute to our pneumatology. This requires that we do not attempt to speak theologically of Israel apart from Israel's king and head, or of God apart from the one and the many whom he has made the means of his self-revelation. Christ is *totus Christus,* Christ-*with-his-people,* with and by the Spirit. This pneumatological discourse is, of course, not a sufficient discourse. It must be accompanied by a separate discourse that employs the language of two natures to distinguish the human from the divine, creature from Creator. The distinction between God and man is driven by God-*who-is-with-man,*

21. Jenson, *Systematic Theology,* vol. 1, p. 83, explains that there must be a "difference between an Israelite who stands over against Israel and the people without whom this one is not himself. . . . Were there only a singular creature who in his own person is 'one of the Trinity', in his instance, the difference between God and creature would simply be abolished; but, in that the one person is the one he is only as identified with a community whose members are not, in their singular persons, identities of God, the one Israelite's membership in God in fact sustains the difference between God and creature." An Aristotelian logic of either-or is (necessary but) not sufficient for theological statements involving relation, perichoresis, and transformation. N. Appel, *Kanon und Kirche,* p. 376, argues that "The self-awareness of the church is ultimately the *self-awareness of the whole Christ,* head and body. Christ is determinative of the awareness and self-awareness of his body"; quoted in John Webster, "The Dogmatic Location of the Canon," *Neue Zeitschrift für Systematische Theologie und Religionsphilosophie* 43, no. 1 (2001): 27.

the Father who keeps the Son, clothed as creature, at his right hand. Pneumatological discourse enables the discourse of Father and Son and therefore of persons.

3.1.3. The Attempt to Separate Israel and Jesus

The Old Testament addresses itself to the many societies that come into confrontation with it. The New Testament is the way it does so.[22] Much biblical scholarship, however, treats the New Testament as a separate and autonomous testament. Such scholarship deals with the first century as though, in this century alone, Israel had to start to articulate its relationship with the world. It deals with the first century in ignorance of all previous and subsequent centuries. It asks simply whether the New Testament is a Jewish or Greco-Roman book. Scott Hafemann points out that our view of Paul, for instance,

> will be determined, above all, by whether one interprets his letters, predominantly against the Greco-Roman philosophical and religious world of Paul's day, as Bultmann argued over fifty years ago, or in the light of the Hellenistic-Jewish world of the first century and its scriptures, as Adolf Schlatter proposed in the early decades of this century.[23]

It is my argument that the New Testament is the public vindication of Israel by Israel's king before all other empires, and thus the witness of the Jewish people to all other peoples. Israel has seen many gentile regimes. Now Israel's Scriptures are opened and made readable to the gentiles by this New Testament, the witness raised by God. They express Israel's knowledge of itself as steward of the world and of Israel's mandate to rule it. We therefore have to ask whether modern biblical exegesis can read Israel's Scriptures as political-cosmological world-claim and understand the public and performative nature of Israel's action as one that anticipates

22. Markus Bockmuehl, *Revelation and Mystery in Ancient Judaism and Pauline Christianity* (Grand Rapids: Eerdmans, 1997), p. 124, argues that "[N]ew and Old stand in a reciprocal relationship: new revelation is always meta-revelation, given shape and texture by a charismatic reading of the old; yet once accepted and accorded its rightful status, this new disclosure becomes in turn instrumental for the understanding of the old, the 'proto-revelation.'"

23. Scott Hafemann, "Paul and His Interpreters," in *Dictionary of Paul and His Letters*, ed. Gerald F. Hawthorne, Ralph P. Martin, and Daniel G. Reid (Leicester: IVP, 1993), p. 678.

and practices a new economy of action. That exegesis which makes Israel's rites, purity teaching, sacrifice, and temple problematic serves only to render invisible the action given to Israel for our sake.

Jesus is the Son who makes all Israel the Son of God. This messiah makes all Israel the single entity that receives its identity from him. Together with his people Israel, Jesus is the oneness and indivisibility of God in his work. God's work and being are not divided into before Jesus and after him. If it were, Jesus would represent the division, and therefore the destruction, of God's work. Historical criticism identified Jesus as the first individual, and we must therefore ask whether it has not used Jesus to separate God from his work. The work of Bruce Malina and Dominic Crossan, along with René Girard and some liberation theologians, may be said to be based on the accusation that rabbinic Judaism had become an oppressive regime from which Jesus was defending the exploited. Susannah Heschel criticizes Ernst Käsemann for insisting that Jesus cannot be integrated into the background of Jewish piety of his time, so making him a figure suffering an oppression — inevitably imposed by Jews. The old polemical opposition of law and grace has, she believes, been replaced by the opposition of purity and compassion.[24] The criterion of dissimilarity by which the authenticity of a teaching ascribed to Jesus is determined by uniqueness, "found not in the things he shares with his contemporaries, but in the things wherein he differs from them," is the principle driving the scholarship of the historical Jesus.[25]

New Testament scholarship that does not allow the unity of Christ and Israel would be in continuity with the idealist or modern theology that seeks an individual. This scholarship would be looking for someone it has decided does not belong to his people, or they to him, an individual subject of narrative (Jesus), or a notional individual author of narrative (Paul). It would be searching the first century for the pioneer of twentieth-century humanity.[26] Such scholarship would be looking for the psychol-

---

24. Susannah Heschel, *Abraham Geiger and the Jewish Jesus* (Chicago: University of Chicago Press, 1998), p. 232.

25. Heschel, *Abraham Geiger and the Jewish Jesus*, p. 241, quoting Käsemann.

26. Making this accusation are, for example, Stephen C. Neill and N. T. Wright, *The Interpretation of the New Testament, 1861-1986* (Cambridge: Cambridge University Press, 1988); N. T. Wright, *The New Testament and the People of God* (London: SPCK, 1992), pp. 6-28; Francis Watson, *Text, Church and World: Biblical Interpretation in Theological Perspective* (Edinburgh: T&T Clark, 1994), pp. 30-45; and Watson, *Text and Truth: Redefining Biblical*

ogy of Jesus, understood as an individual, whereas it should relate this distinctly human mind, will, and set of opinions to the mind and *sensus communis* of the whole people of Israel. The rationale of Jesus' action comes, not from a psychology, but from the mandate of Israel displayed in Scripture. If biblical exegesis cannot do this, it will be merely reproducing a modern concept of mind, a psychology of interiority, that is not publicly responsible or contestable. On this basis Jesus would be the first of many people defined without relation, the object of historical critical science who must be identified by separating him from the people he gathers around him.[27] Such a New Testament studies would be unitarian. It would remove Jesus from Israel and refuse to take with him the manyness of the hands employed by the Word of God. This would be to impose an extrinsic criterion and create a new time, modernity, that defines itself by contrast with the time of God for Israel. It would tend to resist the claim that Jesus is the messiah whose world-rule all Israel participates in. Instead, we must say that Jesus, with his people Israel, is the oneness and indivisibility of God in his work.

Now we must hear two voices that offer a contrary view of the relationship of Israel and the Son. For Michael Wyschogrod "the divinity of Jesus is . . . incompatible with true monotheism." Wyschogrod is of course right to say "there cannot be any individual . . . whose relationship to God is unilateral . . . with the people of Israel not being the decisive presence

---

Theology (Edinburgh: T&T Clark, 1997), pp. 127-68. Marius Reiser, *Jesus and Judgement: The Eschatological Proclamation in Its Jewish Context* (Minneapolis: Fortress, 1997), p. 161, argues that "the decision of the individual for one or [the] other group [that determines one's eschatological lot] assumes greater significance; indeed this is the first moment at which such a thing is demanded at all. Liberal Protestantism, however, saw precisely in this the unique character of Jesus's message." Susannah Heschel, *Abraham Geiger and the Jewish Jesus*, p. 223: "Whereas the Jesus of the past hundred years has been portrayed primarily in opposition to the allegedly materialistic, superficial and even oppressive Judaism of his day, in recent years Jesus has been portrayed as opposing the Jewish laws of ritual purity."

27. It is certainly true, as Ian McFarland argues in "Christ, Spirit and Atonement," *International Journal of Systematic Theology* 3, no. 1 (2001): 86, that "if Jesus is to be confessed as fully human, his actions must have their source in a distinctly human mind and will." But this distinctly human mind must be related to the mind and *sensus communis* of the whole people of Israel. A theological pneumatology must answer Rogers's demand (see the previous section) that it represents the plurality and community brought into being by the Spirit, so the people of Israel is the source of Jesus' thoughts: he had learned from them, and thus he was in a measure their work.

serving as the purpose of the relation."[28] But we can reply that this does not justify Wyschogrod's assertion that God, who is not alone, without company or glory, may not become human. God may make humanity the proper predicate of his work. God is Spirit. He is able to move freely on both sides of a Creator-creature, divine-human line. Two-natures language is intended to state the doctrine of creation, not to problematize it. Such a line is a barrier to us, not to God. Rather, the distinction between Creator and creature is of God's making and is sustained with the single purpose of preparing us to receive him. It is the Spirit who guards this line. He distinguishes us from God by raising the Son out of our grasp, and he holds us in relationship with God, his divine action deciding the future of our nature. We are not different from God by *nature* but by God's *action*.

The result of Wyschogrod's view would seem to be that God may not be at home in the world, not at home in his own work. Is the divine-human or Creator-creature distinction absolute and prior to any divine action, so that this creaturely world is closed to God? But surely Israel may not be considered apart from its relationship with God. If what is perfect may not be broken, is it conceptually coherent to say that Israel was perfect and entire but then ceased to be so? The doctrine of the church is that Israel *will become* entire and perfect. Does such supersessionism come from a failure to understand the eschatological nature of scriptural statement?

Alan Segal concedes that God was found in this Jewish flesh. He believes that the term "the form of God" (Phil. 2:6) is ambiguous enough to make it applicable to the many "sons of God" portrayed in the Scriptures and Jewish apocalypticism.[29] The Christian community awarded to Jesus

---

28. Michael Wyschogrod, "A Jewish Perspective on the Incarnation," *Modern Theology* 12 (1996): 198. He goes on to argue that "the Church found God in this Jewish flesh. Perhaps this was possible because God is in all Jewish flesh." This is not a doctrine of election and freedom, but of substance and therefore necessity.

29. Alan F. Segal, "Paul's Thinking about Resurrection in Its Jewish Context," in *New Testament Studies* 44 (1998): 400-419. The relationship of notions of suffering and martyrdom to the idea that God is at work in and with the diaspora will be discussed in the next chapter. In "He who did not spare his own son . . . ," in *From Jesus to Paul,* ed. J. C. Hurd (Waterloo, Ont.: Wilfrid Laurier University Press, 1984), Segal argues that there was pre-Christian use of Isaac's martyrdom, and exegesis did understand martyrology and vicarious atonement. The concept of resurrection is linked to the problem of theodicy raised in the period of the Maccabean revolt, when resurrection was understood to be the reward for martyrdom. Isaac is preeminent among the martyrs. The Christians joined the messiah conceptuality to that of the servant who suffers.

"the name which is above every name," Lord *(Kyrios)*, the term used to translate and avoid the unutterable tetragrammaton *(YHWH)*. Philippians 2 says that Christ has the divine form *(morphē)*. But Segal does not want to link this divine form to what Paul has to say about this divine Son taking the form of a servant who labors, suffers, and is put to death by the gentiles. The Christian confession is not only that Jesus took the form of God, but that suffering our opposition is the form God's working took. There is no other form of God available to us, no other mode of access to God, than that opened by God coming to us, and in this coming, resisting our resistance — and overcoming it.

> [T]he Christ was depicted as an eternal aspect of divinity which was not proud of its high station but consented to take on human shape and suffer the fate of humanity, even death on a cross. . . . This transformation is followed by the converse, the retransformation into God.[30]

This is to understand the incarnation as reversible and reversed. In disagreement with Segal, therefore, we must say that the form of God is his being with his people, in the form of a servant who works and, in his working, suffers.[31] It is a suffering that must be related to God's ongoing relationship both with the exiled people of his election and with the waiting creation. The whole appearing of God, and thus the whole form and content of our knowledge of him, is as servant. Since we must be reminded that God is at work here, we could equally say that he takes the form of a laborer. God is a laborer, and we are his labor. The physical-bodily being of Jesus is not merely enthroned and restored to divine mode, but both enthroned and therefore at work, now bearing his people. Segal understands Jesus, Paul, and every other visionary to be an "incarnation" of Yahweh.[32] But this is an account that can be made only in the absence of discussion of the ongoing history of God's action with Israel — a work that includes bearing the resistance that Israel itself inflicts on God.

Has this New Testament and biblical scholarship properly represented

---

30. Segal, "Paul's Thinking about Resurrection in Its Jewish Context," p. 411.

31. See N. T. Wright, "Jesus Christ Is Lord: Philippians 2.5-11," in *The Climax of the Covenant: Christ and the Law in Pauline Theology* (Edinburgh: T&T Clark, 1991), pp. 57-71.

32. Segal, "Paul's Thinking about Resurrection in Its Jewish Context," p. 413 n. 21, argues that "This glorious body of the Christ is the spiritual body into which the believer will be subsumed, not the physical body of Jesus."

Israel as the servant of this Lord? Or is this representation not rather a continuation of "the tradition's tendency to undo the incarnation"?[33] The starting point of religious studies is that Israel must be resolved into some more general religious phenomenon, to ask whether Israel is a religion, ethnicity, or ethic. Israel must refuse any identification that involves division by these autonomous domains and insist that Israel's actions receive their proper definition only from Israel's Lord. Israel is knowable to him, not to any definition offered by the gentile world, until that gentile world comes to Israel through baptism for its own redefinition. In becoming that faithful servant, Jesus makes all Israel righteous, and so inaugurates the rule that Israel must exercise over the world, even in the face of its resistance. The reading of Jesus offered by Wyschogrod and Segal demonstrates the unitarian temptation to modern readers of the Scriptures. Beneath it is the constant monist tug of the protological ontology that tends to dissolve plurality in order to create individuals.

3.2. Israel as Son

3.2.1. The Priestly Work of the Son

The next question we have to ask is whether biblical studies allows for this theological definition of Israel as God's ongoing work. Will Adam take up the work God gives him and so be truly God's son? Although New Testament scholarship is familiar with the idea of an Adam Christology, it has not given it any serious employment. Yet an Adam Christology provides a narrative of an action. It allows us to say that Jesus has been *made* the Son by the Spirit. It is not enough to say solely that he *is* the Son. We must see him *becoming* that Son. He *learned* obedience. We must watch him learn it. We must see him taking up the discipline laid on a son, and in obedience taking on the work of a servant and laborer. The point, James Scott argues, is to provide an account of the *becoming* of the Son. "By ignoring this methodological starting point, Pauline studies currently labors under some confusion about the subject of divine sonship in general."[34] Of

33. Farrow, *Ascension and Ecclesia*, p. 249.

34. James M. Scott, *Adoption as Sons of God* (Tübingen: Mohr, 1992), p. 267. He goes on to say that *huiothesia, being made* a son, "is part of the stock of Hellenistic terms of adop-

course it is not only Pauline studies, but Christian doctrine more generally, that is deficient here. This and the next chapter will suggest that this deficiency can be remedied by more closely relating the identity of Israel, exhibited in the scriptural instruction on holiness and purity, to the question of the bringing up of a Son who is an obedient servant, and so linking Adam to Israel's cosmology and creation theology.[35] This is also to ask whether New Testament studies has not been driven by a continued antipathy to the frankly biological character of what it finds in the Bible. It has to be asked whether this antipathy drives it to maintain a dichotomy of spirit and flesh, to hold Israel's theological claims apart from its biological claims and so to reduce the degree to which Israel's cult looks like a fertility cult. I will suggest that we should understand that biology may be adopted as one idiom and instrument of the Spirit's preparation of many sons.

The Scriptures demonstrate Israel's concern with the producing of sons. Does Israel assume that the gentiles will either be attracted or defeated by Israel's own greater fecundity and success at producing sons for Abraham?[36] Does the priestly teaching on Israel's purity and holiness represent the coming into being of this Son, a theology of the coming of the

---

tion, and as such it denotes 'adoption as son(s).' Hence any attempt to translate *huiothesia* in Paul as simply 'sonship' sets the study on the wrong foot from the start" (267). "Christ is *the* heir of Abraham (Galatians 3.6) and *the* messianic Son of God promised in 2 Samuel 7.12 and 14 respectively" (268). "Adoption" is the appropriate concept for divine sonship. "By ignoring this methodological starting point, Pauline studies currently labours under some confusion about the subject of divine sonship in general" (269). Despite the argument of Frances Young, "Understanding Romans in the Light of 2 Corinthians," *Scottish Journal of Theology* 48 (1991): 434, that "Paul will not operate according to the patronage system," patronage, adopting sons and making them members of your household, is precisely the right concept. *Patronage* means making sons by what we could call "elective biology"; the term "affiliation" could also properly serve to translate *being made* a son.

35. T. D. Alexander, "Messianic Ideology in Genesis," in *The Lord's Anointed: Interpretation of Old Testament Messianic Texts*, ed. Philip E. Satterthwaite, Richard S. Hess, and Gordon J. Wenham (Carlisle: Paternoster, 1995), and Christopher Whitsett, "Son of God, Seed of David: Paul's Messianic Exegesis in Romans [1]:3-4," *Journal of Biblical Literature* 119, no. 4 (2000): 661-81, attempt to make this connection. Interest in the biological idiom of Israel's claim did not continue to serve discussion of Israel's theology, and in the nineteenth century it became a separate discipline, that of the history of religions.

36. The concept of the seed of Abraham is the concept that unites the two testaments. Kraus, *Das Volk Gottes*, p. 359, argues that "here we have the single master-concept that Paul employed to express the unity of the Old and New Testament people of God — the seed of Abraham."

Christ and thus of the coming into being of Adam? For want of a more adequate account I will attempt to sketch the biological idiom of Israel's political claim. The Israelite who sees semen on the sheets (Lev. 15:16) sees something more consequential than himself there.[37] He sees the life-substance of Israel, the combined presence of all generations, preceding and succeeding. Though it came out of him, it is the life-stuff of Adam and Abraham: it is not his, but theirs, and it returns to them. The single Israelite is no complete instantiation of Israel; his children are not the affirmation of his individuality, but the gift he must return to the Lord. God gives children, and a man must take them, sow them in his wife, nurture and bring them up. He must present them to the Lord in the temple where God accepts them back from him and accepts that Israelite by accepting his gift of his children.[38] Without children, he has no continuing being in Israel. A man's membership of Israel is confirmed by the arrival of the fruit of the seed given to him to plant in his wife. If his children also turn out to be obediently fertile, he is born again, not of a potential intrinsic to the flesh, but of the Spirit, or Seed, of Israel. Not all are Israel who are simply born to people who are, or whose parents were, Israel: they are Israel when they are born again of the living and enduring Seed and Spirit.

This seed does not always succeed in making a child for Abraham. The child becomes a son for Abraham when later he himself produces a son who is himself obedient, and himself produces a son, and so on. My eschatological reading of Genesis 22 indicates that the status of the whole line is

37. Jacob Milgrom, *Leviticus*, vol. 1 (New York: Doubleday, 1991), pp. 927-33, talks about the seed only in terms of impurity, not giving semen any theological significance or distinguishing it from any other discharge; Milgrom, Maccoby, and Neusner agree that the rules about washing out semen relate to the distinction between life and death, but leave life and death uninterpreted. This is surely not life as such, gentile life, life held in common with the world, but God's life for Israel. Social anthropology does not share the fastidiousness about sex and reproduction biblical studies has inherited from Christian distaste for talking about the demands and products of bodies. Biblical studies has not yet managed to talk about fertility as motive and explanation of human behavior.

38. Lawrence A. Hoffman, *Covenant of Blood: Circumcision and Gender in Rabbinic Judaism* (Chicago: University of Chicago Press, 1996), and Howard Eilberg-Schwartz, *The Savage in Judaism: An Anthropology of Israelite Religion and Ancient Judaism* (Bloomington: Indiana University Press, 1990), provide discussions of paternity. Only gender studies is prepared to talk about reproduction. Nancy Jay, *Throughout Your Generations Forever: Sacrifice, Religion and Paternity* (Chicago: University of Chicago Press, 1992), argues that sacrifice is the idiom of male reproduction.

waiting on the obedience of the very last son. Israel is a function of the obedience and arrival of the last and completing event of Israel-sonship. The period of seven days (Lev. 15:13) allows the seed time to come to fruition in the marriage, or to return to the temple. An Israelite went to the temple to show what moral and procreative acts his husbandry of the seed-and-blood of Israel had produced. The semen is as much the life of Israel as the blood in the temple. It must not remain with the individual Israelite. As long as purification sacrifice has not yet returned it to the temple where it belongs, it is out of place and makes impure whoever comes into contact with it. The blood of Israel is not confined to this present generation but is the function of all generations past and to come. The men of this generation are not of themselves capable of giving their wives children: the men and women together have to have children fathered on them by the patriarchs. The blood is the living and enduring life of Israel, and each individual Israelite must, by the observation of purity, demonstrate his obedience to the task of the production of sons for Israel.

3.2.2. The Economy of Sonship

Now we must turn to what we may call an Adam Christology. Adam is the father of humankind. This is not simply an ontological, but an eschatologically ontological, statement. Adam is the father of humankind *by promise*. He is being made a son, and a father of many sons.[39] Adam's seed does not of itself succeed in making many obedient sons. But Christ, set upstream of Adam, can transform the effect of Adam's death-replicating gene into that of a life-replicating gene. Adam's failed metabolism is set working again by being integrated into a larger and more complex metabolism. Here Adam's permanently activated death-gene functions healthily at its place in the whole life-generating economy of the God of Israel.

Christ adopts us as his sons. Then, like a good son, he presents us to his Father. Jesus has supplanted Adam in his position as father and de-

---

39. See Richard B. Hays, *The Faith of Jesus Christ: The Narrative Substructure of Galatians 3:1–4:11* (Grand Rapids: Eerdmans, 2002), pp. 131-32, and James D. G. Dunn, *Theology of Paul the Apostle* (Edinburgh: T&T Clark, 1998), pp. 379-85, on the discussion that renders *pistis Christou* "the faithfulness of Christ," rather than "faith in Christ." On the genealogy of Jesus, see W. D. Davies and Dale C. Allison, *Matthew*, The International Critical Commentary, vol. 1 (Edinburgh: T&T Clark, 1988), pp. 167-88, and Richard Bauckham, *Jude and the Relatives of Jesus* (Edinburgh: T&T Clark, 1990), pp. 326-42, 376-77.

moted him to a new position as son. Jesus recapitulates humanity; he re-fathers Adam. He is able not only to make sons of us, but to make of us *obedient* sons, ourselves able to bear sons to the Father. Then he hands back this lordship and fatherhood to his Father, to receive us again as brothers. In this relationship what is biological is not prior but serves as a mode of his determination to be father to us. The relationship into which we are adopted is spiritual, the work of the Spirit. It is the possibility of, and acknowledgment and realization of the possibility of, that decision of Son for Father and Father for Son by which the Son presents, and the Father adopts, many sons.

The Father extends time to the Son. The Son returns this time, well-used and full of fruit, to the Father. He honors his Father. The Father and the Son determine that we be both sons and fathers, and live in a generation that succeeds and is succeeded, in time. Our time takes a serial or narrative form.[40] We are bound to exert a lordship and selfhood against our fathers and have it exerted against us by the generation that succeeds us. The one wish of fathers is to produce sons to keep their name alive in the world.[41] To do this, the ancestors work with each generation to recycle the material of life. Blood is supplied to the ancestors, and it returns as seed and another generation of sons. Adam Christology is a successful response to this logic of life in the many formulations of pagan cosmologies. Our environment is constituted by a miasma of seed and spores. The regulations of Leviticus 13–15 are dedicated to ensuring that these alien elements *(stoicheia)* do not contaminate Israel but that Israel continues to be determined purely by the seed of Israel, the life of God.

So far we have seen that Israel is concerned to produce not only sons, but sons who were *holy.* Next we must say something about the work performed, and the life lived, by the people of Israel. We will do this by tackling the contentious issue of sacrifice, which, though it is the subject of a significant proportion of the Scriptures, became problematic first for Christian doctrine and subsequently for modern sensibilities.

Sacrifice represented the commissioning of Israel to the office of steward of creation. Sacrifice *(sacri-ficere),* it must be remembered, means

---

40. This was the argument of John Zizioulas that we examined in Chapter 1.

41. See R. Albertz, *A History of Israelite Religion in the Old Testament Period* (Louisville: Westminster, 1994), vol. 1, pp. 96-101, on the family cult. According to Hebrews a priest is the man who by continuing the family line is going to do the right thing by his fathers, to ensure their continuation by redeeming them.

making holy. The temple sacrifice represents the work of the Son in making holy sons and presenting them to the Father. In the modern anthropology in which all already have the full status of persons, there is no room for understanding the being of a person as a work shared among many.[42] In the first chapter, I introduced Kant's criticism of the Christian account of atonement in which Christ bears our sins. Kant's charge was this:

> Moreover, so far as we can judge by our reason's standards of right, this original debt, or at any rate the debt that precedes whatever good a human being may ever do . . . cannot be erased by somebody else. For it is not a transmissible liability which can be made over to someone else, [in] the manner of a financial debt (where it is all the same to the creditor whether the debtor himself pays up or somebody else for him), but the most personal of all liabilities, namely a debt of sins which only a culprit, not the innocent can bear, however magnanimous the innocent might be in wanting to take the debt upon himself for the other.[43]

Modern theological anthropology has largely followed Kant in this. It does not allow that persons receive their personhood from God, and thus it has had the greatest difficulty in setting out an account of the death of Jesus Christ in terms of a single work shared by the Father, Son, and Holy Spirit. This difficulty is itself the result of a long failure to relate the work of Christ to the sacrificial, liturgical creation theology by which Israel displays this economy of sonship before the world.[44] The rationality of sacrifice is dependent on such a view of Israel's commissioning and employment in the persons-formative work of Israel's God. To modern theology, Kant's anthropology of ontologically unrelated individuals seemed to deliver a blow to a representational and substitutionary view of the purpose of sacrifice, which Western theology had long understood in expiatory and propitiatory, rather than paideutic and ontological, terms. E. P. Sanders, for example, argues that ancient Israel did not understand sacrifices to re-

---

42. We saw in Chapter 2 that being a person involves multiple roles, in which a person represents other persons in multiply-nested conversations and roles without being any the less himself or herself.

43. Immanuel Kant, *Religion within the Boundaries of Mere Reason,* trans. and ed. Alan Wood and George di Giovanni (Cambridge: Cambridge University Press, 1998), 6.72.

44. Ingolf Dalferth, *Der auferweckte Gekreuzigte. Zur Grammatik der Christologie* (Tübingen: Mohr Siebeck, 1994), pp. 237-315, provides an important theological discussion of sacrifice.

move the sin of the individual by representation or substitution, as Christian doctrine had seemed to teach.[45] In Dalferth's summary,

> It is not enough to say he has died instead of us, or in the place of us . . .
> nor for the sake of us — these are all vicarious, whether legal/penal or
> sacrificial/cultic. They involve the substitution of one party for the other
> and these presuppose an ontological individualism.[46]

According to Sanders, atonement for Israel was not so much a response to something that had gone wrong, but the constant process of keeping Israelites in the covenant. This was secured by the everyday business by which the temple registered all the status changes through which members of Israel progressed in the course of life.[47] Temple sacrifices were not related to individual moral misdemeanors, so they were not in the first place about guilt-removal. The atonement rituals do not describe a priest atoning an individual Israelite. They describe the atonement of the temple. Stowers and McLean believe this disallows talk of one man atoning for another and so of Jesus taking our place and atoning for us.[48] Although individuals came to the temple to have their sins removed, this should be understood as part of the maintenance of the whole body of Israel, by which marginalized Israelites were brought back into communion with God and his people. Such reincorporation was a regular task and the purpose of the temple sacrifices.

All New Testament scholarship is confronted by the problem created by Kant's rejection of the possibility that one person represents another.

---

45. E. P. Sanders, *Paul and Palestinian Judaism: A Comparison of Patterns of Religion* (London: SCM, 1977), pp. 474-511.

46. Ingolf U. Dalferth, "Christ Died for Us," in *Sacrifice and Redemption: Durham Essays in Theology,* ed. Stephen W. Sykes (Cambridge: Cambridge University Press, 1991), p. 320.

47. E. P. Sanders, *Judaism: Practice and Belief* (London: SCM, 1992), pp. 112-16.

48. Stanley K. Stowers, *A Rereading of Romans: Justice, Jews, and Gentiles* (New Haven: Yale University Press, 1994), pp. 206-13; B. H. McLean, *The Cursed Christ: Mediterranean Expulsion Rituals and Pauline Soteriology* (Sheffield: Sheffield Academic Press, 1996), and David Seeley, *The Noble Death: Graeco-Roman Martyrology and Paul's Concept of Salvation* (Sheffield: JSOT Press, 1990), dismiss theology informed by the sacrificial conceptualities presented by the Old Testament in favor of the portrayal of Christ's death as an example of (Hellenistic) martyrdom in the tradition of the Maccabeans. I owe these references to Dan Bailey and Richard Bell.

German scholarship in particular has recognized that it must find an expression of biblical anthropology able to withstand Kant's criticism.[49] According to Gese and Stuhlmacher, an inclusive event of cultic representation of the people's life before God was effected for Israel when sacrificial blood, the life substance (Lev. 17:11), was splashed over the holy objects, in particular the mercy-seat *(hilastērion)*. Blood was the medium that "brings people to God."[50] Worshipers experienced death and resurrection in the death of the animal they brought into the temple and with which they identified. Stuhlmacher argues that sins were saved up to be dealt with in yearly installments. In order to deal with them, Jesus was made the *hilastērion*. With Christ, the new age of the righteousness of God has broken through to sweep all sins finally away. Whether *hilastērion* means the event or the site of atonement, the sins of Israel were all dealt with together on that one day in the year. The atonement of the high priest is not merely a technical matter of preparing the place to perform that function, but is the atonement of the whole people.[51] Missing from the account offered by these scholars is what makes blood symbolic and the meaning of this death obvious. But we cannot be content with natural symbols if this is to be a theological account. A more theological interpretation of death might suggest that it is that gentile existence from which Israel is redeemed, and since this is a passing form of existence it may be said to be dying. This scholarship refers to extrinsic theories of symbol, with little indication of who determines these symbols.[52] It transfers the problem from one of atonement to one of hermeneutics and epistemology, rather than of the theological self-understanding of the community addressed and formed by the word of God.

Resources for a more robust account now seem to be forthcoming

49. Summarized by Dalferth as "the Tübingen response," in "Sühnopfer," in *Der auferweckte Gekreuzigte*, pp. 241-83.

50. This is the argument of Peter Stuhlmacher, *Biblische Theologie des Neuen Testaments* (Göttingen: Vandenhoeck & Ruprecht, 1992-99), vol. 2, pp. 316-48; assessed by Dunn, *The Theology of Paul the Apostle*, pp. 212-23.

51. This is argued for by Daniel P. Bailey, "Christ as *Kapporet*" (Ph.D. thesis, Cambridge, 1999).

52. The contributors to Bernd Janowski and Michael Welker, *Opfer: Theologische und kulturelle Kontexte* (Frankfurt am Main: Suhrkamp, 2000), do not seem to have attempted the sort of creation theology or cosmology required here or to have learned from Mary Douglas the semiotics by which this can be done.

from Bernd Janowski and Ingolf Dalferth. Janowski argues that retribution does not mean revenge.[53] Instead it means restitution, by which the act is returned to its originator. The deed returns to its doer, not by any necessity, but in an economy of response, in which it is not objects that are exchanged but those forms of action that promote the relatedness of their agents.[54] In Dalferth's view "the relational ontological structure of the total soteriological event calls for interpretations of the credal statement that Christ has died for us which do justice to the irreducible relationality of the reality expressed."[55] "Identification is reciprocal," says Dalferth:

> Localising something is identifying, not merely describing it. . . . It is a cognitive process in which something is identified to someone in such a way that the addressees of the identification are localised relative to one another.[56]

We expect others to situate themselves so we can orient ourselves by them. This return of identity is what the concepts of *talion* and retaliation refer to. Though *talion* means *paying back,* it does not mean getting your own back, but returning to others the being and relationship missing from their action toward you. It means supplying to others what they were not able to supply to you.[57]

---

53. Janowski, "'Die Tat kehrt zum Täter zurück'. Offene Fragen in Umkreis des 'tun-ergehen-Zusammenhangs,'" in *Die Rettende Gerechtigkeit* (Neukirchener: Neukirchen-Vluyn, 1999), links the concepts of retribution, *talion*, and return.

54. Janowski, "'Die Tat kehrt zum Täter zurück,'" pp. 190-91.

55. Dalferth, "Christ Died for Us," p. 320.

56. Dalferth, *Theology and Philosophy* (Oxford: Blackwell, 1988), p. 204.

57. Janowski, "'Die Tat kehrt zum Täter zurück,'" calls it "a category of social interaction that refers to our acting-to-and-for-one-another in a complex economy in which we may have confidence that, despite all appearances, there will be justice and our being will be returned to us." I have called this nexus of action-and-reaction *(Tun-ergehen Zusammenhang)* an economy of response. Bruce J. Malina, *The New Testament World: Insights from Cultural Anthropology* (London: SCM, 1983), argues for such a single nexus, an economy of honor. René Girard, *Violence and the Sacred* (Baltimore: Johns Hopkins University Press, 1977), argues for an economy of emulation or rivalry. Some part of the theological tradition opposes ransom or penalty because it believes this punishment or penalty can be owed only to Satan. Yet the concept of ransom belongs to the perichoretic metaphysic, referred to in Chapter 1, within which we all own and possess and account for each other and bear account to each other. When this metaphysic is abandoned, ransom is certainly a problem, but so also is representation. Payability to *someone else* is problematic precisely because the status

Kant believed that the person was irreducible, and so there could be no exchange of action or being between persons. Now we are able to make a response, using the concepts of task and office. In reply to Sanders's claim that Lutheran talk of representation and substitution is alien to Israelite sacrifice, I suggest that we should see Old Testament talk of atonement of place as a solution, not a problem. If we make a hard distinction between individuals and persons defined by relation, we can say that Israelites came to the temple as individuals and left as persons. They arrived alienated and left reconciled with God and his people. They came friendless and left befriended. This is what Christian doctrine terms "justification." God says to them, "You are with me," and by this announcement these people are brought into the people of God, so that no other power may touch them. It is precisely individuality, the state of being with insufficient relationship, that was atoned for by the supply of relationship with God.

This is not an event in which places are simply swapped. The Son of Man comes to us in our place, but he occupies a bigger area of the place than we do. We are not pushed out of it, but out of our way of occupying it and into his way of occupying it. We are given place, and, as we become ready for it, we are given *more* place, and given the means to occupy it, so by a process of paideia we are levered up into a fuller and more complex appropriation of the place God has for us.[58] Much biblical and theological scholarship relies on an underdetermined hermeneutic of symbol. I argued in Chapter 2 that symbols have meanings in structures, and structures grow out of the life of a community and have meanings because they have functions. They *do* things and *transform* things; they open and close ways of life within that community. An account of persons requires an account of the world as sets of regularities, local purposes, and openings. In the course of any theological account of persons, the world is set into, and transformed by, an eschatological context. It is identified and received as

---

of *anyone else,* of *others* as such, is a problem. The work of Janowski and Dalferth complements the scholarship of the faithfulness of Christ *(pistis Christou),* which understands that persons are made by mutual constitution (determined by the decision of Christ), for which see Hays, *The Faith of Jesus Christ.*

58. Dalferth, *Der auferweckte Gekreuzigte,* p. 306, refers to a "creaturely place." The relational character of the salvific action of God in Christ Jesus would be quite obscured if we did not understand that it is above all not about what Jesus did or suffered, but about who, in this doing and suffering, he is: the creaturely place of the self-disclosing presence of the Creatorly and new-creating love of God.

creation, the proper place of creatures. As Janowski points out, what we are given is not an object, but a new action, a new behavior and behavior-world.[59] Humankind is given a place and a job to do in it.

3.3. Israel and Its King

3.3.1. Israel and the World

The next question to ask is about place. Has New Testament studies found a way to accommodate Israel's claim that God has given the world to Israel, that it is Israel's place and mandate? Can New Testament studies read the Old Testament as Israel's response to, and refusal of, the empires of the world? Can it understand Israel's cosmology as the whole idiom of her polity, politics, and self-understanding? Or has New Testament studies succeeded only in making the New Testament a discussion of the impact on Israel of the Hellenic and Roman empires? Can it concede that the Torah resisted many empires before Greece and Rome and is equally able to resist all subsequent foreign political claims, even including those of our own time? If New Testament studies reads the New Testament as a separate testament, and in deliberate ignorance of all the previous and subsequent centuries of Israel's address to the gentiles, it will treat the first century as though Israel had never encountered gentiles before, and perhaps thus as utterly vulnerable to Hellenism. We must look for a less Marcionite New Testament studies, better able to contribute to a politically more sophisticated theology.

N. T. Wright has provided a strong version of the meaning of messiah, and so of the claim of Israel. The all-embracing royal and religious claims of Caesar are directly challenged by the equally all-embracing claims of Israel's God.

> The more Jewish we make Paul's 'gospel', the more it confronts directly the pretensions of the Imperial cult, and indeed all other paganisms whether 'religious' or 'secular'. It is because of Jewish monotheism that there can be 'no king but God'. . . . The Pauline *euangelion* is based firmly in Judaism; at the same time, and indeed precisely for this reason,

---

59. Janowski, "'Die Tat kehrt zum Täter zurück,'" p. 190.

it functions as the royal announcement which challenges the pagan principalities and powers.[60]

Wright holds together the covenant and the apocalyptic. "The real apocalypse has taken place in the resurrection of the messiah Jesus but that event can only be understood and its significance elaborated through an exploration of the covenant to Abraham."[61] Israel had a clear idea what restoration would look like, and what has happened to Jesus unmistakably fits this idea. "Judaism in Paul's day, as all Jews knew, had not in fact been redeemed within its own terms of expectation."[62] Paul saw that God had really given Israel justice. Jesus had won this restoration, which was clearly what was promised to, but not won by, anyone else in Israel. According to Wright, Paul realized that Jesus was therefore

> that which his supporters had claimed, namely Israel's messiah; that this Jesus, the crucified and risen messiah of Israel, was now enthroned as Lord of all, Jew and Gentile alike; that these events were indeed the inauguration of 'the age to come'. . . . As a result of this whole complex of thought (complex for us, reconstructing it; plain sailing for a first century Pharisee) the pagan idolatry of the world has been decisively defeated, and those who adhered to it — that is, the gentiles — were to be summoned to give allegiance to this strange and subversive Jewish messiah.[63]

Wright argues that Jesus is the arrival of Yahweh in a world of real and political conflict, hence "the gospel of Christ" is the arrival of the ruler named Jesus.

60. N. T. Wright, "Gospel and Theology in Galatians," in *Gospel in Paul: Studies on Corinthians, Galatians and Romans for Richard N. Longenecker*, ed. L. Ann Jervis and Peter Richardson (Sheffield: Sheffield Academic Press, 1994), pp. 228-29. Wright goes on to say: "When their god, Jahweh, acted within history to deliver his people, the spurious gods of the heathen would be defeated. If and when Jahweh set up his own king as the true ruler, his true earthly representative, all other kingdoms would be confronted with their rightful overlord." Wright's argument depends on a conceptual henotheism, also argued for by Christopher Seitz, *Word without End*, p. 255. I shall use this conceptual henotheism in Chapter 6 to argue against a dichotomy of religious language and nonreligious language that would confine theological claims to a domain of untestable and therefore non-public religious discourse.

61. Wright, "Gospel and Theology in Galatians," p. 232.

62. Wright, "Gospel and Theology in Galatians," p. 234.

63. Wright, "Gospel and Theology in Galatians," p. 234. This discussion of messiah now also appears in Wright, *The Resurrection of the Son of God* (London: SPCK, 2003), pp. 553-78.

The temple was the court of the great king who gives justice; the nations were attracted to Jerusalem because it was their belief that there was justice for them there. But the first-century leadership of Israel had managed to create a divided, oppressed, and therefore unclean nation. The temple had become the possession of Israel, the envious elder brother. Jesus enacted Israel's king riding into Jerusalem, simultaneously in vindication of Israel and in judgment of it, the revenge of the gentiles against it.[64] The temple cleansing was a claim to kingship, judgment, and revenge. The gentiles who crucified Jesus and destroyed the temple were doing God's work, so God was acting here, publicly and politically. As the gentiles represent all that is cursed and separated, dead and dead-making, the arrival of the God of Israel took the form of Israel hanging curse-like on a tree. Israel handed its king over to the gentiles, and Israel's God handed Israel over to the gentiles, making Israel, in the single figure of the messiah, the gentiles' king, too.[65]

3.3.2. Jesus Inaugurates the Rule of Israel

Israel is God's word of refusal to the gentiles. God's word is No. Israel can really be said to speak, and to be, this speech-act in which Israel is distinguished from the gentiles and made holy. It is not Israel's word alone, but God's word. Israel may long deny its election and delay setting to work. But God's word does not return to him empty. Israel participates in the defeat of the gentiles and is their new hope.[66]

Israel is the lord of the nations. It is not by chance that Israel finds itself subjected to the nations and fighting for its identity. Israel is always under the threat of absorption, which would make Israel indistinguishable from them and no longer holy. The new gentile (Christian) form of Israel's being

---

64. N. T. Wright, *Jesus and the Victory of God* (London: SPCK, 1996), p. 639; Jesus came into Jerusalem at Passover, on a donkey, and crying for Jerusalem, "the symbol and embodiment of YHWH's return to Zion."

65. Wright, "Curse and Covenant: Galatians 3.10-14," in *The Climax of the Covenant*, p. 151: "The crucifixion of the Messiah is . . . the *quintessence* of the curse of exile, and its climatic act."

66. The relationship is not causal. Israel does not change anything or cause anything, but Israel is the medium in which everything is made utterly different, as we will see in the next chapter. I argue with Wright that Israel participates in the defeat of the gentiles, and against Wright that the obedience on the cross of one member of Israel is "retroactively" causative of the obedience of all Israel.

is distinguished by the realization that what is significant is not that Israel is oppressed by this or that nation, but that Israel has to bear all the nations. Israel may not fight or disown them, but may only confess itself to be, in fact, both servant and lord of all. The messiah who is king of Israel is king of the nations, too, rival to Caesar and to every individual and institutional world-hegemony. He is king of kings. To make the same point again, if Jesus is messiah, all Israel is messiah. Christ and Israel are not yet synonyms, but when the new Adam is at once one and many, they will be. Warnings against trinitarianism rely on an individualism that would leave God without servants or speech. The first clause of the Decalogue, that God is alone and is the only God, does not clash with the equal imperative that his servants are his and have no identity other than the identity he gives them. The Spirit, in the history of Israel, built and assembled one full man, and when that man was successfully entirely with God, creature at the right hand of his Creator, the Holy Spirit was able to replicate his character in a new community. This community spans and unites heaven and earth.

3.4. Who Can Tell the Story of the Son?

Next we must ask who is able to tell Israel's story. Who can recount the Scriptures such that they are the word of God that not only goes out to humanity but also returns, bringing with it humanity to God? The question of who can read the Scriptures is the question of who can read Israel. If, as Leo Purdue believes, narrative (literature) is replacing history as the major interpretative paradigm for Scripture, the question becomes "Who has the right to any scriptural narrative?"[67] Stephen Fowl asks, "Who can read Abraham's story?"[68] Fowl argues that every narrative places its teller and hearers, so a

---

67. Leo G. Perdue, *The Collapse of History: Reconstructing Old Testament Theology* (Minneapolis: Fortress, 1994), pp. 232-34. The different metaphors of New Testament studies and patristic or early Christian studies derive from the different hermeneutical histories of the two disciplines. New Testament studies relate to text as the record of history. But without salvation history or teleology, can there be history? Can New Testament studies work on the paradigm of history if it has ruled out talk of God's dealings with humanity?

68. Stephen E. Fowl, "Who Can Read Abraham's Story?" in *Engaging Scripture: A Model for Theological Interpretation* (London: Blackwell, 1998). He points out that "the internal coherence of Paul's reading presupposes and requires that Abraham's story be read within the context of an *ecclesia*" (p. 134).

story cannot be told by just anybody, but only by those who participate in it. Whoever can tell this story must know how it ends, and to do this they must be able to distinguish themselves from the story, such that they can tell it — it is not just the sum of the things they are. The God who raised one of our number from the dead can tell our story in such a way as to make it not necessary, so that our failures do not become finally definitive of us. God is both audience of the story we tell about ourselves and its judge and corrector, who can improve on our endings, turning our disaster into redemption.[69] This, I will argue, makes the story of the collapse of mediation a warning story, not a story the truth of which is finally settled. The task of telling the story of Israel must be accompanied by a separate conceptual work that maintains the language of the story in good order.[70] Such conceptual work Israel calls the law. The story and the law are in mutually constitutive relationship. The law makes holy the community, and only the holy community can tell its story in a way that follows the account of it given by God.

Some New Testament scholars have recently started to understand Scripture again as commentary on other Scripture. Richard Hays argues that the reader is required to interpret a citation or allusion by recalling aspects of the original context not explicitly quoted. In this manner Scripture comes to inform all the instincts and imagination of its readers.[71] It is the sons who may read the Scriptures and tell the story of Israel, but equally reading the Scripture makes a son of you.[72] Narrative, parable, and enacted symbol are

69. Christopher Seitz, *Word without End*, p. 11, argues that "historical-critical methods and hermeneutics of assent will stand outside and fail to grasp that God is reading us, not we him."

70. In Chapter 5 I will argue that exegesis must understand itself to be in conversation both with dogmatics, as the tradition of exegesis, and with philosophy, as the work of referring the conceptuality of exegesis and dogmatics to the discipline of wider public speech.

71. Richard B. Hays, *Echoes of Scripture in the Letters of Paul* (New Haven: Yale University Press, 1989); Scott J. Hafemann, "Paul, Moses and the History of Israel," in *Paul and the Scriptures of Israel*, ed. Craig A. Evans and James A. Sanders (Sheffield: JSOT Press, 1993), and N. T. Wright, *The New Testament and the People of God*, pp. 137-43, and *Jesus and the Victory of God*, pp. 133-44, set out similar hermeneutics of texts and reading communities in mutual constitution.

72. Scott, *Adoption as Sons of God*, p. 268, argues that "Christ is *the* heir of Abraham (Galatians 3.6) and *the* messianic Son of God promised in 2 Samuel 7.12 and 14 respectively. . . . Believers who are thus baptised into the messianic Son of God and take up his very cry of 'Abba' to the Father (Galatians 4.6) participate with him in the Davidic promise of divine adoption."

means to conceptualize the Scripture reading in which audiences find themselves not only implicated but constituted.[73] Parable telling obliges listeners to assess for themselves which roles in the Scriptures they are involuntarily playing out. It gives them an opportunity to identify which story is going to end badly, and so to swap to the winning side in the history of Israel. These stories constitute the whole grammar that allows the society to say and do some things and not others.[74] This performative hermeneutic of echoes and resonances relies on a single world-fabric of motives and purposes set in teleology and narrative. It is a theory about an affective continuum that is a function of all that is said within it. For the sake of our comprehension of the Bible these scholars are building a theory about the cement that holds a society together and makes it a single, albeit warring, entity.[75]

New Testament studies approaches Scripture as text. Until the advent of reader theory, New Testament studies most often dealt with texts as though they were things, with essences to be reached by stripping away the exterior. But a text is not a simple object in this sense, but a fabric of associations and relations. In the case of the Scriptures, this is a fabric of sociality that must be related to the determination of God to make us persons in relation.[76] We cannot strip away the relationship to find what is beneath either texts or persons. Questions about the identity of the embodied person of Jesus, the Son who sits at the Father's right hand, can be answered only by pointing to events of relationship of Father and Spirit. Jesus is the source and definition of all the relationship and history that he names Israel. We have to find a way of understanding Scripture as *action*, initiated by God, in which God brings up Israel.

73. See Fowl, *Engaging Scripture*, pp. 75-91 and 113-19, for a similar argument.

74. See Wright, *Jesus and the Victory of God*, pp. 125-44, for this argument.

75. Despite the new interest in performance, in honor, and in speech acts, Hays, Wright, and Fowl have not bought far into the philosophy of performance but still hold most stock in the voluntarist philosophy of reflection, in which the effective assumption is that a fabric of obligations, expectations, narratives, and forms of contracting-together is truer of first-century society than of our own because moderns are not in the same way the creatures of narrative and relationship.

76. Webster, "The Dogmatic Location of the Canon," *Neue Zeitschrift für Systematische Theologie und Religionsphilosophie* 43, no. 1 (2001): 26, argues that "Paying attention to the canon as ecclesial concept may help extract a theological account of the Scripture from giving too formal or juridical an account of the relation of the canon to the church by stressing that canonicity is best understood in terms of its function in 'establishing and governing certain networks of relationships'" (quoting Fowl, *Engaging Scripture*, p. 3).

3.4.1. Who Can Read the Scriptures?

Which comity has a right to the Scriptures of Israel? The question of who can read the Scriptures is the question of who can correctly discern the identity of Israel. Jon Levenson argues that there is a significant difference between the Scripture reading of the two communities, Jewish and gentile. In Jewish reading of Scripture, Jewish history has wrongly come to overtake Jewish belief as determinative of Jewish being.[77] But it is not "history" or ethnicity but confession that determines who is a member of this community, for it is the faithful confessing Jewish community that is really Jewish. Scripture is the live and continuing history of this people in biblical and post-biblical periods, which has to be lived and performed correctly again by each generation. The telling of the law as story belongs together with the keeping of the law as commandment. "Nothing is more delicate than the interplay of universalism and particularism in traditional Jewish theology. Take away the theology, and the interplay disappears or mutates."[78]

But Levenson plays down the difference expressed by the doctrine of election. He informs us that "Israel was not chosen on merit."[79] Yet this is scarcely the issue. What is at issue is whether we can and even must say that, having been chosen and tested, Israel becomes different from the nations. This is not to say that the gentiles can discern that difference, although it is for their benefit that Israel is different. Equally, the difference (even, superiority) of the Jews is not the possession of the Jews, and it may be empirically as inaccessible to them as it is to the gentiles. Yet they must confess that they have a better law because they have a better master than the other nations. It might be countered that Jewish reluctance to speak more clearly on the doctrine of election is a matter of good taste or realism born of an instinct for survival. Is it bad taste to do anything but leave the matter alone, or must Christian theology assert itself to express the difference? Israel is not claiming to know only what any nation really might know. It must claim that the nations fail to worship the one God and his

77. J. D. Levenson, "Why Jews Are Not Interested in Biblical Theology," in *Judaic Perspectives on Ancient Israel,* ed. Jacob Neusner, Baruch A. Levine, and Ernest S. Frerichs (Minneapolis: Fortress, 1987), pp. 281-307.

78. Jon D. Levenson, "The Universal Horizon of Biblical Particularism," in *Ethnicity and the Bible,* ed. Mark G. Brett (Leiden: Brill, 1996), p. 169.

79. Levenson, "The Universal Horizon of Biblical Particularism," p. 159.

one covenant and law and that they worship instead many other rival gods by whom they are held in misery.

Is there one set of Scriptures shared between two communities, Jewish and Christian? Has one of them better right to these Scriptures by virtue of having acquired them first, such that the community that came to them later has a weaker claim or even represents a falsification of them? Alternatively, are there two distinct sets of Scriptures for two communities, for Jews the Jewish Scriptures, and for Christians the Old and New Testaments? In "Why Jews Are Not Interested in Biblical Theology," Levenson has argued that biblical theology is in fact always Protestant exegesis rather than engagement with Jews or Jewish Scripture.[80] Is it the case that the Old Testament is Jewish and the New Testament Christian, so that there is the Hebrew Bible, but no book called the Old Testament? Is the inclusion of the Torah and Prophets in the Christian Scriptures even a "scandalous annexation"?[81] Is Levenson right in saying that neither Jewish nor Christian scholarship is anything but very marginally either Jewish or Christian, both neutered by that third worldview that reigns in universities? The extent to which Christians read the Old Testament is precisely the extent to which they are Christian. The extent to which they read the New Testament to the exclusion of the Old Testament is the extent to which they are Marcionite rather than Christian. Do students of the Christian Scriptures too glibly refer to their discipline as New Testament studies, failing to realize how much we are all the unwitting students of Gabler, de Wette, and others responsible for the disciplinary division between New Testament and Old Testament scholarship? Does this disciplinary division divide the indivisible witness and testament of the one God?[82]

---

80. Levenson, "Why Jews Are Not Interested in Biblical Theology," pp. 303-4; see also Levenson, "Theological Consensus or Historicist Evasion?" in *Hebrew Bible or Old Testament?* ed. Roger Brooks and John J. Collins (Notre Dame: Notre Dame University Press, 1990). Roland E. Murphy, "Old Testament/Tanakh — Canon and Interpretation," in Brooks and Collins, eds., *Hebrew Bible or Old Testament?* pp. 12-27, rightly argues that the Hebrew Bible and the Old Testament are different books, and that this is a question of canon, a fact of literary description, not a matter that historical criticism can determine.

81. This is the suggestion of Hans-Georg Geyer, "Solus Christus," in *Ja und Nein: Christliche Theologie im Angesicht Israels,* ed. Klaus Wengst and Gerhard Sass (Neukirchen-Vluyn: Neukirchener, 1998), p. 16.

82. Christopher R. Seitz, "Two Testaments and the Failure of One Tradition-History," in *Figured Out: Typology and Providence in Christian Scripture* (Louisville: Westminster John Knox, 2001), discusses the unity of this witness.

3.4.2. Supersession and Dialogue

Why has the church called this Testament *Old?*[83] It could perhaps be that it was from the beginning, original and therefore genuine. Because it is the original Testament it is the actual and continuing basis of creation and re-creation. It is ever alive and new, and makes all things new. The structure and logic of this house, which determines the life possible within it, was laid down as the house was built. Any other logic or testament written later, unrelated to the event of its building, is spurious. This Testament is ever alive because it is that covenant and economy within which the world was built, and by which it is sustained in life and allowed to come to no ending other than that which satisfies the original testator. The *New* Testament is an introduction to the Scriptures written for gentiles, a special form of attachment whereby gentiles are brought into compatibility with the Jewish Scriptures, and thus enabled to draw life and sustenance from them. Of course, a testament is the work of a testator, the witness of someone who witnesses to himself.[84]

Does reading the Bible and offering any summary of its contents — by, for example, taking one concept such as salvation history or covenant as central and confessional — do violence to the plurality of what is there? Does it impose a limit on the communities that may read it and be liberated by it? Is Gerhard von Rad or Brevard Childs, or any Christian reader, attempting to bring the variety of the material in the biblical text under a control not theirs to impose? Walter Brueggemann wants to maintain in complete freshness the admission that God's action is violent, sheerly

---

83. Watson, *Text and Truth*, pp. 179-80, argues that it is called the Old Testament in relation to the New, but also to some degree because the New Testament brings something not present in the Old Testament. Watson asks whether Childs sets the Old Testament alongside the New "in a relationship of pure simultaneity" and whether this threatens their proper difference. Seitz, "Christological Interpretation of Texts and Trinitarian Claims to Truth," *Scottish Journal of Theology* 52 (1999) asks whether Watson is able to establish that the Old Testament is determinative of the meanings of the New, albeit that the meanings of the New may not be read out of the Old apart from the New.

84. Lindbeck, "Postcritical Canonical Interpretation," in *Theological Exegesis: Essays in Honor of Brevard S. Childs,* ed. Christopher R. Seitz and Kathryn Greene-McCreight (Grand Rapids: Eerdmans, 1999), argues that Childs's use of the concept of witness must be augmented by the narrative-symbolic approach, represented by Hays, and the authorial discourse approach, exemplified by Wolterstorff.

other, and bafflingly unknowable.[85] But the action of God is surprising and alarming not only because God is unknowable, but much more because God is knowable.

It is not in the gift either of Christianity or of Judaism to prevent itself making too expansive or too modest a reading of Scripture. Neither can prevent itself from effectively ruling out the real and different reading the other community makes. Any reading of the Old Testament runs the risk of being a reduction of it, and a closing of the possibilities of reading the Hebrew Bible. Any reading of the Hebrew Bible risks being a closure of the possibilities of reading the Old Testament. Has academic biblical studies decided that the community that wrote the Scriptures, and did so for its own benefit, is the community from whose clutches this text must be taken? Is it the mission of biblical studies to rescue the biblical texts from the Christian and Jewish communities?[86] But neither the Christian nor the Jewish community, neither half of the single community of God, is autonomous. The Old Testament, the record of the history of the people of Israel, is not diminished by the New Testament, for among other things the New Testament is the teaching that God is not here and the end is not yet.

Is not a chief part of the unaccountable, and therefore perhaps violent, action of God that he elects a people? Might it not be that it is precisely the elect who lead the protest about this action? Israel might well try to find some less conspicuous form of being. It is unaccountable that God chooses, and he chooses a number. It is no more reasonable that he choose many than that he choose few, or one rather than none. This is scandalous to the supersessionism represented by the modern understanding of time, which thinks first that each particular thing is offensive until it is reabsorbed back into the universal, and then that each particular thing is by necessity replaced by the next particular thing. It understands only that, because God is one and humankind plural, God must represent a threat to that plurality. I have already argued that the fully trinitarian doctrine of God witnesses to the communion of divine persons, who solely guarantee the possibility of communion, plurality, and particularity for us.

---

85. Walter Brueggemann, *Theology of the Old Testament: Testimony, Dispute, Advocacy* (Minneapolis: Augsburg Fortress, 1997), pp. 359-99.

86. Markus Bockmühl, "'To Be or Not to Be': The Possible Futures of New Testament Scholarship," *Scottish Journal of Theology* 51 (1998): 290, makes the criticism that Philip Davies wants to confiscate the Bible from the community that owes its existence to it. Biblical studies must always be tempted to claim the Bible as its exclusive object.

We have asked whether the scholarship of dialogue may not represent a playing down of the scandalous particularity of Israel's status and a refusal of the doctrine of Israel's election. The question of who has the right to read which Scriptures reflects the politics of twentieth-century Jewish-Christian dialogue. Some scholarship has preferred to read the New Testament as a Greco-Roman phenomenon, rather than as an expression of Israel's cult, in order to avoid offense to religious or political sensibilities. Anti-supersessionism may become so scrupulous that it becomes a falsification of Jewish theology, against which the new perspective on Paul scarcely prevails. Can New Testament scholarship join the notions of suffering and martyrdom to the idea that God is at work, and at work in and with the scattered and gathered people of God, and therefore still at work today? Is the New Testament the outworking of the political theology and cosmology of the Old Testament? This is surely required by the theological claim that Israel's work is directed toward the world and that a public claim on the world is intrinsic to the identity of Israel. In the course of examining the doctrine of election, and considering it as a doctrine about God and his servant, we have asked about the status and responsibility of Israel. I have suggested that Israel is not autonomous and not without responsibility to the nations. Israel is, under God, still in dialogue and in contest with the nations, for their sake and its own. Now we must ask about the resistance represented by the economy of modernity to the doctrine that takes the form of the Western understanding of time.

3.5. The Work of God

Israel is the work of God in progress. Eschatology is the theological concept that reminds us of the reserve with which we must speak about any work in progress. Israel may not be separated from God to be analyzed under alien criteria. Israel cannot be accounted either as singular or plural, until God is accounted the determinative member of Israel. If there are two, and one is perfect, both are perfect, for the perfect one perfects the other. The obedient priest sets his hand on the head of the creature, supplying what the creature lacks, so it no longer lacks anything. This is the relation of the Creator and his creature. The activity of many members of Israel together make the One. They do not merely symbolize him, or stand in for him, but are adopted by the Spirit as the constituents from which the

One is assembled. They stand in for him in the sense that they are proved to have been really practicing, waiting, and being integrated by his Spirit into him. Thus, eschatologically and retrospectively, all those in the history of Scripture who appear to have been simply waiting for something to happen were in fact waiting faithfully and were being built together to become the faithful witness. The modern view sees a steadily increasing distance between ourselves and the first-century event of Jesus Christ. But Israel is not confined to the past. The survival of the Jewish people is evidence of God's faithfulness and obliges us to an eschatological redefinition even of our time as the joint time of Israel and God, into which the peoples of the world are also called and gathered.

How successful are Jewish scholars at the demythologization of this time of modernity? Is there a Jewish eschatology? Could the doctrine of the sabbath function in this way? Is the history of the West the history of the supplanting of the election of this people, the specific people of God's choosing, with a generalized version by which God's action was abstracted to meaninglessness? The idea of progress was the beginning of the reduction of the people of Israel to the *idea* of election, and the turning of a generalized idea of election against Israel. When time is used to name the relationship of God and Israel, it must be understood to be determined by their movements toward each other. Israel grows into the space God provides, for God on the trinitarian conception is not only agent but also the host and enabler of all other agents. It is because God came to Israel that it can be said that Israel comes to God. Then we can say that time is nothing but the determination of God for Israel and Israel for God, and this is the ground of possibility for a world of agency.

3.5.1. The Hospitality of the Estate

This chapter inquires into the relation of the two doctrines of God's immediate work of election and his mediate work of making holy. It attempts to understand each as the basis and expression of the other. God is the mediation of his work, so it may be said to be both mediate and immediate. This chapter argues that God is a worker, that he works a people to become participants in his work. Israel's liturgical task is the labor of imagining, modeling, and preparing for the new creation, and so participating in its arrival. Israel will participate in the work of God that sustains creation. We need an account of the resistance to the work of God in the form of the son who would not work, the person described by the history of Western secularization, who seeks no participation in the work and working of God, but who succeeds in establishing no alternative economy.

God will not allow any form of human life to determine his creation other than the form he intends for it. He will have a creature who is no less than free. Israel represents the knitting together of the various ends of the gentile world into the single end of participant in the economy of God. Israel's theology is therefore creation theology: it understands the world as the estate God cultivates for humankind. This work of God is driven by an end, the hope God has for humanity; we need the concept of eschatology to represent this hope-driven labor of God that is both ongoing and already vindicated. God speaks and is heard, and the world returns his speech. The Word of God halts, defeats, breaks up, re-gathers, and re-employs the words of the world and returns them to God as his Word. All other rival words are merely estranged creatures of God. Because they belong to God's estate, it is God's logic that, unknown to them, will come to inform them so that they are no longer opponents but creatures. Those who consume the Lord's substance live off his estate, are being taught his work, and will gain the economy of action he intends for them.

The question of being is the question of to whom the economy of being belongs. It is thus a question of the identity of its Creator and of his ability to sustain it against rival economies.[87] Israel is the servant of its Lord inasmuch as it takes up its work as steward of the economy of God's creation. The doctrine of creation therefore entails that it is Israel's task to host the peoples of the world. It is for Israel to lead the gentiles. Israel must bring them into the house of its Lord. Israel must supply to them the being its Lord intends for them. Life is the specific life that a particular lord and his economy supplies. There is no life in general, no life outside one or another lordship. The rationale of Israel's holiness and purity teaching is to witness to Israel's freedom from the claims of other lordships and forms of life. This freedom derives from Israel's office as servant of God. The exercise of this hospitality involves allowing its recipients also to become participants in it. Israel's host gives his people the means to play host and

---

87. Oliver O'Donovan, *The Desire of the Nations: Rediscovering the Roots of Political Theology* (Cambridge: Cambridge University Press, 1996), p. 148, believes that "If one of the three elements of political authority could be seen as privileged in Israel it must surely be that of possession."

return hospitality.[88] Lordship is not about the simple exercise of domination but about the exercise of bringing up people into the form of life enabled by that economy. Who will, by successfully hospitable dominion, be confirmed in the task of stewardship of land and people?

In Israel's cosmology Israel itself works the ecosystem of the world. The world does not work without Israel's effort. Sacrifice displays the fruits of the obedient husbandry of the land given to Israel, among which must be accounted the well-being of all members of Israel. Israelites understand that they host and feed each other. Food always belongs to someone and represents their invitation to eat. Nourishment is inseparable from the obligation to play host and have your property affirmed to you by sharing it with the poor.[89] In the concept of bread is included all the work of providing this bread — planting, harvesting, and all the husbandry required to put bread on the table when the guest arrives. All food is accompanied by a set of obligations to which, by eating, we make ourselves subject. Food is related to the possession, control, and constitution of our own body. If we eat someone's bread, his work enters and constitutes us, and he has some claim, even an ontological claim, on us. The world does not produce bread for us of itself. It is by God's hospitality that it does this.[90]

3.5.2. Liturgy as Work

We must now link the sacrifice, worship, and teaching of Israel to the work of God. Israel's liturgy and ministry are the work of the Son and conse-

88. See Patrick D. Miller, "Israel as Host to Strangers," in *Israelite Religion and Biblical Theology,* Journal for the Study of the Old Testament — Supplement Series (Sheffield: Sheffield Academic Press, 2000), on this hospitality. Bruce D. Chilton, *Feast of Meanings: Eucharistic Theologies from Jesus through Johannine Circles* (Leiden: Brill, 1994), p. 50, believes that Jesus taught that what is offered should be and should be seen to be one's property. Israel is the tenant of the vineyard and is given talents to invest in it.

89. See Jacob Neusner, "Judaism after the Destruction of the Temple," in *Israelite and Judaean History,* ed. John H. Hayes and J. Maxwell Miller (London: SCM, 1977). The land is a metonym for all the persons that live on it and the ecosystem that binds land and people to each other as creatures of God; the Creator is householder and husbander of his property and estate, and his land and its product count as his substance and being.

90. Peder Borgen, *Bread from Heaven: An Exegetical Study of the Concept of Manna in the Gospel of John and the Writing of Philo* (Leiden: Brill, 1965), shows that Jesus' response, "I have bread," to the disciples in John 4:32 indicates that he is not ready to sit down and eat, for he is still working to bring to the table another, not-yet-gathered set of people.

quently of his people. The concepts of performance and commentary that we met in Chapter 2 may help us make sense of this liturgy and ministry. The temple was the place of worship. Here those made weary by the burdens of many masters could confess, and appeal to, one sole God and master. This confession made them free. This public act of confession and worship was the whole rationale of all temple activity. Subordinate to this worship was teaching and learning the record of God's generosity to Israel. This took place in the synagogues and the courts of the Jerusalem temple. Rabbinic colleges addressed problems of scriptural interpretation in the same healthily competitive way modern interpreters do.[91] Their members took part in the worship, and they discussed right worship and right exegesis of Scripture. Teaching took place in the cloisters, while the sacrifices took place in the center of the temple courtyard. All action was watched by the audience, who commented on it, and their commentary shaped the next round of action. Their reading of Scripture determined the sacrifice, and their understanding of the sacrifice impacted on their reading of Scripture. Reading Scripture involves the ancillary work of writing, copying, and collating, of learning by rote, and of commentating and maintaining all the interpretative skills of the oral law.[92] Ritual and Scripture constituted a single work of the formation of this people. This work and tradition did not cease with the first-century destruction of the temple.[93]

91. See Sanders, *Judaism*, pp. 170-82. Bockmuehl, *Revelation and Mystery in Ancient Judaism*, p. 9, argues that "The bearer of revelation whether priest or prophet (or both) is almost never properly independent of the cult." Christopher Rowland, *The Open Heaven: A Study of Apocalyptic in Judaism and Early Christianity* (London: SPCK, 1982), p. 318, shows the diversity of opinion in the second-century rabbinic debates, a diversity demonstrated by the story of the four rabbis who entered the garden, only one of whose hermeneutic procedures allowed him to survive in it.

92. According to Bockmuehl, *Revelation and Mystery in Ancient Judaism*, p. 98, God himself has taught Torah to the tribes of Israel, and he spends three hours a day studying Torah: "The idea of the dynamic presence of revelation in both written Torah and oral tradition is present at least *in nuce* already prior to the fall of Jerusalem" (p. 113). Bockmuehl asserts that Ina Willi-Plein "regards the angel as almost a hypostasis of interpretation" (p. 30 n. 40). Rainer Riesner, "Jesus as Preacher and Teacher," in *Jesus and the Oral Gospel Tradition*, ed. Henry Wansbrough (Sheffield: JSOT Press, 1991), p. 191, argues that "One cannot overstress the importance of the synagogal teaching system as a background for the formation and transmission of the Gospel tradition."

93. Bockmuehl, *Revelation and Mystery in Ancient Judaism*, p. 61, argues that "There are sufficient indications to show that at least some form of priestly or Levitical 'prophecy' continued in the post-exilic age." David E. Aune, *Prophecy in Early Christianity and the Ancient*

Temple ritual interpreted Scripture. The congregation of Israel assembled before the high priest. In the high priest, the congregation saw God in the form of his servant; and in the congregation, the priest saw God in the form of his servant people. Each took one part of the conversation of the Father and the Son and spoke their part in the conversation of God into which this liturgy incorporated them. Each aided the other into the role and office of obedient servant. God elected and transformed their parts in the liturgical repetition of this conversation into his own work and speech.

It is Israel's liturgical labor to participate in this conversation of Father and Son. The event of being made witnesses of the action of God, termed "apocalyptic," is one mode of Israel's formation in this dramaturgy.[94] As the narrative is repeated, events become perceptible to its participants. This communal visualization serves their induction into the proper action of the Israelite toward Israel's God, set out by this liturgy and Scripture. The Father speaks, and the Son hears and receives his speech. The Father tells about his Son to those he intends to add to his Son. The Son is telling those he wants to present to the Father about his Father. God is telling us about himself in the third person. In this way God draws and assembles us into his narration, so the story of God's action is a story about our coming into his action, and this narration constitutes the two-dimensional form of our coming to participate in this action. The action of God in telling, hearing, and receiving constitutes the whole economy in which we will receive our being. God's telling us about himself, in the story of himself and his servant, is his means of letting us find our identity and place in this servant and so become that servant. The story gives us a place, office, and work. God tells us about God by playing alternately his role and ours in order that we come to play our role for ourselves. By this telling and acting out, Israel is drawn into the character and action of God.

All that is performed in the temple and synagogue serves to demonstrate the office God has given to Israel and the history of Israel's attempt to fill it. The actions of the priest have a place in a series familiar to all Is-

---

Mediterranean World (Grand Rapids: Eerdmans, 1983), p. 104, agrees: "It has become increasingly recognized that prophecy did not disappear in Judaism during the hellenistic and Roman periods."

94. Apocalyptic is Israel's political witness to the nations in pictorial mode. We will return to it in §4.5. See Crispin Fletcher-Louis, *Luke-Acts: Angels, Christology and Soteriology* (Tübingen: Mohr, 1997), pp. 205-11.

rael. Where everybody already knows what is going on, or is united in offering competing versions of it, each action is interpreted by the next action in the series. The priest may be telling more than one story at a time, telling one story in the mode of another, undoing and re-performing the version of a story told by rivals. All of these represent a parody and deconstruction of the ideologies and claims of the nations of the gentile world. This cultic parodying created by the public performance of sacrifice required mastery of the modalities of the animal-lexicon of the ancient world.[95] Though it was subject to the processes of dispute and translation, it did not allow itself to be interpreted into alien terms.[96] The congregation saw what they saw because they had been taught it; what they saw was not visible to non-practitioners.[97] The being of Israel was constitutively reiterated and shaped by these movements of priest and congregation, to make a nation shaped by a single paideutic effort.

The liturgy and ritual performed by Israel describe a new form of public being. The first five books of the Old Testament, the Law, is the set of propositions that display the action of a particular human being and that particular form of human life that comes from him. They portray the eschatological-biological body of Jesus Christ, the Son who vindicates Israel. They not only display him but also serve to bring him into being. They bring him into being both as one man and as many people. He is present to a single generation of his people, so within a moment of time and space, but he also brings into being a whole history and set of skills and relationships, themselves available as experience and propositions arising from them. The skills and relationships represented by Scripture

95. In the animal semiotics of Israel and the ancient world each dynasty and nation has an animal emblem, which may serve as a proper name for that nation or its ruling house. See the discussion of Mary Douglas, "The Pangolin Revisited: A New Approach to Animal Symbolism," in *Signifying Animals: Human Meaning in the Natural World*, ed. R. G. Willis (London: Unwin Hyman, 1990).

96. Aristeas gives a description of the movements of the priest in the sacrifices, though without naming them; see C. T. R. Haywood, *The Second Temple: A Non-Biblical Sourcebook* (London: Routledge, 1998). It may be that much of the action of the priests is lost to us, or remains before us in Scripture that has not been recognized as priestly stage directions.

97. Christopher Rowland, *The Open Heaven: A Study of Apocalyptic in Judaism and Early Christianity* (London: SPCK, 1982), p. 347, argues that "Rabbinic exegesis of Genesis 1 and Ezekiel 1 has left us with the impression that what started as an expository exercise soon turned into a vision, as parts of the chariot and the cosmos appeared in the imagination of the visionary."

constitute our induction into his life, and so our transition from a simpler to a more complex form of creaturehood. In what we have said so far, we have assembled some means of showing how God and Israel may be in one action together, because Israel is drawn into the greater complexity and freedom opened by the action of God.

3.5.3. Biblical Studies on Liturgy as Israel's Work

Israel has no work that is not first God's. Worship of God is Israel's work. This work of worship includes the confession that the life God intends for Israel is to extend through Israel to all creation. Some Old Testament scholarship understands worship in this way.[98] Samuel Balentine believes that "covenant-making and covenant-keeping recall and renew God's creational designs" and that "the liturgy of covenant-making can be properly understood as a liturgy of creation-keeping."[99] He argues that Israel's temple represents the practice of a creation theology. "The Torah also presents worship as the principal means through which God's creative design for the world is established, sustained and restored." Balentine believes that the claim to participate in the labor of creation is the key to Israel's understanding of history.

> With the collapse of the history paradigm has come the move to reconceive history in terms of creation theology. . . . [W]hile this has led to a more balanced view, it has not produced an alternative to the history paradigm. It simply subordinates historical (human) time to "cosmic time."[100]

Can the turn to performance in Old Testament studies produce the conceptuality of transformation that would allow God as agent and as pro-

---

98. See Brueggemann, *Theology of the Old Testament*, pp. 117-228; Miller, *Israelite Religion and Biblical Theology*, pp. 269-336; and Bernhard W. Anderson, *From Creation to New Creation: Old Testament Perspectives* (Minneapolis: Fortress, 1994), pp. 208-11, for examples.

99. Samuel E. Balentine, *The Torah's Vision of Worship* (Minneapolis: Augsburg Fortress, 1999), p. 126. Balentine believes that as symbolic act "ritual has the capacity both to mirror and to transform a society's worldview and ethos, and priestly ritual must be understood with priestly creation theology" (p. 75). F. H. Gorman Jr., *The Ideology of Ritual: Space Time and Status in the Priestly Theology* (Sheffield: JSOT Press, 1990), p. 59, describes ritual as a means of "world construction."

100. Balentine, *The Torah's Vision of Worship*, p. 22.

vider of the first account of his agency?[101] As Perdue identified the move from history to text, Balentine intends to identify the movement from text to worship understood as liturgical work. By it Israel is brought up to the status of God's co-worker.[102]

3.5.4. Work Complete with Its Outcome

The rest of the sabbath is the vindication of work. The sabbath is not the end of work or the opposite of work. It is the teaching that the outcome of God's work is already present to him in that working. The sabbath is God's work understood both as present action and as completed action together with its result, an action completed in his time, not ours, but which provides a time that is still future promise to us. To understand the doctrine of the sabbath as an eschatology in this way enables us to maintain parallel accounts. In one, God now suffers the resistance of the world and waits for what he does not yet have, while in the other, the outcome of God's work is always present with him.[103]

The majority of scholars, however, understand the sabbath in a differ-

---

101. Balentine seems to dichotomize worship and teaching, arguing that the historical-critical approach has given way to an emphasis on doxology. See also Gorman, "Ritual Studies and Biblical Studies: Assessments of the Past, Prospects of the Future," *Semeia* 67 (1994): 13-36. Brueggemann, *Theology of the Old Testament*, p. 653, counters that "it is in worship, not in contextless, cerebral activity, that Israel worked out its peculiar identity and sustained its odd life in the world. Worship life, over time, takes on an internal logic of its own in the community of practice, an internal logic not available to outsiders and about which the community does not trouble to speak very clearly or precisely."

102. Balentine, *The Torah's Vision of Worship*, p. 87, believes that "treated separately Genesis 1 and 2 have traditionally been construed as affirmation of two ideas: God's independent (or in religious terms, transcendent) and unassisted creation of the world (Genesis 1); and humankind's dependent and totally passive receipt of divine imperatives (Genesis 2). . . . In the vision of Genesis 1–2, however such a simple view of God's cosmic design is inadequate. Close attention to creation's liturgy makes it clear that in the world God creates, God chooses to remain open and responsive to acts of 'creaturely creativity.' God and creation are portrayed as engaged in a relationship of mutual creativity."

103. Bernhard W. Anderson, "Creation," *The Interpreter's Dictionary of the Bible* (Nashville: Abingdon Press, 1986), vol. 1, p. 730, states: "Creation is fundamentally an eschatological doctrine." Jon D. Levenson, *Creation and the Persistence of Evil: The Jewish Drama of Divine Omnipotence*, 2nd ed. (Princeton: Princeton University Press, 1988), p. 109, is skeptical about the coherence of the view that the sabbath could mean that God stops work and withdraws.

ent fashion. They see work and rest as opposites. So in the view of Jacob Neusner and Bruce Chilton, for example, "keeping the Sabbath makes us like God. Not working on the Sabbath . . . is a way of imitating God."[104] God is not at work, but at rest. The more we work, the less we are like him. The sabbath stands apart from the profane week of the gentiles, whom Israel has to meet and do business with.[105] Neusner and Chilton ask, Why did Jesus not heal during the week and then, like God, observe the day that timelessly reflects the finishedness of heaven? We must reply that the work is not over, the earth is not yet a finished article, ready to be appreciated in stillness. The sabbath now takes the form of our suffering participation in Jesus' labor, and therefore in the cross; this labor is constant, but it is the light yoke of priestly office. The sabbath prevents those who, by adding day to day in unbroken series, intend to accumulate the fruit of other people's work in order to build an alternative creation of their own.[106] All God's working is entire and complete, a single sabbath that other days cannot interrupt.[107] The sabbath restricts and brings to nothing all other projects and destinies. It keeps the world open and prevents it from knitting itself together into any other form.[108] The active absenting work of God tells us that the messiah is not here and that what is here does not amount to the totality of what is to be. What the world presently is, is not the end. The temple worship is the product of the celebration that overflows from around the throne and interrupts life below.[109] The king is not here, but

---

104. Jacob Neusner and Bruce D. Chilton, *Judaism in the New Testament* (London: Routledge, 1995), p. 136.

105. Neusner and Chilton, *Judaism in the New Testament*, p. 136.

106. André LaCocque and Paul Ricoeur, *Thinking Biblically: Exegetical and Hermeneutical Studies* (Chicago: University of Chicago Press, 1998), p. 46: "According to Leviticus, at some point the earth can decide to take the Sabbaths that Israel did not grant her; she may refuse to produce."

107. Terence Fretheim, *Exodus* (Atlanta: John Knox, 1991), p. 230, argues that "Sabbath-keeping is an act of creation-keeping." Jon D. Levenson, "The Jerusalem Temple," in *Jewish Spirituality*, ed. Arthur Green (London: Routledge & Kegan Paul, 1986), p. 52, also believes that "The Sabbath is a kind of democratisation of the Temple experience, and the land of Israel is an extended Temple. . . . The Temple is the world as it ought to be."

108. The seventh day is the unity of the six days, and thus "rest" is the whole of what God has worked, not something experienced after this work by giving up or ceasing this effort.

109. See Otfried Hofius, "Gemeinschaft mit den Engeln im Gottesdienst der Kirche," *Zeitung für Theologie und Kirche* 89 (1992); see also Horst Dietrich Preuss, *Old Testament Theology*, 2 vols. (Edinburgh: T&T Clark, 1995-96), vol. 1, pp. 256-58.

nonetheless he ensures that nothing else comes to usurp his place. To say he is not here is to say only that we are not yet made ready to receive from him our co-presence with each other. It is part of our liturgical labor to say this — and to lament it. To this end we must maintain this double account of time that the concept of eschatology represents. If we do not do so we simply oppose God's timelessness with the forces of decay to which our own deficiency of being exposes us. This is to confuse our creatureliness with fallenness. We saw Pannenberg charge Augustine with opposing time and eternity in this way, such that eternity appeared to be timelessness, rather than the fullness of time. Instead, we have to confess that the fullness of time, the sabbath, sends out to us what we presently receive, so that the whole slowly and serially supplies the parts, one to another.

3.6. The Work of the Servant

3.6.1. The Son and the Father Work Together

The Son does not act alone. The Son works with the Father to do the Father's work. The Son is bringing many sons to the Father, a work we could call, not inappropriately, *affiliation*. According to Hengel, Paul assumes that both the Father and the Son can be addressed as "Lord" *(Kyrios)*.[110] Both are addressed as the coming judge and credited with creation. There is a "unique soteriological connection between Psalm 110.1 and 4, between the 'sitting at the right hand of God' and the heavenly high priesthood of Christ including his soteriological *intercessio*."[111] The throne is a bench where Father and Son sit together. The high priesthood of God is God's whole mode of being for us. The high priest takes what is the Father's and gives it back to him in the form of the Son who pleases the Father. The Son is the form of the creature in full. The Father intends to extend this form to

110. Martin Hengel, "Sit at My Right Hand," in *Studies in Early Christology* (Edinburgh: T&T Clark, 1995), p. vii. Seyoon Kim, *The "Son of Man" as the Son of God* (Tübingen: Mohr, 1983), p. 99, argues that "With the 'Son of Man' Jesus designated himself in reference to the heavenly figure who appeared to Daniel. . . . Jesus saw himself destined to realise the heavenly counsel revealed to Daniel."

111. Hengel, "Sit at My Right Hand," p. 147. See also O. Keel, *The Symbolism of the Biblical World: Ancient Near Eastern Iconography and the Book of Psalms* (London: SPCK, 1978), pp. 256-68.

all his creatures and, through them, to all the natural history of the world of his creation. The creed correctly maintains that the Son sits at the right hand of the Father, in opposition to that Gnostic docetism which cannot tolerate the bodily resurrection of a creature to God.[112] The Jesus who sits at the right hand of the Father is the whole *plērōma*. With the entire creation we are with him there, waiting to be brought to life.[113] There is a single speech and conversation of Father and Son, and the Son — as both creature and the world of the creature — returns the word of the Father to the Father, now not only as the Father's word but also as the word of the world.[114] Accounts of the resistance of the world, of loss, and of fall may be told only as resistance overcome.

From the right hand of the Father the Son sends the Spirit. The Spirit replicates the Son to us and us to the Son. According to Douglas Farrow, we must begin from "God with us," the "descent and ascent of the God-man."[115] This is provided by a trinitarian identification of God and Jesus, the new Adam in which all human beings and their world have their future. This will provide a correction for "the tradition's tendency to undo the incarnation."[116] Whereas the gnostics saw in the redemptive work of the *Logos* "the separation of what was unnaturally united," Irenaeus saw in Jesus the reunion of what was unnaturally separated. "In teaching the coherence of all things around the incarnate Word, Irenaeus was safeguarding not only the integrity of Jesus but the integrity of every particular."[117] Farrow asserts that Irenaeus understands the Christ-event as the climactic moment in a long history of God's approach to humanity.

---

112. According to Hengel, "Sit at My Right Hand," p. 159, "the exalted Lord is no *deus otiosus*. His continual *intercessio* as the consequence of his atoning death . . . has its parallel in the *intercessio* of the Spirit in the believer on earth."

113. Israel's aniconism understood that the creation could be fully itself in the meso-form of one person. The creation is the macro-version of Jesus, the person of the creation who includes and sustains all persons. He waits, looks forward, re-members and assembles the dismembered and scattered limbs of past and future. Jesus is the creation as pure object present to the Father, though not yet present as object to us.

114. This must be our answer to the question of the location and reality of the church. Jenson, *Systematic Theology*, vol. 1, p. 206, asserts: "Heaven is where God takes space in his creation to be present to the whole of it; he does that in the church."

115. Farrow, *Ascension and Ecclesia*, p. 249.

116. Farrow, *Ascension and Ecclesia*, p. 249.

117. Farrow, *Ascension and Ecclesia*, p. 55.

Only after a protracted period of preparation does the Word appear among us — not as a retort to the old covenant or its deity, but as that very deity in person. . . . [I]t is under [the prophets'] tutelage that we are slowly readied to receive him, for he does not come to us unannounced. When he finally does come of course a great threshold is crossed and a new age begun; under the tutelage of the incarnate one, in the communion of the Spirit, we ourselves may now advance towards God.[118]

The conversation of the Father and the Son is spread by the Spirit from heaven to earth. It is received and repeated in the worship of Israel. The *sessio* of the Father and the Son makes itself present in the temple as the dialectic of people and priest in the dramaturgy of apocalyptic, the condensed theological product of Israel's liturgical labor. Their conversation narrates the story of God and his servant. To understand Israelite sacrifice as *killing* is to ignore the dramatic and didactic character of this event and its liturgical remembering in temple sacrifice. Israel intends to represent this as the horrible act of the gentiles who can know no better. It is a dumb-show of son-killing that Israel is performing in the knowledge that the son-killer nations are watching and know that they are meant. Only the non-expert (modern) onlooker, who is ignorant of this complex mimetic relationship of Israel with its audience, could conclude that this is an act of son-killing rather than of halting the son-killers. By ignoring the audience of the surrounding gentile nations, modern hermeneutics, refusing to be the audience shaped by Scripture, reads this lesson in ignorance. It understands Israel's sacrifice as precisely the reverse of what Israel intends. As Israel has represented it, so with the Spirit's mediation it comes to be. Congregation and priest are together bound to God in the economy of his action. All sacrifice and worship reiterate God and humankind being together, bound by the many modes of the mediating action of God.

Israel is the work of God. Israel's worship is the theological description and deconstruction of the world of the gentiles and its transformation into the finished creation of Israel's God. The habits and behavioral traits of the nations of the world are diverted from their own ultimately inconsequential trajectories into this path. By its action Israel's worship captures the whole phenotype of the alternative creation of old Adam, undoing it

---

118. Farrow, *Ascension and Ecclesia*, p. 76. Farrow goes on to argue that "As Irenaeus sees it, our evolution has actually become our devolution. The Son does not appear at the middle of history, then, but at the end; not somewhere near the top, but at the bottom" (p. 77).

and rebinding it into the living and lasting creation of God. Israel deconstructs the myth of the single agent in combat with his fate. The Father and Son are in this work together. The Father is the receiver and guarantor of the Son's action. The Son is able to gather up and replay the whole behavioral history of the world, transformatively and redemptively, so that it becomes the record of the arrival of humankind, the free and obedient creature of God. It is the argument of this chapter that Israel demonstrates that isolated individuals have no action of their own, but that they are drawn into the action of God. Israel has an action precisely because it is the dual action of creature exercised with his Creator. The Son is the one who acts as servant. The servant who is raised by the Father is the Son.

3.6.2. The Son Who Would Not Work

Two sons, two versions of Adam, are contrasted in a parable of Jesus. Both sons were instructed to go to work in the Father's vineyard, but only one of them went.[119] One son would not hear his father's command, would not serve or receive the discipline that makes a good son. Like the kings of the earth, he would rather be served than go to work himself.[120] This son is the individual, the product of the economy of modernity. There is no work that originates in the individual. His work may be credited to him only if it is built with God as master workman, thus only inasmuch as he does not work alone and is no individual. Otherwise he is building his house on sand, tearing down his barn to store what he will never live to enjoy, sowing for another man to reap. Nothing belongs to the individual, and his action brings him no gain. The belief that sacrifice is the violent act by which the individual wrests something from another individual, or by which one individual overcomes and consumes another, is the myth of Marduk and Tiamat. It is the myth that the Genesis account of creation refutes. One individual cannot propel another into being or motion. Human action, including sacrifice, cannot be understood as the action of propelling an inert other into action, thereby bringing something out of nothing.

Without God, their host, mediating between them and the fruit, the first man and woman were unable to find a reply to the serpent and exer-

---

119. The parable of the two sons appears in Matthew 21:28-31.
120. Hebrews 5:8-10; 12:7-10; Mark 10:42-45.

cise their authority over it. Adam lost the faculty by which he could take what God gave. Christof Gestrich points out that "Adam has not moved into a position directly under the position of God *by a fall into sin*. On the contrary, Adam's authority to name all living beings and gain power over them was decisively reduced by the fall."[121] As a result Adam has only the moment of his choosing in which he surveys the world (the fruit) and God's work (the garden), and yet does not receive it, and the commission it represents, from God. He is stalled in this moment, in which he, a human being, weighs God against some other possibility of his own invention. The Adam believed in by the Western history of secularization is the individual who cannot make his choice stick. He can only continue to choose and choose again, such that he can never actually decisively choose anything, be satisfied by his choice, and let it inform his future. He cannot finish any act and be ready for another. The biblical story of the fall and separation of humankind from God, divorced from humanity's place in the evangelical narrative, has become the foundation story of the West. But it is not Christian. It is not entirely Augustine's fault that his account of the fall has tended to eclipse the deeper theological story. The Alexandrian fathers were also unable to be entirely rid of the deep ontological pessimism of the pagan Hellenic worldview that found the story of humanity's separation compelling.

The Western tradition, for which Kant is now representative, teaches that everything is subsequent to, and constituted by, the fall of Adam.[122] Yet the Adam who fell thereby ceased to be the first and constitutive Adam. A second Adam has become the source and beginning of Adam's race.[123] The supersession debate has its origin within a protology, an assumption that what is, is already autonomous and settled. But we may not measure God's work by how far he succeeds in returning the situation to one that

---

121. Christof Gestrich, *The Return of Splendor in the World: The Christian Doctrine of Sin and Forgiveness* (Grand Rapids: Eerdmans, 1997), p. 88.

122. Immanuel Kant, "Speculative Beginning of Human History," in *Perpetual Peace and Other Essays*, ed. T. Humphrey (Indianapolis: Hackett, 1983), p. 51. See also Gestrich, *The Return of Splendor in the World*, pp. 84-117.

123. According to James D. G. Dunn, "1 Corinthians 15.45," in *Christ and the Spirit in the New Testament*, ed. Barnabas Lindars and Stephen S. Smalley (London: Cambridge University Press, 1973), p. 140, "Jesus became Last Adam at his resurrection. As the first Adam came into existence at creation, so the last Adam (as such) came into existence at resurrection, so the resurrection marks the beginning of the humanity of the second Adam."

preceded this fall. This would problematize the relationship of our action and his by making it a question of who initiates and permits the action of whom, God or humankind. But the work of God is its own measure; he gives it its autonomy, pronounces when it has that autonomy, and ensures that all that *shall be* does not detract from or threaten, but fits and renders perfect, all that *has been made.*

The first Adam understood his encounter with God as a meeting with an equal. He believed that he could agree with God on separate fields of operation, to cooperate or to conduct turf-wars. This Adam did not recognize that his own body and resources were the possession and work of the God who addressed him. The sum of things that Adam did, did not belong to him, and the things of his world did not recognize Adam or come willingly to him. Had Adam acted as the priest of creation, acting within the freedom of the end rather than the constraint of his origin, he would have overcome the mortality inherent in these beginnings and ends and so freed all creation for the eschatological and free life of the creature of God. But, not having learned and grown into his freedom, Adam did not have the maturity to be the priest of creation and could not succeed in liberating creation from its mortality. We have already seen that it is not the beginning but the end that is determinative. The new Adam liberates creation from the failed priesthood of Adam the individual, re-fathers Adam, and allows the future to be determined by the Adam who is man-with-God, the creature who is with his Creator. In Chapter 5 I will argue that the story of secularization and the evolution of the economy of the modern West derives from this story of the man who does not understand himself as creature of God. In the last chapter I will argue that this son has already been overcome by the obedient Son who does the Father's work.

3.7. Sacrifice and Law

The new being and action, sent as the Spirit by the Father, are supplied to Israel. They are supplied only as fast as Israel receives them, learns them, and employs them, making them part of Israel's own character. God gives Israel the law as the set of skills by which to live on the estate and in the household of God. Led and determined by their head, this people lives by hope and is obedient to what they are promised.

3.7.1. Abraham and Isaac

The Ten Commandments announce the character of God and the freedom of the people who belong to him.[124] Each commandment amplifies the first command to worship the one God. The sixth, the command not to murder, represents one description of the new life set out by the first command. Israel is the people no longer subject to the imperative of murder. Abraham's sacrifice of Isaac — known also as the *Aqedah* — is the first enactment of the sixth commandment and so the inauguration of a new economy of freedom. The majority approach here is unsatisfactory, because it displays no hope or eschatology. I will set out a new reading of Genesis 22, which, if correct, must also be an old one. It tells the sacrifice as the whole story of Israel, the story of the Son who goes to do his Father's work.[125]

The climax of the story has commonly been understood to be the moment when Abraham raises his knife. The tension of this moment in the story is not because Abraham knows he is going to do a horrible thing. Abraham is an Aramean, for whom child sacrifice is a customary, not an awful, thing.[126] The tension here is because we do not know how God's promise is going to win out over this ancestral practice. In this event the act of child sacrifice is for the first time portrayed under the new concept of murder and understood to be horrible. It is understood in this way precisely by that holy people who are to spring from Abraham as a result.[127] So the instruction "take your only son and sacrifice him as a burnt-

124. This is argued by Stanley Hauerwas in "The Truth about God: The Decalogue as Condition for Truthful Speech," in *Sanctify Them in the Truth* (Edinburgh: T&T Clark, 1998); see also Brevard S. Childs, *Exodus: A Commentary* (London: SCM, 1974), pp. 393-427.

125. The majority approach is represented by James L. Crenshaw, *A Whirlpool of Torment: Israelite Traditions of God as Oppressive Presence* (Philadelphia: Fortress, 1984); Philip R. Davies and Bruce Chilton, "The Aqedah: A Revised Tradition History," *Catholic Biblical Quarterly* 40 (1978): 514-46; Raymond E. Brown, *The Death of the Messiah from Gethsemane to the Grave: A Commentary on the Passion Narratives in the Four Gospels,* Anchor Bible (New York: Doubleday, 1994), vol. 2, pp. 1435-44. R. W. L. Moberly, *The Bible, Theology and Faith: A Study of Abraham and Jesus* (Cambridge: Cambridge University Press, 2000), seems to be moving in a direction similar to the one taken here.

126. Milgrom, *Leviticus,* vol. 2, p. 1588. See also Jon D. Levenson, *The Death and Resurrection of the Beloved Son: The Transformation of Child Sacrifice in Judaism and Christianity* (New Haven, CT: Yale University Press, 1993).

127. Attributing horror to Abraham's state of mind is a reading back, one of those anachronisms resorted to for heuristic reasons.

offering" is not the story, and the raising of the knife not its climax. They are the scene setting. It is the divine command that follows which constitutes the climax.

Abraham's hand is halted by a word from God. The sense of the whole story is located in the command, "Do not lay a hand on the boy."[128] This is the climax and punch line. Does God command Abraham to kill his son, or does he forbid killing, with the result that he gets many sons who are holy? Which way to read this story? We have to employ the whole of the Scriptures to determine that this is a teaching about the whole work of God with humankind. It embraces generations and millennia, but it flattens out the eschatology into a palimpsest, as though a three-frame cartoon, illustrating past, present, and future, were redrawn superimposed in a single frame. We have to decide whether this is a story about an origin, and thus about how we got to be the way we are, or whether it illustrates timeless truths, or whether it teaches that we are to receive a future that is different from our past.

As an Aramean, Abraham believed that the death of a son would release a stream of sons and prosperity, an economic conceptuality in which to get something out you have to put something in.[129] The original commandment of self-restraint reflects humankind's subjection to nature and necessity. But the *Aqedah* commandment, "Do no murder," establishes that Israel is not subject to this economic logic that determines the rest of the earth. The identification of the death of the firstborn as murder frees Israel from the forces and compulsions of nature. God's staying the knife is the first lesson in the establishment of a new polity; and the meaning of this knife-staying lesson, and the accomplishment it represents, is only slowly subsequently realized. It requires many generations of life with God for Israel to begin to learn the character of God, summarized in the Sinai Decalogue of freedoms.

The gospel is promise. Yet the majority tradition reads Genesis 22 without eschatology, and thus not as an announcement creating hope. It

128. Genesis 22:12: "Do not lay a hand on the boy. . . . Now I know that you fear God because you have not withheld from me your son, your only son."

129. According to Albertz, *A History of Israelite Religion*, vol. 1, pp. 102-3, if you want sons and offspring for your flocks you have to prepare a place for them in the body of a son given as a firstfruits offering. For a social anthropological statement of this sacrificial logic see Walter Burkert, *Homo Necans: The Anthropology of Ancient Greek Sacrificial Ritual and Myth* (Berkeley: University of California Press, 1983), p. 39.

interprets it either as a story about the fall as the origin of humanity's freedom, or as a timeless truth about the seizing of freedom through breaking moral limits — "the suspension of the ethical." Both interpretations understand that Abraham was selected because he was obedient — that is, because in some way he chose himself. This story has been read as the founding moment of humankind's antinomianism, of the invitation to break the law of God and leave it behind. It would encourage us to believe that choosing yourself is the real form of choosing. Such readings, led by that of Kierkegaard, have ignored the Decalogue and the rest of the Bible, which is reason enough to make us suspicious.[130] Jon Levenson provides a substantial recent treatment of the *Aqedah* in this tradition. He finds that Reformed discussions of Abraham's faith, such as von Rad's, ignore the contextual verses around Genesis 15:6, the Bible as a whole, and rabbinic commentary.[131] Yet Levenson argues that child sacrifice played a continuing part in the religion of Israel.[132] It was the continuation of the sacrifices to Baal, the god who offers his son for immolation.[133] "The impulse to sacrifice the firstborn remained potent long after the literal practice had become odious and fallen into desuetude," becoming transformed into "a sublime paradigm of the religious

130. Søren Kierkegaard, *Fear and Trembling*, ed. W. Lowrie (Princeton: Princeton University Press, 1941). Before Kierkegaard's reading, the tension was between divine command and paternal affection, not between divine and moral law. Jacques Derrida, *Given Time* (Chicago: University of Chicago Press, 1992), follows *Fear and Trembling* in reading the *Aqedah* as a Jewish potlatch that, by giving everything for nothing, intended to wreck the rationality of bourgeois faith in deferred gratification. John D. Caputo, *The Prayers and Tears of Jacques Derrida: Religion without Religion* (Bloomington: Indiana University Press, 1997), p. 196, believes that Abraham sacrifices all the time he has but has no idea if this will buy the future promised: "When Abraham raised the dagger and resolved to plunge ahead, to give [death] without a return, without knowing where this mad leap would land him in the next moment, then, in that very moment when the angel stayed his dagger from Isaac's breast, Abraham severed the circle of time and left it gaping open" (p. 162). John Milbank, "The Sublime in Kierkegaard," *Heythrop Journal* 37 (1996), also believes that this is a reckless gift: "This is a total sacrifice of self and others" (p. 143); "Abraham's sacrifice of Isaac is an anti-sacrifice because it is a completely pointless sacrifice: *not* the ancient sacrifice performed within the city to ensure its survival" (p. 144).

131. Levenson, "Why Jews Are Not Interested in Biblical Theology," p. 137.

132. See Levenson, *The Death and Resurrection of the Beloved Son*. On human sacrifice see R. de Vaux, *Ancient Israel: Its Life and Institutions* (London: Darton, Longman & Todd, 1961), pp. 441-46.

133. Levenson, *The Death and Resurrection of the Beloved Son*, p. 34.

life."[134] The sacrifice of the firstborn son is part of a larger biblical theology of the firstborn and his relationship to his father, which is "a matter of more significance to the relationship of the theologies of the people Israel and the Church than has heretofore been recognised."[135] If Abraham had not obeyed the command to sacrifice Israel, he would, according to Levenson, have elected Isaac as his own son over Isaac the Beloved Son and a place in the "larger providential drama." The *Aqedah* "tests whether Abraham is prepared to surrender his son to God who gave him. To say with Kierkegaard and von Rad, that he is prepared to do so because through faith he expects to receive Isaac anew (as indeed happens) is to minimise the frightfulness of what Abraham is commanded to do."[136] Levenson, in line with Jewish medieval commentary, sees the sacrifice as a test of Isaac more than of Abraham, and sees father and son as undivided in their obedience to God. Ivan Strenski asks Levenson whether we can "move so easily from deploring the 'obviously' barbaric to the plainly 'sublime.'"[137]

But all these ever more extravagant portrayals of Abraham as individual and originator of subjectivity represent a failure of eschatology, and thus a false start. Israel's sacrifices should be seen not as killing but as commentary on the practices of the world that feature killing sons. Israel's theology is the refutation of accounts of violence or necessity as origins of moral or economic rationality. The Aramean practices of Abraham predate the election of Abraham and the commencement of the training and character formation of Israel. Israel's sacrificial practice does not originate in the sacrifice of the firstborn. The *Aqedah* represents the election from the gentiles of a new, holy, God-dedicated line. Abraham is a gentile plucked from the gentiles. At the origin of Israel's coming into being are all the practices of the gentiles from which Israel has been elected and removed. Israel is elected and re-created against the background of this chaos and violence. These are not the basis of Israel's election, however,

---

134. Levenson, *The Death and Resurrection of the Beloved Son*, pp. 52, x.

135. Levenson, *The Death and Resurrection of the Beloved Son*, p. 34.

136. Levenson, *The Death and Resurrection of the Beloved Son*, p. 126.

137. Strenski, "Between Theories and Speciality," p. 10, asks, "What kind of religion or society could place child sacrifice anywhere, much less apparently at the centre of their ceremonial life?" Strenski, *Durkheim and the Jews of France*, p. 103, points out that "Frazer wrote that ancient Hebrew human sacrifice and the death of Jesus were part of a 'surviving' Jewish culture trait of bloody sacrificial victimisation."

and Israel refuses them as violence and chaos only as this people has been trained to identify them as such. That all the behavior of the world is chaotic and violent is not obvious to gentiles, but the elect community has to learn to identify it as such. Violence is what the gentiles amount to, and this violence is the background against which, and even on which, Israel's new character is written and formed.

Abraham is not tested to see what he is as an individual, to see whether there is enough faith-substance in him to make him worth God's while. Testing and judgment belong only with the process of the formation of the elect community.[138] It is the fiction of individualism that the individual contains the whole world in microcosm, a sufficient source of world to himself. But that this is a fiction is precisely what Israel is teaching us. It is only a story about Abraham inasmuch as it is about the generations who, by obediently referring to him as father, make him their father. He tests positive for fatherhood because of their obedience, not because of any property of Abraham the individual. The redemption of Isaac from Abraham's knife is not a second event subsequent to Abraham's call, but a second lesson that tells us what that call is. It teaches that Abraham is recruited to the task of making many holy generations. It is the teaching in summary and the story in diagram form. The situation is that humankind is inseparable from the habit of killing; the story is that one instance of humankind is prevented from killing, and the consequence is that this character is the father of many children who are to become strangers to the earlier ways of humankind. Out of the "Do no murder" command comes Isaac, the guarantee of Abraham's line.

3.7.2. Delayed Beginning

Does God test Abraham by telling him to sacrifice his son? Is Abraham's readiness to defy instinct and moral convention rewarded by freedom? If we understand the story in this way, it becomes a repetition of Adam's fall. Abraham's significance would then be as an individual constituted by his own decision, in absence of relationship. He decided to break the conven-

---

138. Moberly, *The Bible, Theology and Faith*, p. 99, interprets the word "tests" as "refines," not "tempts." If refining relates to training and becoming, it allows for the paideutic version of sacrifice that I am arguing for and the necessary expressivist rather than causal logic that it requires. Brevard S. Childs, *Biblical Theology of the Old and New Testaments* (London: SCM Press, 1992), p. 327, also opts for a sense of "tests" that looks forward to God's ongoing action.

tions of human sociality, to set up on his own, and he received his reward. He succeeded in doing something precisely inasmuch as he did it himself, without God. This is the Kantian account of human history *(ordo salutis)*, on the basis of which humankind's separation from God would be the beginning of the real history of humanity. In Kant's exegesis of the fall, as the "speculative beginning of human history," the human person "discovered in himself an ability to choose his own way of life and thus not to be bound like other animals to just one."[139] The fall was humanity's breakthrough into self-production. "Whether man has gained or lost as a result of this change can no longer be asked, at least if one looks to the vocation of his species, which consists in nothing other than *progress* towards perfection."[140] Human beings have clearly come into their own, so this fall away from God was the real beginning of human beings standing on their own two feet. In such a secular understanding, the fall represents humanity's own act of self-construction — that is, the creation of a space and time of human beings' own making, which they must defend against the unfriendly incursions of God.

But there is another possibility. We can follow Irenaeus and speak of the fall only in terms of its correction and recapitulation by the second Adam, which show that the fall did not succeed in creating a separation from God.[141] Humankind is in its infancy, an infancy now unnecessarily

---

139. Immanuel Kant, "Speculative Beginning of Human History," in *Perpetual Peace and Other Essays*, p. 51. Similarly G. W. F. Hegel, *Lectures on the Philosophy of Religion*, volume 3: *The Consummate Religion*, ed. Peter C. Hodgson (Berkeley: University of California Press, 1985), pp. 104-8. According to Gestrich, *The Return of Splendor in the World*, p. 86: "Hegel believed he could take from this verse [Gen. 3:22, 'The man has become one of us, knowing good and evil'] the idea that Adam and Eve's sinful falling away from the image of God given to them when they were created was not only a source of evil in the world but at the same time the source of a very positive opportunity for the development of humanity since now the knowledge of the good also became possible." See the remarks of Wolfhart Pannenberg, *Anthropology in Theological Perspective* (Edinburgh: T&T Clark, 1985), pp. 47-60; and Karl Barth, *Church Dogmatics*, IV/1, p. 382.

140. Kant, "Speculative Beginning of Human History," p. 53.

141. According to Irenaeus, *Against Heresies* 3.21.10: "So also by the obedience of one man, righteousness having been introduced, shall cause life to fructify in those persons who in times past were dead . . . so did he who is the Word, recapitulating Adam in himself, rightly receive a birth, enabling him to gather up Adam [into himself] from Mary." Irenaeus goes on to say: "Luke points out that the pedigree which traces the generation of our Lord back to Adam contains seventy-two generations connecting the end with the beginning, and implying that it is he who has summed up in himself all nations dispersed from Adam downwards" (3.22.3).

prolonged by a sullen adolescence. Human beings are not able to create anything, much less construct themselves or be by themselves. Not only was Adam immature, but he is still immature. He is still not ready to pass on to his fellows what he has received from God.[142] But Adam does not succeed by the fall in putting any distance between God and himself. The Creator was not too feeble to hold on, and his creature did not slip from his grasp. The fall was not a free fall through empty space but was a falling and being caught and placed in a particular God-determined time and place, a soft place within which, though we are sin-damaged, sin is effectively limited by death and cannot make an end of us. Sin and death are theological concepts, not otherwise evident. Death is not its own master but is confined to this world-enclosure, placed from the beginning by God, for God's purposes. So within this death-delimited place of our falling and landing is the world that, because it is the world of God's working, has enough "give" and flexibility in it to withstand the whole excess and deficiency that our sin represents.

Rather than attributing the fall to any necessity or nature as the Western *ordo salutis* seems to do, we may learn a more paideutic account. The fall was a wandering, a failure to maintain a direction or to discover any orientation. Adam's being is that of being in a house without a host, a society without other members: it is a kind of autism. By never getting around to the work of participation in God's creation-sustaining work, Adam commenced by default another work. This amounted to dismantling God's creation to make with it something much poorer, never reckoning whether he had the wherewithal to complete a city of his own. By following Adam in failing to recognize the owner of this creation and its own implicit order, we also fail to take advantage of the place intended by God for our flourishing, and we succeed only in running it down. In the wilderness Jesus declined to continue this refusal or to be party to this estrangement. He turned away from Adam's refusal and Satan's account of alternative creations and took up God's work again. Jesus did not come to a business gone into receivership but to his own vineyard and house; he reassumed the office of householder, and the estate recognized the voice of its master. He has put his hand to the plow and gone to prepare a place for us. So to

---

142. Irenaeus understood Adam as immature. Adam and Eve "having been created a short time previously had no understanding of the procreation of children; for it was necessary that they should first come to adult age" (*Against Heresies* 3.22).

apply this more Irenaean version of Adam to Abraham, we must understand Abraham not as individual but as Israel, the obedient son and witness of God.[143]

3.7.3. Murder — Israel's Estimate of Gentile Being

God's giving of the concept of murder corresponds to his election of the people of Israel. The concept of murder is not one apparent to all the world, a commandment that the gentiles could keep if they wished. The commandment is precisely to be *not-gentile*, to have nothing to do with those forms of life that Israel lumps together under that term.[144] The command "Do no murder" is therefore the election of Israel in imperative mood. God's word is the unity of description and imperative, of speech and its being heard and acted on. Within this concept of murder come all species of gentile being, all summed up as "death." The command returns to the idolaters what they have offered, a case of paying them back in their own coin. Worship of some other god is death, and putting to death what is death belongs to the act of confession of God as the only Lord.[145]

According to tradition, the sacrifice of Isaac took place on the hill on which the Jerusalem temple was later built. The sacrifice of Isaac is therefore the first of the sacrifices taught in Leviticus and Deuteronomy and performed in the temple.[146] This worship informs the practice of the

143. Wyschogrod is mistaken in understanding either Jesus or God as individual, unaccompanied by his Word and the hearer of that Word. With the personhood he has from the Father by the Holy Spirit, Jesus persons Abraham too.

144. E. Feldman, *Biblical and Post-Biblical Defilement and Mourning: Law as Theology* (New York: Yeshiva University, 1977), believes that Israel is not so much concerned with death as a physical phenomenon as with demythologizing death by demonstrably rejecting those routines and observances that surround death in other societies. Gerhard von Rad, *Old Testament Theology* (London: SCM, 1975), vol. 2, p. 350, agrees: "What is astonishing is the way in which this mysterious world [of death] is entirely divested of its sacred character."

145. According to R. W. L. Moberly, "Towards a Definition of the Shema," in Seitz and Greene-McCreight, eds., *Theological Exegesis*, p. 135: "Deuteronomy 7 presents ḥerem as a metaphor for religious fidelity. . . . The rationale for ḥerem is election and holiness, the essential counterpart to the confession that Yahweh is One and Israel is to love him unreservedly." Ḥerem, "putting to the ban," means destroying everything and everyone associated with pagan cult and tolerating no mixture or intermarriage. It is to put offenders outside Israel, thus sending them out to where death rules.

146. See Moberly, *The Bible, Theology and Faith*, pp. 108-18.

husbandry of the creation into which Israel has been set.[147] It is a creation theology, which prepares and trains Israel up to become that entirely unforeseen creature, the human being who is with God. By unlearning the patterns and orientation-less deviations that represent Adam's endless failure to make a start on the job, and starting on an apprenticeship as priest of creation, the old creature becomes the new creature. What goes on in the Jerusalem temple is the training by which this people will come to realize that killing, which characterizes all other nations, is a way no longer open to them. No blood whatsoever may touch the ground of the holy land of Israel. No intrinsic significance is given to blood, but all the practices of the gentiles involving blood for the ancestors are demonstrably reversed in the temple — the blood is simply poured away down the drain around the altar.[148] It is, as Jacob Milgrom shows, not a matter of safely disposing of a dangerous substance, but of comprehensively disarming and depaganizing death, sin, blood, and purity. It is part of the heuristic intent of the liturgical practices that teach the status of Israel and the character of Israel's God.[149] Comprehension and appropriation of these practices are not secondary to the rituals of atonement themselves, for the rituals are responsible for the formation of Israel's new mind.

According to Milgrom, all Israel's sacrifice is about demonstrating publicly, and thus at the altar, that the animal killed falls within the definition of meat that may be eaten by Israel. Each killing must be shown to be the permitted killing of the animals within the covenant and thus to be not a case of murder. To make the killing a permissible sacrifice, the Israelite is required to return the blood, otherwise his own blood will be forfeit. Only the permitted animals may be killed, and that only when the blood of a proportion of them is publicly disempowered at the temple. Human beings' violent nature cannot change, but it need not pollute the earth if, according to Leviticus 17, they obey one law, to abstain from blood: human blood must not be shed and animal blood must not be eaten. The life is God's and must be returned to God. Israel enjoys the repeated use-value of the permitted animals by not consuming the whole life (blood) of the

147. See Perdue, *Collapse of History*, pp. 115-40.

148. See Milgrom, *Leviticus*, vol. 1, pp. 704-6, 49. The gentiles are told just to pour the blood out, but Israel must do this on the altar (Lev. 17:11). See §5.4, Maimonides on Israel's sacrifice as reversal of pagan practices.

149. See Milgrom, *Leviticus*, vol. 1, pp. 44-45.

creature. Since this blood prohibition is not to be found in Israel's neighbors it "must be adjudged as the product of a rational, deliberate opposition to the prevailing practice of its environment."[150]

The liturgical labor of the temple represents the becoming-holy of the nation. The temple is the process of the establishment of the new creation in which Israel is Adam, finally set to work. Jesus is the Israel, who having undergone baptism, turns away from the possibilities of alternative regimes and creations of the gentiles to take up the Father's work.

3.7.4. The Office of Sacrifice

Humankind is given a new action. Human beings are to be drawn into the co-work of creation, and that action we can summarize as "sacrifice." This is the means by which they are drawn into this new action.[151] Leviticus instructs that the Israelite "is to lay his hand on the head of the burnt offering, and it will be accepted on his behalf to make atonement for him" (Lev. 1:4). "In the Old Testament cult the consecration takes place by placing the hand on the head of the sacrificial animal, extending to it the personhood of the sacrificer, to identify the sacrificial animal and the offerer of the sacrifice."[152] The high point of the sacrifice is the laying of hands on the sacrificial animal. In laying his hands on this creature the sacrificer is appointed its steward. He is given the office of priest mandated to exercise the authority of Israel's God over his creation.[153] With this office the sacrificer re-

---

150. See Milgrom, *Leviticus*, vol. 1, p. 706. In the same way, semen is holy because it is the life-substance of Israel, and it has a periodicity longer than the individual Israelite who produces it.

151. See Dalferth, *Der auferweckte Gekreuzigte*, pp. 271-83; Preuss, *Old Testament Theology*, vol. 2, pp. 238-44; and Pannenberg, *Systematic Theology*, vol. 2, pp. 421-28, on christological employment of Old Testament concepts of sacrifice.

152. Ingolf U. Dalferth, "Mythos, Ritual, Dogmatik: Strukturen der religiösen Text-Welt," *Evangelische Theologie* 47.4 (1987): 278. According to Dalferth, there are "three stages to the action of the Old Testament sin-offering: the act of consecration by which an animal became the symbol of the Lord of the sacrifice, the act of killing the animal which is significant only as the means of obtaining blood, and the act of symbolic incorporation of the man into salvific communion with God." It creates a transfer or extension of agency and an identification of the offerer and his offering.

153. See John D. Zizioulas, "Preserving God's Creation: Three Lectures on Theology and Ecology," *King's Theological Review* 12-13 (1989-90): third lecture, p. 6; and Anderson, *From Creation to New Creation*, pp. 111-31, "Human dominion over nature."

ceives a new mode of personhood and new existence. But it is not only a single event but part of the process of training and instructing him in this task. By this hand gesture the Israelite takes up his task. Through the sacrificial animal the obedient Israelite has access into the court and presence of the Lord.[154] Israel put its hands on the Son and handed him over. Thus the death of Jesus is the meeting in one place of God and humanity. This meeting creates the place in which the two of them may remain together.[155]

In Israel's economy, sacrifice refers to, and instructs the sacrificer in, the grateful recognition and return of the life and being received from God. We saw Janowski refer to a complex economy in which we act to and for one another.[156] Being is what is supplied, and it is supplied as a particular opportunity of action. Old action gives way to, and creates the place for, new action. New action does not remove old action but secures it and supplies what is missing from it. *Paying back* (retribution) means responding to the demand to be offered some token of relationship. We have already seen that we all demand that others give us something of themselves, and that this should be an account of themselves in which we feature. They have to lay out for us some place that we share with them. The law of return of like for like *(talion)* is not only about criminal law and vengefulness. It is also the basis of civil law, compensation, and the provision of a basis for negotiation to start the process of making good. The satisfaction theory should be understood not in terms of punishment but in terms of the giving and receiving of being from one another. Wrath and punishment refer to that moment when this process has stalled and there is a collapse in Israel's economy of being. God restarts the process of giving and receiving with a new injection of giving. "Anselm and the Bible agree that satisfaction is not opposed to the idea

154. See Bernd Janowski, *Sühne als Heilsgeschehen* (Neukirchen-Vluyn: Neukirchener, 2000), pp. 199-221, for discussion of the laying on of hands. The animal's persona and therefore death is extended to include the Israelite who offers him in the temple.

155. Wolfgang Kraus, *Der Tod Jesu als Heiligtumsweihe* (Neukirchen-Vluyn: Neukirchener, 1991), argues that the death of Jesus is the consecration of the temple in which humanity will be with God.

156. Bernd Janowski, "Der Tat kehrt zum Täter zurück," in *Die Rettende Gerechtigkeit* Neukirchen-Vluyn: Neukirchener, 1999), pp. 190-91. See also C. Gestrich, "God Takes Our Place: A Religious-Philosophical Approach to the Concept of *Stellvertretung*," *Modern Theology* 17.3 (2001).

of forgiveness but is its presupposition, and reconciliation takes place at the initiative of the guilty."[157]

The animal represents the whole ecosystem, medium, and world that God provides for his people. Because animals represent places in an ecosystem, they function as a semiotic technology, the basis and middle term of all communicative action. Animals bear political meanings. Leviticus lists those animals which may enter the temple and be sacrificed to represent the elect nation, and those animals which are not acceptable, which represent the gentiles outside the covenant.[158] The animal is the creature and instrument of the Lord of creation, a creation that is made up of all animals and nations. To grasp the animal in the way instructed in Leviticus is to accept the appointment as the officer of God over the gentile and animal world. To take this animal is to receive the word and command of the Lord. God has his hand on the animal; when by this consecration a human hand is placed on the animal too, the animal represents the united agency of the two of them. The human being enters the place of the Lord, sponsored and accompanied by the animal. As the animal is the servant and representative of the Lord, we can say that the Lord escorts the human being into the place of the Lord. Person and animal do not swap places, but the agency of the animal is extended to include the person. Like a court usher, the sacrificial animal accompanies the human being through the courts of the king to the throne room where the king sits. In this place he will receive from his king his own place. The animal is the whole world and medium that God gives to humankind and humankind obediently receives. It is a lease and commission. It is given only as long as it is obediently received, and returned, and received again.

Though there are two parties to every sacrifice, it is not the case that one is sacrificed to the other. Rather, the one is inducting the other into creaturehood in a process of paideia. This is an event in which one party mandates the other, and a process in which one is trained by another into the skills by which he can receive and exercise this mandate. The two parties comprise a teacher and a learner, a human being sacrificing, and his Lord supervising his learning and correct exercise of this priestly office. The sac-

---

157. Colin Gunton, in a review of Steindl, *Genugtuung: Biblisches Versöhnungsdenken — eine Quelle für Anselms Satisfaktionstheorie?* in *Journal of Theological Studies* 43 (1992): 285.

158. See Mary Douglas, *Leviticus as Literature* (Oxford: Oxford University Press, 1999), p. 225.

rifice is not for the benefit of the Lord but is part of the practice of the husbandry into which the Lord inducts his servant. Every process of teaching and learning is accompanied by a process of testing and inspection. We saw in Chapter 2 that the identification and isolation of sin is part of this process of progress-checking, which is itself part of learning. By the performance of sacrifice and bringing some of the results of its husbandry to the temple for inspection, Israel's progress in appropriating the land and learning the holy practices of husbandry of God is tested and approved.

The book of Leviticus tells us that God puts his hand on the world in the form of the animal and keeps his hand on it to ward off other gods and claimants. The instruction that the Israelite "shall put his hand on the sacrifice and it will be an atonement for him" (Lev. 1:4) summarizes the relationship of God to his creature. This description of this gesture represents Israel's deconstruction of the many obeisances of the pagans. It is the relationship expressed in the sacrifice of Isaac, in which Abraham obediently played the part God gave him to play, God's own office. He put his hand on Isaac, the future of Israel, gaining for humankind a place at the head of creation, a place he is to keep his hand on. We can therefore say that, at one point, Israel has only and precisely one member. God is this member. God distinguishes himself from us. The Son is at the right hand of the Father, one God, with humankind as his work. Other than God, no member of Israel is capable of sustaining his or her own identity or supplying identity to others. Perhaps we can also say that Israel never expected anything else than that God be its vindication. The ancestor through whom all Israel must march is not Abraham, but Jesus. Only as a result of passing through Jesus does Abraham's line continue and his fatherhood achieve duration. We may therefore say that the product of the eucharistic industry and economy of Israel is no divisible commodity but creatures who have the character and image of the God of Israel. They are members of his staff and household and are therefore persons, free and able to open new action and freedom to each other. Next we must say something about the medium employed by this account.

We have established in this chapter that the Spirit brings us into being. God makes us sons and daughters. Sometimes he does this ostensibly by biology, at others by election, though it must be said this is all by election — that is, by his sovereign choice. This election is the whole point and purpose of all biology. God makes us material and embodied, available and locatable to one another, in this biological medium. He makes us not alone, but accompanied, set in a world of people. In the next chapter we must establish that God does this by his Spirit — that is, he does this himself. God works with his own hands, not using the work of another, with no other resources than his own. Yet he works with, and against, our recalcitrance. He works with what we seek to withhold but what he takes from us in order to give us again. He is the medium of his own work, and he provides the medium within which we can come into being.

CHAPTER 4

The Medium of God's Work

We must now ask about the medium and economy in which God distinguishes himself from us and reconciles us to himself. God is the medium of his work. This theology requires a pneumatology that will manifest the many forms of this work of God. This chapter indicates what that pneumatology will involve. It will start with the doctrine of the atonement, proceed to discussion of sanctification, and end by relating these to Israel's political cosmology or doctrine of creation.

4.1. Accounting for Cost: The Destruction of the Gentile Economy

The Lord is the Spirit. He divides but is not himself divisible. He can open and pass through; nothing can hold him out. He is impervious, so he cannot be opened or entered. He can search and examine; but to our cognizance he is imperceptible and will not be summoned to our scrutiny. The Spirit is one, and he makes his work one with him; he can keep possession of it, so it cannot be separated or even distinguished from him. The Son is employed in the work of the Father. Their unity cannot be anatomized, analyzed, or known except where the Spirit makes the Son known. The Spirit can penetrate our economy, but nothing in our economy can cut the Spirit off from the Son. The Spirit is therefore able to act as the medium by which we are brought out of our many economies into the single economy of their action. The medium of God's action is first God himself. Subsidiarily it is also those other economies God brings to an end, and to a new beginning, in the economy of his creation.

I have argued for the importance of a medium by which to articulate performance and by which to recognize failure in order to improve that performance. Sin is the conceptuality by which an account of the holy character of Israel's God may be given and his holiness brought into being in his people. The sins of Israel do not succeed in coming between Israel and God. The enmity of Israel does not prevent God from coming to this people; the earth can cope with Israel's sins. This much must be said, though we cannot stop there. In the first place sin is childishness. God does not do anything with Israel's sin but puts up with it, as a parent puts up with the imperfect pronunciation of a child that will disappear as that child becomes an adult. This sin has no cost. Since the gentiles are without any parent or instructor to bring them up, they cannot develop and do not leave sin behind. But where mixing with the gentiles means that Israel continues to pick up their behavior and be reinfected by it, sin is also serious and in need of atonement. The scattered people of Israel (the diaspora) are threatened by proximity with the gentiles. With the end of Israel-Judah as an autonomous kingdom, the gentiles, and thus the exile existence, come to the land of Israel itself. The pollution of the land caused by the mixture and mayhem of uncontrolled, murderous, gentile appetites really does threaten the whole world. Where else will salvation for the gentiles come from if not from the holy people?

In Israel's infancy, God overlooks Israel's sin and counts it for nothing. We will see Milgrom and others offer such an account below. But this is not yet an adequate account. God is also angry at sin. He condemns it and destroys it.[1] Israel is the judgment of God against the gentiles. Gentiles kill and eat, fail to hold together, die and are reclaimed by the earth. Death is built into them and is the working-out of what they are and do.[2] Fallen creation goes beyond its boundaries, yet it fails to grow into its proper limits.

---

1. See James D. G. Dunn, *The Theology of Paul the Apostle* (Edinburgh: T&T Clark, 1998), pp. 62-70, and for an account of judgment of sin, pp. 102-14; H. D. Preuss, *Old Testament Theology* (Edinburgh: T&T Clark, 1995), vol. 1, pp. 128-37, on Yahweh as warrior and as war; W. Brueggemann, *Theology of the Old Testament* (Minneapolis: Augsburg Fortress, 1997), pp. 373-84, on where God's judgment seems to become God's violence, negativity, and irrationality.

2. See John D. Zizioulas, *Being as Communion: Studies in Personhood and the Church* (London: Darton, Longman & Todd, 1985), pp. 51-53.

The boundaries given to enable it to progress to fullness of life now serve only to keep it from progressing from one stage to another. It is stalled in an earlier form of life. Mortality is necessary at every stage, so the organism can move through and out of that stage; but, considered apart from the causality of the end, the whole adds up only to mortality and futility. The doctrine of sin defines chasing, rutting, tearing, and killing as typical of humankind as a species. This species will never become anything that it is not already. It is only the arrival of the law to one people, the elect community of Israel, that makes the behavior of human beings *murder*. We must say this as a corrective to the Kantian anthropology that makes guilt and sin almost intrinsic to our dignity. That humankind is given over to death is not a piece of natural theology.[3] It is only Israel that terms all that human beings do as sin and all that they are as death. Death is what the gentiles do and what they amount to. It is Israel's name for the gentile world.[4]

But more than this, the gentiles are also the judgment of God against Israel. Sin is most visible in Israel, for Israel is a worse sinner than the gentiles. Gentiles are even employed in Israel's punishment. Yet even in disobedience, Israel still bears witness to the action of God. All prognosis of disaster coming upon Israel is the speech of the prophets to Israel and is not intended to be overheard by the gentiles. So we must say that, on the one hand the gentiles are innocents and what they do is not yet even sin. And on the other hand, they are the dogs, outside any law, and therefore *are* sin. Their sin threatens even the holy people.

Jesus is handed over to the world. He is made passive. Passivity and passion become his action. Although Jesus is the circumcision, baptism, and

3. Stanley Hauerwas, *Sanctify Them in the Truth* (Edinburgh: T&T Clark, 1998), p. 66, asks: "Why is talk of Christ considered 'fideistic' but not talk [i.e., natural theology] of sin?"

4. Mary Douglas, *In the Wilderness: The Doctrine of Defilement in the Book of Numbers* (Sheffield: Sheffield Academic Press, 1993), p. 24, argues that "The nature of the living God is in opposition to dead bodies. Total incompatibility holds between God's presence and bodily corruption. God is living, life is his. Other gods belong to death, contagion and decay." Similarly Jon D. Levenson, *Creation and the Persistence of Evil: The Jewish Drama of Divine Omnipotence* (Princeton: Princeton University Press, 1988), p. 29, explains that "The Adversary overcome in Isaiah 25:6-9 is not Leviathan under whatever name, but 'Death'. It is best to see in this term the name of a deity, because the same word *(mt)* denotes in Ugaritic the name of one of Baal's foes, *Mot*, the deadly son of El, who succeeds in swallowing Baal." Yahweh swallows Death rather than the reverse. Against Levenson we must say that the opponents of Yahweh are opposed to him only in being his rivals for us, not because they are intrinsically able to oppose him.

anointing, he is circumcised, baptized, and anointed.[5] Although he is the resurrection, the one who may never die, he suffers and dies. He suffers the world. If we are allowed to abuse the language a little, we could say that Jesus is *worlded*. He calls out from the world what is most intrinsic to it — death — and summons it together to a single point, that of the cross. When Jesus calls, death comes out of the world. Jesus is able to break open the world and separate death from it.[6] The indivisible Spirit drives division out. The world is *Jesused*. Death has no claim on him, so it finds nothing in him by which it can gain purchase. Death is *deathed*. The Spirit makes the Son indivisible and so impregnable: the world cannot break him. God has allowed the tares to grow in the field, and though, like the kings of the earth, they grow very confident, their destruction is assured, for he has all this time prepared a place for them, a no-place. In entering the enclosure of death the Son is not enclosed, but breaks open what only he had held shut.

As Israel suffers the gentile onslaughts, Israel is half-persuaded that it has to compete with the gentiles as an equal rather than as their lord; Israel has to fight them as though it were one of them, rather than bear them as a parent does a child. Inasmuch as Israel succumbs to this temptation, Israel sins — Israel *gentiles*. In persecuting the followers of Jesus, Saul of Tarsus had been opposing the God of Israel. He had understood himself to be doing a righteous thing in ridding Israel of all traces of the rebellion led by Jesus, a man publicly displayed as shamed and punished for rebellion. But the confrontation with God on the Damascus road showed Paul that all Israel is rebellion against God, acting as wildly as any gentile people. The man on the cross was the righteous Israelite who did what it was given to the whole people of God to do. He bore the aggression of the world. He bore it until the force of it was broken and exhausted by fighting against God and was taken captive to God. The act of crucifying Jesus was a pagan attack on the God of Israel, a pagan sacrifice.[7] In killing Jesus, the regime

---

5. Jesus is baptized by John "to fulfill all righteousness" (Matt. 3:15); see the discussion of Marius Reiser, *Jesus and Judgement: The Eschatological Proclamation in Its Jewish Context* (Minneapolis: Fortress, 1997), pp. 181-86.

6. See, for example, Luke 4:35: "Be quiet," Jesus said sternly; Mark 5:8: "[Jesus] had said to him, 'Come out of this man, you evil spirit.'" The legion of spirits return to the gentile animals to which they belong.

7. Martin Hengel, *Crucifixion in the Ancient World and the Folly of the Message of the Cross* (London: SCM, 1977); J. Harries, *Law and Empire in Late Antiquity* (New York: Cambridge University Press, 1999), p. 140, and D. G. Kyle, *Spectacles of Death in Ancient Rome*

made the sacrifice that put the whole people out of relationship with their God. Yet this was not finally definitive of this event. Jesus made this the sacrifice that was righteous and life-generating. The cross was the act by which the regime *gentiled* itself and Jesus *righteoused* himself, and as such this was the joint act of God and human beings, in which the act of humankind was redeemed by God.

Jesus bears the fighting and resistance that are the gentile mode of the world. Whose blood flows? The statements "It is by his wounds that you are healed" (1 Pet. 2:24) and "We have redemption through his blood, the forgiveness of sins" (Eph. 1:7; cf. Rom. 3:25; 5:9) have different intentions: their middle terms have to be supplied with reference to the whole evangelical narrative. We need two accounts. His blood flowed for the healing of the nations. But this blood does not flow from wounds opened by the blows inflicted on him by the nations. Jesus judged the nations.[8] The gen-

---

(London: Routledge, 2001), p. 168, show that types of punishment represent places on the shame scale. On the cross Jesus was hung up and displayed: "The God of our fathers raised Jesus from the dead, whom you had killed by hanging him on a tree" (Acts 5:30; see also 10:39; 13:29); "As Moses lifted up the snake in the wilderness, so the Son of man must be lifted up" (John 3:14).

1. To be hung up is to be shamed, to have all the honor and life drain out of you, until you have no honor or resources or reputation or support left to you. In the course of this being hung up, the Son descends through all intermediary levels of status and being until he has no being left — a state of total shame. When he is raised from this lowest status those who shamed him are now shamed because they could not keep him down.

2. The animal is demonstrably lifted up and waved so that it can be seen to be distinguished from all others (Lev. 7:30). The blood is shown, and if the blood is acceptable in this firstborn, then the blood of the whole flock is acceptable (Rom. 11:16). It is made acceptable because in this event this particular lamb and sacrifice and intercession has been accepted by God.

3. The animal is held up so that the blood pours out, in such a way that it can be seen that blood is flowing (Exod. 29:12; Lev. 4:18) — like a drink offering (Phil. 2:17) — that is, not exhausted or interrupted because this is a living sacrificer (Rom. 12:1) who pours, and continues to pour, his inexhaustible life into our economy, with the result that it is redetermined by him.

8. Reiser, *Jesus and Judgement*, p. 255, believes the scholarship of apocalyptic "separates judgement and salvation as if they were not two sides of the same coin, two aspects of the one eschatological event. . . . Judgement is the obverse of salvation, and its necessary precondition." Oliver O'Donovan, *Desire of the Nations: Rediscovering the Roots of Political Theology* (Cambridge: Cambridge University Press, 1996), p. 141, understands restoration of Christ from death as judgment against Israel and for Israel.

tiles are punished.[9] Though it is the blow delivered by God, it is struck by each against all. The gentiles become the punishment of God to each other. They have to drink from their own cup. But this takes place in the idiom of the blood of only one of their number, one of the nations elect for this purpose — Israel. Her blood runs, and therefore their blood has run. The gentiles are let, and Israel is the blood that flows out. All the blood shed by the gentiles is pointless suffering from the wounds they inflict on each other. Yet Israel's king really suffers, in that his people, those he regards as his own substance, are wounded. He bears them and is covered in their blood. But because he has determined that they belong to him, their blood is his blood. Because it is his determination to drive them to atonement through this crisis, it must be laid to his account, yet he did not shed it. He is wounded because those who are his fight him and each other and bleed. He is not wounded because they inflict wounds on him: they have no means of touching him. Death inflicts injuries on Jesus that the resurrection demonstrates have no duration or lasting reality. Yet their wounds are healed and lacks are supplied by him, in the form of his own substance — his blood. This blood — the reviving substance of life — comes from his generosity. It does not come from his wounds. It is the opponent who receives the wound that is fatal and whose blood runs. The wounds are returned to the wounder.[10] God redeems his people from Egypt, but he does not have to pay Egypt for them in some neutral currency (blood). God pays Egypt back in Egypt's currency, that of violence and fury. God refuses and returns this currency. The medium of this atonement is the whole economy of humanity, which is commandeered, seized, and given a new function within the eschatological economy of God.

4.1.1. God Withstands Us and Suffers No Resistance

The Son is one with the Father. They are together in the work of the cross. For this reason it is a mistake to think that death dealt finally with Jesus on

---

9. The cross is the event of putting to the ban (ḥerem). The holiness of God is such that his very approach causes things to burst into flame and what is not holy is burned away.

10. Mary Douglas, *Leviticus as Literature* (Oxford: Oxford University Press, 1999), suggests that this is the sense of retribution. Colin Gunton, *The Actuality of Atonement: A Study of Metaphor, Rationality and the Christian Tradition* (Edinburgh: T&T Clark, 1988), p. 88, suggests that the question of to whom the payment is made should be avoided. But here we see the devil paid back in his own currency.

the cross. The cross was our act of attempting to separate the Son from the Father, but this act of ours was itself our death. On the cross Jesus called death together and *deathed* it.[11] The cross extracted death from the world and balled it together into a place of no extension. The crucifixion is therefore one event with two agents. We crucified Jesus, and God raised him. The cross is our act transformed by God into God's act with us and against us — resurrection.[12] There are not two acts here involving two agents; thus there is no problem of how the second agent engages and refers to the first act. It is not we, alone and by ourselves, who make a first act. Our rebellion does not construct some real position that we succeed in holding against God. From the first our rebellion is contained and co-opted by God and made to serve no other future and hypostasis than resurrection. Jesus' resurrection is his being with human beings, albeit that this *being-with* takes the form of God *being-against* us. It sets humankind permanently under the canopy of the cross. The resurrection is not a moving away from the cross but is the vanishing of the sinful hypostasis that contained and secured us and the appearance of the Son who was always ahead of us. It was the coming together of humanity with God.

Our crucifixion of Jesus was not an act we succeeded in exerting over him by ourselves. The crucifixion was not our sole act that made God's act

11. My argument will be in line with that of Thomas Weinandy, *Does God Suffer?* (Edinburgh: T&T Clark, 2000), to which the answer is a sophisticated but emphatic No. It will be against that of G. W. F. Hegel, *Lectures on the Philosophy of Religion,* Volume III: *The Consummate Religion,* ed. Peter C. Hodgson (Berkeley: University of California Press, 1985), pp. 322-27: "But this humanity in God — and indeed the most abstract form of humanity, the greatest dependent, the ultimate weakness, the utmost fragility — [is] natural death. 'God himself is dead', it says in a Lutheran hymn, expressing an awareness that the human, the finite, the fragile, the weak, the negative, are themselves a moment of the divine, that they are within God himself" (p. 326). Rather than follow Hegel, and the twentieth-century theology that has followed him in this (e.g., J. Moltmann, *The Crucified God: The Cross of Christ as the Foundation and Criticism of Christian Theology* [London: SCM, 1974]), I will attempt an approach that brings the cross into closer relation to the Old Testament portrayal of the utter refusal by the God of Israel of the gods of the nations. He names them *death,* engages them in battle, suffers their resistance, and breaks it.

12. John D. Zizioulas, "Towards an Eschatological Ontology" (paper given at King's College, London, 1999), p. 9: "Since the end decides finally about the truth of history only those events leading to the end will be shown to possess true being or being *tout court.* The historical events of revelation, therefore, are true and real only because they lead to the end from which they came into being, not in themselves. In such a view, not even the cross can have a meaning of its own; it is the Resurrection that reveals the meaning of the cross."

of resurrection possible. Rather, resurrection is what becomes of our act of crucifying him. The cross — our attack on God — is not the first act that sets us up as autonomous beings who have sent God away.[13] Rather, this death is just the sum of the deviations that represent the gentile mode. God has protected us from the consequences of our acts, but in the cross God no longer holds back. He lets us have the consequences of all our acts. We are punished by the return of all the violence we released into the world. He unites us with our act. It is not the act that we did alone, but our act with him, and thus his and our single co-work.[14] Crucifixion of us, in the form of the crucifixion of our one representative, is the form in which resurrection comes to us.

4.1.2. Who Pays? The End of the Time of the Son Who Would Not Take Up the Father's Work

Everything that the pagans do amounts to grief, decay, waste, and fruitless suffering. They want what will never come. Their striving is therefore bitter and pointless. Christ's suffering consists in refusing and returning to them the projects of the gentiles.[15] Their designs shatter on Christ. He retrieves the gentiles and bears them to that other set of designs which God has for them. Paul's own pre-conversion life consisted of avoiding suffering the gentiles. Now Paul understands that it is God's will precisely that Israel bears and suffers the gentiles. This realization becomes a hermeneutic of the cross. From the very beginning of God's history with Israel, God had borne Israel, and borne her against Israel's own resistance.[16] He bore Israel not so that Israel should suffer a gentile fate, but that by re-birth Israel should be delivered from the gentile hypostasis. God has suffered and waited and been patient,

---

13. On Luther and Nietzsche's "God is dead," see Eberhard Jüngel, *God as Mystery of the World* (Edinburgh: T&T Clark, 1983), pp. 55-104.

14. Death and crucifixion are Christ in our medium; resurrection is Christ in his own medium. But our medium has no purpose other than to allow us to be readied for emergence into his medium — so our medium is only ours because it is his for us. I have reduced an explanation to a description.

15. O'Donovan, *The Desire of the Nations*, p. 276: "The first consequence of this reorientation of society to individual wants is that suffering becomes unintelligible."

16. See Markus Bockmuehl, *Revelation and Mystery in Ancient Judaism and Pauline Christianity* (Grand Rapids: Eerdmans, 1997), pp. 142-44, and Dunn, *The Theology of Paul the Apostle*, pp. 499-532, for discussion.

not so that this state should continue and be ratified, but so that it should come to an end and Israel be elect and released from slavery to the gentile mode. The cross is therefore two sorts of suffering: it is the suffering of the gentiles, which is without purpose, and which God refuses; and it is the suffering of God, which is patient, merciful, and purposeful. Apart from God we are subjected to pointless, fruitless suffering — the problem identified by theodicy. Such suffering has no time and no end. But the suffering of God is the patient and purposeful waiting that redeems a people from futility. Since they are not their own but God's, the suffering of Christians is not fruitless but God's purposeful suffering and laboring by which the world is borne into new life.[17] The purposeless gentile mode will pay.

The event of the cross represents the gentiles having their way with Israel. The cross is a compressed symbol for the temple and thus for the whole cosmology of Israel in microcosm. The tree that is induced to bear a single fruit represents Israel's Son-reproduction cosmology. By his performance of the cross Jesus imitates and parodies the world, performing the world's script in such a way as to take its script away from it and leave it bereft.[18] The obedience of the Son takes the form of suffering alone the contradiction and resistance of the whole world. There is no one who follows the messiah to the cross, so Israel is a set with a single member. Jesus' recognition of what he has to do comes with the realization that he is alone against the world. The Servant is not a mass movement but a single Israelite who has to undergo the baptism of the enmity of all. They are not his hosts and fellows, but his enemy, the river he has to go through and the drink he has to drink. Only by passing through him can they become the river of healing that flows from him, and through which even the gentiles may pass into Israel. God has fulfilled his righteousness against Israel, in Israel's despite, doing what Israel could not do.

17. See Dunn, *The Theology of Paul the Apostle*, pp. 482-87; and also S. J. Hafemann, *Suffering and the Spirit* (Tübingen: Mohr, 1986), p. 219, on Paul's "imagery of a triumphal procession, with himself as the captive slave of God who is constantly being led to death. With this image Paul graphically portrays that it is through his daily experience of death = suffering that the glory and power of God are being revealed."

18. The gentiles act alone, without and against the God of Israel. In Israel the God of Israel shows them that he holds all their action and that they have no answer to his challenges. This theory of the cross and Israel as deconstructive imitation relies on a continuum of action, such that action must be seen as new, so if it is foreseen (pre-parodied) it is not free and cannot be action, as we saw in §2.7.

Now we can see how this equation of being and honor works biblically. Jesus was abandoned by all. He was hung on the cross to display his complete isolation and shame. All resources of support drained away from him, until he had nothing. In this visible world he was cleared out of all resources of public reputation and recognition. He descended through all intermediary levels of status and being until he reached the lowest point, left altogether without being, in total shame. But the forces of this world could not keep him down. Being unable to make their judgment stick, they have been publicly revealed to be without power. When he was raised by the Father, Jesus was set at the highest place.[19] The Father reversed the action of humankind by overturning this public assessment of his servant. Because Jesus is raised from this total absence of status, those who shamed him are now shamed. By his resurrection ride back up through all levels of the cosmos, the God-man intimidates all would-be rebellious forces, stiffening the resolve of all the faithful, demonstrating to the wavering that his forces are greater and that he will therefore prevail.[20] The troops of the rebellious forces reassess the chances of their winning under their leaders, and desert, returning to the leadership of the one God.[21] By his Spirit the victorious Son calls and draws out of the earth all the dispersed elements, all the bodies of the poor, hidden by wicked people, and brings them together to form one bright new body — the resurrection body, united with himself. This human being is reassembled from the divided and plundered spoils held by the various rulers of the eons.

Western theology has made the cross of Christ unintelligible by explicating about it in the very logic it resists. The cross is itself cut off, separated, isolated by the analytic individuating logic of the ontology of "nature." This has naturalized death, relating it to the state of our bodies rather than our persons, and so concealed the idea that death is a breakdown of connection

19. "The God of our fathers raised Jesus from the dead, whom you had killed by hanging him on a tree" (Acts 5:30; cf. 10:39; 13:29).

20. Clinton E. Arnold, *Ephesians, Power and Magic: The Concept of Power in Ephesians in Light of Its Historical Setting* (Cambridge: Cambridge University Press, 1989), pp. 123-34, 155, describes the cross and Christ's ascension journey as a military campaign by which order is restored to the cosmos.

21. "In that day the Lord will punish the powers in the heavens above and the kings on the earth below. They will be herded together like prisoners bound in a dungeon" (Isa. 24:21-22). Now Jesus Christ "has gone into heaven and is at God's right hand — with angels, authorities and powers in submission to him"(1 Pet. 3:22).

and the end of participation. The gospel provides and requires a relational and doxological ontology that maintains that we come alive when people include us, and we die when we are excluded. Our life is a function of their action. We die when we are "cut off." Modern theology has not taken seriously enough this preaching that "You put him to death but God raised him from the dead" (Acts 5:30). God simply refused and reversed the verdict and action of humankind. The one who was thrown out is the one who was sent back to become decisive and constitutive of the life and being now available to us.

4.1.3. Resurrection as God's Time for Us: God's Time Redetermines Ours

The cross is the work of God. God works, but the outcome of his work is already present to him, so he is seated on a throne, at rest, publicly vindicated and given glory.[22] The cross took the form of the alien sacrifice in which Israel played the part of the enemies of God and was defiled. The resurrection demonstrated the cross to be the enthronement and exaltation of the God of Israel over his enemies. He is raised from them, but the cross, which is the form of his exaltation over us, remains the covering thrown over us. It characterizes us permanently as the conquered.[23] The resurrection baptized the world in this work and the medium it created, so this medium lies over the world as the protective covering of this present age *(saeculum)*. Baptism is the outer, and circumcision the inner, mode of this new medium in which we now live.

---

22. Thus Wolfhart Pannenberg, *Jesus — God and Man* (London: SCM, 1968), p. 278: "Luther agrees with the main line of the patristic doctrine of reconciliation in seeing the cross as an action of God in and through Jesus, not as an accomplishment of the man Jesus in relation to God." According to Martin Hengel, "Sit at My Right Hand," in *Studies in Early Christology* (Edinburgh: T&T Clark, 1995), p. 162, the unity of action of the Son and the Father in the death of Christ on the cross (2 Cor. 5:19) parallels the heavenly communion of Father and Son on the throne.

23. The cross becomes that tragic or biological hypostasis in which we are confined until we are readied for a greater economy. T. F. Torrance, *Space, Time and Incarnation* (Edinburgh: T&T Clark, 1969), p. 85, believes that "If we refuse to abstract it (the resurrection of Jesus Christ) from the field of living power disclosed in the Person of Christ, who is after all the subject of the resurrection, and think of it not only in terms of the successive and coherent structures of his life and work on earth but in terms of his whole space-time track in the cosmos" then "we are able to discern the operational principles which . . . emerge at this level and control the boundary conditions left open at the lower level without abrogating them."

By our baptism into this medium, the cross also becomes our support and our light and easy yoke. The resurrection is not the undoing of the event of the cross, but the transfer of that event from our fallen cosmology to God's place in which it is the finished work. The cross is a new environment that we are baptized and immersed in. It redetermines our metabolism. In it we learn to make one another present. The cross is the path, opened up by the Son, along which the Spirit now leads us, so that in the wilderness territory of the cross we are taught the practices and life of the resurrected Son. Our way through this territory must be learned as a set of skills and form of action. We are the ones who must become other than we presently are. He will meet us, not as we have been, but as we will be, transformed to become the people of his household. He has come to us, as the one Son. He is with us as the many, the Spirit, in such a way that we are graspable to him, while he is not graspable for us. The coming again — the general resurrection — will be the completion of the resurrection in which this one will lead and stay with this many.

The cross replaces and reestablishes the earlier abortive beginnings of the world. It is the moment when God was united with his work and creature. The cross is, and remains, the beginning and basis of the creation, the coincidence of creation and new creation. It is the ongoing work of the Son of Man who opens to us the two territories of earth and heaven as a single territory.[24] It is because he is the end, who works this end for us, that the cross is this beginning for us. Thus it is the true beginning of time. The reconciliation of God and humankind in this event is the beginning that corresponds to the end God has prepared. We call the action of God new because it makes all complete, present, and ever new. The question is therefore not how much is old and how much is new. This would be to ask what units the work of God lets itself be measured in. The work of God lets itself be measured only by the units of his devising: these units measure it by the end that God intends for it and direct it toward that end. This measure achieves that good shape and dimension that fits uniquely each par-

---

24. By traveling through all levels of the cosmos the God-man intimidates all would-be rebellious forces. "The rest seized his servants, ill-treated them and killed them. The king was enraged. He sent his army and destroyed those murderers and burned their city" (Matt. 22:6-7). In the face of this threat the rebellious forces abandon their masters and return to the king. "In that day the Lord will punish the powers in the heavens above and the kings on the earth below. They will be herded together like prisoners bound in a dungeon" (Isa. 24:21-22).

ticular, and fits each particular to the one end of its Creator. Because it is new, all the old is present, at last in its proper place.[25] Now the old will always be new and will never be disparaged or threatened by the possibility of being overtaken. It will be originating, of the beginning and thus original and true. The Father places Jesus first. He is appointed to the position of origin, pattern, and principle. He is the first man, and time has no other meaning than proximity, orientation, and movement in relation to him. Thus he is before Abraham and Adam. He is before all the founding figures named in the genealogies of the gentiles. He is, as it seems to us, retrospectively, first. It is not the case that a first draft was abandoned, but rather that the world was completing drafts without number. It is not then preexistence but repositioning the existence of everything that comes to compose the whole world.

The resurrection of Jesus was precisely not the general resurrection, but the provision of a longer, gentler way to the general resurrection. This resurrection, which is both commenced and delayed, is the mode of God's hidden work of holding and training a people.[26] By the resurrection, the crucifixion of Christ was lifted from Christ and placed instead on the many who had crucified him. Their act rebounded to catch them. The many have been corralled by the death that his resurrection has imposed upon them. Their death is now not at all their death, but entirely his death, the death that holds, not him, but them on whom he has imposed it. Now they can be slowly supplied, by the Spirit, with the resurrection. It can be supplied by the one who has risen from them and is therefore able to be with them, without their sin and death. The resurrected one is the Lord, the Spirit, the true and faithful servant who will not waste his talents or lose a single member of the flock he has gathered. He has worked, and his work is united with its harvest. He has paid with his labor, and he now receives the reward due to him.

---

25. Bockmuehl, *Revelation and Mystery in Ancient Judaism and Pauline Christianity*, p. 124, argues that "new and old stand in a reciprocal relationship: new revelation is always meta-revelation, given shape and texture by a charismatic reading of the old . . . instrumental for the understanding of the old, the 'proto-revelation.'"

26. Pannenberg, *Jesus — God and Man*, p. 66: "The earthly Jesus' expectation was . . . directed . . . toward the universal resurrection of the dead, which would of course include himself should his death precede it. Then when his disciples were confronted by the resurrected Jesus they no doubt also understood this as the beginning of the universal resurrection of the dead."

4.2. The Indivisibility of God's Time:
The One Testament and Witness

Does the Spirit work in the same way in the Old Testament and the New? Does he work differently after the crucifixion, or resurrection, or ascension? The character of the worker and of his labor does not change, but the work itself alters. On the seventh day, the day that includes all days, this Servant sat down at the right hand of the Father. The Old Testament action of the Spirit, the spiritual salvation history of Israel, is woven together to make one man, a single exemplum of the creature who is with God. The trauma involved in the impact of this meeting of God and his creation registers as the crucifixion.[27] It is an impact only because the creation is fallen, not perfected, but this impact represents the instantaneous perfecting of that creation. The resurrection is the joining of that finished work with the worker who has finished his creation and is together with it. The crucifixion is the instant of the completion of the work, the world transformed from fall to completion in a moment. It is the completion of the single testament of the one God.[28]

In the course of the history of Israel, the Spirit assembled and built up Israel to the status of the one completed and ascended man who sits with the Father. When that man was with God, creature and Creator together on the same bench, the Holy Spirit could replicate that man, and the freedom of creation that he represented, everywhere. So though there were many false starts, they were not finally false because as a result of them the full man arrived, born of the virgin. There was no discernible process building up to him other than that represented by the whole history of this people. The fullness of time, the Ancient of Days, himself arrived. By the arrival of this fullness of time, all Israel's time and waiting were redeemed.

---

27. See Gerhard Forde, "The Work of Christ," in *Christian Dogmatics*, ed. C. Braaten and R. W. Jenson (Philadelphia: Fortress, 1984), on the encounter of God and humankind as collision. This account does not place the encounter of humankind with God on neutral ground, so the question of *how* does not seek an extrinsic answer and thus one in terms of a mechanism, an outside causal and explanatory nexus. The encounter is on God's territory and terms, or, in the terms I shall use in Chapter 5, in the medium and economy he provides.

28. Thus N. T. Wright, *Climax of the Covenant: Christ and the Law in Pauline Theology* (Edinburgh: T&T Clark, 1991), p. 151: "Because the messiah represents Israel, he is able to take on himself Israel's curse and exhaust it. . . . The crucifixion of the Messiah is, one might say, the quintessence of the curse of exile, and its climatic act."

Time, on this theological definition, is the union of God's work and its fruit, time complete with its outcome. The eschatological economy of God, which we have already introduced once as the Sabbath, cannot be interrupted by the other economies of time created by rival lordships. The seventh day creates these six days. He creates for us these defined economies of time in which we may increasingly participate in the fullness of the resurrection, the eschatological economy of God.

The activity of the many together make one man, the Son.[29] They do not merely symbolize him; rather, they are the parts adopted by the Spirit out of which the Son is assembled and made. They stand in for him in the sense that they are proved to have been really practicing, waiting, building, and so by his Spirit properly *being* him in anticipation, the Coming Man. Thus eschatologically and retrospectively, all those in the history of Israel who appear to have been waiting vainly were in fact waiting for him, and were therefore faithful witnesses. If he would never come this time would be wasted time, invested but without return. Until he comes we cannot say in what sense this has been time at all. But if we wait for him, it will be not lost time but the time in which we learned to ask him to come to us to do his work, to receive him and become his people. Then we will be entrusted with much more time.

Since the Son did come in the single person of the God-man, time was redeemed and none of this waiting was in vain. The man who is with God can count time and tell history complete with its end. He can open the scroll and from it bring Israel alive. This instructor can make the Scriptures of Israel's own self-articulation effective for the transformation of the gentiles, too. He can tell times apart, setting live and formative time on one side, and barren and still-born time on the other. This sort of lived time will be found to have been the time in which God's servant learned his work. The righteousness of Israel that achieved no actuality has ceded its place to the righteousness that did. Since no previous Adam succeeded in holding on to his office and place, the God-man has become on the cross the retrospectively real and lasting Adam.

If Jesus is Christ, all Israel now is in Christ. Israel has been vindicated because its office has been carried out, albeit this has been the work of this

---

29. Here *homoousion* means "one," "united"; it does not mean one entity or one single stuff defined by a concept of substance. Being does not qualify oneness: triune oneness and manyness qualifies being.

single Israelite. The obedience of the Son takes the form of suffering contradiction and being alone against his own, so that Israel is a set with one member. If Christ triumphs, and he insists that Israel is with him, then Israel has triumphed with him. Then retrospectively we can say that the children of Israel were indeed waiting for him, and that they were also rewarded with him. He is their reward, for they have become children of Abraham by the faithfulness of Christ.

I have suggested that Israel's political claim must be related to Israel's cosmology. The work of the Servant takes the biological idioms of reproduction, respiration, and consumption and commandeers all would-be autonomous nature for the work of God. The issues sketched in this chapter can scarcely be answered by a biblical studies that does not understand itself as biblical *theology*. I argue in the next chapter that autonomous exegesis that does not stay in conversation with doctrine and philosophy cannot read Israel's Scriptures as a political-cosmological world-claim. Without learning from doctrine and political philosophy, would-be exegetes of the Bible are unlikely to understand Israel's cosmology as a public claim to commandeer, transform, and reemploy the world. Without an understanding of the commanded nature of Israel's action, as action that points to and participates in the new economy of action opened to God's people, modern biblical studies problematizes Israel's liturgical labor and therefore its ritual action, sacrifice, and temple. Must the academic attempt to give an account of Israel divide Israel from Israel's God? Must it fail to hear Israel's word as offer and command? Can autonomous biblical studies represent anything but a claim to be able to divide the one work and creation of God into the separate and autonomous realms of nature, on the one hand, and the intellectual, cultural, and religious realms of subjectivity, on the other? Such an academic project divides the people of Israel from their king, the body from the head, the people from their theological purpose and eschatological determination. It divides the indivisible work of God. We have discussed the world as God's task, place, and reward for Israel. I have suggested that the conceptuality, on the one hand, of relatedness, participation, and incorporation and, on the other, of command and transformation must form the whole center of theology.[30] Jesus Christ appears

---

30. Such participative conceptuality appears in this thesis as affiliation, adoption, friendship, kinship, the exercise of hospitality and possession, righteousness, the economy of response, and affective continuum.

against the resistance of what is, in the twofold form of (1) substance, nature, biology, and (2) politics, violence, and the contest of claims. Twentieth-century New Testament studies has perpetuated the modern division of discourse between cosmology and politics, between nature and action.

Theological biblical studies must recognize Israel's cosmological claim as a theological claim. It is a claim to be the first creature of the creation of God. The cosmological and political idiom of the *Old* and *New* Testaments has been neglected by biblical studies. Perhaps this neglect is inevitable to any New Testament studies that does not understand itself to be fully a study of the *Old Testament*.[31] I have suggested that pneumatology must include discussion of blood and seed, of sonship and the messiah, of holiness and purity. This cosmology must play a greater part in the theological account. It is a cosmology of creaturehood, an economy that receives its definition, not from an autonomous economy of nature, but from the action of God who draws his creatures into his action. We must understand "spiritual" to mean greater biological reality, not less — greater embodiment, not disembodiment. The language of biology that describes reproduction is not to be set in any strong contrast with the language of spiritual election. Kinship requires the two modes of elective and biological kinship. One may not be set over another.[32] It makes little difference whether we say it is the concerted obedience of many generations, or the failure of obe-

---

31. The problem is recognized by H. H. Schmid, "Creation, Righteousness and Salvation" (1973), in *Creation in the Old Testament*, ed. B. W. Anderson (Philadelphia: Fortress, 1984), p. 102: "In recent decades the concept of creation has been largely ignored in theology. According to the broad *communis opinio* it has been agreed that a theology of creation does indeed belong to Christian theology but that it must be accorded a secondary position to christology or soteriology."

32. New Testament studies has tended to approach Jesus' faith in abstraction from the cosmology of Israel and so individualistically or morally, in contrast to the relational-participational view that understands it as the function of the adherence of Spirit and Father that brings success and glory — in the form of a host of sons, as I argue here. H. Moxnes, *Constructing Early Christian Families* (London: Routledge, 1997), p. 32, for example, treats "fictive kinship" as though it were the opposite of real, because biological, kinship. I suggest we should understand "fictive" as a synonym for "adoptive," "elective." A household head can adopt a son, say by raising a freed slave to this status, and this elective kinship will be cemented by marriage and the arrival of heirs biologically related to both parties. On this basis fictive kinship means only kin elect, the source of future kin. Elective relationships, relationships "by faith," are in the long run constitutive of biological relationships.

141

dience of many generations made good by the obedience of one, that makes Israel obedient to the political and paideutic task Israel is given.

4.3. Sacrifice: Creation Theology as Action

4.3.1. Ecology Mediates

God makes Israel holy. The Son presents his people perfect to the Father. He enables them to worship and return thanks to God. The Son sacrifices and presents Israel holy to the Father. He passes on this action of his to Israel, so that it becomes the proper action of the body because of the head. Thus Israel can present the Son to the Father, and we can finally say that Israel sacrifices to God. Sacrifice is the whole thankful action of the people made holy. The greater part of the Scriptures are concerned with sacrifice on this definition. We have arrived at the doctrine of sanctification.

In common with the greater part of the Western and in particular Protestant tradition, Karl Barth decided against employing sacrifice as a model for his discussion of the work of Christ. Though the atonement could be presented in sacrificial and priestly terms, Barth believes that these are now antiquated and so presents his account of reconciliation in terms of the court of law familiar to Western theology.[33] But in his brief discussion of sacrifice, it is clear that Barth has a thoroughly forensic understanding of sacrifice. Sacrificial petitioners come to God only because they are guilty and need atonement, and they come with a restitution payment for sin offering *(ḥaṭṭaʾt)*. Barth explores sacrifice only briefly because this is "a form which is now rather remote from us."[34] This remoteness is of course "only a particular form of the problem of time."[35] The issue of sacrifice is bound up with the status of the Old Testament and of the people of Israel, and so it is also bound up with the question, introduced at the beginning of the previous chapter, of whether Israel is now cut off from us, superseded.

Colin Gunton argues for the continuing usefulness of the concept of sacrifice. He believes that it can be supported by an appeal to its derivation

---

33. Karl Barth, *Church Dogmatics*, ed. G. W. Bromiley and T. F. Torrance (Edinburgh: T. & T. Clark, 1956-75), IV/1, pp. 275-83.

34. Barth, *Church Dogmatics*, IV/1, p. 275.

35. Barth, *Church Dogmatics*, IV/1, p. 287.

"from something deep in human nature, of such a kind that it appears to be rooted in a universal or near universal feature of our life on earth."[36] One problem, though, is that sacrifice is archaic. "We no longer slaughter animals ritually." So "to call the death of Jesus a sacrifice is obviously a metaphor: although there is a death, it is not on an altar."[37] Metaphor allows us, Gunton argues, to extrapolate from what the ancients did to what God does for us. Sacrifice of animals has been replaced by a sacrifice of thanks and praise, and yet this represents no diminution of the cost of this sacrifice.[38] According to Hebrews, "It is impossible for the blood of bulls and goats to take away sins" (Heb. 10:4). Gunton believes that this blood did not take away sin. Yet blood was offered in the temple precisely because it did indeed — not finally, but yearly — take sins away. Of course it is God who removed this sin. But we refer to blood as a summary statement of all those constituents of the world of his creation, bulls and goats included, that are adopted and employed by God as the medium by which he effects this atonement for Israel.[39] These specific constituents do not have this function intrinsically. They are not natural symbols. They have this function within and as a result of the history that Israel and Israel's God have shared. They are the private language and conversation of Israel and God, of which gentiles have no knowledge. This theological hermeneutic of sacrifice has to be supplied to Gunton's understanding of sacrifice as the costly self-giving of God.

36. Colin E. Gunton, "The Sacrifice and the Sacrifices: From Metaphor to Transcendental?" in *Trinity, Incarnation and Philosophy: Philosophical and Theological Essays*, ed. R. J. Feenstra and C. Plantinga (Notre Dame: Notre Dame University Press, 1989), p. 210.

37. Gunton, "The Sacrifice and the Sacrifices," p. 217. F. M. Young, *Sacrifice and the Death of Christ* (London: SPCK, 1975), pp. 101-4, believes we can empathize with ancient societies that practiced sacrifice. Gunton, *The Actuality of Atonement*, pp. 111 and 122, argues that the concept of metaphor is the means by which to understand sacrifice as transcendental.

38. Gunton, *The Actuality of Atonement*, pp. 120-25.

39. Theories of sacraments represent an unfortunately abbreviated doctrine of creation that does not adequately proclaim that God is able to make all the products of the earth of his creation serve to nourish and build up his community and make it present to himself as his people. In this creation anything will serve as 'bread', as that means whereby we are made holy and presentable to him and brought into his presence, but only that does serve as bread which in a joint history (described as the history of instructor and learner in §2.1) has been agreed and understood between God and Israel. God and Israel create the symbols in the course of their conversation which takes the idiom of Israel's learning and increasing participation in the life God extends to Israel.

Sacrifice, then, is not simply the forgoing of one thing for another. These are not natural symbols in a zero-sum economy. It is "not simply the offering of a human life but of the concentrated summation of humanity: it is the kind of offering that, so to speak, longs to offer not only itself but all flesh. That one offering can stand in for the others because, in anticipation of the eschatological presenting of all spotless before the throne, it takes the representative and random sample of fallen flesh and offers it, through the Spirit, perfect to the Father." It intends to teach all flesh to present itself to God, by inducting it into a new medium, a new currency of human relating and account-giving. "Sacrifice, in this concrete realisation of the transcendental, is the expression and outworking of the inner-trinitarian relations of giving and receiving. The inner being of God is a taxis, a dynamic orderedness, of love construed in terms of mutual and reciprocal gift and reception. If the sacrifice that is Jesus's human life and death is a realisation in time of the eternal taxis, then it is indeed universal."[40]

As Gunton says elsewhere,

> God the Father "gives up" his only Son, allows him to be delivered into the hands of sinful men. Jesus lays down his life, and . . . offers his humanity, made perfect through suffering to the Father. So it is with the Spirit. As the gift of the Father he is the *aparchai*, first fruits, of the perfecting action of God in Christ. Although, under the conditions of the Fall, the sacrifice of Jesus must take the form of spilling of blood, that aspect is not of the essence of sacrifice, which is rather to be found in the notion of gift. It is the Father's giving of the Son, the Son's giving of himself to the Father and the Spirit's enabling of the creation's giving in response that is at the centre. . . . It is as a dynamic of giving and receiving, asymmetrical rather than merely reciprocal, that the communion that is the triune life must be understood.[41]

We must now ask what else must be said in order to say this.

Israel exists in a single economy with the peoples of the world and with the natural world in the form of the land of Israel. On both these definitions Israel makes a strong distinction between itself, as the people elect and becoming holy, and the world. The natural world is the proper loca-

---

40. Gunton, "The Sacrifice and the Sacrifices," p. 221.

41. Gunton, *The One, the Three, and the Many: God, Creation and the Culture of Modernity* (Cambridge: Cambridge University Press, 1993), p. 225 n. 19.

tion of this work of Israel's political self-identification and witness, and it provides the biological idiom in which this witness takes place.[42] It is the medium that makes sacrifice intelligible. It is the teaching of Genesis 2 that none of the animals are sufficient for the purpose of friendship with humankind, and that humankind is given the task of stewarding and representing them. On Israel's estimation the gentiles are also animals, the helpless functions of their animal appetites.[43] Yet because Israel also shares with the gentiles a complex system of what we could call animal semiotics, Israel can bear witness to the lordship of the God of Israel over the nations. This Israel does in the terms set out in Leviticus of the atonement of a human being by an animal, in which the man with his hand on the head of the sheep recapitulates the relationship of humankind with the rest of the natural world.[44] The human being is both one animal among many, in a single ecosystem with them, and the priest of creation. He calls and names creation and is its head and highpoint. Israel is the priest of the gentile-animals, and Israel puts his hand on their head, for this is the proper relationship between them.

4.3.2. Sacrifice and Meaning

Sacrifice is an act of selection of one animal from many animals; by this process the whole natural and political world is ordered. Killing is just one moment in the intricate and multiple processes that define the use human beings may make of the animal world and so define their own relationship to it.[45] The social body is formed in selecting and processing animal bod-

---

42. C. T. R. Haywood links Israel's sacrifice to its cosmology in "Sacrifice and World Order: Some Observations on ben Sira's Attitude to the Temple Service, Sacrifice and Redemption," in *Sacrifice and Redemption: Durham Essays in Theology*, ed. S. W. Sykes (Cambridge: Cambridge University Press, 1991).

43. Richard H. Bell, *No One Seeks for God: An Exegetical and Theological Study of Romans 1.18–3.20* (Tübingen: Mohr, 1998), p. 131: "Paul believes that not only are the gentiles like beasts; Jews also have become like animals."

44. Leviticus 1:4: "He is to lay his hand on the head of the burnt offering, and it will be accepted on his behalf to make atonement for him."

45. This must go some way to answering the question of the intelligibility of sacrifice asked by N. T. Wright in *The New Testament and the People of God* (London: SPCK, 1992), p. 274: "We know that the great majority of Jews took part in the sacrificial system, but we do not know *why*. . . . [A]ccording to what inner rationale was the killing of animals or birds thought to *effect* atonement and forgiveness?" See the discussion of Bruce D. Chilton, "The

ies. Such selection takes the form of killing because — like planting and breeding, harvesting and processing — killing and eating is intrinsic to our physical presence in the world. Eating animals is the way we navigate through the food-chain and moral world. Killing, eating, and mating are forms in which we give and receive life, and, consequent on that, in which we make and receive meaning. They bear meaning because the human species lives by means of reaching out, selecting and communicating, taking to themselves, and killing and eating. In attempting to say why the killing of animals plays a part in the worship of the God of Israel, the modern theological literature of sacrifice addresses the wrong question.[46] It is not the killing, but the whole complex action of *choosing* and *taking*, that is given to humankind.

There is of course a risk that we will again muddle what is distinctively theological about this discussion, with an indifferent matter of the history of human employment of animal bodies in communication. The new discussion of sacrifice relies at base on a noncontentious understanding of animal sacrifice as a technology of persuasion, making contracts and records. We established in Chapter 2 that, in addition to mundane use for sustenance and in other economic functions, previous generations used animals as props in all communication in the public arena. What we now do with books and other media of communication and record is an extension of what they did with the carcasses of animals. They modeled social arrangements by making cuts and incising marks on the carcass, in particular the parchment made of its skin, which evolved over millennia into writing, printing, and the whole media of communicating and ordering the social body.

A sacrifice is a public act of investiture. To sacrifice means to present or show someone or something to an expert audience, in such a way that what is shown is publicly accepted. What is shown and received becomes constitutive over the long term. If "to sacrifice" is allowed to mean only "to kill," it can refer only to a pagan act. By understanding "to sacrifice" not as "to kill" but as "to present," we concede the possibility that Israel's sacrifice is that heuristic and orthopedic action by which Israel is brought to partic-

Hungry Knife: Towards a Sense of Sacrifice," in *The Bible in Human Society: Essays in Honour of John Rogerson*, ed. Carroll M. Daniel, David J. A. Clines, and Philip R. Davies (Sheffield: Sheffield Academic Press, 1995).

46. See §3.2 and Stanley K. Stowers, *Rereading of Romans: Justice, Jews, and Gentiles* (New Haven: Yale University Press, 1994), pp. 206-13.

ipate in the action of God and is made holy.[47] In the law this action is given to Israel as the proper and permitted mode for human beings. We must sow and plant and reap and kill and eat to live. For Israel a proportion of this whole complex of mundane action, which includes killing and eating, must be done before God in his temple. By it, Israel understands that the creation represents God's hospitality and invitation; Israel's action in the world is the means of life God licenses, and by returning to God as gift a proportion of the creation God leases to Israel, Israel demonstrated its progress toward competence as custodian of God's creation.

Sacrifice represents humankind's mediatorial role in creation. The temple is a sophisticated semiotic mechanism that is able to link divine presence in the temple to a physical outworking in the fertility of land and people.[48] In the Jerusalem temple one lamb is burned, in the morning, and one in the evening. It is an unceasing event that generates time, just as the sabbath generates the days that precede it. The smoke of the lamb, wine, grain cakes, incense, and prayers of the worshipers rise to connect earth to heaven as though forming an umbilical cord.[49] The sacrifices and incense

47. This does not entirely clarify the sense in which (in John 1:29; Acts 8:32; 1 Cor. 5:7; and Rev. 13:8) the Lamb dies for us. Revelation 13:8 does not tell us that the Lamb was slain from the creation of the world. This would be to revert to the pagan definition of sacrifice as violent expiation. Rather, those whose names have been written from the creation of the world in the book of life belong to the Lamb that was slain. The reorientation work in which we have been engaged makes it easier to see this as the combination of a number of teachings about the action of God that can also be distinguished.

48. See William P. Brown, *The Ethos of the Cosmos: The Genesis of Moral Imagination in the Bible* (Grand Rapids: Eerdmans, 1999), pp. 73-74, and Brueggemann, *Theology of the Old Testament*, pp. 54-79, for discussion of the connection between divine presence and the fertility of the land.

49. The burnt offering represents the action of heaven's reaching down to earth, by which earth is brought into union with heaven and made one circulation and economy with it, the union of humanity's stewardship of their flock with God's stewardship of his flock. The sacrificed lamb is not going on a single journey upward from humankind to God: Israel is not in a simple sense giving a lamb to God. Israel is returning one of God's lambs to God. Israel does this to demonstrate good use of the flock God has entrusted to Israel. Husbandry and livestock are the idiom of this single economy (communion) of God with humankind. The sign "lamb" represents this complex asymmetrical reciprocity and stewardship. The lamb becomes fire — communion that makes itself visible. The equation of bread (and meat) and body ("This is my body given for you") is an invitation to eat what the host provides from the harvest and the permitted animals of his estate. Bread and world are metonyms. Jesus fills not only bread (the archetypal seed-product), but the whole elemental stuff

create the smoke that fills and covers the temple. This cloud of smoke is the presence *(Shekinah)* of the Lord who leads his people, and the protection of the Lord who fills and covers them.[50] The Lord's presence generates this cloud and this sacrifice by providing the animals and the prosperity they represent. The smoke rises and turns to cloud; the clouds gather and water falls on the land, making the crops grow and animals and people flourish. Rain and plant life, and the animals and children that result from them, are idioms of God's mercy. The *Shekinah* is both God's arrival and the priest's protection from the effects of God's arrival.[51] Each sacrifice is consumed to nothing. But taken together as the single project of the formation of this people, the temple sacrifices are not burned to no purpose. If this people does not give up, but continues to sacrifice and keep the lamp alight, the bridegroom will find them. The light and fire of the old covenant will result in the appearing of the new. It will be demonstrated that Israel's obedient labor in the place given him in the material world will have served in the preparation of this people and the final coming to them of their king. The biological nexus will be taken up and adopted by the Spirit for the place of the coming together of God and humankind.

---

that the cosmos is, so bread represents the whole of the rest of the material creation and ecosystem. As bread the whole earth goes through human beings to be reconstituted as itself. See the discussion in Mary Douglas, "The Eucharist: Its Continuity with the Bread Sacrifice of Leviticus," *Modern Theology* 15 (1999): 209-24.

50. According to Douglas, *Leviticus as Literature*, pp. 79-80, the book of Leviticus works on complex sets of analogies. When the carcass of the slaughtered animal is opened, the organs lie in a set of relationships also used for purposes of theological illustration. The soft inner organs are protected by a layer of fat: every opened carcass looks like a figure of eight, the fat separating the top half from the bottom, but equally holding the top and bottom together and comprising the whole medium by which they meet. This fatty section is the animal equivalent of the layer of cloud that hides the top of Mount Sinai from the bottom. The *Shekinah* by which Israel is brought together with God at Sinai is reiterated in every sacrifice in which the fat is set between the top and bottom parts of the animal carcass, so the three-level construction of meat on the sacrificial fire reiterates the coming together of God and Israel. The concept of place within structure is the key to reading the theology on display in Israelite sacrifice.

51. David Kupp, *Matthew's Emmanuel: Divine Presence and God's People in the First Gospel* (Cambridge: Cambridge University Press, 1996), asks how the *Shekinah* can be both the presence of God and the hiding of the presence of God. I am arguing that apocalyptic should be understood as the process of learning to see what goes on in the temple. Scripture protects us from, and prepares us for, the impact of this glory.

4.4. The Temple:
The World of Gentiles Is God's Task for Israel

4.4.1. Creation and the Temple

Israel's natural cosmology is its description of the world, constituted by the world's peoples, and of the task entrusted to Israel of bringing these peoples to the one God. The world, in the form of the land of Israel, is the medium of God's action. The temple is a complex sign system and working model of creation that relies on the logic of microcosm. The temple represents the land and provides a matrix of analogies with which complex theological statements about God's relationship to his people and the world he gives them may be made.[52] The tree-shaped menorah, for example, joins the idiom of light and flame to that of growth. The light of the menorah and the smoke of incense and the sacrifices compose the cloud that represents the presence of God with his people and the single divine economy he prepares them for.[53] The temple represents the garden, and the tree at the center of it, featured in the first chapters of Genesis. The temple is Eden come to Zion.[54] Zion is the highest among the mountains that holds down the forces of chaos and sustains the first act of creation: separation of sea from land.[55] Zion is the foundation, cornerstone, and navel. Creation continues to be a strenuous work. It involves a battle against the forces. "The language of combat, victory and enthronement" must continue to appear in any account of the createdness of the world.[56] The world is in rebellion. Adam has

---

52. Samuel E. Balentine, *The Torah's Vision of Worship* (Minneapolis: Augsburg Fortress, 1999), pp. 126-31, understands the "Covenant as sanctuary building and world building." Balentine, like Fretheim, thinks "the liturgy of covenant-making can be properly understood as a liturgy of creation-keeping" (p. 126).

53. Fire is analogous to the divine creative action. Fire and light relate to the natural processes of growth and decay. In §4.6 I will link fire, light, and becoming to the cosmology that gives meaning to practices involving sacrificial fire and light.

54. See Brown, *The Ethos of the Cosmos*, pp. 133-43, and also Othmar Keel, *The Symbolism of the Biblical World: Ancient Near Eastern Iconography and the Book of Psalms* (London: SPCK, 1978), pp. 112-76.

55. See J. D. Levenson, *Sinai and Zion: An Entry into the Jewish Bible* (Minneapolis: Winston, 1985), pp. 133-35.

56. Levenson, *Creation and the Persistence of Evil*, believes that "the language of combat, victory and enthronement . . . is not given its due" (p. xxv). The writer of Psalm 74, for ex-

not given the creaturely forces the leadership and discipline they need, with the result that they have become unruly local centers of recalcitrance where power is hoarded rather than returned to God.

The doctrine of creation declares that the world is the possession of God for us. It is his on two counts: first, he made it; second, he went to war to win it back from rebellious forces, and he did win it back from them. We need not only the static account, in which the trauma of creation is finished and we look back *(anamnesis)* in celebration of this victory. We need also the account in which the struggle of the creation-battle (cosmogony) is ongoing. We must watch as pockets of resistance are mopped up, and so learn the skills of policing the powers, and maintaining order, so we know what the establishment and reestablishment of peace has cost. We saw above that this obliges us to make use of a Christus Victor Christology. Here Israel is given an action, and this action gives Israel life. This is a minimal requirement of the doctrine of creation required by a theology of persons who are being made free.

The building and maintenance of the temple form an analogy for and microcosm of the cultivation and rule of the world.[57] In the temple the now-ordered waters of chaos appear as the spring that waters the world. The temple displays justice and warns all unjust rulers of all the benighted peoples. It is the stronghold that stands against all other forces and polities that rise up against Israel.[58] It is also the throne where God invites the Son to sit with him, to declare that the labor of creation is done, and that people may no longer force one another to work. The sabbath is here, and all things in the completed creation are very good.

Recent scholarship of Israel's cosmology seems to avoid making at least a couple of connections. Do the temple and the ritual that takes place within it represent the future creation and Adam within it? Does Adam function as the priest of creation? Does the high priest portray Adam, the first and last man, on the Day of Atonement?[59] These themes, familiar to patristic theol-

---

ample, "acknowledges the reality of militant, triumphant and persistent evil, but he steadfastly and resolutely refuses to accept this evil as final and absolute" (p. 24).

57. Brown, *The Ethos of the Cosmos*, pp. 141-51, agrees.

58. Levenson, *Sinai to Zion*, p. 147: "The Temple city complex was thought to be a source of revelation in and of itself." Keel, *The Symbolism of the Biblical World*, pp. 269-79, shows the iconography of the king as temple builder and priest.

59. Bockmuehl, *Revelation and Mystery in Ancient Judaism and Pauline Christianity*, pp. 37-38, discusses the Son of Man and Messiah as the mystery that is hidden.

ogy, appear not to interest contemporary biblical studies, with the result that we can only speculate.[60] The temple can also be regarded as a tree. Perhaps this tree represents all Israel, past, present, and future. The temple is the tree of good and evil and its fruit.[61] The roots of this tree go down and its branches reach up, like those of the menorah, to fill the world and secure it to the heavens. Should we understand the whole line of humankind as a single organism, the future generations of which might be likened to the branches and the patriarchs to its roots? Should we see the man crucified on the tree as the stem of the new and united humankind, who sums up and recapitulates the being of the whole cosmos? By his resurrection, the new Adam returns to his place in the garden of the world, its summation and priest. He knits together and recapitulates all modes and behaviors to make a single cosmos that is alive, beautiful, and eternal. Such would be the result of linking Israel's teaching about holiness to an Adam Christology.

Our next section links purity and holiness to the election of Israel as servant and witness to the holy God. God's faithfulness and Israel's obedience result in many sons. There is a reluctance in the literature to say what the purpose of purity is. In Chapter 2 I suggested that, because God keeps Israel apart from other influences, Israel learns its character solely from him. Israel's life is a learning from God and transformation by him for the sake of the world to which Israel is his witness. We may therefore say that Israel is holy *for the world*.

60. Margaret Barker, in *The Gate of Heaven: The History and Symbolism of the Temple in Jerusalem* (London: SPCK, 1991) and *The Revelation of Jesus Christ* (Edinburgh: T&T Clark, 2000), leads the way with work on the temple cosmology, but perhaps her results remain to be established.

61. Discussion of the relationship of man and tree is scarce. "The God of our fathers raised Jesus from the dead, whom you had killed by hanging him on a tree" (Acts 5:30; cf. 10:39; 13:29). He was hung up and displayed on this tree. "As Moses lifted up the snake in the wilderness, so the Son of man must be lifted up" (John 3:14). Are tree and mountain metonyms for the complete future earth that is heaven-and-earth, the glory of the appearance of God? Is the curse of the law (Deut. 21:22-23) cause or effect? Does Deuteronomy tell us that a man on the tree pollutes and kills off the tree? Does the messiah hung on the tree render the law and temple cult barren or even malignant? Do the words "He became sin for us" mean that, being hung on a tree, he rendered the land "sin," barren, extinguishing the continuum of divine action? The tree appears as wisdom and its fruit in the wisdom literature. By being hung on it, does he kill off one version of the tree, change the fruit of the tree from evil to good? Is the cross the tree or trees of Genesis 2? The man hung on the tree is its fruit. Does the man bear the tree, such that it grows from him, so he is the continuation of the family line of Israel? Is Jesus claiming to be the true tree and fruit, such that present Jerusalem is a false tree and fruit?

4.4.2. The House That Makes the People Holy

A number of accounts of holiness and purity are now on offer from scholars of the Old Testament or Hebrew Bible. Together they represent a conceptual revolution, for which much credit is due to Mary Douglas, the social anthropologist whose own Catholic understanding of sacrament has allowed her to decipher some of not only Israel's public and ritual actions but also the ritual and purity codes of our own modern societies.[62] Purity means readiness directed to the achievement of holiness. It is the means by which changes and growth in holiness may be accounted for. Accounting for holiness is the means by which growth in holiness is achieved. Purity indicates where holiness has been, should be, or is but should not be. It is evidence of the work of the generation and regeneration of a holy people.

Philip Jenson argues that "Israel existed in the midst of the nations, and some of the laws imply that Israel had a distinctive identity in relation to them. Various laws reflect this awareness of a distinction between Israel and the nations."[63] It is possible to extend the parallel to include a correspondence between the three classes of the animal world (sacrificial, clean, and unclean animals), and the three divisions of the human world (priests, Israelites, and gentiles). This is evidenced by the alignment between sacrificial animals and the priestly class. In the two lists of blemishes, the defects that disqualify a priest from entering a sanctuary to offer sacrifice (Lev. 21:17-21) are very similar to the defects that bar a sacrificial animal from being slaughtered (Lev. 22:17-25).[64]

---

62. See Richard Fardon, *Mary Douglas: An Intellectual Biography* (London: Routledge, 1998).

63. Philip Jenson, *Graded Holiness: A Key to the Priestly Perception of the World* (Sheffield: Sheffield Academic Press, 1992), p. 145. Further discussion is provided by Walter Houston, *Purity and Monotheism: Clean and Unclean Animals in Biblical Law* (Sheffield: Sheffield Academic Press, 1993), and M. Haran, *Temples and Temple Services in Ancient Israel: An Inquiry into the Character of Cult Phenomena and the Historical Setting of the Priestly School* (Oxford: Clarendon, 1978). Of these, only Douglas's work seems to allow that Israel's cultic performance may include parody and deconstruction of the nations.

64. Jenson, *Graded Holiness*, p. 146. Jenson explores the issue of classification. Holiness is wholeness and freedom from imperfection and anomaly, which assumes stable structures and processes in terms of which deviations can be measured. The architecture of the tabernacle and camp classifies space into zones that we might relate to stages of sanctification, though much of the biblical studies literature gives a merely structuralist account, refusing

According to Jacob Milgrom, no single theory will cover the entire complex of sacrifices. The whole is a matter of ongoing negotiation as Israel progressively refines its understanding and frees itself from clumsier and more pagan formulations.[65] We may not insist on too much consistency, for Leviticus, like any biblical book, is a work in progress, the work of the oral Torah. The incompleteness of Scripture indicates that Israel's battle against pagan beliefs was a gradual process.[66] Central to Milgrom's view is his "Priestly Picture of Dorian Gray." Sin does not scar the face of the sinner because it flies from the scene of its occurrence to the temple to take its toll there.[67] But even those who do not sin are guilty if they have allowed the wicked to flourish and so contributed to the pollution of the sanctuary. The sanctuary is holy and awesome because it is powerful enough to process away the insufficiencies of Israel. Like any powerful piece of machinery, it is out-of-bounds. Because it is utterly pure, it draws to itself the insufficiencies from all over the land, and they accumulate there until they are dealt with. The sanctuary gathers and holds sin as a filter gathers dirt: this dirt represents the cleaning work it has done on Israel over the year.[68] On the day of atonement it is swept finally into the center of the sanctuary through the *hilastērion* and into oblivion.

Leviticus is a polemic against the idea that physical impurity arises from the activity of demons who must be appeased or exorcised. In Israel, impurity was harmless.[69] Purification is neither healing nor theurgy. Lay

---

to ask about the purpose of these visible gradations in holiness. See also Brueggemann, *Theology of the Old Testament*, pp. 650-79, and Brevard S. Childs, *Old Testament in a Canonical Context* (Minneapolis: Fortress, 1989), pp. 84-90.

65. Jacob Milgrom, *Leviticus,* 3 volumes, Anchor Bible Commentaries (New York: Doubleday, 1991), vol. 2, pp. 1368-71. Emanuel Feldman, *Biblical and Post-Biblical Defilement and Mourning: Law as Theology* (New York: Yeshiva University, 1977), similarly argues that Israel is concerned not so much with death as with demonstrably not doing those things the pagans do, not repeating their respect payment to ancestors. Feldman's subtitle provides the all-important context for our discussion in this chapter.

66. In §5.4 we will see Maimonides arguing that this incompleteness was also a function of the particular gentile behavior it had to challenge and oppose.

67. Milgrom, *Leviticus,* vol. 1, pp. 257-60.

68. Milgrom, *Leviticus,* vol. 1, p. 260: "On the analogy of Oscar Wilde's novel [*The Picture of Dorian Gray*], the Priestly Writers would claim that sin may not leave its mark on the face of the sinner, but it is certain to mark the face of the sanctuary; and unless it is expunged, God's presence will depart."

69. Preuss, *Old Testament Theology*, vol. 1, pp. 258-59, also believes Israel showed little concern with demons. J. D. Crossan, *The Historical Jesus: The Life of a Mediterranean Jewish*

persons, but not priests, might contact impurity with impunity, though they must not delay their purification in case their impurity affects the sanctuary.[70] Scale disease is part of a symbolic system that sorts anything that looks like death with death.[71] The highly visible, biblically impure scale disease symbolizes the death process as much as does the loss of vaginal blood and semen. Based on the Mishnah's association of skin disease with slanderous gossip, destructive of people's reputations and appearances, Robert Kugler suggests that "skin disease" represents an identity damaged by slander.[72] Ambiguous appearances and false representations in Israel are a theological problem. The purity legislation is the means by which those who have been victims of slander and false witness are publicly re-honored and given as it were a new public face. The appearance on a body of a skin "disease," the analogical message of "death," is used as an opportunity to review the life-renewing power of the God of Israel. The concern of this legislation is not in the biological pathology of bodies but in the incorporation of all Israel's members into Israel. The forces pitted in cosmic struggle are the forces of life and death set loose by humankind itself through obedience to, or defiance of, God's commandments.[73] Despite all the changes manifested in the evolution of Israel's impurity laws, the objective remains to sever impurity from the demonic and to reinterpret it as the divine imperative to Israel to reject as death whatever God does not command.

Peasant (Edinburgh: T&T Clark, 1991), pp. 313-18, suggests demons are representations of foreign, gentile forces.

70. Robert Kugler, "Holiness, Purity, the Body and Society: The Evidence for Theological Conflict in Leviticus," *Journal for the Study of the Old Testament* 76 (1997): 3-27, argues that Leviticus 16–27 shows an Israel-wide pervasive democratic holiness system, and that holiness, contained within the sanctuary, is largely unaffected by the impurity of the general population. In Leviticus 1–16 things are intrinsically impure, and debate is about what goes in and out of the body. In Leviticus 16–27 all Israel is holy, any incursion of impurity meets the sacred head-on, the violator stands no chance of survival, and impurities are fatal to their bearers before they can take any sacrificial remedial action.

71. Milgrom, *Leviticus*, vol. 1, p. 44: "The cultic sphere attests a progressive reduction of religious impurity in all three primary human sources: scale disease, pathological flux, and corpse contamination."

72. Kugler, "Holiness, Purity, the Body and Society," p. 25. Jacob Neusner, "Judaism after the Destruction of the Temple," in *Israelite and Judaean History*, ed. John H. Hayes and J. Maxwell Miller (London: SCM, 1977), p. 676, argues that skin disease was given a spiritualized explanation, as caused by slander, so that now it is gossip that makes one unclean.

73. Milgrom, *Leviticus*, vol. 1, p. 59.

Murder is the central theme of the purity laws.[74] All life is inviolable. A small number of edible animals are excepted when they are slaughtered properly, their blood drained and thereby returned to God. According to Milgrom, "[Man] wants meat and he has to kill to get it. Man is a criminal only if he appropriates the animal's lifeblood. But if he returns it to its divine source via the altar he commits no crime."[75] The blood of the purification offering purges the sanctuary by absorbing its impurities. The priest eats the flesh of the purification offering: impurity does not pollute him as long as he serves God in his sanctuary. The fundamental premise of the purity law is that human beings can curb their violent nature through ritual means — specifically, through a dietary discipline. This will drive home the point that all life is shared, even with the animals, and inviolable. The only exception is the meat of the animals given by God. Means of meeting the demands of holiness multiplied in order to provide for everyone atonement and membership in Israel. The reddish substances made cheap blood surrogates in purificatory rites for the scale-diseased and corpse-contaminated persons.[76] The central concern is not to let poverty prevent the very poor from bringing some offering: they must not be disbarred from Israel.

Hyam Maccoby summarizes purity as the ritual proper to the court of the great king. Ritual purity has to do with the temple.

> It is simply the protocol for entry into the palace of the King. The priestly people is privileged to have his residence in their midst, and must consequently comport themselves in accordance with the prescribed etiquette. . . . [T]he Israelites have this privilege of service in the portals of God . . . instead of wiping their feet, they must cleanse their whole body of impurities which, outside the Temple, have no negative meaning. . . . The rest of mankind . . . are not unclean in the special sense of Temple-uncleanness; only Israelites can incur this uncleanness, because they are the chosen house-servants of God.[77]

---

74. Feldman, *Biblical and Post-Biblical Defilement and Mourning*, pp. 139-40.

75. Milgrom, *Leviticus*, vol. 1, p. 736.

76. Milgrom, *Leviticus*, vol. 1, p. 46, explains that the law-makers interpreted sacrificial rules to foster the individual conscience. They ordained that repentance converts an intentional sin into an unintentional one, making it eligible for expiation.

77. Hyam Maccoby, *Ritual and Morality: The Ritual Purity System and Its Place in Judaism* (Cambridge: Cambridge University Press, 1999), p. 206. Maccoby believes that the purity

Conceiving the temple as a palace and priests as its retainers does much to clarify Israel's liturgical action. Those who receive no justice from their own rulers may go to the court of appeal made available to all the peoples of the world by the overlord resident there. Gaining purity is not something that has to be done before a priest may go in and serve. It is the commencement of the demonstration at the temple, and thus before the nations, of the holy character of God.[78] Maccoby argues that purity is an issue for priests only.[79] Off-duty priests and all Israel are in a state of impurity, which we might interpret as "unreadiness." Since the demise of the temple, all Israel has been in this state all the time. "Impurity" is the state or moment of starting to get ready to do purity, and even this starting to get ready is part of doing purity, part of the temple service.

This approach allows us to relate purity and holiness to Israel's task of exercising hospitality, building the house, and becoming the people that can live with the great king on his estate and in his palace. God is king, the earth his property, and its people his creatures and servants, who owe their whole being to him. This is the atonement model that relates to the doctrine of creation, but the relationship between them has received only the sketchiest description in modern theology.[80] God owns us, and we are his property. We have been too long on our own out on the far fringes of the estate, and we need to come out of the field and into the house to be refreshed, served, and restored. That God is not only king but owner, and not only owner but his own estate manager, is presupposed everywhere in the Scriptures. Maccoby, Feldman, and Milgrom discuss the achievement of purity only in terms of the insiders, as only Jewish scholars may. They

teaching is about the cycle of *birth and* death, not merely death, as Feldman and Milgrom argue, but he is less successful than either at making death and life theological categories that relate to God's character and intention for Israel. Maccoby belongs at the idealist pole of Feldmann's schema, with none of the link to the doctrine of creation seen by Levenson.

78. This starting to get ready, though it commences out on the land or in the city because it is a matter of *putting aside* things to take to the temple and *going up* to the temple, is all part of the service. Milgrom, *Leviticus*, vol. 1, p. 485: "If a person sets aside an animal for a given sacrifice the animal becomes holy . . . when the householder wishes to separate the heave offering, he must both form the proper intention to do so and orally announce that intention, designating the portion of the crop to be deemed holy." E. P. Sanders, *Judaism: Practice and Belief, 63 BCE–66 CE* (London: SCM, 1992), pp. 147-54.

79. Maccoby, *Ritual and Morality*, pp. 9-11.

80. See also the conceptuality of possession, sketched in Chapter 1, and of participation, sketched in Chapter 2.

therefore rely on models of the uncontested sovereignty of God — as the king, shepherd, and father who gives order, shelter, support, and nourishment. They do not deal, as Christian theology must, with how the outsider can be made an insider, so they give no account of the cost of this event or of the violence of the defeat of the powers from whom the gentiles must be redeemed. Their account is therefore different from that of Janowski and Stuhlmacher, as it is from Levenson's account of the violence involved in defending God's rule over rebellious forces that challenge his sovereignty over his creation.

Mary Douglas gives a strong version of an assumption shared by all Old Testament commentators: "The nature of the living God is in opposition to dead bodies. Total incompatibility holds between God's presence and bodily corruption. God is living, life is his. Other gods belong to death, contagion and decay."[81] Milgrom minimizes magic and argues that all Israel's effort is now dedicated only to showing that Israel precisely does not do, but rather subverts, what the pagans do. A history-of-religion background and greater interest in the mechanics of the semiotics convince Mary Douglas that magic, miracle, and rite are useful concepts.[82] She is not convinced that Israel is quite free from pagan rites or belief in demons or occult forces and sees no point in crediting Israel with unique sophistication here. Milgrom is concerned to show that, though the process is not complete, by a successful employment of the semiotics Israel has already gone a considerable way in removing itself from what the gentiles do. The animals that may be offered as gifts represent those behaviors that have a place before God. Those behaviors and animals forbidden have no access to God and may not be brought into the temple.[83]

Douglas demonstrates that the organization of the temple, its servers, and the place of the tribes around it point to a cosmological order, and that the same is true of the literary composition of Leviticus and Numbers.

---

81. Douglas, *In the Wilderness*, p. 24.

82. Douglas, *In the Wilderness*, pp. 34, 165-66. The following two issues are related: the fact that the Scriptures are never quite self-consistent because they are unfinished (there is always an evolution of thought discernible) and the fact, which concerns Milgrom (but not Douglas), that Israel seems never to be quite rid of pagan influences.

83. Douglas, *Leviticus as Literature*, p. 225: "The noble domestic animals to whom the covenant is extended stand opposite the zoo of animal kinds not to be eaten or touched." See also David Bryan, *Cosmos, Chaos and the Kosher Mentality* (Sheffield: Sheffield Academic Press, 1995).

In Scripture and in the temple building we are dealing with a single artistry in two media. The structure of the biblical books repeats the structure of the sacrifices and rites.[84] Sacrifice is therefore not primarily about killing, but about the selection of one body from the many and the rearrangement of it as analogy of the relationships Israel is in. Israel is engaged in the process of rebuilding and maintaining this microcosm of its relationship with God, constantly arranging and grooming itself back into its proper location in this relationship.[85] Liturgical processing within the temple is one mode of this rebuilding, hearing the scroll read is another, seeing the tripartite construction of the meat on the sacrificial fire is another. The chapters about physical impurity present the body in a series of covers: first the fat covers the organs, then this is covered by the skin; the body is covered by a garment; over the Israelite comes the roof of the tabernacle; and over the whole lot is the covenant.[86] Atonement means being covered and protected. We can also understand this as God weaving together the fabric of Israel when it gets torn, and unpicking the fabric that the gentiles have prematurely woven together, separating what they have confused. Adam is given animal skins so that he is no longer exposed and vulnerable; the ark of the covenant prevents the land from becoming barren or exposed; the high priest's garment represents the heavenly bodies, Israel's history, and the glory of God, all of which cover and protect the people of Israel. Reading and writing, and the resulting Scripture too, are simply idioms of weaving and processing. Their logic is expressivist, not causal.

Each of these scholars argues that the temple made the people holy. I have expanded on their argument to claim that the temple inducts and educates the elect people into a new action and economy. Biblical scholarship seems reluctant to set out such a paideutic meta-narrative. It has therefore tended to explain Israel's action in terms of rationalities that are taxonomic or economic, serving a purpose unrelated to Israel's witness to its God. Theological reason is composed of just such rationales as these; so, in some sense at least, sociological and functionalist descriptions do not threaten theological description. Nonetheless, theology has its own work to do from this wide range of Old Testament sciences to reveal a gospel.

---

84. See Douglas, *Leviticus as Literature*, pp. 195, 218.
85. See Douglas, *In the Wilderness*, pp. 83-101.
86. See Douglas, *Leviticus as Literature*, p. 244.

4.5. Israel Scattered: Israel as God's Place for the World

4.5.1. Hospitality as Liturgy

The liturgy and service of the temple make holy the elect people. This work includes the teaching and Scripture necessitated by exile, by which those away from the holy city nevertheless participate in its work. Temple and synagogue are one in a single work of Scripture and oral Torah in which Israel witnesses to its God's lordship over the gods of the nations. The loss of Israel's land to the gentiles and the destruction of the temple do not mean that this liturgical service is halted. Rather, it leads to an entire reliance, rather than merely partial reliance as before, on the medium of synagogue and Scripture.[87] Centralized animal sacrifice ceases, but the cult continues where it had originated, at home where Israel meets, eats, and teaches.[88] Israelites are properly understood as pure, so that what extends from a person, and what one is and does and has, manifests that purity.[89] Central to sacrifice is the identity of the host and of the guests who bear him gifts. The gifts supply their introduction to the great king. Members of Israel host each other, and they are to exercise a more expansive hospitality to outsiders that extends to the whole world. The gifts borne by members of Israel are first one another, and then all other creatures of the world that is the royal estate. Giving meals is the form in which a member of Israel makes the other his guest and a member of his household, itself part of the household of the great king. God's action in circumcision and baptism re-determines the world: it transforms it from being contested territory to being entirely his own creature and estate, the medium in which his people may be undividedly with him.

We now have to relate the medium established in circumcision and baptism to what is visible to this world, and thus to the related themes of vision and apocalyptic.

---

87. For which see Donald D. Binder, *Into the Temple Courts: The Place of Synagogues in the Second Temple Period* (Atlanta: Society of Biblical Literature, 1999), and James T. Burtchaell, *From Synagogue to Church: Public Services and Offices in the Earliest Christian Communities* (Cambridge: Cambridge University Press, 1992).

88. According to Berakhot 55a: "Now a man's table atones for him" (quoted by Neusner, "Judaism after the Destruction of the Temple," p. 670).

89. See Bruce D. Chilton, *Pure Kingdom: Jesus' Vision of God* (London: SPCK, 1996), pp. 123, 125.

4.5.2. Circumcision: Discipline as Transformation

I suggested that we interpret the holiness-purity code in terms of the seed and line of Israel. Israel is intended to be not a mere son, but the *obedient* Son. We must now attempt to link this strong thesis about the biological idiom of the reproduction of Israel to the meeting of God and humanity in the person of Jesus Christ and in the event of the defeat of all other forces. From the cross and the right hand of the Father, Jesus sends the *Pneuma* of Israel. The blood and seed of Israel issue from him. This pneumatology is a teaching about the new mediation of creation. The Spirit baptizes and immerses the world in a new and holy environment that only the elect community can receive. Their breathing and speaking will create a creature able to live in this medium with them.

How far has Christian biblical studies employed this theme? Daniel Boyarin argues that rabbinic Judaism opposes Christian insistence on transforming bodily Judaism into an affair of the spirit. Circumcision is the idiom of sacrifice that forms the body of Israel. The cutting is visible because the community watches, and because it has a physical effect on the body of the individual Israelite. Bruce Longenecker believes that Paul distinguishes outward physical circumcision and inward circumcision of the heart, so we have on the one hand the ethnic symbol, and on the other, inner piety.[90] Boyarin objects to this distinction. This physical mark is copyright to Israel: this cut on the skin *means* Jewish and *makes* Jewish. Judaism is a set of physical practices, so to look underneath the skin is illegitimate: there are no changes or mechanism there. Boyarin argues that Paul's claim about an inward circumcision and "spiritual" Israel is illegitimate.[91]

A greater interest in the cosmology of Israel set out by the holiness teaching of the Pentateuch might help us here. It would allow us to understand that, for Paul and his contemporaries, circumcision was a medical operation on the vessels between "heart" and sex organs. The ancient world supposed that the various forms of behavior came from the various organs of the body, and among these, whether in leading or subordinate

90. See Bruce Longenecker, *Eschatology and the Covenant: A Comparison of 4 Ezra and Romans 1–11* (Sheffield: Journal for the Study of the Old Testament Press, 1991), p. 193, and Dunn, *The Theology of Paul the Apostle*, pp. 454-55.

91. See Daniel Boyarin, *A Radical Jew: Paul and the Politics of Identity* (Berkeley: University of California Press, 1994), pp. 93-94.

position, were the sex organs.[92] The seed of Israel came out of the "heart," the organ from which the spirit *(pneuma)* overflows, and overflowed into the sex organs to determine the character of the child. The ancient world did not believe that the design of the body was complete at conception, but that the body needed continual intervention through the earliest years of life. It held that a medical-and-moral regime was necessary to turn the wild body born into the crafted body of a son and heir.[93] This would make circumcision more like a foreseeable adjustment of, or supplement to, the capacities of the body. Circumcisions close the channels to organs that produce only animal-gentile behavior and open the channels to spiritual behavior of the spirit *(pneuma)* of Israel. The only distinction made by Paul and his world was between those circumcisions that succeed at this difficult hormonal switch-work and those that do not. Paul would therefore be contrasting the familiar circumcision by the community, which starts as a cut on the skin, the effect of which is intended to work upward to alter the connections, with a new circumcision that enters the lungs, as spirit, and fills all the organs of the body at once. Its first evidence is a new form of behavior rather than an alteration to the skin. The secret of circumcision must then be found outside the body, in the environment from which it breathes. This environment has been decisively altered by the resurrection of Jesus. Circumcision must be related to the baptism that brings the character of God in suffering and bearing the world to the people of Israel, who are scattered like seed over the nations of the world. Baptism makes circumcision the condition of the whole world and so redetermines the continuum of Israel's action.

The ancient world had no strong dualism of physical and mental. It assumed that both the body and the continuum in which it moved were full of components and forces, and that there was no strong distinction between the two. The ancient world understood the world to be composed of algorithms operating in an environment made up of other algorithms, as does contemporary biological science. The physical and mental elements were pumped round in one circulation that constituted the whole cos-

---

92. Aline Rousselle, *Porneia: On Desire and the Body in Antiquity* (Oxford: Blackwell, 1988), pp. 13-20, provides a good discussion of ancient physiology.

93. The case is easy to make for the Greek world, more difficult for Judaea. The cosmology of Israel, everywhere presupposed in the Old Testament and nowhere explicit, is only fragmentarily being brought to the surface by Mary Douglas and the comparative history of religions scholarship of Israel's ancient Near Eastern neighbors.

mos.[94] In this single economy the *Logos spermatikos,* the resurrected body of Jesus, available to us as the transforming meta-biology of his Holy Spirit, makes our life-environment new. Though the old man did not foresee it, the new man becomes — through the Spirit-assisted, normal processes — the rightful heir of the old man. It takes only the (spiritual) joining of the new man with the old man to make all the old stock produce new men. The consumption of animals that belong to other powers was understood to make us open to possession by those powers, which could then determine the thought and behavior available to us.[95] This possibility is excluded by Israel's circumcision. This is not just a circumcision of the people of Israel, but, by the event of the cross, a baptism of the world-environment, by which the whole environment is circumcised to the gentiles. Baptism is the circumcision of the environment. It involves God's action as Spirit and breath, as spore and power, transforming the old body into the new, meta-biological, obedient creature.

4.6. Seeing and Being Brought into Being

We must now link this spiritual metabolism of the cult to Israel's eschatological doctrine of creation. Israel must confess itself a people being brought into being. This is being brought into increasing comprehension of this process, articulated in an eschatological doctrine of creation. Creation is now under way and will not be complete until redeemed and consummated by the arrival of humankind, the grateful, free, and obedient creature of God. The whole creaturely economy created by baptism serves to produce this obedient son. The temple issues knowledge of itself, not only in the form of images (*eidola,* models) of itself but also as the faculty of vision itself. Israel's doctrine of creation comes with its own theory of perception. We must therefore look briefly at how vision and apocalyptic fit within Israel's cosmos and how it is treated by New Testament exegesis. What I have said about the production of obedient sons, and the idiom of seed and blood, must also be said in terms of fire, light, sight, and knowledge, where a similar logic holds good.

94. See the Stoic pneumatology in §5.5.

95. See Dale B. Martin, *The Corinthian Body* (New Haven: Yale University Press, 1995), pp. 176-78 and 209, on "the logic of invasion."

4.6.1. Light, Sight, Fire, and Heat

We find in the Bible some of the discussion of light, sight, fire, and heat, which the ancient world understood as a single moral and physical continuum. This continuum enabled certain sorts of behavior and prevented certain others. New Testament studies, however, seems to identify the occasional appearance of this continuum in terms of a modern understanding of light, and so as individual exegetical problems. The saying of Matthew, that "the eye is the lamp of the body," is an example.[96] The eye allows light in. It also, like a valve, keeps it in, so it adds to the heat in your body. It is this heat that also allows your body to function as a lamp, giving light and sight out again by which others can see, and by which they can also see you for who you are. Weak eyes fail to keep your proper spirit and fire in, allowing what fire there is inside to leak away, and putting you at risk of being taken over by a stronger alien spirit. Your eyes are bad if they produce no light, because the fire and spirit in you are not strong enough to generate any light.[97] We are the functions of the thermodynamic at work in us — though of course it is not *in* us; it *is* us. This thermodynamic metaphysic, which relates to the Greek conceptuality of spirit *(thymos)*, appears in the New Testament as the phenomenon of *doxa*, presence, glory, and light.

Does this help us with 2 Corinthians 3:18: "and we who with unveiled faces all reflect the Lord's glory"? N. T. Wright believes that "the mirror in which Christians see the glory of the Lord . . . is one another . . . when they come face to face with one another they are beholding as in a mirror the glory itself."[98] Light shines on a mirror and is reflected off. These faces reflect light from Christ and like multiple in-turned mirrors keep it reflect-

---

96. Matthew 6:22; for discussion of this passage see Dale C. Allison, "The Eye Is the Lamp of the Body," *New Testament Studies* 33 (1987): 61-83.

97. In the ancient world, light was understood not only to enter eyes but also to *issue from* them, as simulacra that issue from the whole body, so that what we receive is not a single stuff that we can always call light but the self-presencing of each object in that economy. According to Ruth Padel, *In and Out of the Mind: Greek Images of the Tragic Self* (Princeton: Princeton University Press, 1992), the ancients understood that "Something *comes into* the eye" (p. 42); "Eyes . . . are involved in two-way traffic" (p. 61). See also David Park, *The Fire within the Eye: A Historical Essay on the Nature and Meaning of Light* (Princeton: Princeton University Press, 1997), pp. 39-43, and Martin, *The Corinthian Body*, p. 24.

98. N. T. Wright, "Reflected Glory: 2 Corinthians 3," in *The Climax of the Covenant*, p. 181, translating *katoptrizomenoi*.

ing back and forth between them. That much is true, but there is more, for which the concept of reflection is not adequate. Like the good eye, they receive light, and hold it, as a good stove holds its heat. It is then also able to act like a lamp and send that light out again. Light makes fire make more light, with the result that there is more light at the end than at the beginning. "Reflect" or "behold as in a mirror" cannot translate this growth in light. The Spirit makes light grow by making believers not only its transmitters but also its co-producers.

Christians are light-generating as long as they recognize one other as actualizations of the shining of the face of Christ. There is no strong distinction to be made here between the face, the light it radiates, and the image it casts. Christ is the face that shines its own light with such brightness that it not only reflects off other faces but also heats their fire, making it not their fire but his, so that it is not merely their exteriors that shine Christ's light but their interiors that host his fire. More than that, it is not only the light of Christ's face that reflects off other faces, it is Christ's face that shines through and refigures these faces, creating a family resemblance. Prolonged exposure to him makes you look and act more like Christ. Not all fire is the same: the fire you generate is as personal to you as your voice. There are both a hierarchy of fire and the issue of how benign any particular source of fire is.[99] The first point is that there is no strictly zero-sum economy of light, so one must spread this fire by tending it and being a custodian and householder of it. The second point is that light, fire, and glory are the possession and function of persons, and they function as concepts for the formation of persons.

Richard Hays also discusses 2 Corinthians 3. First there was the old covenant, and then there was the new covenant. The new covenant is much brighter than the old. But what is cause and what is effect here?[100] "The old-covenant glory did not just peter out like a battery-powered flashlight;

99. A person of dignity would not condescend to take fire from a more humble hearth to relight his own. Foreign fire is what Nadab and Ahibu offer in Leviticus 10:1.

100. Richard B. Hays, *Echoes of Scripture in the Letters of Paul* (New Haven: Yale University Press, 1989), p. 135, offers this paraphrase of 2 Corinthians 3:7-8: "But if the ministry of death chiselled in stone script, came with such glory that the sons of Israel were not able to gaze upon the face of Moses because of the glory of his face (a glory now nullified in Christ), how much more will the ministry of the Spirit come with glory." As Moses was eclipsed by the intimation of Christ, so the sight of Christ on the cross represents to us the utter unreadability and veiledness of the intentions of God.

rather it was done away by the greater glory of the new covenant in Christ."[101] The old did not end; it was just rendered redundant. It is the comparison with the new that brings it to an end, no failing of its own. Was there no use for it anymore, and so in this sense the one covenant was done away with by the greater glory of the other? Perhaps Hays's analogy can be improved upon. Here are two other options. When the sun comes up, we are no longer reliant on the oil lamp that gave us light all night long: the lamp is not rendered nonfunctional by the daylight; it does continue to add its small light to the light of day; but since no one is concerned to tend it, it eventually goes out. Or consider a second analogy: the glory of the old covenant was the pilot light; when the main burner of the boiler roars into life, it does not extinguish the pilot light, but the pilot light now cannot be distinguished from the rest of the flame. The old covenant cannot be made out from the new. In each case the relationship between the glory of Christ and of Moses is not one of either-or, but one that demands a more participative logic. The one is the means of the other.[102] The new covenant is the glory of the old. The old has worked successfully in that it has brought about the new and self-renewing covenant; it has created both the conditions for its success and the occasion of its bursting into appearance. The old covenant worked alone, was faithful to its purpose, and was vindicated; it has borne fruit and no longer bears the burden alone.

Wright assumed reflection in a zero-sum economy of light; Hays assumed that because the new is bigger and better than the old, the old is shamed rather than vindicated. But the saying about the eye in Matthew and the discussion of glory in 2 Corinthians relate to a single cosmology in which fire, light, and vision all function equally as action, reception, and means of both. Why are these exegetes attempting to understand them in terms of reception alone? Does this misreading of Israel's cosmology result from the assumption that what is new can only serve to displace what is old? Could such a logic be the result of residual supersessionism? Is it not the inevitable result of modern New Testament studies — that is, of a New Testament studies determined to establish its identity independent of the conversation with other theological disciplines?

---

101. Hays, *Echoes of Scripture in the Letters of Paul*, p. 135.

102. In the second case the pilot light enables the main flame. In the first case the oil burned by the oil lamp is the function of last season's sunlight converted into oil by an olive tree.

4.6.2. Fire and Becoming

Fire, light, and vision belong with the issue of what is visible in the temple. A remark from Christopher Rowland illustrates how the issue of vision arises in discussion of the temple. "When Paul sees the risen Lord, we may describe it as a vision of a heavenly being, but within the thought-world of Paul's day that meant the drawing-back of the veil to disclose that other dimension of reality which was normally hidden."[103] Apocalypticism requires an ontology that does not simply oppose presence and absence but uses biological description and an account of the development of an educated audience to determine the modalities of God's action.[104] In a *non-modern* cosmology, vision is the function not of the one doing the looking, but of the one looked at, who must release vision of himself before anyone may see him. Vision is a matter not only of receiving light, but also of giving light, for the giving of light is the giving of authority. You can see the lord only when you are in his court and thus in his favor.

Fire and light belong together to the ancient world's metaphysic of becoming. They are the idiom in which things come to be and pass away again.[105] The total processes of nature, which come into being and pass

103. Christopher Rowland, *The Open Heaven: A Study of Apocalyptic in Judaism and Early Christianity* (London: SPCK, 1982), p. 378. "Entry into the garden was . . . the exposition of the Scriptures. . . . There was great responsibility resting upon the student of the Scriptures . . . it was a potentially dangerous exercise which could have dire consequences for the unwary" (p. 318). See also Bockmuehl, *Revelation and Mystery:* "Much as in an apocalyptic, even the visionary revelation of 'mysteries' does not come 'out of the blue', but is mediated by a meditative exegesis of Scripture passages — be it Genesis 1, Ezekiel 1 or Isaiah 6" (p. 117); "The exposition of the *merkabah* (Ezekiel 1) was explicitly permitted only to mature and experienced rabbis working in camera; similar restrictions applied to other passages" (p. 122).

104. For accounts of biblical apocalyptic, see, for example, John J. Collins, *The Apocalyptic Imagination: An Interpretation of the Jewish Matrix of Christianity* (New York: Crossroad, 1984); Haywood, "Sacrifice and World Order"; and Margaret Barker, "Beyond the Veil of the Temple: The High Priestly Origins of the Apocalypses," *Scottish Journal of Theology* 51 (1998).

105. "Fire" is what the cosmos most essentially is. Though this fire remains fire, it also devolves into other elements. Fire gives birth successively to air, to water, and to earth, but it does so without ceasing to be fire: everything comes out of fire and passes back into it again. So we have:

> Fire
> Fire-air
> Fire-air-water
> Fire-air-water-earth (Fire), or

out of being again, were regarded by the ancient world as fire and as spirit. They are conceptualized most conveniently for us by the Stoics. The issue of whether we can use Hellenic thought to discuss Israel's practice arises because, for the sake of academic convenience, we deal only in discrete intellectual systems (Stoic, platonic, neoplatonic), rather than understanding these merely as formal versions of a continuum of folk beliefs and practices and a commonsense cosmology of the ancient world. This is not a single cosmology, to be sure, but sets of practices and beliefs with family resemblances. Fire, heat, and light are not simply about vision and knowledge, but constitute the whole medium of the natural and moral world. In Israel the temple sacrifices drove the single economy of people, the land and its products, producing the cloud of the *Shekinah* that functioned as their common medium. This was not an autonomous system that could be described by biology alone, but was determined by the God of Israel who moved his people on to holiness, a project in which all the processes of biology must play their part, and by which they would also be redeemed. Fire, heat, and light equally represent the moral component of this continuum. Being in someone's view allows you to see (only) what he sees, and seeing something amounts to admitting it and giving it approval. There is no light as such, but only the light and vision exercised by some particular authority and the set of objects admissible to it. The ancient, and therefore also the biblical, world understood epistemological and ontological issues to be inextricably connected. Seeing is the function of respect-paying to some authority by which you are granted an audience, a vision. An angel or apocalyptic appearance in the temple to a figure from Israel's Scriptures

---

$$A$$
$$A \, (A - A^1)$$
$$A \, (A^1 - A^2)$$
$$A \, (A^1 - A^2 - A^3) \to A$$

The lower spheres of the cosmos represent either the presence of the furthest of these from pure fire itself or the presence of these elements in increasing degrees of mixture. The cosmos simply occasionally returns to being what it most essentially is, as though it periodically cleans itself up. Fire seeks to return upward toward its origin; even mixtures of the other elements that we see in the growth of other entities such as plants seek upward toward their origin as fire does. All this becoming is what being *does*, without ever ceasing to be immutable. See K. F. Johansen, *A History of Ancient Philosophy* (London: Routledge, 1998), p. 329, and G. E. R. Lloyd, *Polarity and Analogy: Two Types of Argumentation in Early Greek Thought* (Cambridge: Cambridge University Press, 1966), pp. 236-37.

refers to a particular moment or characteristic of the action of God in Israel's history. With a more developmental conception of light or fire, which understands it as an act of giving and receiving authority and being, New Testament scholarship would be able to link the vision of apocalyptic to the issue of the community that has been taught it and brought up in it that I argued for in Chapter 2.[106] This allows us to say that that Scripture is closed to gentile eyes, not for their punishment only, but also for their protection.

4.7. Biblical Scholarship on Israel's Cultic Action

I have argued that the temple represents Israel's liturgical work of worship of the one God and comprises that complex set of activities that build the people of God's household. The building that stands on Zion, and the image of it displayed in every synagogue, is the house of God to the extent that it contributes to this project. While it is no longer controversial to understand all New Testament theology, Paul's included, as temple theology, there remains the question of how far New Testament scholarship has been able to see the temple as Israel's liturgical labor and performance, before the world, of its office as its Lord's under-laborer.

In Chapter 2 I introduced the conceptuality of participation as a resource for discussion of paideia and eschatology. In this chapter I have asked whether the scholarship of biblical exegesis, theology, and (political) philosophy employs the logic of participation, which would allow it to talk about incorporation and transformation and so to follow the claim of Israel's eschatological political cosmology. I have asked whether biblical studies has found the means to account for transformation. Can it represent Israel's claim to be the mediator of the transformation of the material-biological world from autonomy to creaturehood? I have asked whether the literature that discusses Israel's temple cult is willing to understand it as the theological and liturgical work that opens a new and wider modality of action. I have tried to show that this literature has not yet adequately engaged with the themes of sacrifice and of sacrificial fire and

106. Bockmuehl, *Revelation and Mystery*, p. 113: "If therefore the exposition of Torah constitutes an event of revelation, it may not come as a great surprise that the rabbis even employ language reminiscent of the fiery Sinai theophany in describing the study of Scripture."

light, or with the conceptuality of clothing, covering, and tabernacle, that I related to atonement. It makes too little of the conceptuality of baptism and circumcision. It does not, for example, relate this conceptuality to the eschatological redetermination of the environment, or to the writing, binding, and weaving that, for Israel, conceptualize the growth and thickening out of relationship. Accounting for the becoming of this holy people requires a thermodynamic metaphysic able to relate light, heat, and seeing to growing and coming into appearance. A concept of elective biology is required to demonstrate that sons are born to Israel in the mixed media of biology and adoption, in which the material processes of the earth are taken up by the Spirit. Can biblical scholarship avoid setting spirit in opposition to body, or biology in opposition to moral and meaningful action?[107] Must biblical scholarship rely on this problematic dichotomy of biology and culture, produced by a univocal modern concept of presence and representation, being and its reflection? I have suggested that modern biblical exegesis lacks the conceptuality of performance that I sketched in Chapter 2 and that I will relate to the public practices of paideia represented by non-modern political philosophy in the last chapter of this book. I have suggested that it makes Israel's ritual, liturgy, sacrifice, and temple problematic for this reason. I have asked whether biblical exegesis gives an adequate account of the responsibility of Scripture to the community it forms and of the (asymmetrically) co-constitutive relationship of Scripture and that community. Can it concede that Scripture instructs and forms the people of God?

These brief forays into the person and work of Christ represent something of a new approach. I have presented my atonement theory as a general anthropological theory. I have developed a Christology that serves as a general anthropology. I am not setting out first an argument about Christology, which I then have to argue for again in terms of its wider application to anthropology and humanity. Christ is the criterion of humanity. I have set out a theology that is already fully an address and challenge to the world, not a hermetic religious discourse. Diagnosis of modernity that is mission to and judgment of the world is intrinsic to theological statement, not subsequent or external to it. I am not trying to secure a religious

---

107. In §5.4 we will discuss Funkenstein, who asks why Christianity has not made more use of the Stoic metaphysic, which does not create this dichotomy.

conceptuality but to refute it. Such a new anthropology and anthropological ontology are perfectly permissible. These are not religious theories; they are general theories discerned and stated by theology.

It may be countered that it is not the task of biblical or New Testament studies to discuss the meaningfulness of their subject matter outside the text, but that this is rather the job of systematic theology or hermeneutics. It is the task of systematic theology, in conversation with the other disciplines of the university representing the various claims of the economy of modernity, to discuss the meaningfulness of these biblical texts. It is the job of theology to perform in the university the evangelical task of hearing and, under God, passing on God's word to our own society. This brings us to the issue of which models and metaphors to adopt for this purpose. I have suggested that this hermeneutical task must be continually resubordinated to the doctrine of God who is for us. The question of the status of biblical language — its models and metaphors — is not to be settled by a distinct discipline of hermeneutics to which the political and theological nature of biblical statement can be referred. This question is intrinsic to the theological task of making the doctrine of God obediently evangelical. This can be done only by a more convincing performance of theology, including what might be called a typological interpretation that belongs to a logic and ontology of participation. The question is not which metaphors we should adopt in talking about the person and work of God. Rather, it is the task of theology to commandeer every modern concept in turn and bring it under the discipline of Scripture and the doctrine of the church. Thereby we may see that the action of God in Israel is the mediation whereby, through baptism, even we moderns may be made properly present to each other. Israel, in the person of Jesus Christ, is our lesson, teacher, and supervisor. So I have come to the uncontroversial conclusion that there must be more, and more robust, interaction between biblical studies and political and systematic theology. There must be a biblical theology.

In these last two chapters I have argued that Jesus makes a better performance of the world than does the self-professedly secular world. The secular world puts in a fallen and failing performance, he a perfecting and enduring performance. He does this world-performance necessarily in the face of the world and against the world. He does it on the cross. He is God and man. He is man. We are not yet truly human. True human beings are the creature, servant, and friend of God. We are not yet this. Jesus can do us better than we can do ourselves. We cannot do anything that Jesus cannot repeat and do better. He can take away our claim to have done something new and unrepeatable, which would put us decisively beyond God and make us autonomous. He can put in a performance of greater virtuosity that shows that all our doing is just a failure of his doing. He mimics and portrays us, both in our present truculence and misery and in the glory that we will receive from him. On the cross he plays us as we are, and as we will be, with him. These chapters have offered an account of atonement that does not rest on a choice between models that requires a resultant separate work of hermeneutics and epistemology, with further separate discussion of the appropriateness of such models for today, and thus of the issue of time and modernity.[108] Rather, I have attempted to provide a theology of time in which time is what God provides for us. God ushers us into his time. He brings his servant-community up into the skill of receiving time and giving his time. His time describes and contains the time of modernity. These chapters have prepared us for the final chapters of this book, in which our claim to be the knower and measurer, because the actor and creator, of our world is dethroned.

---

108. The contributors in John Goldingay, ed., *Atonement Today* (London: SPCK, 1995), and John T. Carroll and Joel B. Green, eds., *The Death of Jesus in Early Christianity* (Peabody, MA: Hendrickson, 1995), intend to give an account of the atonement, and then a separate account of the atonement for us today.

CHAPTER 5

Mediation and History

The modern West believes that there has been a loss of mediation. It tells a story of individuals who dispense with mediation and so make themselves autonomous. But the church may tell such a story of collapse and loss only as one moment in its confession of God. God overcomes the fall of humankind, supplies human beings with the resources for mediation, and gives them a proper freedom.

5.1. Paideia

I will now lay out two contrasting versions of history and economies of time. One of these is broadly the history the West tells of itself. This is a history of growing autonomy from God; it is the story of secularization. The other is a salvation history in which God is readying humankind for relationship with himself. It insists that, despite itself, modernity also has its part in this movement. This is not new, of course. These two economies of time are the two cities described by Augustine, which I shall discuss in the final chapter.

To situate the discussion of the loss of mediation I must present its context, and I will do so by setting out an ethic. We can tell the history only by saying something about purposes. The object of all human doing is the formation of a people. Christian theology claims that God makes himself a people and is now in the process of making them holy. It therefore also claims that participation in the talk of Father and Son is the end and guarantee of all public life and discourse. As commentary on what is said, theology — and, in conversation with it, philosophy — is designed to serve this end.[1] Such a theology, in conversation with philosophy, will relate to the world, and thus to the discourse of science. It will relate also to law, as a set of propositions about what that life could be, and a set of skills by which to regulate talk about that life, in order to move toward it. Law educates. The formation of a people is the proper task of law. All leadership must be subordinate to this paideutic task and judged deficient when it does not lead toward the formation of a people. It is the task of critical philosophy to respond to law and to articulate for the law the problems arising in the course of this project. Philosophy and criticism must understand themselves to be in dialogue with law and on law. They must remind the state that it is to teach and to lead, by encouraging certain discourse and limiting other types of discourse.[2] Reason and enlightenment are about the ongoing task of leading that project and judging that leadership.[3] Philosophy, often known

1. See Pierre Hadot, *Philosophy as a Way of Life* (Chicago: University of Chicago Press, 1995), and Martha C. Nussbaum, *The Therapy of Desire: Theory and Practice in Hellenistic Ethics* (Princeton: Princeton University Press, 1994), who make the case that philosophy is therapy intended to serve formation, though these two authors understand this formation in individual rather than corporate terms. Political philosophy represented by Quentin Skinner, *The Foundations of Modern Political Thought* (Cambridge: Cambridge University Press, 1978), is notionally at least about positive freedom and the formation of sociality through concerted public action and by means of state-building, which itself forms a public character *(sensus communis)*. Moral philosophy, on the other hand — represented, for example, by Jerome B. Schneewind, *The Invention of Autonomy: A History of Modern Moral Philosophy* (Cambridge: Cambridge University Press, 1998) — describes a negative (formal) freedom, which understands that the wise person must retire from the fray of public life and action to theory and contemplation. Ian Hunter, *Rival Enlightenments: Civil and Metaphysical Philosophy in Early Modern Germany* (Cambridge: Cambridge University Press, 2001), argues for ethical philosophy as serving political philosophy.

2. In *The Contest of the Faculties,* Immanuel Kant rejected any sense that philosophy is subordinate to law or that law is to be understood as the education of a people and enlargement of its imagination. He detached philosophy from any responsibility other than to itself.

3. Robert R. Williams, *Hegel's Ethics of Recognition* (Berkeley: University of California Press, 1997), p. 21, finds that "Recognition names not only a structure of intersubjectivity but also a teleological process in which freedom is progressively mediated and realized. This process proceeds in the direction of an increasing recognition of freedom and an increasing realization of freedom. The state is supposed to complete this process of freedom and recognition as its telos." Michael N. Forster, *Hegel's Idea of a Phenomenology of Spirit* (Chicago: University of Chicago Press, 1998), believes that we must judge paideia, which he calls "law and purpose historicism," as "philosophically indefensible, merely one of the more seductive and persistent of the many philosophical damp squibs developed during this period" (p. 294

also as criticism, or critique, must understand itself to be in dialogue with law, so that together with law it can remind the state of its mandate to teach, lead, and enable. The university is the place in which professors of law (let us call them philosophers) dispute about ends and means, about ethics and law-making. They do this in order to refine their own performance as trainers of leaders and legislators. The church is at different moments participant in, leader of, and critic of this project.[4] Legislators are commentators on public speech. They demonstrate the bounds and direction of good speech by modeling good action and by ruling out whatever action does not contribute to it. The purpose of law is not to rule a vast number of actions out, but to bring about a large number of competencies. It is speech-therapy designed to bring the whole people into speech and action.

Most cases of speech can be handled on the floor of the market. Common sense deals with them. The cases the market cannot handle it passes up to law. Law passes the hardest cases up again to philosophy. But what happens if philosophy does not refer its conclusions back to the speech of the law court and back again to the whole speech of the market of public discourse?[5] In the belief that there was no control of talk about the world, Socrates gave up talk about the world to concentrate on the education of legislators.[6] In giving up the world, he gave up the vocabulary in which all action takes place. He took the world away from the *polis,* with the result that explanation became a referring everything back to an ideal earlier state before the first event. In the same way Kant brought to an end the subordination of philosophy to law. Law was no longer understood as the education of a people.[7] As a result, philosophy understood that it was only

---

n. 10), "the perpetuation in a modified guise of recently discredited Christian theological dogmas" (p. 294).

4. On the question of whether the state is part of the church's responsibility, see Oliver O'Donovan, *The Desire of the Nations: Rediscovering the Roots of Political Theology* (Cambridge: Cambridge University Press, 1996), pp. 193-242, and Reinhard Hütter, *Suffering Divine Things: Theology as Church Practice* (Grand Rapids: Eerdmans, 2000), pp. 166-68.

5. It is intrinsic to the possession of power that the powerful are not aware of what they are doing and are as likely as anyone to protest their powerlessness.

6. Schneewind, *The Invention of Autonomy,* p. 534. According to Xenophon, *Memorabilia* 1.11-12, "Socrates broke with his predecessors by attending to a new set of issues. He did not dispute, as they did, about the cosmos and the nature of things in general. He asked instead about human affairs."

7. T. J. Hochstrasser, *Natural Law Theories in the Early Enlightenment* (Cambridge: Cambridge University Press, 2000), pp. 196-97; in *The Contest of the Faculties* Kant "suggests

ever to talk about thought, never about public action. It became an all-forbidding law that determined that the only thing to be discussed is pure reason.[8] Philosophy must service the speech of the community that employs it, but the philosophy that disdains to attend to the speech and hopes of any community cannot do this. Oliver O'Donovan believes that our "communities of discourse do not interact to construct a catholic vision of the common good. They conglobulate into would-be philosophies which are both sectarian in outlook and totalitarian in pretension."[9]

Modernity identifies religion as separate from ethics, the discussion of ends. It supposes that we all know what end has been agreed upon and have now only to concern ourselves with how to get there, and so with comparing one means with another. The modern concept of religion belongs to this idea that there is one single end and all talk is only about *how*, not about *what*. Theology should refuse this definition and identify religion as talk about ends, assume open discourse about what the ends are, and insist that there is no meta-discourse that can settle this for us. Then we can say that religion is a matter of the good performance of talk about ends. It is not to

---

that nothing but confusion and argument would result from trying to deduce normative principles from empirical materials (ie intellect from the realm of sensations). For Kant the jurist's approach will inevitably be that of trying to deduce general principles from the law of the land, whereas properly it was the role of philosophy to identify the background *a priori* principles of moral philosophy. While the state required the lawyers to make the current law codes their proper object of study, philosophy should be freed from such restrictions. Philosophy served the cause of truth, whereas the other three faculties existed to serve the utility of the government." Gillian Rose, *Dialectic of Nihilism: Post-Structuralism and Law* (Oxford: Blackwell, 1984), pp. 11-24, describes modern "Reason" as a tyrant that refuses the possibility of there being anything other than itself to which it has to be responsible. I have argued that reason (which in Chapter 2 I termed "commentary" or "articulation") is agreed upon by the parties as a subsidiary work to the work of improving their performance.

8. Charles Taylor, "What Is Wrong with Foundationalism?" in *Heidegger: Coping and Cognitive Science — Essays in Honour of Hubert L. Dreyfus*, vol. 2, ed. Mark Wrathall and Jeff Malpas (Cambridge, MA: MIT Press, 2000), p. 133, argues that Kant formalized the strong form-content distinction made by contract theory, for which what matters is not the good society, but just meeting the procedural requirements of consent. All ethical discussion is in the idiom of the will, without reference to positive content, making it a matter of form, not content, unhooking right from any substantive good.

9. O'Donovan, *The Desire of the Nations*, p.283. O'Donovan continues, "The term 'ideology' best expresses this meltdown of the democratic idea, an implosion of critical speech upon itself in which the very act of speaking is crushed beneath the ambitions speech is made to serve. Self-posited speech destroys its own point and collapses into silence."

be reduced to reaching agreement so that talk can stop, but it aims at getting better at the give-and-take of converse, so the talk can grow, become a good of its own, and open space for other goods to emerge. Our talk is then both preparation for, and already good performance of, life in common.[10]

Religion, or practical philosophy, is the science and skill of talking about ends. Talk about ends is the means to developing the ability to tell the difference between ends. It must always refer itself to the world and receive comment back from it, so religion and the world are in a single conversation, in which each passes judgment on the performance of the other. Our academic talk therefore must understand itself as a commentary on the whole economy of bodiliness that constitutes the world. It should concern itself not only with the formation of the intellective soul, but also with the speaking to and hearing of many, and the enabling of many in hearing and speaking.[11]

A quite different definition of religion was proposed by Hobbes and Spinoza. Religion is the opposite of secular. The secular is the state in which all are free of external and therefore coercive political and intellectual authorities, in particular of explicit traditions of public and political discipline. Religion represents a constraint on humankind; secularity is freedom from that constraint.

---

10. Until the eighteenth century, the concept of rhetoric dealt with all the issues of performance. Public speech was not reckoned to be easy, so it was taught and learned. Jerome B. Schneewind, "The Divine Corporation and the History of Ethics," in *Philosophy in History: Essays on the Historiography of Philosophy*, ed. Richard Rorty, J. B. Schneewind, and Quentin Skinner (Cambridge: Cambridge University Press, 1984), does not relate the good to freedom or to a sense of the development and growing up into freedom and maturity of the agents within the "Divine Corporation," nor does he define goodness further as goodness for a range of specific ends that require choices. Similarly, Frederick C. Beiser, *The Sovereignty of Reason: The Defense of Rationality in the Early English Enlightenment* (Princeton: Princeton University Press, 1996), does not relate "reason" to reasoning together, converse, public talk, and the skills of the development of public talk. Reason therefore for him never appears as faith doing what it must do to remain faithful — taking instruction, learning to think. Reason for Beiser appears to be precisely *not* tradition, inspiration, or Scripture. I have defined reason as what these three do together.

11. The case for theology as the mode of the truly public life is made in Chapter 6. Hadot, *Philosophy as a Way of Life*, p. 32: "Christianity was presented as a *philosophia*, a way of life in conformity with the divine Logos[;] as the Middle Ages developed, one witnessed a complete 'total separation' of ancient spiritual exercises, which were no longer considered a part of philosophy but were integrated into Christian spirituality, and philosophy itself, which became a 'simple theoretical tool' at the service of theology, an *ancilla theologiae*."

But we must reply with an alternative definition. "Secularity" is the term for the determination of an elite to be autonomous and to make the polis the servant and expression of their autonomy. Some are then free of external intellectual authority, but they themselves comprise an undeclared intellectual authority over others. The state would then not be the project of the formation of plural acting and enabling; rather, it would be a closed economy and property of a clique. This redefinition of religion created a sphere of tight control over public discourse with the intention of extinguishing disunity and disagreement and of bringing about acquiescence and unity under the state.[12] Religion ceased to be public discourse and became instead private discourse and the private sphere. It divided the world into the two spheres of public and private such that even the public sphere was absorbed into the private sphere. The sphere of politics became the private function of a small group, and the leadership that had been the function of the formation in conversation of a whole people became the property of that group, and government became a clerisy and technocracy. Within this new sphere, the resources of memory, imagination, and desire are under the control of authorities who do not refer their authority to the project of public speech and formation and are not themselves subject to the discipline of public speech.[13] They control what we may commend and hope for. Subordinating the church to this type of state means subordinating talk about ends to talk about means as they relate to an end that is non-negotiable and about which no public expression is allowed. They subordinate all speech to the penalties of the civil power.[14] Such a state rests on

12. Steven Nadler, *Spinoza: A Life* (Cambridge: Cambridge University Press, 1999), p. 272, argues that "Spinoza's ultimate interpretation is to undercut the political power exercised in the Republic by religious authorities." John Milbank, *Theology and Social Theory: Beyond Secular Reason* (Oxford: Blackwell, 1990), pp. 17-20, has a similar argument. Hunter, *Rival Enlightenments*, p. 27, argues that "By replacing the Aristotelian anthropology of man's rational and social being with an Epicurean conception of man as a passion-driven self-destructive being, and by using a voluntarist theology to exclude theo-rational conceptions of justice from the civil domain, the civil philosophers literally (Hobbes) or in effect (Pufendorf) identified natural law with the commands of the civil sovereign."

13. Peter J. Leithart, "The Gospel, Gregory VII and Modern Theology," *Modern Theology* 19, no. 1 (2003): 15, argues that "the Gregorian reversion to the antique order of priest/non-priest is at the heart of the project of modern secularism." See also Bernd Wannenwetsch, "The Political Worship of the Church: A Critical and Empowering Practice," *Modern Theology* 12 (1996): 269-99.

14. Hunter, *Rival Enlightenments*, p. 26, argues that "rather than restricting religion to

the belief that the church has no regulative or governmental function over groups and public persons, but is to govern only the individual solitarily.[15] It represents the determination to drive together all the *how* questions of the practice of a good life and to give them technical solutions. We now call these solutions "political economy," or "economics and administration."

Historical biblical criticism has its origins here. Like the philosophers, the biblical scholars made a claim to autonomy that involved reading the Bible without its formative community, the church, and without the formation of any community as its purpose. Deconstruction of claims in the Bible was a way of deconstructing the political claims of political hierarchies and law. So, for example, Kant:

> There is, therefore, no norm of ecclesiastical faith except Scripture, and no other expositor of it except the religion of reason and scholarship (which deals with the historical element of Scripture). And, of these two, the first alone is authentic and valid for the whole world, whereas the second is merely doctrinal. Its aim is the transformation of the ecclesiastical faith for a given people at a given time into a definite and self-maintaining system.[16]

Truth cannot create or even tolerate any community, for any community is a failure of universality. So modern exegesis understands itself to be autonomous from doctrine (the tradition of an ecclesial community) and philosophy (public political responsibility). According to Jon Levenson, "historical criticism is the form of biblical studies that corresponds to the classical liberal ideal. . . . Like citizens in the classical liberal state, scholars practising historical criticism of the Bible are expected to eliminate or minimise their communal loyalties, to see them as legitimately operative only within associations that are private, non-scholarly and altogether vol-

---

the private sphere in order to effect the de-sacralisation of politics, Leibniz, Wolff, and Kant all attempted to receive a secular equivalent for religion — in the form of their own natural theologies — through which they hoped to provide a moral basis for a resacralised state."

15. Amos Funkenstein, *Theology and the Scientific Imagination from the Middle Ages to the Seventeenth Century* (Princeton: Princeton University Press, 1986), p. 17, argues that "The view of the state as a human artifact through and through rather than as a natural product of a built-in *inclinatio ad societatem,* though it had never before been defended so radically and systematically, replaced pure natural law traditions."

16. Immanuel Kant, *Religion within the Boundaries of Mere Reason,* trans. and ed. Alan Wood and George di Giovanni (Cambridge: Cambridge University Press, 1998), 6.114.

untary."[17] The rationale of this type of biblical studies is no longer obvious. A more constructive approach must understand law, philosophy, exegesis, and theology as in conversation with one another. The two tasks of reading the world and of reading the Bible both require exegesis, and concepts, and doctrines.[18] In each of these disciplines what is said must be related to the whole history of what has been said, to continuity with the tradition, and to internal and external consistency. It is a matter not only of what the biblical exegetes say they find in the biblical texts, but also of what theologians say that all previous generations of exegetes have found there, and of what philosophers say about the language that these exegetes and theologians use. If left to their own devices, the exegetes would be making a claim to immediacy. But the philosophers and theologians, as long as they understand themselves to be in conversation with the exegetes, together function as the control on exegesis. The biblical exegete uses concepts kept in serviceable order by the philosopher and provided by that keeper of the thesaurus of the tradition, the theologian.

The Bible is the commentary on and technique of navigation through all the forms of writing and institution building that make up the world, as well as their redirection to the formation of the community of God's witness in the world. Scripture is itself already exegesis. Scripture is exegesis *of the world*. So Scripture is first the subject of exegesis, not first its object. Exegesis of Scripture is subsidiary to Scripture's work of reading the world. This work of world-reading is not merely a looking at the world; it is bringing various worlds into confrontation. The end is not to look at the world as one single mute object, and so to imagine ourselves as imperious, disengaged subject. The world is not one thing, but many conflicting voices that address us and will answer for us if we do not answer for our-

---

17. Jon D. Levenson, "The Hebrew Bible, the OT and Historical Criticism," in *Reading in Communion: Scripture and Ethics in Christian Life*, ed. S. E. Fowl and L. G. Jones (Grand Rapids: Eerdmans, 1991), p. 47. Jonathan I. Israel, *Radical Enlightenment: Philosophy and the Making of Modernity, 1650-1750* (Oxford: Oxford University Press, 2001), pp. 258-74, 447-56, indicates some of the history of the political imperative that drove this early modern secularizing biblical hermeneutic.

18. See Gerard Loughlin, "The Basis and Authority of Doctrine," in *Cambridge Companion to Christian Doctrine*, ed. Colin E. Gunton (Cambridge: Cambridge University Press, 1997), p. 42: "Scripture and tradition were transformed into history and experience"; see also Oswald Bayer, *Gott als Autor* (Tübingen: Mohr Siebeck, 1999), p. 10: "All three dimensions (history, philosophy, literature) belong together, and may not cut themselves off from one another or set themselves up as absolutes."

selves. The point is not to assert our detachment from the world, but to join in conversation with it.

To read Scripture is to be equipped with an additional means by which the world may make itself visible to us. It provides us with a greater bandwidth, enhancing our ability to receive the complexity of the world. Through Scripture we may follow the trajectory of our acts and so see them together with their outcome and see relationships in their completeness. Scripture understands the world not as a thing without speech but as complexes of conversations. It does not merely see it but hears it, is heard by it, and interacts with it. It shows us the world as history and therefore as the place for humans, the animal with history and therefore with a future. Inasmuch as biblical studies understands itself to be alone before the text, able to take in everything at once as though it were all at once present like an illustration, it misidentifies the end. It abstracts the time in which the thing is, so it sees only a flat field without event or interactivity.

5.2. Enlightenment as Immediacy

The project of the economy of modernity is to *see*. It intends to see through the obstacles to seeing. It is a claim to pure knowledge. It understands that it must do without practical knowledge, and become purer and clearer by ridding itself of all considerations of the practices and means of knowing. It is the claim to dispense with the whole population of intermediaries. For this reason it intends to look past the elect people that God has appointed to steward and husband us into knowledge. It understands all discussion of the medium of knowing as unnecessary restraint that prevents it gaining an immediate knowledge.[19] The project of the economy of

---

19. Garrett Green, *Theology, Hermeneutics and Imagination: The Crisis of Interpretation at the End of Modernity* (Cambridge: Cambridge University Press, 2000), p. 54, argues that Kant characterized "leading reins" as illegitimate restraint, while Johann Georg Hamann countered that Kant (contradictorily) made immaturity "self-incurred," blaming the nation for a tutelage forced on it by the self-appointed guardian and exploiter, Frederick II. Ingolf Dalferth, *Gedeutete Gegenwart: Zur Wahrnehmung Gottes in den Erfahrungen der Zeit* (Tübingen: Mohr Siebeck, 1997), p. 147, argues that Hegel indicated that the apparently complete victory of the Enlightenment was a Pyrrhic victory that had resulted in the difference between theology and philosophy, in the form of the opposition of faith and knowledge, being now "relocated into philosophy itself."

modernity has shunted the question of *how* into a number of special domains — aesthetics, politics, or technical expertise. It tolerates no plurality, crowds, or complexity; no range of time-scales; nor the non-linearity and asymmetry of the dual agency of God with humankind. It is the attempt to do entirely without consideration of performance and to go directly to the object, filtering out whatever is not amenable to the conceptuality of immediacy. It promises to free us from the tutelage of another, to provide a cheaper grace that gets to the object faster, doing so at the expense of being able to identify the object that is the goal. It wants to get us there without our being altered or matured by the process. In all this it represents simply a failure of patience.

The enlightened are enlightened only because they sit at the summit. The world writhes below them. They can see it, but they no longer feel it. But equally they are *unenlightened*. They do not know what everyone in the heap beneath them knows. The world is a thing of conflict, a matter of pushing forward, acquiring leverage, and accruing the wherewithal to see purely and be enlightened.[20] There cannot be universal enlightenment because this vision is achieved only at the expense of someone who cannot see because he is not given the leisure. Yet the poor can see what we cannot — that we are exploiting them. Our view, being incomplete, is false and represents no enlightenment.[21]

Modernity is constituted by the belief that it merely receives what is there without contributing to it. Robert Jenson provides the most categorical statement of the dominance of vision in the Western tradition:

> The organ of truth, in the classic tradition, is the "mind's eye"; knowledge is *theoria, seeing*. . . .
>
> . . . To knowledge for which sight is the metaphor, the response or solicitation of the other is not *constitutive*. In the final versions of Greek reflection, which became the theology of all late antiquity's cults, this ideal of knowledge is paradigmatically and foundationally instantiated

20. In *Phenomenology of Spirit* B.IV.a 194-96, G. W. F. Hegel discusses the different knowledge and consciousnesses of a master and a servant.

21. We may say that the church succeeds in making the best claim to universality and catholicity. It is the real university. It knows what the university does not, that knowledge is inseparable from work and the overcoming of resistance. With the concept of the bondage of the will, the church knows that knowledge is not all known, that it is closed, and that it is we who prevent it from becoming open.

in Aristotle's Unmoved Mover under various aliases. This God is a sheer act of vision, wholly agent and not at all sufferer, receiving and expecting nothing from what is seen — if, indeed, it is acknowledged that anything other than itself comes within its purview. . . .

When the Enlightenment revolted against theology in the name of reason, it thus revolted also against philosophy as anciently practiced, since it was theology by which that practice was now carried on. Thus in the Enlightenment's understanding and practice of "reason," the countervailing factor [talk and hearing] is gone. Reason becomes what even Aristotle did not make it: sheerly the individual's ability to see truth.[22]

We command the object of our vision, but we do not hold ourselves responsible for it, for it is purely object. Could we go even further than this and say that modernity is the belief that we merely receive but do not contribute? Is modernity intrinsically this posture of detachment? Is it simply a mode of being, one that is deficient because it is a being without responsibility? Modernity claims that looking is a simple act of reception, and thus of passivity, which has no constitutive impact on us and for which no training is required.[23] It claims that knowledge is effortless vision, that everything can equally well be seen through anything, and that there is no requirement to discover a proper implicit order. All knowledge is just a beatific vision of the object. We can see right through to the very object utterly without interference of any intermediaries. But it is not so. Looking is an idiom by which we interact with the world and have an impact on it.

I have indicated that there is still a non-Kantian *a posteriori* philosophy of technique that deals with all the issues of how.[24] Theology is a form of this practical knowledge. It insists that knowledge is not instantly visible, that the body is more than the eye, that things have to be learned and worked for, and that there is an inevitable and proper toil of translation. I

---

22. Robert W. Jenson, "On the Renewing of the Mind," in *Essays in Theology of Culture* (Grand Rapids: Eerdmans, 1995), pp. 166-68.

23. It also claims to project the time and space in which there may be objects, and so to constitute the object it sees.

24. In Chapters 1 and 2 we related *being* (and thus objects) to affordance. The thing-in-itself is a paradox: if it is a thing it is a tool and a "for-a-purpose," not a "for-itself" or "in-itself." Thus pure knowledge (pure reason) is not about all that most purely *is*, but about control of, commentary on, and correction of practical knowledge. Practical knowledge is about all that mostly purely *is*, for all that is can and must be regarded and examined as an affordance, as a tool, as a thing.

argued in Chapter 2 that all our knowledge and world are mediated to us. Everything we see, we see through the skills honed by many generations, and in their generations these people always remain the media of all our seeing. Seeing, and the apparatus of reading and literacy we have built on it, does not represent the whole range of bodiliness, but only a part of that range. It is the result of the remembering of some skills and promoting them to become our dominant vocabulary while pushing into the background other skills and modes of embodiment. The Western nominalist reading of Augustine mistakes the order of *knowing* (the heuristic purpose) for the order of *being*. It confuses the *articulation* — that is, the *means* and *method* of learning — for the end, which is relationship with and knowledge of God. The vocabulary of vision, counting, and "clear and distinct ideas" may be properly employed as the *means to improve on our performance*, which I introduced in Chapter 2 as "articulation." Such a vocabulary of counting and vision has its proper place as the instruction that promotes the development of learners, taking them on from stage to stage by introducing a new lesson as they are ready for it, and which they have to learn before they may pass on to the next. Understood to refer to the possibility of an immediate vision of the end and possibility of the abolition of mediation, the vocabulary of vision and enlightenment is disastrous. But understood as the means by which learner and instructor articulate the means to improve the learner's performance, it has a proper function. We must therefore understand all the claims of vision, of clear and distinct ideas, and of enlightenment to have their place only with discussion of contemplation and beatific vision through liturgical mediation. They are heuristics that belong to the concept of paideia.

A doxological ontology would allow us to relate vision to *being*. Any power broker sees us because he allows us to come into his view. He allows us to see what he sees as he sees. All those who pay court to the power broker contribute to making him the man he is. It is only by virtue of our looking up to him that there comes to be an orientation schema of up and down that is second nature to the population brought up within it.[25] Our looking and seeing have a history; the history forms a continuum that acts

25. Martin Jay, *Downcast Eyes: The Denigration of Vision in Twentieth-Century French Thought* (Berkeley: University of California Press, 1993), p. 49, attributes the "rationalization of sight" to the "increasingly formalized and distant social space of the courtly societies of the era . . . elaborate courtly rituals of display devised to mark the articulations of social hierarchy."

as the medium of our action. Every sort of looking is a certain mode of de-
liberately seeing some persons and overlooking others, while forgetting
that this is what we are doing. All this pure and immediate seeing is refusal
of mediation. But it is not at all what it claims. It is not the absence of mediation. It is the mediation of that concept of the strong man, whose body
language our society has internalized. In the next chapter I will argue that
this power broker is the executive arm of the many autonomous domains
that constitute the economy of modernity.

Leadership is the ability to describe what we do in terms of its
paideutic effect and to do so successfully, so people follow us. The state is
therefore the activity of adducing reasons for what we are doing that relate
to the project of the formation of the body.[26] The reasons we give always
claim that my individual good also corresponds with the social good so my
way will serve for all of us. Reason and rationality serve as the accoutre-
ments of our display, the tools and tokens by which we amplify our gestures.[27] I give reasons, and I may employ whole academies to produce reasons for me, but they all serve to make me the arbiter and criterion of
reason. I elevate myself, and I explain how that is good for the rest of you,
and you find that my reasons are persuasive, but nevertheless this is all a
matter of my self-elevation. The self-elevation of the strong man has established an entire economy of reason and long become the general mode of
self-elevation. Yet still it is one person's act against all others, which all oth-

26. John H. Yoder, *The Priestly Kingdom: Social Ethics as Gospel* (Notre Dame: Notre
Dame University Press, 1984), p. 158, argues that "If the ruler claims to be my benefactor, and
he always does, then that claim provides me as his subject with the language I can use to call
him to be more humane in his ways of governing me and my neighbors. The language of his
moral claims is not the language of my discipleship, nor are the standards of his decency
usually to be identified with those of my servanthood. Yet I am quite free to use his language
to reach him."

27. Alasdair MacIntyre is aghast at the cynicism represented by Erving Goffman in *Interaction Ritual: Essays on Face-to-Face Behaviour* (New York: Doubleday, Anchor Books,
1967). MacIntyre writes: "The goal of the Goffmanesque role-player is effectiveness and success in Goffman's social universe is nothing but what passes for success" (*After Virtue: A
Study in Moral Theory*, 2nd ed. [London: Duckworth, 1985], p. 115). MacIntyre is right in saying that we regard him for his particular (institutionally determined and therefore objective) expertise (such as that of the sportsman at his sport), but Goffman is also right in insisting that we also recognize him for the charisma and élan that converts him into the
object of emulation, a natural leader outside his institutional role. In Chapter 2 we found
that play within the game is informed by speech in the form of commentary and a range of
para-game considerations and activities.

ers have interiorized and now replicate. All the rationality of the economy of modernity is still the self-elevation of the strong man, who leads, but leads us only to variations on his own self-exaltation.

For all the greatness of the rationality of the economy of modernity, the Western intellectual tradition, it is also just the flamboyance that hides the act of a bully. When used together, the concepts of power and aesthetics serve to account for the magnificent redundancy of much of our performance. Where there is no proper account of performance as the whole medium of our being, the issues of aesthetics and power appear to be stray ends. I suggest that if we hold together aesthetics and power with the other concepts to which I have drawn attention, they contribute to the proper description of our action as complexly reciprocal creaturely action, allowing a theological account of the action of God and human being together in the medium of God's provision. The claim of pure knowledge is to dismiss the other person's medium, refuse his help in coming to know him, and so come to know him without his cooperation, violently. It is to decide that the other person's medium should be understood only as a threat that must be rebuffed. The claim of modernity to exert its own pure vision is a claim to see past Israel, the medium of God, and impose on Israel our own medium. So the claim is to see the objects and purposes of God's imagination and desire, even though, without the Scriptures that are Israel's own self-commentary, we have no medium of imagination by which we could identify these as those objects.

The ancients conceptualized the givenness of limits as the weaving of the fates.[28] Without the Scriptures as the source of its imagination, modernity has no concept of law and no means of conceptualizing givenness or of conceding the otherness of others. Modernity does not understand that the action of others leaves us only certain room, not an absolute freedom, although, on the other hand, it does license us a freedom with definition. Modernity understands only that we weave ourselves — and thus we have no means of saying that we do not like the results.[29]

---

28. See R. B. Onians, *The Origins of European Thought about the Body, the Mind, the Soul, the World, Time and Fate* (Cambridge: Cambridge University Press, 1951), pp. 349-51.

29. Early Christian studies, however, has a more mature understanding of power than New Testament studies. The early Christians rewrote the definition of power and manliness (*virtù*) by outperforming the Roman definition of manliness by the practice of asceticism, continence, and self-control. The more sophisticated hermeneutic of early Christian studies, conscious of the issue of rhetoric, persuasion, and the possibility of, by suffering, winning a

We receive our place, and in it some things are given. We need to cultivate the conceptuality by which we can say that a state of affairs, constituted by other people, is given. They make up the platform on which our formation becomes possible. Modern theology has let all the conceptuality of sociality and reciprocity drift out of the safekeeping of theology and philosophy. Instead, it has become the fiefdom of economics and administration and of the *technique* claimed by the sub-Hegelian sciences of theory, sociology, anthropology, and gender that know nothing of paideia. Without this conceptuality we do not realize that all our theological autonomy is moved by the shifts in the tectonics of the tradition, in slow but constant change under pressures that it is our specifically theological task to identify. Theology is a matter of *theologic* — that is, of logic and method. It allows us to name these extrinsic logics that separate life into various forms of administrative engineering and science. Theological diagnosis of changes in our social logic must not be divorced from the *theologic,* so God-talk does not become method as such.[30] Without the resources for talking about excess of human acting over and beyond the true and the good, theology cannot be science, with a proper respect for the sheer exuberance of the world. It must recover the discipline to allow talk of the world for its own sake and become more than merely morality. Without logic it cannot discern which moments demand truth discourse, which require discourse about what is good, and which need discourse simply about performance, with the result that everything it says risks becoming trivial.

---

world, employs the concept of performance and understands power as the modality of knowledge. See Frances M. Young, *Biblical Exegesis and the Formation of Christian Culture* (Cambridge: Cambridge University Press, 1997), for an example of the concept of paideia at work in exegesis; and see Ellen T. Charry, *By the Renewing of Your Minds: The Pastoral Function of Christian Doctrine* (New York: Oxford University Press, 1997), for the concept at work in doctrine. Denise K. Buell, *Making Christians: Clement of Alexandria and the Rhetoric of Legitimacy* (Princeton: Princeton University Press, 1999), and Elizabeth A. Clark, *Reading and Renunciation: Asceticism and Scripture in Early Christianity* (Princeton: Princeton University Press, 1999), show the idea at work in early Christian studies, their hermeneutic derived via Foucault and Kojève from Hegel's use of the concept of performance.

30. Hegel argued that all sciences have histories and that a law or logic is needed to control the telling of their history within any history of humankind. He believed that we will be defined by the gods or forces of "nature" until, by renegotiating the concept of nature with the life sciences, we can proceed beyond the Stoic cosmology of "nature," a nature made absolute and unreachable by Kant's epistemology, but within which Schleiermacher was content to build his religion of inwardness.

I have argued that the state was once a public project but, from the seventeenth century, became an autonomous sphere and the possession of a clique that declined constitutive relationship with the whole conversation of society. According to this story, there was once a united world of practical philosophy, then a fall and the division of the world into separate domains, of which I have identified the three domains of exegesis, philosophy, and theology. What point is there in such a story? This story can be told only as a heuristic and as warning of what would happen if we were not concerned to demonstrate the *theologic* — that is, to tell the greater story of the whole act of God for humanity, represented by the totality of Christian doctrine. It is not to say that this *is* the history, but that this *will be* the history if we do not apply ourselves to the task we are set. The story of the fall has its place within the sum of doctrines, which themselves have not only a doxological (truth) function but also a paideutic function in the formation of the community that can praise God. The Son who does the Father's work has the right to tell the story of the fall such that it is a story that only refers to a threat vanquished.

5.3. The Collapse of Mediation

The seventeenth century saw the beginning of a collapse of mediation. Alasdair MacIntyre believes that

> It was in the seventeenth and eighteenth centuries that morality came generally to be understood as offering a solution to the problems posed by human egoism and that the content of morality came to be largely equated with altruism. For it was in that same period that men came to be thought of as in some dangerous measure egoistic by nature; and it is only once we think of mankind as by nature dangerously egoistic that altruism becomes at once socially necessary and yet apparently impossible.[31]

---

31. MacIntyre, *After Virtue*, pp. 228-29. Similarly Funkenstein, *Theology and the Scientific Imagination*, p. 72, suggests that "Only in the seventeenth century did both trends converge into one world picture: namely the Nominalists' passion for unequivocation with the Renaissance sense of the homogeneity of nature — *one* nature with forces to replace the many Aristotelian static natures."

This is the most common account of secularization, and this is the story that determines who we moderns are and what place we occupy. It is the story of how action came apart from being, freedom from nature, humankind from creaturehood. I have said that an ontology of intermediary duties, powers, and media allows us to understand human action as nested in the world of other creatures. It enables us to acknowledge that action creates, and is created by, character and capabilities, and creates and is created by an environment and world. The economy of modernity replaces such Aristotelian accounts of intermediaries with notions and practices of immediacy. From the seventeenth century on, humankind was distinguished from nature and separated from it, and ceased to be either an animal or a creature. The new account of a culture-nature split redefined the concepts of nature and culture, the latter seen as separation from a God-given creaturely place. Nature ceased to be the place prepared for us and became instead the triumphant mechanical world-picture. It is the claim of Weber that the story of desire, and the work of imagination, has out-worked itself and is being replaced by rationality, which will fill the world and leave no place for narrative or imagination.[32]

When histories become too successful they succeed only in showing their inevitability. A history that attributes a breakdown to one historical moment problematizes how we recover from that breakdown.[33] Gerard Loughlin offers a discussion of the loss of authority of Christian doctrine. He believes that Christian doctrine became attenuated as it was increasingly set within an alien metaphysic. Stoic and Epicurean metaphysics, introduced in the Renaissance by new translations of Latin and Greek texts, came to replace the Aristotelian metaphysic with which Christian doctrine had been in long conversation.[34] In an Epicurean metaphysic, space is uni-

32. Max Weber, *The Protestant Ethic and the Spirit of Capitalism,* trans. Talcott Parsons (New York: Scribner, 1958), p. 182.

33. Stephen N. Williams, *Revelation and Reconciliation: A Window on Modernity* (Cambridge: Cambridge University Press, 1995), p. 7, points out that the story of the loss of mediation told by Gunton and Newbigin does not demonstrate that anything has become inevitable or that human beings have thereby lost responsibility for their acts.

34. See Funkenstein, *Theology and the Scientific Imagination,* pp. 39-46. Declination conceptualizes every movement as entry into new never-before-entered space; every thing is a new thing, confined within its own time-cell. In this metaphysic there is no responsiveness or relationship, and therefore no cause-and-effect. The Latin concept of absolute property may be related to this atomist conception of the thing without relation.

form and empty, and nothing in it needs mediation to be present to us. The void, the very absence of mediation, became the metaphysic that framed Christian doctrine and effectively subverted it.[35] Michael Buckley holds this Epicurean metaphysic responsible for Descartes's and Newton's account of infinite space, in which, since it has no intrinsic structure, order has to be imposed on the world by the observer.[36] But Scripture, along with other texts, must be understood to have intrinsic structure. Texts, and Scripture, are not all of the same sort, or immediately readable, but require a process of learning.

John Milbank and Nicholas Lash try to determine when the dissolution of the mediation of doctrine began.[37] Did the process start in the seventeenth century, or earlier, with Scotus in the fourteenth or Aquinas in the thirteenth century? Colin Gunton understands Buckley to argue that Aquinas's form of analogy, the "erection of theological structures independently of christology and pneumatology," was the underlying cause of modern atheism.[38] Gunton believes Aquinas made the assumption that two sorts of knowledge have access to the same being of God, such that one form of knowledge is immediate and the other mediate. It is no surprise when the doctrine that demands work is replaced by the one that does not, the expensive version by the cheaper. But Lash points out that the cheaper version, the "classical doctrine" of God, is of course not knowledge of God but of the logic of knowledge of God, a retrospective demonstration of the proper use of concepts. Aquinas understands that there must be a propaedeutic to prepare the reader for the knowledge of God that was to follow. The first part of the *Summa* intends to prepare us to read the doctrine of God as Father, Son, and Holy Spirit, set out in the third part. It is not another way of teaching what the third part teaches, but

35. See Loughlin, "The Basis and Authority of Doctrine," pp. 44-46.

36. Michael J. Buckley, S.J., *At the Origins of Modern Atheism* (New Haven: Yale University Press, 1987), pp. 47-50.

37. John Milbank, "Only Theology Overcomes Metaphysics," in *The Word Made Strange: Theology, Language, Culture* (Oxford: Blackwell, 1997), pp. 41-48; Nicholas Lash, "When Did the Theologians Lose Interest in Theology?" in *Theology and Dialogue: Essays in Conversation with George Lindbeck*, ed. Bruce Marshall (Notre Dame: University of Notre Dame Press, 1990).

38. Colin Gunton, *The One, the Three and the Many: God, Creation and the Culture of Modernity* (Cambridge: Cambridge University Press, 1993), pp. 138-39, cited by Loughlin, "The Basis and Authority of Doctrine."

of giving readers that conceptual competence with which they may embark on the real work.[39] There is a pure knowledge of God, a philosophy and beatific vision; the question is, who is holy enough to embark upon it? Loughlin argues that "the Summa is really no more than grammatical notes upon the Church's reading of scripture, being entirely determined by the scriptural story . . . first and last a narrative of the Word."[40]

Lash and Milbank want to show that Aquinas understood that the knowledge of God has to be obediently performed in worship and in the continuous expression and re-expression of doctrine.[41] We need to practice speaking about God, but we can practice only by actually speaking about God; by God's faithfulness our speaking may improve. Writing such a *Summa* was a dynamic, ongoing, and even liturgical act, an unceasing procession around the *loci,* such that every point is mediated by every other. Writing theology is a practice of the church obedient to its master and thus servant to the world; it is not an act that intends to come to an end with a final statement. Milbank argues that Aquinas understood each science to bring its fruit to theology, and *philosophia* is what all this theologically obedient science amounts to. Theology is the organizing principle for other sciences, the science of sciences, and *philosophia* is the practice of this theology. But are there levels and hierarchy of different sciences? Lash asks whether Milbank is not trying to turn all knowledge into theology, and to do away with other sorts of knowledge. This would threaten the real claim of theology, which would then not be allowing the world to be itself.[42]

Loughlin argues that a slow collapse of mediation meant that all texts

---

39. Charry, *By the Renewing of Your Minds,* pp. 134-35, makes the same point for Augustine.

40. Loughlin, "The Basis and Authority of Doctrine," p. 45. Alasdair MacIntyre, *Three Rival Versions of Moral Enquiry: Encyclopaedia, Genealogy and Tradition* (London: Duckworth, 1990), pp. 140-41, 162, 169, makes a similar argument for Aquinas.

41. Lash, "When Did the Theologians Lose Interest in Theology?"; and Lash, "Where Does Holy Teaching Leave Philosophy? Questions on Milbank's Aquinas," *Modern Theology* 15 (1999): 433-44.

42. Lash, "When Did the Theologians Lose Interest in Theology?" Milbank replies in "Intensities," *Modern Theology* 15 (1999): 445-97. See also Hadot, *Philosophy as Way of Life,* p. 107: "With the advent of medieval scholasticism however we find a clear distinction being drawn between *theologia* and *philosophia.* Theology became conscious of its autonomy *qua* supreme science, while philosophy was emptied of its spiritual exercises which from now on were relegated to Christian mysticism and ethics."

become uniform. As all being is the same, so is all knowledge of being, so there is crisis about how to tell one sort of text from another. Loughlin connects Frei's and Buckley's discussion of text as performance and learned, mediated, and mediation-making praxis, to the discussion by Lash and Milbank of whether philosophy has its own separate realm.[43] Buckley shows that Lessius, for example, employed the argument of Cicero in *On the Nature of the Gods* to attempt to make Scripture comprehensible to those who had newly rediscovered Stoic and Epicurean deism.[44] To do this, Lessius separated Scripture from the doctrine that represents the church's deliberation on centuries of Scripture reading. Perhaps modern biblical hermeneutics derive from these Stoic- and Epicurean-addressed apologetics of Lessius. The thought that the texts of the Bible and of the church can simply be handed over to some non-taught other originates in the *via moderna* belief that the knowledge of God is available apart from God's own conceptual mediation of it. The *via moderna* had abandoned a complex ontology in favor of a univocal ontology, in which God was one being among others, and therefore an object of the same immediate knowledge.[45] If all being is the same, there need only be one sort of inquiry to say what being any particular thing has. This defines theology and philosophy in opposition to one another, respectively as knowledge that does, and knowledge that does not, require mediation. It allows a stand-off between theology and philosophy to emerge. Philosophy had once meant the practices of knowing, and the various sciences in their order, and theology had meant the knowledge of God who orders and enables our knowing. Now philosophy and theology became rival means of access to identical knowledge: philosophy was public and concerned that that knowledge be known, while theology was esoteric and concerned to prevent it being known.

43. This is the issue of natural theology, of whether there are two gods, the first known in and by what is, a god of the Greeks, known by nature and indistinguishable from nature, and the other the God of the theologians, in charge of his own mediation, and yet who commandeers and transforms the grammar not only of "divinity" but also of "nature" into the grammar of creatureliness and triune Creator.

44. Buckley, *At the Origins of Modern Atheism*, pp. 40-45, 54-55.

45. Loughlin, "The Basis and Authority of Doctrine," p. 46, explains that "Once the univocity of concept and language had been established, analogy and metaphor belittled and God conceived as but another, if unique, 'extended' thing *(res extensa)* it was only a matter of time before Ockham's razor was used to remove an unnecessary hypothesis."

Aquinas's achievement did not succeed in preventing the impoverishing ontology of the *via moderna*. Failure to appreciate Aquinas's *Summa* as part of its obedient ongoing doxological training and character formation work left the church's liturgical action vulnerable to analysis in terms of the metaphysic of absolute absence of relation and mediation, and so to dissolution.

The result of the collapse of mediation is that being is substance — all the same, and all measurable. A proliferation of measure made everything infinitely divisible. When all being is of one sort, how can one being be distinguished from another, other than by pure "measure"? This pure measure is time. A new definition of time as uniform resulted from this univocal ontology, which distinguished between all being on one hand, and all relationship, structure, similarity, analogy, language, and symbol on the other. The media of relationship — measure, time, money — exist in an economy in which everything can stand in for everything else.

What is the status of these accounts of the collapse of mediation? Is the loss irrecoverable and the problem insuperable? Is it really the case that mediation is lost, or does it just shift into a different vocabulary? Perhaps giving an account of the loss of mediation is, like a contrite confession, a proper part of the redemption of that loss? But we must clearly say that the mediation is not lost. It remains the possession and work of God and has never been the possession of humankind apart from God. In the form of Israel, God always provides this mediation to the world. Nothing has been made impossible by a fall in history. Secularization has made nothing impossible or irrecoverable. The Christian confession of our fall, within the context given by the whole liturgy of Christian confession, belongs to the process of our learning our salvation. So the question that ends this section is, Who can tell this history? Who can confess that they have become separated from God, except the persons that God has redeemed? The Western tradition has no means of substantiating its story of separation, its purely secular history. It has nothing it could ground this history in, no independent witness to hear this history and acknowledge it as truth. The Western history is itself about the abolition of any Other who could be such a witness. God — and, in the Eucharist, his servant — is able successfully to tell the story of salvation, which includes an account of the fall. But this telling does not represent the reassertion of the fall and separation, but confesses that God has made this separation of no account. This confession is made by the world-bearing Word who returns to God.

5.4. Law and Accommodation

The law is the medium of instruction for the elect community. That was one conclusion of Chapter 2. The purpose of the law is to drive the community on to holiness. Without that purpose, law is a pointless restraint on the world. But this pedagogic concept of law and its control on salvation history became, if not lost, certainly in large part replaced by the concept of law without teleology. The story of the collapse of mediation, confined to a dualist, Platonist metaphysic, serves to make the fall timeless. As a result it ceases to be a story and becomes a cosmology of upper and lower realms. We can therefore counter a dualist with a non-dualist metaphysic. This is what we did in Chapter 2 with our examination of contemporary non-dualist accounts offered by cognitive science. Under the non-dualist account there is no collapse from a mediated to a non-mediated economy. Attention to non-dualist metaphysics, therefore, would enable us to reduce the extent to which modernity thrives on its story of its estrangement from God. Amos Funkenstein asks why the church did not make more use of the Stoic cosmology. This would have prevented the dualism that allowed the Epicurean void and atomism to become our decisive metaphysic, and the concept of the detached observer our controlling hermeneutic.[46]

As the teleology and the practices of mediation became more attenuated, Israel and the church ceased to be considered competent and articulate agents of mediation. They were no longer taken seriously as actors in their history or ours. Israel's practice was divorced from its teaching, the meaning of Israel's sacrificial practices was lost, and with it all understanding of Israel's status as critic of the world of the pagans. Israel came to be understood as just one example of primitive society. Israel's sacrifice was understood by Western anthropology as one of the many commutations of (human) sacrifice and of the social contract that controls violence.

Theology that starts from the fall cannot understand sacrifice. And indeed large parts of the tradition have followed the wrong path on this, the central issue of Christian action. Where there is no comprehension of the process of paideia and formation, sacrifice is taken to be the propitiation

---

46. Funkenstein, *Theology and the Scientific Imagination*, p. 43. Funkenstein continues: "Only in the seventeenth century did both trends converge into one world picture: namely the Nominalists' passion for unequivocation with the Renaissance sense of the homogeneity of nature — *one* nature with forces to replace the many Aristotelian static natures" (p. 72).

of an angry, and needy, tyrant. According to Deborah Shuger, Augustine found Israel's sacrifice a difficult issue.[47] Augustine believed that "it befitted God to request sacrifices in earlier times; now, however, things are different, and he commands that which befits this time."[48] Augustine believed that the law was handed over to Israel in installments as Israel became ready to receive them. "In question was the wisdom of the sacrificial ritual in ancient Israel. The pagans ask: If they were not good, why were they instituted? And if they were good, why were they abolished by a new dispensation?"[49] Pagan polemics were directed not at the idea of the one God but at the notion of God acting arbitrarily. Augustine replied that the process of history is not arbitrary. Like the cosmos, its parts need not be intrinsically beautiful, but need only fit together to make a beautiful whole.[50]

God opposes polytheism throughout all ages. In *The Guide to the Perplexed* Maimonides argued that it is Israel's task to be God's witness and to endure all the trials of world history.[51] The action of the gentiles is directed against Israel. Every apparently irrational precept of the law is a countermeasure to some practice of the culture of the archetypal gentiles, the "Sabeans." There were one-to-one inverted correspondences between each law and the pagan practices it was intended to oppose. The fact that the reasons for certain commandments have been forgotten demonstrates the success of divine teaching. God uses contingent elements within nature to

47. Deborah K. Shuger, *The Renaissance Bible: Scholarship, Sacrifice and Subjectivity* (Berkeley: University of California Press, 1994), p. 223.

48. Augustine, *Epistulae* 138.1.5. In the *City of God*, Book 10.5 (quoted by Shuger, *The Renaissance Bible*, p. 378), Augustine said: "For if he had not wished the sacrifices he desires (and there is only one, the heart bruised and humbled in the sorrow of penitence) to be signified by those sacrifices which he was supposed to long for as if they gave him pleasure, then he certainly would not have prescribed their offering in the old Law. And the reason why they had to be changed at the fitting and predestined time, was to prevent the belief that those things were objects of desire to God himself . . . and to make us realise that what was required was what they signified. . . . Hence the meaning of the text, 'I desire mercy rather than sacrifice' (Hosea 6,6), is simply that one sacrifice is preferred to another; for what is generally called sacrifice is really a sign of the true sacrifice. Mercy is in fact the true sacrifice."

49. Funkenstein, *Theology and the Scientific Imagination*, p. 224.

50. Augustine, *Epistulae* 138.1.5: "It befitted God to request sacrifices in earlier times; now, however, things are different, and he commands that which befits this time. He, who knows better than man what pertains by accommodation to each period of time, commands, adds, augments or diminishes institutions . . . until the beauty of the whole history, whose parts these periods are, unfolds like a beautiful melody."

51. Funkenstein, *Theology and the Scientific Imagination*, p. 237.

change it, and sacrifices are elements of the polytheistic mentality used to transform this mentality by degrees.[52]

I argued in the previous chapter that Israel's statement of the law is its response to pagan law-systems. It is driven by confrontation with the pagans, so it may not be explained by simple reference to nature or the requirements of biological survival. The law is the work of the tutor who prepares Israel for each new lesson. But the accommodationist schema dichotomizes the concepts of law and time, so it is the mere passing of time that determines when the law must change to accommodate change. There were different rules and laws for different times: sacrifice had been legitimate for ancient Israel, but God had since made a new law, so now it was not.

Funkenstein believes that the patristic and medieval explanation of Israelite sacrifice led, during the Renaissance, to a "search for correspondences and concordances of legal, religious and political institutions that express the *qualitas temporum* and hence that sixteenth century legal historicism may itself have been inspired by the traditional Christian explanation of sacrifice."[53] Renaissance legal theory came with a developmental theory: primitives have simpler and more savage laws, law develops the morals of nations, societies move on and up a single developmental path, and as they do the law needs to change to impose a regime of greater civility. The belief that God's law first allowed sacrifice and later abolished it resulted in the idea that laws change with their societies through an inexorable process of time. Shuger finds Grotius collecting examples of sacrificial rites with all the anthropological glee of Frazer, all understood as variations on commuted human sacrifice.[54] Study of the change or development of

---

52. Shuger, *The Renaissance Bible,* believes that Maimonides' accommodationist interpretation entered late scholasticism and inspired the first comparative studies of religion. Shuger argues that John Spencer, *On the Ritual Laws of the Hebrews* (1685), attempted to give every precept a precise historical rationale, so by demonstrating the time-boundness of every biblical institution he hoped to combat Jews, Catholics, and "fanatics." Rather than relate what Israel did to any intention of Israel's to refute the pagans, Spencer tried to reconstruct the primitive mentality to which Israel had been assimilated, and he saw Israel's laws as attempts to wean Israel from the Egyptian religion.

53. Funkenstein, *Theology and the Scientific Imagination,* p. 241.

54. Grotius, *De Satisfactione Christi* (1617). Shuger herself believes that "the essential rites and narratives of Christianity embody the logic of blood sacrifice and originate within an archaic episteme . . . [to] penetrate behind the civilised veneer of western ideology to its violent hinterground" (*The Renaissance Bible,* p. 83).

laws was the beginning of anthropology, and discussion of sacrificial substitution in the context of Roman law became discussion of property rights, economics, and anthropology.[55]

If God is faithful, what has been good for Israel may be good for us too. Israel, and the church of any earlier generation, may then be the medium of our instruction. Our age may be measured against other ages, even when other decisions and dispensations held good. This faithfulness makes God responsible to the law, which, as we have seen, expresses the narrative and the character of his relationship with his people. Without the conception that God is faithful to his own rulings, there is no set of his promises that can be quoted back to him by which he is content that we hold him to account. If God is not understood to be bound by his own faithfulness to his own previous rulings, and so as the guarantor of the law that enables paideia, the possibility of learning from previous generations is gone. If God is understood only as wielder of absolute and unaccountable power, there can be no comparisons between law in one age and law in another, and there is no possibility of paideia. With no understanding of law as paideia, history is not purposeful. It is just the passing of time, understood in terms of some unspecified concept of development. Without a theological concept of law and covenant, paideia evaporates into the idea of progress.

Earlier centuries distinguished between God as mediator *(rector)* and as owner *(dominus)*. As mediator, God is responsible for justice and for the purity of the whole language and currency of relationship. This medium is provided by God, but it belongs to the whole population: all its interaction takes place within it. The owner can forgive or remit a debt that is owed privately to him, and creation is God's own property. Yet this creation consists of the many persons whom he has given a stake in it. For their sake God does not act as though he were alone and simply remit debt.[56] God

---

55. Adam Kuper, *The Invention of Primitive Society: Transformations of an Illusion* (London: Routledge, 1988), traces the origins of anthropology to nineteenth-century historians of law. The pedigree is traced further through the Scottish enlighteners by MacIntyre, *Three Rival Versions of Moral Enquiry*, pp. 177-89, and, via Montesquieu and Herder, back to Grotius. See also Hochstrasser, *Natural Law Theories in the Early Enlightenment*, pp. 4-37.

56. Oliver O'Donovan and Joan Lockwood O'Donovan, *From Irenaeus to Grotius: A Sourcebook in Christian Political Thought* (Grand Rapids: Eerdmans, 1999), p. 792, argue that "The intelligibility of the doctrine turned on the understanding that God acted as the ruler of the universe, and the atonement was an 'act of jurisdiction.' A ruler, like a creditor, is free

acts as a just arbitrator, which means that he is wrathful when being is withheld from those who need it by those who can afford to give it. Whatever is defaulted is owed not to him alone, but to all the members of his economy to whom, as the creatures of God, it also belongs. It is God's task to provide justice and restore the medium of creaturely interaction, by supplying whatever it lacks.

But the *via moderna* decision to emphasize the absolute power of God over the faithfulness of God resulted in a receding understanding of God's ongoing responsibility to, and maintenance of, his creation. The seventeenth-century jurist Grotius represents a transition from one understanding to the other. "God is no longer *rector,* constrained by the law, which is (the law of) what he has done, but *dominus* who may dispose as he will."[57] Under the increasing influence of Roman law, known to the early modern era as *natural law,* the Aristotelian suspicion of the right of exchange over use gave way to an absolute right to control one's person and property. This movement was the anthropological complement to voluntarist theology. Humans best exemplify the image of God when exercising unrestricted sovereignty and property rights.[58]

We have seen that we need two terms to ascribe two roles to God. One role is private. God is owner; he can dispose of the world of his possession as he wills. But the other role is a public role. God is manager and arbitrator, responsible for the maintenance of the whole economy. The manager must see that debts are paid, in order that there be fairness between members of the household. But Christ can also take over our debts because he is not only manager but also the owner, who can introduce something new to the economy. He can supply the new substance with which debts can be paid. Where there is something missing, he can supply it. He does not in-

---

to forgive, unlike a judge entrusted with the administration of a law. But a ruler, unlike a creditor, cannot simply waive the right, but has responsibility for upholding justice for the whole community."

57. Shuger, *The Renaissance Bible,* p. 70. Gunton, "The Doctrine of Creation," in *The Cambridge Companion to Christian Doctrine,* p. 151, indicates the *via moderna* origins of this move.

58. William T. Cavanaugh, "The City — Beyond Secular Parodies," in *Radical Orthodoxy: A New Theology,* ed. John Milbank, Catherine Pickstock, and Graham Ward (London: Routledge, 1999), finds that, for Aquinas, Adam's right of property was based on *dominium utile,* justified by its usefulness to society in general. See Cavanaugh, pp. 187, 195, and Milbank, *Theology and Social Theory,* pp. 12-13, on this voluntarist anthropology of rights.

tend to supply it in such a way as to make our action meaningless, but precisely in order to give our action time to become more proficient. Thus the stricture expressed by the Socinians and Kant that God cannot transfer debt from one person to another, even to himself, does not allow the claim that God is also owner of this creation and can therefore do something new. He can create and re-create. He can step in to re-float our economy, because, being the underwriter of all our interaction, he already is in our economy; our economy is a subsystem of his. There is a circulation. Our praise must be not only received from God but also given again back to God. God has to receive it again. He creates, and what he has created he also takes back from us again. He gives, and he takes away. It is this last term that modern and Western theology cannot bring itself to utter. He takes it away again. He takes a tithe. This is the charge to us of keeping what we have in good order. But this cost, of having some of the world we have been given taken away again, is borne by him. He does not leave us to bear this cost. This cost, of sin, has concerned the West more than the East, precisely because the West failed to keep it integrated into an account of creation as present work that requires God's present maintenance, his liturgical work.

The result of this loss of law is that the whole economy of Israel's action — *sacrifice* — is no longer recognizable as parody and demythologization of the nations. Instead it is understood as an act of propitiatory violence. Israel was accused of doing precisely what Israel's deconstructive mimicry accused the nations of doing. The loss of the law as hermeneutical medium resulted from the loss of the law as paideia. Sacrifice has no basis in human sacrifice.[59] The appearance of sacrifice as problem stems from the failure to realize that Israel is the community that can correctly read the Scriptures as the deconstruction of the gentiles and violence. The meaning of all Israel's ritual and sacrificial action is given by its place in the conversation of God with his people.

The Western political tradition has been formed by reading the history of Israel. This tradition believes that the Scriptures are open to us, that

---

59. I argued this against Levenson in Chapter 3, where we saw that "violence" is simply a synonym for "gentile world." See also Milbank, *Theology and Social Theory*, pp. 392-98, and his "Stories of Sacrifice," *Modern Theology* 12 (1996). Girard and Milbank argue that the death of Christ is the end of sacrifice, but because their understanding of sacrifice is not derived from Israel's own teaching, but from some more general account of violence, it is no easy matter for them to show this.

we can clearly make Israel out in them. The West has set out to copy Israel, surpass Israel, and leave Israel behind. All the political and constitutional construction of the West represents our engagement in Israel's project, but without Israel, so modernity builds where it understands Israel to have failed. It claims that Israel must be seen through and seen past so that we gentiles can make our own start.[60] We do not allow conversation with Israel, and Israel is not allowed to host our learning. We have to learn without Israel. This rules out the people provided to be our hosts, intermediaries, instructors, and medium of our learning. It rules out the whole middle world of persons. But if gentile vision had not succeeded in making Israel its object, the Western tradition would have been laboring in vain and would have succeeded neither in following nor in overtaking Israel.

5.5. Inside and Outside

Next in this discussion of mediation we must be reminded that there has always been a single account of the world, available to the Western tradition. We have seen that a Stoic metaphysic gives us a non-dualist account of the world as a single continuum of forces and motion.[61] The total movement of this continuum is a function not only of the individuals that presently compose it, but also of the movement of all previous generations. In the course of the seventeenth century, however, this single continuum of motion separated into a dualism of motion on the one hand and emotion on the other. Motion was what could be seen in the physical world. But emotion ceased to be understood as an aspect of motion generally, and became instead a matter of psychology, of what happens *within*.[62]

---

60. Kant, *Religion within the Boundaries of Mere Reason*, 6.127: "We cannot therefore begin the universal history of the Church (inasmuch as this history is to constitute a system) anywhere but from the origin of Christianity, which as a total abandonment of the Judaism in which it originated, grounded on an entirely new principle, effected a total revolution in doctrines of faith."

61. Protestant theology has tended to offer only a univocal account of the individual will, in a vacuum, without adequate consideration of time or others.

62. See Daniel Garber, "New Doctrines of the Body, Its Powers and Place," and Susan James, "The Passions in Metaphysics and the Theory of Action," in *Cambridge History of Seventeenth-Century Philosophy*, ed. Daniel Garber and Michael Ayers (Cambridge: Cambridge University Press, 1998), pp. 553-623, 913-51.

The inner emotions of the individual were distinguished from the public interaction of persons, reducing action to either psychology or politics. Subjectivity and sentiment, located in head or heart, became individualistic, released from any location in a tradition, and unaccountable. Without trinitarian mediation, Christian doctrine became locked into a cosmology that referred everything to that sealed container, the soul, with the result that each person cultivates, not the world given to us by God as our task, but his or her own soul, which is a whole world to itself. This led to the consequent discourse of subjectivity, first as the soul, visible as religious pietism, then as the self, popularized by late-eighteenth-century Romanticism. Coleridge, Schleiermacher, and the most recent of the affective theologians, René Girard, vainly tried to establish that we occupy and ourselves constitute a continuum of emulation and envy, of motion and emotion.

But there is no reason why this dualism should prevail. The Western tradition tends to assume that first there is the thing, and then there is the motion invested in it. First it has *being,* and then subsequently it has *life.* The Western tradition sees each entity as a vehicle invested with movement from outside. But there is no reason why we should always put things this way around. We could equally put things the other way around. We could say that motion comes first, and the individual body comes second, that movement is prior to substance. Then we could say that the continuum of movement brings particular things into being, and thus that the Spirit brings particularity into being. It is also healthy to put things this way around. We saw in Chapter 2 that the life sciences, which have to account for change, do in fact do this. We must use both approaches and not subject emotion and motion to that dualist cosmology that attributes priority to the individual soul over the world of many persons.[63] We should keep two definitions of the soul in operation. In one of these the soul is the microcosm that participates in the continuum of the movement of the cosmos. In the other "the soul" is simply an archaic term for "mind." Mind itself, we saw in Chapter 2, may be regarded as a way of talking about the unity of those articulations and corrections that serve to improve on the way we relate to other people. Our discussion of our own soul or self should be understood to serve this paideutic articulation that serves our

---

63. Bernd Wannenwetsch, "The Political Worship of the Church," *Modern Theology* 12 (1996): 278, argues that "the Church's worship of God is the overcoming of political antinomies, the most important of which is that between public and private."

being for other persons.[64] Always to make mind prior is to give the world a lesser and merely temporary value.

The result of always making substance prior, and everything else subsequent to it, is that we have a systemic division between interior and exterior. One consequence is that moderns do not see how their public and economic behavior impacts on those beyond their field of view. They are insulated from the consequences of their (economic, public) actions. Religion has become a discourse without impact on the world, an inoffensive metaphorical talk about our own inner spiritual or emotional states. We have divided the theological confession of sin. We have invented two parallel worlds, one in which the language of guilt describes our own private emotional state, the other in which the language of credit and debt describes the external world but is not thought to impact on our own inner being.

The seventeenth-century discussion of passions has also become the modern discussion of time. Time ceased to be a moral concept and has become naturalized. Modernity believes that individuals give and receive nothing in their encounter with peers. They do not suffer either gain of being or loss of being from these encounters. I said in Chapter 1 that the result of denying ourselves the conceptuality of ontological credit and debt is that we are utterly unable to say what it is we suffer, lack, or inflict on one another. Suffering that is not identified as the impact on us of specific groups of others becomes simply fate, and in the economy of modernity this fate appears as time. Time is a debt that is unrelated to any action in the world, either our own or anybody else's. But temporality is the question of what change is undergone. We must relate this to the question of who inflicts change on whom, and who is master of whom. The question of time is, Whose time is it? Who can measure and out-measure whom? God's time for humankind and being for humankind are not what hu-

---

64. For the seventeenth-century abandonment of these in favor of the soul as internal to the individual, see Isabel Rivers, *Reason, Grace and Sentiment: A Study of the Language of Religion and Ethics in England, 1660-1780*, Volume 2: *Shaftesbury to Hume* (Cambridge: Cambridge University Press, 2000); Frederick C. Beiser, *The Sovereignty of Reason: The Defense of Rationality in the Early English Enlightenment* (Princeton: Princeton University Press, 1996), pp. 139-40, 165-71; Susan James, *Passion and Action: The Emotions in Seventeenth-Century Philosophy* (Oxford: Clarendon, 1997); Raymond Martin and John Barresi, *Naturalization of the Soul: Self and Personal Identity in the Eighteenth Century* (London: Routledge, 2000); Michael Losonsky, *Enlightenment and Action from Descartes to Kant: Passionate Thought* (Cambridge: Cambridge University Press, 2001).

mankind inflicts on God or what God must suffer involuntarily, but is God's determination to be for human beings and with them. Time must be understood not as non-personal substance (or equally, absence), but as the action of God who has time for us.[65] Only thus is it a question about God's condescension to suffer and bear us, to take our weight, to be measured (and timed) by us.

The modern concept of time represents our refusal to concede the continuing personhood of the persons of the past. The refusal to understand temporality as debit and credit of being makes all being the same. Time is then only what passes without in any way effecting what is. These two concepts of fleeting time and unchanging being constitute the economy of modernity.[66] Christianity was being reduced to mere pietistic soul-talk and subjectivity that reproduces a dualism of intellectual and sensible realms.[67] Spirit, the concept of God at work in the world, without theological conceptual maintenance work slowly separates under the pressure of the idealism of the tradition, reverting to serve a dualism between body and spirit, between physics and metaphysics, teleology and human action. We have to ensure that our theological concepts remain in touch with the biological, chemical, and physical. In this way theology can refer to the world and be scientific, and science can be brought into conversation with teleology, so that discus-

---

65. The oneness and indivisibility of space (infinitely and uniformly divisible) we associated with Newton is the concept of the oneness, simplicity, and indivisibility of God. The concept of space derives from that of spirit: it is a displaced pneumatology. Newton's space is all-equal, absolute sameness, identity, endless divisibility, and multipliability of all things equally, and thus the abolition of difference. Time (= the uniformity of time) represents the idiom of spirituality in the economy of modernity.

66. We can ask whether modernity is any more than a shrill discourse of the accelerating rate of change that results from the separation of time from event and teleology.

67. Alan M. Olson, *Hegel and the Spirit: Philosophy and Pneumatology* (Princeton: Princeton University Press, 1992), p. 151, explains that Hegel was concerned that theology was being taken over by a conception of Spirit reduced to mere subjectivity. This subjectivist reduction was particularly pronounced in Christology in which Christianity is reduced to an emotivistic mystery cult focused on the personality of Jesus. Schleiermacher encouraged this subjectivism by failing to address adequately the content implicit in the trinitarian conception. Hegel therefore opted for "speculative pneumatology as the center of his system, since it was his conviction that only Spirit, considered in its fullness, could reconcile without compromise faith and knowledge." Michael Welker, *God the Spirit* (Minneapolis: Fortress, 1994), p. 289, asserts that "Hegel is correct when he notes with sadness that the 'speculative consideration and knowledge of the nature and activity of spirit has declined . . . in recent times, even to the point of losing even a vague notion of it.'"

sion of human action is kept in conversation with what is.[68] Without reference to the work and ends of God, we have no way of distinguishing between needs and desires, no means of discerning the proper necessity laid on us. We only really know and act when we receive our knowledge and action as the gifts that give us our place in the purpose of God.

This conception of a continuum of movement helps to take us beyond the dualism of inside and outside. With it we do not have to think in terms of the opposed domains of mind and the world. We can avoid some of the effects of dualism by a concept of continuum. A continuum is in fact a concept of spirit, a pneumatology. The logic of the many relationships of this continuum is complex, recursive, even contrapuntal. But such conceptuality gives us another set of tools. Our intention is not at all to do away with the old subject-object logic. We need to make contrasts, so we need subject-object logic for a Christology, the means by which we can confess that we are not God, that creation is not divine. But we will need this additional non-dualist logic for a pneumatology, by which we can confess that the world is held united to God by God, that the Spirit makes it known, but that it may not be known without him.

5.6. Metaphysics as Theological Task

5.6.1. Theology and the Economy of Modernity

The belief that we are post-metaphysical and that knowledge is unproblematic is an indication of how securely we have set ourselves within a one-world economy. I have indicated that this claim to be one is a function of a

---

68. Dietrich Ritschl, *The Logic of Theology: A Brief Account of the Relationship between Basic Concepts in Theology* (London: SCM, 1986), calls for a theology that can engage in a more energetic conversation with the whole range of metaphysics, which requires a more trinitarian, less dualist theology. "Over against the (Augustinian) restriction of theology to the relationship between God and humanity (or the soul) there were constant serious attempts to think in terms of the triangle God-humanity-nature" (p. 51). And similarly D. W. Hardy, "Christ and Creation," in *The Incarnation: Ecumenical Studies in the Nicene-Constantinopolitan Creed,* ed. T. F. Torrance (Edinburgh: Handsel Press, 1981), points out that "Our inherited presuppositions cause us to read the Gospel in thoroughly mentalistic and moral terms, giving most attention to Jesus' self-consciousness and intentions, rather than in spatio-temporal, physico-chemical, biological and socio-cultural terms" (p. 100).

totalitarian claim to comprehend everything. This oneness is a function of many worldviews and metaphysics that constitute an illusory plurality. Christianity is an address to all metaphysics that cooperate in this single economy. These metaphysics are the languages of the nations of the world, and the gospel speaks all languages to speak to all nations. For four centuries and more, the critical and skeptical effort of philosophy has been directed solely against ontology; meanwhile our everyday practices, without ontology as the conceptuality of participation by which we could recognize them and unthink them, are lost, mired in the habits of criticism itself become ontology. Because we have not cultivated the conceptuality by which to see our everyday action as determined by our own history, our everyday habits have become to us a nature.[69] The theological task involves interaction with the metaphysical tradition to identify competing orientation schemas, to contest them, and to play them off one against the other. I have argued that theology must respond to and — where it is required in correction — employ a dualist metaphysic that allows us to distinguish one economy from another and to say that what we presently have is not yet what God intends for us. And I have argued that theology must also respond to and employ a *non*-dualist metaphysic that does not contrast body and mind, material and spiritual, but allows that there are modes of bodiliness, and that some constitute a better performance of bodiliness than others. God intends for us that performance which brings us from poorer modes, through richer modes, into one economy with him. Since this economy is the work of the Holy Spirit, we should call this properly bodily and creaturely performance "spiritual."

There is therefore no abdication from the work of metaphysics. The Enlightenment has not removed this responsibility from us. Ian Hunter argues that there was not one but several rival enlightenments, each with its own abjuration of ontology and its replacement by an anthropology of its own.[70]

---

69. Norbert Samuelson, "The Death and Revival of Jewish Philosophy," *Journal of the American Academy of Religion* 70, no. 1 (2002): 121, argues that "Most of the concerns that characterised pre-twentieth century philosophy have moved to disciplines other than philosophy. . . . [T]he places today to master this art are departments of mathematics, linguistics, cognitive sciences and the life sciences, not departments of philosophy."

70. Hunter, *Rival Enlightenments*, pp. 23-24: "In Pufendorf's natural law we discover a political anthropology of man as a creature whose violent passions threaten his capacity for sociality, thereby necessitating the creation of a sovereign power capable of imposing the rules of sociability as law. Leibniz's practical philosophy, however, is grounded in his platonic 'monadology', treating man as an intellectual soul capable of participating in the di-

There is "no sharp break between these philosophies and Christian theology, and no epochal shift from a religious age to a secular 'age of reason.'"[71] Milbank argues that there must be an ongoing metaphysical task. Doctrine must not become constrained by a metaphysic that dichotomizes inner and outer space. Being and space must be kept complex.[72]

I suggested in Chapter 2 that there is not one time, but many warring times. We must therefore say again that there has been no collapse of mediation. There is no linear development from mediate to immediate, from religion to secularity, from heteronomy to autonomy. As it is told by the Western tradition, the myth of progress is myth, not history. Modernity and postmodernity are no more than these two beliefs, first in the steady coming into being of new time, and secondly in the singleness of time. They are the conceptual equivalent of what previous ages knew as *spirit*. This myth of a single, seamless, and inexorable time, the protological ontology, understands us to be both pushed and pushing forward, out of the ground of dead materiality, up into the air of new open space. But it is our theological task to subject this monistic time to theological criticism. In our discussion of secularity, the collapse of mediation, and modernity, therefore, it is not a matter of preferring one metaphysic, metaphor, or model. It is about responding to, and transforming, all such pagan cosmologies and metaphysics.[73] The problem is not excessive Platonism or

---

vine intellection of the substance, and thereby perfecting himself through contemplation. Following Pufendorf's footsteps, Thomasius' quasi-epicurean anthropology of passional man necessitates an ethics of self-restraint and a jurisprudence of sovereign command. Finally, in Kant's anthropology of man's dual intelligible-sensible natures, we encounter a further elaboration of the metaphysical *homo duplex* driving Kant to construct an ethics and politics in terms of man's self-purifying recovery of his self-governing rational being."

71. Hunter, *Rival Enlightenments*, p. 25.

72. John Milbank, "Sacred Triads: Augustine and the Indo-European Soul," *Modern Theology* 13 (1997): 461, argues that "properly speaking, there are no internal spaces: an internal space is only a fold which can be unfolded and so re-externalised. Every inside can be penetrated because we really remain always on the outside: we go inside a house, because the outer walls fold inwards, while remaining strictly speaking exterior." A clearer version of this argument is presented by Wolfgang Iser, *The Range of Interpretation* (New York: Columbia University Press, 2000), pp. 102-3. In Chapter 2 I argued for this complex space that is the function of alternation, of recursivity, and therefore of persons.

73. In Chapter 6 I argue that theology must confront not only the dualism produced by the complex history of the interrelationship of Aristotelianisms and Platonisms, but also the non-dualist discourses of Epicureanism and Stoicism that account for the concept of nature that supports the economy of modernity.

Aristotelianism, nor is the object the achievement of a Christian world-view or metaphysic. There are many competing paganisms, and Christianity is in conflict with them. Christian theology is even, according to Bayer, "a science of conflict."[74]

5.6.2. *Scripture and the Economy of Modernity*

Scripture is the resource of imagination and desire. The church reads this resource in order to cultivate a new desire and calls on God to release us from our self-imposed predicament, whatever it might be. This way it can give a more theological definition to the concepts of emotion, passion, and time. This allows us to regard things in the world, not as alien to us, but as our own (plural) action and product and as the frame of future action. Then we can see things as the products of the generosity of God, passed to us by previous generations and renewed by the relationships and gratitude in which they are received. Modernity can discern no difference between Israel's Scripture, doctrine, and law and all Western writing and institution building. Without Scripture there is no law, and without law there is no concept of givenness or otherness. There is no understanding of creation as an act of hospitality, with the result that the things of the world remain inert and unredeemed, openings not taken. The disappearance of the concept of law, of Scripture as the address of God to humanity, is the story of accommodation to human autonomy and the disintegration of law and Scripture into the mere marking of successive ages, the passing of that time which is the currency of modernity.[75] The attempt to say that Israel has no place in the West or that the West has taken its ethics and self-identity not from Israel, but from some other source purely its own, is an attempt to make the economy of modernity safe from the threat of the economy of the one God.[76]

The Bible is a resource for the imaging of possible futures. The claim

---

74. Oswald Bayer, "Theology in the Conflict of Interpretations — Before the Text," *Modern Theology* 16 (2000): 501.

75. Rose, *Dialectic of Nihilism*, pp. 131-70, makes this argument.

76. Rose, *Mourning Becomes the Law* (Cambridge: Cambridge University Press, 1996), p. 86, argues that the "desire to conceive of law and coercion as absolutely distinct from the good and the community . . . represents one of the main ways in which modern Jewish thought participates in a methodological and substantive divorce which characterises the development of modern philosophy in its separation of ethics from the social analysis of the ways in which authority is legitimised."

of the Scriptures of Israel is that they are about God only because God is not only their speaker but their first hearer, reader, and performer. The Scriptures have their reception, implementation, and confirmation in him. On this basis alone can the Bible be properly read as literature of the development of the imagination and desire of a people. Indeed, all Western institution building can equally be understood as a work of imagination, for politics, contract making, and conventions of autonomy all claim to open and enable a future. The category of literature is therefore essential for the Scriptures. But equally essential is the category of history, talk of the world in terms of the truth of what has been.[77] The Bible is reducible neither to imagination nor to history — nor even to the two together. "Law" is a third term we can employ in the heuristic and orthopaedic senses set out in Chapter 2. The difference between literature and history is the same as that between the imagination of Israel and the imagination of the gentiles, for whom the future means just more of the past, history without purpose or end. Theology understands that Israel is in charge of the work of imagination, knowing that Israel will use its own resource of its history with its God to that end, not the wish-lists of the nations. As the one elected by God, Israel is the guarantor and medium that there will be a future for the nations. This future will not be in their history, but in Israel's history, the history that the one God shares with Israel. Exploration and recovery of the past is the whole idiom of the future. By the exercise of grief and lament, our expectations may be expanded and we may come to know that nothing has been made impossible yet, because the God of Israel can open again what has been closed. There is such a thing as a future, and it consists in the ability of Israel's God to keep things in play. In this future, the past is no longer past, but is rather opened and sustained in life, and itself becomes alive and life-generating.

We have dealt with the Scriptures as mediation under the rubrics of history, literature, and law. I have suggested that we must understand each of these in terms of its relationship with the others. We must first tell the story and then discuss its grammar and the concepts used in it. There is no talking about history without subsequently making clear who is talking,

---

77. In Chapter 3 we saw Perdue and Balentine argue that Scripture ceased first to be law, and then to be history, and that it has become instead merely imagination, "narrative." We also saw Fowl, Wright, and Hays argue for constitutive narrative, at least for the ancient world by which the economy of modernity assumes Israel is confined.

who it is that is telling that history and is able to tell that history because it is one to which the speaker is party. History cannot be obediently told without regular interruption by commentary work, which clears away the conceptual debris and allows the history to continue. History is the building together of relationship: the work of criticism and judgment and the conceptual ancillary work of philosophy are a necessary part of this building. I set out the charge made by the economy of modernity, most explicitly by Spinoza and Kant, that Israel was incapable of self-government and thus unfit for any wider leadership role. I have said that Israel is the leadership of the West. Only Israel in the person of its Messiah, by the exercise of its Scripture and law, can read the whole entity and action (writing) of the West. Israel can read this Western being as the transformation of the gentiles by baptism into constitutive association with the people of God's election. Israel interrupts and saves Western being from succumbing to utter captivity by imagining for it, and witnessing to it, what it could be within the economy of the one God. The proper basis of such an account is theological, one that relates it to the account God gives of his place.

In summary, then, we have to tell a better story. But now we are able to turn this statement around. We are in a position to apply the logic of the rediscovered hermeneutics of narrative and communitarian ethics, introduced in Chapter 3, to the Western tradition. At last we can say that not only do we write, but we are also *written*. We are the objects of the narration of another. We have to be told again into a better story, by a better historian who is a more expansive and compassionate storyteller. We have to be imagined afresh by a narrator who can sketch a new and larger image of us. We have to be taken out of the place given by that narrative and those master metaphors, in which we have placed ourselves and become trapped. We have to be reunited with our abandoned plotlines and given a new chance to resolve them. We can do this only in dialogue with our narrator — one in which we may play a junior but willing partner. The Western tradition is not just writing, however. It is life, full of interaction and construction. But this life is not free in the sense given by an atomistic metaphysic. It is free because it is to a degree delineated for us. This means that it is a tradition of writing, and as such it is also in a most serious sense our Scripture, for it is the script we have no means of departing from. It describes and determines who we are. It is therefore not just *writing* that is written. The *world* is written, and *we* are written. The pathways available to us are in part laid down ahead of us.

Not only do we build institutions, but we are built and placed by them. They support us or constrict us. The Western tradition is the edifice in which we live. It has been put together by all previous generations of our predecessors, and our own present action also contributes to it. As it stands, this building is too constrictive to enable us to bring one another up to maturity. It has not allowed us the action of investing in one another, presenting one another, and making one another present, which I referred to first as a doxological ontology and then by the properly theological term "sacrifice." The Western edifice allows room for only one protagonist, the individual, and so ensures that every would-be individual is in conflict with every other. The structure of this building is that way of being allowed by the logic of the Western narrative, itself determined by the schemas and templates that make up the economy of modernity. This house has to be taken apart and put back together again. All the elements that form this structure have to be disassembled and properly reassembled. They have to be reordered by the master builder to make it the place in which we can live together.

CHAPTER 6

The Economy of the One God

God sustains a place for humankind. The people of God are the first brought into this hospitable economy. They are to be the witnesses to God of the liberation from alien economies and imperatives that he provides. Rival gods, the world, our mundane practices, and modernity must all feature in our account of the God who is for us.

In Chapters 3 and 4 I examined the relationship between Christian doctrine and biblical studies. I approached this relationship as though it was a dialogue, albeit sometimes a very distant one. I asked how far biblical studies was obeying Kant's injunction to control access to Scripture and delimit the discourse of Christian doctrine, by the exercise of what he claimed was a more universal rationality. I suggested that biblical studies was not the immediate exegesis of what is simply to be found in the Bible. It was also promoting — largely inadvertently, to be sure — the program of an elite anxious to remove itself from public accountability, a program given philosophical expression by Kant. In Chapter 5 we began to ask whether we can see things the other way around. Can we understand the world in the terms Scripture offers? Does the world absorb the Scriptures? Or do the Scriptures open up the world to make it a larger world?

6.1. Scripture in the Economy of God

We have gathered a number of resources to serve as a means of talking about the world, a hermeneutic. With them we can also articulate a hermeneutic of Scripture. Scripture and doctrine have, of course, already had

211

their impact on the formation of this hermeneutic. We have introduced the thought that Scripture is exegesis of the world. In a moment, with these resources, we can attempt to speak about Scripture in a quite new way that will enable us to see Scripture as part of the effort that renews creation.

I argued that God brings his people into agency by processes of learning and sanctification that are led by the creation liturgy of Israel. We saw that the action of Israel goes out from God, is made visible in the liturgy of Israel's priests and worshipers, and returns to be integrated into the economy of God's action. I have argued that performance is accompanied by commentary: action is interpreted in public and expert discussion, which serves to alter and create new action. Sacrifice, and the teaching and worship that offer commentary on it, proceed together; one is not prior to the other. Though it is subject to the usual processes of public discussion, Israel's liturgical action, the participation of this people in its own being made holy, does not allow itself to be interpreted in terms that Israel has not adopted for the purpose. It is not available to the sight of those outside Israel. The question of who can read the Scriptures and interpret the liturgical action is also the question of who can read Israel. God is the constitutive reader and arbiter of Israel.

God is the guarantor that it really is his law that Israel has. The law is the instruction and the process of joint target-setting that enable implementation and compliance. In addition to dialogue and narrative, the law takes the form of propositions. Since those party to these propositions know them, they are able to develop a shorthand for these propositions. As a result, Scripture is full of complex summary statements that are unreadable to outsiders. Israel and its God together share the knowledge that Israel will grow into the action and territory opened to it by God. Because Israel knows this, Israel can say that it is not yet what it will be. This is what Israel does in confessing its deficiency and failure. The concept of sin is therefore meaningful only to the people under this instruction and discipline. Outsiders may not decide that the people of God have forfeited their place before God. The gentiles, and thus Christians, may speak about the failure of the people of God only in the course of learning from Israel, in the form of Israel's Scriptures, how to receive the generosity of God, and so not to fail.

6.1.1. The Role of Scripture

Building on the argument of Chapter 2, we can say that Scripture is the learner's articulation of the lesson she receives from her instructor. This lesson can be read only in partnership with Israel, by the baptized community that has been given the Spirit by the obedient Son. Thus the Christian can learn only within the Christian community, and only as this community itself learns from Israel, properly recapitulated by the Son. The Son transforms our movements into those of the community refigured by him. Scripture is the orthopedic tool by which a new set of practices are taught; it is the set of protocols that learners must learn to internalize so that the Word of God becomes their own mind and word. The single intention of the law is to propel its students toward adulthood and toward the stature of Jesus Christ. The process of the production of the holy people is not finished. The discernment of progress, and thus the exercise of judgment, is part of the process of refinement. But if the law itself has become disordered, or if Scripture is no longer properly heard, the law can no longer order people into the place right for each. The law without the Spirit only has the effect of stalling our growth. If this were the case, the law, good and necessary to us in each specific stage, would confine us within it, just when we should be released and encouraged forward to the next stage. The law is designed to build us up, but it needs to be maintained itself, and Christian doctrine needs to be kept in good order, so that it performs this purpose of building up a people. The law is effective as long as the instructor is present to the learning community in the person of the Spirit. Separated from the Spirit who serves Christ, it cannot do this. When the garment of the law is worn by Christ, it takes its form from him and is able to give us his stature.

Scripture tells us about the Son in order to propel us forward toward him. But it not only moves us toward God; it also protects us from him. Scripture is the screen or visor by which we are protected from the brightness of the Word. Like the veil with which Moses protected those who saw him, Scripture acts as the screen that lets the brilliance of God filter slowly through to us, gently promoting our growth, rather than allowing it to blaze out to endanger us. Scripture protects us, and is the means to discern that the world protects us, from God. It represents the gentle, not-all-at-once-ness of the Word of God.

A community forms Scripture and is formed by it. The action of Israel that we have received in the form of Scripture and liturgy topples the alternative constructions of the gentiles and prevents the world from knitting itself together into any form other than the form of Christ. It is the one action that keeps the world open, reminding us that the Messiah is not here, and that what the world presently is, is not the end. True reading produces the transformation of the readers, so hermeneutics *is* ethics, the reading of people into the church. The spiritual sons of Abraham are the ones who can tell the story of Abraham. Their narration of the action of God is witness to their paternity. God, the first actor of Scripture, creates a community composed of patriarchs, prophets, and saints, into which we are to be integrated. He makes this cloud of witnesses and this diversity of speech and action shape us. God creates these many words and voices, and this crowd, for us. This crowd surrounds and accompanies us and gives us our place. The witnesses of the Old and New Testaments form a single chorus that cheers and shouts warning and encouragement. They line the road on which we now travel after the Son, willing us on, lifting us with their breath, and driving us along after him. They urge us not to give ourselves away to those other lords who prey on us, and they tell us to pass their encouragement and warning on. They are conveyors and amplifiers of prayers, who make the requests we do not yet know how to make for ourselves. The Holy Spirit utters these patriarchs, prophets, and saints and bears their voices to us. In turn they bear and utter the Son and are made holy in the process. But these many witnesses are not replaced by the Son. The New Testament does not replace or displace the Old Testament. These many witnesses, the Old Testament as much as the New, now mediate Christ to us. As he mediates them, they mediate him, and all their mediation is his work.

The one Son does not replace the many people who belong to him. He is the guarantor of their continuing manyness. He starts a community, and he is its definition, but he does not represent its end. Rather, he grows and expands it without limit. The manyness of these witnesses to the Son, themselves provided by him, is our protection against the intensity of his otherwise unmediated presence. Their presence to us in the form of the liturgy and the writtenness of Scripture is the protection the Son presently gives us. Scripture is therefore the screen by which we see the Son at work, while we remain secured within the crowd of witnesses represented by Scripture. This scripturally and liturgically mediated mode of our life means that we cannot see God at work *now*, in the events of our own history. It is a safeguard precisely against that. It means that we can only see

God at work *then,* in that time, a time now closed and removed from us. We can see these witnesses, but only in static form, so though we can see them, they cannot be touched by us. They are separated from us as by a mirrored window. They see us in real time, but we see them only as unchanging portraits and receive their voices only in the form of the liturgy. They hand the deposit and rule of faith to us, as something written and performed, and we must hand this whole tradition on without loss.

Now we can say that theology is commentary on the action of the earthly community, the church, which is learning to understand itself as the work of the company of heaven. If we concede that the plurality represented by the Christian community is inaugurated by heavenly company and assembly, then theology can treat this sociality and community as its proper object, and it will be a science obedient to the self-revelation of the trinitarian and social God. The Father and the Son, two witnesses who agree, send the Spirit to provide many witnesses to themselves. God is not only one witness but many witnesses. What makes this account different, then, is that it does not make unity prior to sociality. Manyness and one-ness are equally fundamental. By putting plurality co-equal with unity, we make the Bible not one object, but many objects, and not objects only, but subjects. These subjects are witnesses and therefore persons, so in this account persons are fundamental. This means that we avoid the problem created by two objects, the Bible and the reader, only one of which can be subject.

6.1.2. Scripture Brings Embodiment

Jesus holds the life of the generations of Israel. Scripture is the clothing by which he holds them and the process by which he prepares them one for another. He is the agent by which this clothing changes from external cladding (Scripture) to internal structure (embodiedness). The patriarchs are bound up with each other in the web and fabric of the Son. He is raised from them, because their bonds — *death* — fail to hold him. His being raised — from them — is the guarantee that they are sealed in him and that his call will raise and assemble them. His resurrection makes them all present to him. Only in him, by his Spirit, will they become present to each other. These many generations of Israel are made present to us only in the mode of Scripture. The Son wears them bound about him, as his garment. They are not immediately present — resurrected — either to each other or to us. They are hidden from each other in different pockets of time, held together only by their one Lord. They look forward to the day of Christ. Then the Spirit will raise them and make them present to the Father as the body of the Son. Their resurrection and perfection are dependent also on us. For Scripture to become the full resurrected presence of Israel, we have to be grown and raised as readers and members of Israel, such that we can read them, return their presence to them, and have our presence returned to us by them. Our being found obedient in Christ is the moment at which their waiting is over, and we will be brought together in one assembly. We are not complete until we are united with the patriarchs, and they are not complete until they are united with us.

Scripture prepares us. To this end it protects us and in stages removes this protection from us. The resurrection has already raised this protection from one of our number. His unity with the Father effects the unity and efficacy of Scripture. The patriarchs are presently mediated to us as one single instantiation of Israel, the co-presence of the whole company in the one person, Jesus Christ. As one and complete, he is the arrival of the many. We are being trained to perceive and receive this host in him, the one they have sent ahead. They are present to us as the fabric of the Scripture. Within the fabric of this tabernacle we grow from smaller and simpler into larger and more complex dimensions, each dimension preparing us for the bigger space beyond it, where God and his hosts wait. When this enclosure has become our own body and clothing, it will give way to bring us immediately before one another because we are brought before God.

In Chapter 4 I suggested that Israel is the proper reader of the written self-commentary of the West. Israel is able to pick up the script the West regards as its own and weave it into Israel's own script, to make one new garment. On the cross Jesus takes the world's script away from the world, undoes it, and out of it writes a new and living script. He takes away the gentile mind and there establishes the mind of Christ, the history and law of God and his people. The Scripture of Israel constitutes the new mind for this new people.[1] It is the case law that determinates the modes of behavior by which its members may grow into relationship with one another. Familiarity with these cases, and the keeping of the first-level rules, is the

---

1. If the Scripture of Israel is the mind of Christ, it is also the answer to the question of the psychology of Jesus — one of the phantoms pursued by (supersessionist) New Testament studies.

means by which a new public mind and *sensus communis* comes into being. This is the basis for the development of further levels of rules and a community able to deduce new rules, which in turn is the means of opening a future for one another.

6.2. Immediacy or Formation?

Every philosophical tradition, like every course of education, can be nothing but a course of paideia. It is not only about human formation, but it is itself a project of human formation. It is not merely a description of a static state of affairs, but is itself an endeavor, an intention to make a new state of affairs. Ostensibly the Western philosophical tradition has repudiated paideia. It does not present itself as an explicit syllabus for change, but as a descriptive statement of the natural flow of change. Its excessive concern with change, and its determination to show that everything changes absolutely, conceals its real conservatism. The philosophy of representation, exemplified by Descartes and Kant, has canonized the eye and the mind that can immediately perceive all that it allows before it. In Chapter 2 we saw that the concepts of discursivity (conversation), embodiedness, and learning, given expression by cognitive science, show that this is not how it must be. We should also remind ourselves of the connection to the ontology that we introduced in Chapter 1. The apparatus of visualization, of which writing is a part, makes things appear and gives them their presence. It takes from the *being* of those behind, thereby putting them behind, and gives it to those up front, thereby bringing them to the front and giving them greater being. This preferment and promotion mean that some are advanced while others are dropped; their being is denied them. The Western modern economy of being can only replace one by another, and thus it is a failure to sustain all. Theology must say that an action other than this zero-sum modern economy of immediacy and visualization is available to us in the people of God and the action given to that people. To say this, theology must identify the habits of which the world consists and argue that they represent a failure of being. It can identify writing, representation, and the whole apparatus of intellect as a way in which we fail to return to each other the whole being that God gives us for one another. The modern ascendancy of the practices of writing and representation represents only one, constrictive, mode of being for one another. I have argued that reason should be understood as public conversation, oriented to form a people and bring that people into one conversation about the good. Writing and reasoning, in which we must include the rationality we call economic rationality, is to serve and commentate on this public doing. Its purpose is neither to form an autonomous realm nor to become the whole and only possible idiom of the realm of public doing.

6.2.1. Writing and Formation

We have said that writing is a mode of bodiliness. But writing is a reduction of, and may be an impoverishment of, the whole action of the body. We attempted to recover a sense of the whole action of the social body of the people of God by our discussion of the temple. Here we saw the employment of the temple as a microcosm and platform for the modeling and maintenance that displayed Israel's political and cosmological claim. Israel's liturgy of public drama used procession and animal semiotics to refer to creation and to the on-looking peoples of the world in the course of presenting this people — embodied — before its God. By contrasting the modern schema and economy of representation and writing with Israel's public liturgy, we may concede that the Western economy of writing is a reduction of the whole action of the body. It is a failure to see that the formation of the social body, the community, cannot but be the whole purpose of our action. The activity of writing suggests that there are two worlds, the real world and the world of written representations that reflects it. But the world is not divided into a world of bodiliness and a second world that simply mirrors it. Israel's economy of action can liberate us from the modern schemas that claim to represent an unchanging reality. The modern dualism of being on the one hand and representation of that being on the other does not allow for plural action. It does not concede that, though what we want to see is hidden from our view, it is visible to others, perhaps only to past or future generations. Modernity represents a particular claim to see everything all at once, without the assistance of other viewers. It claims to be a clear and unaided view of the whole field. We believe that our predecessors have no effect on us, that we are simply pushed along by the outward unidirectional flow of time. The hermeneutics of modernity filters out relatedness and complexity, and so it can understand text only as object with a flat surface visible to all, on which words are as univocal as traffic signs.

I have argued that our place is woven and written for us, and only *co-written by* us. We have seen that we can employ the new hermeneutics of narrative, introduced in Chapter 3 with the ideas of Hays, Fowl, and Wright, to show that we weave one another into narratives. Our public being is a function of other people's writing and construction, not merely a function of our own individual wills. It is the work of society to model and imagine for itself new spaces, places, and idioms of relatedness. The whole effort of society is to imagine what is not yet. It is the task of leadership, by the exercise of imagination, to open places that allow us to grow and develop. Scripture is the education of desire through particular resources of memory and imagination; it weaves and writes us a role and a place in the household of God.

6.2.2. The Apparatus of Formation

We are looking for a theological hermeneutic that will faithfully represent the address of God to the world as the work of God on the world. We must now attempt to relate the scriptural hermeneutic we have just sketched with a general hermeneutic, by which I mean not only a way of seeing, but much more a way of interacting with and participating in the transforming of the world.[2] We have seen how writing (representation) has, in large part, come to function as a synonym for *being* in the economy of modernity. This discussion enables us to see Scripture not merely as writing but as constructing a community and a world. Scripture is a form of interacting with the world by which the world suffers change.

2. John Webster, "Hermeneutics in Modern Theology," *Scottish Journal of Theology* 51 (1998): 307-41, distinguishes between a general hermeneutic (represented by Werner Jeanrond) and a special or theological hermeneutic (represented by Francis Watson). A general or universal hermeneutic is a set of descriptions of social human action, bodiliness, and co-presence of the sort offered in Chapter 2. Webster opts for Watson's theological hermeneutic (pp. 309-11). Theology must provide and defend the hermeneutics that is required by its subject matter. This much is true. But theology must also go on the offense and set out to show the limits of any general and therefore worldly hermeneutics. It must deconstruct these worldly hermeneutics by pointing to the histories from which they arose to demonstrate that these do not have the necessity that they claim. Theology is not obliged to provide answers to questions asked by other disciplines, so we do no correlation method here. But theology must hear the world (and so let its interlocutor give some account of itself) and hear it better than the world hears itself, because theology does so hopefully, and therefore with higher ambitions for the world than the world has for itself.

Here two new thoughts may be introduced. Scripture is an interface with an orthopedic function: it redetermines us from within. Scripture is a body prepared for us, a being located and sheltered within a community and a world. First, Scripture is writing in the same sense that software is written or circuitry etched. Each constitutes a network that creates a new action and new complexity within which new dimensions of action may come into being. Scripture is two dimensions that open a third dimension of *time,* thus drawing us into a many-dimensional world. We have already discussed learning in terms of being drawn from simpler to more complex dimensions, and we have related these dimensions to affordance within environments. New circuitry is driven by the old circuitry, but it also alters the old circuitry's output and over the long term makes the total circuitry new. Both software and the bodies (hardware) that open and read it make that software determinative of the operation of the system — or, in this case, the life of the community. This provides us with an alternative means of conceiving the relationship of Scripture and church. Scripture always comes to us in installments, most obviously when read in a liturgical context to a congregation. Each installment of Scripture represents a package of action that redetermines the behavior and constitution of the community that receives it. To stick with the terms employed in this book, we can see these as packets of being, action, otherness (holiness), opportunity, maturity, and freedom. The Scriptures are a set of instructions, each of which becomes available only when the previous installment has been installed and calls it down. Each installment acts as the operating system for the next. In every case these installments act as the mechanism that opens and makes visible, not a set of propositions, but another and further set of variables, dimensions, and affordances.[3] Each set of instructions becomes active in a variety of ways determined by eventualities that cannot always be anticipated.[4] There is no viewpoint from which the Bible can be seen all

3. Don Ihde, *Expanding Hermeneutics: Visualism in Science* (Evanston: Northwestern University Press, 1998), p. 160, argues that "instrumentation is a complex inscription-making device for a visualisable result." We could then call Scripture an "inscription-making device for a visualisable result." Scripture makes humankind visible and readable to the new mind of the Christian community. Imaging technology does not see what is *inside.* That would return us to Descartes's dichotomy of inside and outside. Imaging technologies are expressivist — they constitute their object into an image for us. We develop the skill of reading such analogical representations as representations of wholes.

4. This is to employ the concepts of discursivity (the alternation involved in conversa-

at once. We are therefore not the first reader of the Bible, and Scripture is not first of all information addressed to us. Rather, each installment of Scripture is a set of instructions that serves to bring into being the obedient reading and acting community. Because in this account Scripture does not rely on a receptive mind, we have found a properly non-Cartesian hermeneutic. Scripture does not release its next installment until previous installments have readied the learner to receive it. The term given by the theological tradition to this conception is "sacrament."

The Holy Spirit drops self-assembling installments of the figure and action of Christ into us. The Spirit bypasses the detached and disaffected mind to reorder us from within and to set us to work. These instructions lay down the pathways and circuitry that produces a people with the mature behavior of the people of God. This people is able to receive God's resources from him, to open them to the world, and from the world to return them to God again. It does this in the time God provides, and with successful reception of the time God releases new time and opportunity. We said that the learner and supervisor together articulate the steps and units by which the learner can progressively achieve the fullness of the action of the game. We learn to improve on our performance by analyzing it in progressively simpler idioms and dimensions. I related Scripture to this skill of articulation and analysis of our *habitus* and called it orthopedic. I have linked Scripture to the project of the formation of a people. Only for this holy people would there be a world distinct from them, for which they would be responsible as God's steward. This community is being drawn into the many dimensions of the inexhaustible economy of God. This economy of God appears as two economies, or two dimensions, of bodies and ideas, things and writing, in order to develop the competence and readiness of this new community for the further economies God has for it.

God is the first knower. He is the first reader, both of the world and of all texts in it.[5] He is the new testament and witness. He can open or hold closed. He can open knowledge of himself and break off pieces to nourish us with. The point of submitting hermeneutics to the doctrine of God as judge and knower is to show that all our knowledge is knowledge under li-

---

tion) and recursivity (by which we query any claim of any account to be the single settled version of what has been) introduced in Chapter 2.

5. Christopher Seitz, *Word without End: The Old Testament as Abiding Theological Witness* (Grand Rapids: Eerdmans, 1998), p. 11, argues that "Historical-critical methods and hermeneutics of assent will stand outside and fail to grasp that God is reading us, not we him."

cense. It can be revoked, from a distance, without our realizing. God is not distant from his word; it is immediately with him. This king can close a gate at the other end of his land simply by a nod. With the Bible we have the whole world in our hands, entirely present to us in microcosm.[6] Yet, without him, we are without means to see what it is. We are in reciprocally constitutive relation with our environment. This environment is formed by the whole history of what we have been, an economy of being. Our every effort to distinguish ourselves from everything that is only confirms that we are not finally able to do so. We cannot distinguish ourselves from the totality: our identity is lost in the lump. We can be identified apart from this economy of being only by the God who is able to read and transform our history, and thus transform the way we are. We can be raised from it only by him. He can give us a new and larger place within the eschatological economy. Here, then, we have linked our hermeneutic of Scripture to the doctrine of God, who is not separate from his knowledge of himself, except as he makes this knowledge gentle enough to do us good. This is a pneumatology, an account of the coming of the Son modulated by the Spirit. And it makes this work, of which Scripture is the medium, ontological: we are reconstituted, brought into being, freed, and made holy. Again, this eschatological ontology understands that we are not ourselves without other people.

6.3. The Protological Ontology

But theology is not only speech about God. It has to start with talk about God, and it has to come back to talk about God; but in order for our speech to become *theological* it also has to talk about the *world*, understood as God's world. Truthful talk about God is a good practice that can turn other practices to the good. Practices constitute the field from which ideas emerge, and ideas constitute the field from which practices emerge. Our discussion is not for the sake of ideas only, but so that better ideas inform us and improve our practices and make a richer life. We must not attempt

---

6. David S. Yeago, "Jesus of Nazareth and Cosmic Redemption: The Relevance of St. Maximus the Confessor," *Modern Theology* 12 (1996): 182, finds Maximus making a similar claim: "The cosmos, then, is a sort of Bible, and the Bible is a cosmos, each at once concealing and revealing the Logos."

to go beyond talk of practices, persons, and their objects, for then what we say would serve only to distinguish and separate the spiritual from the material. It would be dualizing and spiritualizing, and it would result in our failure to know the world as the act of God's hospitality.[7]

The world addressed by the Word of God is not one. It is in itself many words and claims. The Word breaks up this world and commandeers and re-gathers these words to give them a new place and employment within God's economy. God's words return to him and are commissioned by him for us again. In the person of the ascended God-man who sits at the right hand of the Father, humankind returns this Word from the world to God. In him all the speech of the world is caught up in the speech the Father receives again as his own. The world makes the claim to be one. The doctrine of the one God says that it is not the world but God who is one. I have argued that a number of accounts must be present in any attempt to talk about the world. We cannot simply say what the world is or what modernity is. Theology must be aware of the range of conversations to which it must remain committed, for its task is to make such conversations feel the challenge to their autonomy that theological discourse represents. All theological statement intends to make statements about the world properly complex to prevent every would-be definitive statement of the world until the world is reconciled with its Lord.

One moment in our account of the speech of God must include the resistance met by the Word. This resistance is both *us*, the many, in our all reluctance, and the *opponent*, whose grip holds us bound as a single undifferentiated entity. The Word of God must break the grasp of this single opponent on us before we, the many, may even start to hear this Word for

---

7. We must therefore offer three accounts in parallel:
   1. a PERSON-PERSON account.
   2. a PERSON-THING-PERSON account, which is also a PERSON-WORLD-PERSON account.
   3. a GOD-HUMANITY-WORLD-CREATION-WORLD-HUMANITY-GOD account.

The "object" in the term GOD-OBJECT-GOD is the term GOD-WORLD-HUMANITY, in which form God prepares us to take our place in the scheme HUMANITY-CREATION-GOD. Dietrich Ritschl, *The Logic of Theology: A Brief Account of the Relationship between Basic Concepts in Theology* (London: SCM Press, 1986), p. 151, complains that the development of a trinitarian doctrine of creation in terms of the threesome GOD-HUMANITY-NATURE and of new creation was supplanted by an Augustinian restriction of theology to God and humanity (or the soul). The "Greek" PERSON-PERSON schema lacks a world and remains ideational. With less than three terms, theology will not be theological, but only dualizing.

ourselves. All the would-be plurality of the world is sham. It serves only to produce a single homogenous entity that obliterates all particularity. It holds us captive. But it is our action that creates this captivity. The Word of God therefore addresses first two parties: Satan and his world; then three parties: Satan, the world, and us; and finally, with the defeat of Satan, two parties again — the world and us. We can be distinguished from the world only when Satan is defeated, and he is beaten only when the world can be distinguished from us and we from it. Only then do we cease to be everything and become instead creatures who are given our place by God.

Kant did not concede that the Word is met by resistance. The limits he outlined for theology suppose that we are as individuals already ready and able to hear the Word of God and that the world is a place of peace in which every such claim can be freely heard and weighed. A trinitarian theology must meet this Kantian theology and anthropology with an account that says that the world must first be released from the compulsion that creates this single demonic economy of being. This being and this opposition must be addressed both as not-yet-one and as not-yet-many. The world is nothing but opposing forces, one outcome of which is the enforcement of a unity and uniformity that prevent the emergence of the humankind and anthropology that Kant hopes for. This world declares itself one, complete, and autonomous, but the address of God interrupts this world and reveals declaration to be false.

The economy of modernity claims to be one and to be one without God. It denies hearing or receiving anything that is not itself. It therefore claims that the Word of God has given way to the secular word of humankind and has been proved to be just one of its own many words. It is therefore not enough to talk, as modern theology does, only of God's Word, without going on to account for who can hear and receive this Word. It is in its reception and return that this Word becomes act and creates an economy of speech and action. We must account for the reception of God's Word in terms of the defeat and redeployment of other rival words. God is able to recover his Word from the world and from whatever interloper attempts to withhold it from him.

The world of the economy of modernity claims to be a single being that is a function of nature and the totality of all that is. This monist and protological world-claim demands that what knowledge we have of God must meet the criterion it sets for certainty. It believes that we know God, as we know the world, without the mediation of God or any other creature.

Both are ours, as pure object, passively and immediately before us. Indeed, God cannot be anything but this totality. Modernity is an economy of vision based on a cosmology in which we are as serene and disembodied as Olympians, completely able to survey and command all that is. This claim is the result of a development in which criteria for knowledge of God became criteria for the knowledge of the world. But God must first take away from us this world that we know unequivocally and immediately so that we will be saved from becoming the totality we claim — and so that the world is saved from us.

This protology has its own history and is itself a story. In the *Timaeus* and *Republic*, Plato described a hierarchy of being: at the top were the *forms* or *ideas*, and at the bottom was the miasma of this life. In this cosmology the upper realm represented unity, oneness, and good order. All that belongs to the upper realm rises and returns to it, while all materiality and formlessness sink down to form a morass without unity or order. The upper realm has all reality, action, and unity; the lower reality is less real, is passive, and is broken into many contending fragments. It has only whatever reality, action, and unity the upper realm lends it. In the *Timaeus* the two were indissolubly one cosmos, a totality in which the world and humankind and god together constituted a single divine being. Subsequent neo-Platonic developments introduced more complex layers and ladders of intermediaries, a chain of being. Plato's was the most sophisticated version of the world's description of itself as this single being. It therefore rightly featured in the Christian account of the world; it was responded to, condemned, and corrected against the totality of Christian doctrine and the ongoing liturgical work of the Christian confession of the triune God who creates something that is not himself.

In the *Republic* the lower realm was described negatively, as that which had no strong reality or unity. In the course of the philosophical tradition, however, and particularly under the pressure of the positive Christian description of the world, this lower realm became the realm of empirical experience. In the medieval period, the vision of God was the purpose and object of all knowing. But with the loss of the liturgical mediation of knowledge, this object of our vision ceased to be the God who makes himself object for our sake. It became ever more firmly the empirical object of the senses and the world, until the beatific vision became simply a vision of the world understood as an object that could play no part in our coming to know it. The upper realm was all form, number, and oneness itself. But in the course of centuries of complex Christian and Islamic appropriation and development of neo-Platonic and Aristotelian traditions, the lower realm took on much of the attributes of the upper. The result was that by the end of the seventeenth century what was empirical came to have an unproblematic oneness and unity. What was once the lower realm, which had no unity, became the criterion of unity. Where Christian theological mediation was surrendered, in part by a determination to raise God above involvement in earthly concerns, God became more distant and decreasingly the agent of his own mediation. The lower realm of the object of the senses loomed larger until it eclipsed the upper realm altogether. Did the upper realm go into eclipse, declining and then disappearing altogether? We have a quite different story to tell.

The upper realm disappeared *as realm,* but the tradition did not abandon this dualist up-and-down cosmology. The upper realm grew. It did so because we elevated ourselves to it. The observer became the upper realm, and with him all considerations of how he, or rather we, know. The upper realm ceased to be the place of the serene and distant gods.[8] Instead, it became the serene internal Cartesian self that was first sure of himself and then sure of everything that he could make appear before him. The lower realm became the object, things in the world, chief among which are other people. So we still have two worlds, subject (above) and object (below). But their twoness is bogus. One claims to be the control on the other, but neither of them, subject or object, can be this. The object merely reflects the subject, for wherever he looks the subject sees only what he chooses, and whatever he sees serves only to confirm what he has allowed to appear before him. The object may be merely his own reflection. He lives in a world that may be fantasy, but since he does not allow his sole rule to be challenged, he allows no criteria by which this world could be tested for reality. What had been the upper realm became the rule of the knowing subject; the social sciences refer to this unaccountable rule as *theory* or *method.* But is the world then any more than a reflection or fiction of this unaccountable demonic knowing subject?[9]

The economy of modernity believes it knows its world. It admits to a

8. Plato, *Phaedrus* 247.

9. It makes no difference whether we say that the world is the lower realm (object), and we (subject) are the upper realm that looks down on it, or whether we say that our knowing power (subjectivity) is the (hidden) basis and platform on which the world is present to us.

theory of perception — that is, it identifies objects that it claims are not itself. It does not admit to an ontology — that is, it does not admit that it is itself part of what is, and therefore part of what can be identified as an object. It believes it has left behind all questions of the mediation of being. It believes it no longer needs to answer enquiries about how to get from the lower sphere to the upper, from fleeting sense-impressions to knowledge of unchanging forms, from the parts to the whole. It wants to cease to be passive and subject to time and become unchanging and impassive — divine. It believes that it is post-metaphysical. But its very own *action* of knowing *is* that upper realm. It is that realm as *action,* rather than as object. How has it arrived at this serene assurance of its own ability to identify objects and never to be itself an object of inquiry? Modern knowledge, which sees through and pushes aside all mediation, remains indissolubly part of the one indivisible cosmology in which the upper sphere knows — *intellects* — the lower. The modern epistemological constitution, far from being an escape from this dualist cosmology, is a continuation of it. Action, chief of which is *knowing* and *dividing* and *uniting,* continues to represent that upper realm. *Knowing* is not merely mirroring at all: knowing is the whole mode by which we *act* on one another. We define one another as passive to our act of knowing. But on this basis can we know others at all? Modern epistemology or cosmology is dualist. Yet, since it cannot concede that there is anything outside itself, it is monist. It cannot break out of this oscillation between two and one, and so it cannot tolerate the possibility of plurality.

Christian theology must respond to this metaphysics that is now disguised as epistemology. Theology requires a set of protocols that control the claims of knowledge. It identifies the claim to immediate knowledge as a theological claim, in the sense that the Platonic cosmology represents a pre-Socratic *theology.* It is not secular, but religious, just where it takes itself to be most secular. Christian theology must say that humankind does not know God where God does not give himself to be known. Equally importantly, it must say that humankind does not know the *world* where God does not give the world to be known. This latter claim is missing from modern theology, which has been taken in by the mock modesty with which science has relinquished the claim to have knowledge of God for the apparently more limited claim to have knowledge of the world. Just as in the Platonic cosmology the intellect or sphere of theory knew and mastered the lower realm, so the modern practices of perception do not allow that anything could resist being known by the knowing subject. In Platonic cosmology the upper and lower realms made one cosmos and one being, so the knower is not finally different from what he knows. It is precisely this belief of the Western tradition — that it has, by its theory of perception, escaped ontology — that keeps the Western tradition firmly within this cosmology in which the divine *knows* the earthly, and, by its being known, the earthly confirms this self-perception of the divine, and the two make a single entity and god.

The world we now claim to know makes a claim to unity that is derived from this protological ontology. The object status of the world is the reflection of our status as intellect and subject. We know the world because it is brought into being precisely by our knowing. We have a non-mediate knowledge of it. When the question of God is raised, we seek a non-mediate knowledge of God as just another object-in-the-world. Does God have existence, or does he give this sort of empirical evidence of himself? The two spheres of the Intellect and Sense, now the Subject and his Object, have drawn the world into two poles and swept away all complexity and reciprocity of relation to leave a clear floor between them. The question of the otherness of God — of there being something outside this totality — has become only the question of our knowing and the perpetual labor of the confirmation of our status as subject. The subject of the economy of modernity does not care to accept external discipline or to receive his place and purpose from others. He does not find them authoritative for saying who he is, for his inner self is prior to such an external world, and external restraint is inimical to his being. In this economy we are each of us a god and participate in that god that is totality.

The economy of modernity claims totality. This timeless being produces new social and ideological configurations but is itself unchanging. Its whole action effects to clear away a whole world of complex intermediate relations and replace it with a concept of vision and immediacy. Theology must challenge this world and world-belief. Theology is a complex, time-tensed, account of the world, dualist in that it maintains a now and not yet, an account of two times or two cities. It teaches that there are not two types of knowledge, taught *(doctrine)* and non-taught *(immediate)* knowledge, but that all knowledge is taught and mediated. It teaches that only God knows in the non-mediate, non-taught way in which the economy of modernity assumes it knows.

The economy of modernity understands its whole action as the exercise of subjectivity and choice. From the correct belief that we can choose *which* persons and authorities to acknowledge, we have moved on to think that we may choose whether or not to acknowledge others and their authority at all. Following the collapse of the complex medieval account of being and beings, a distinction arose between two sorts of knowing that distinguished between (1) knowledge of the other mediated by the other and (2) immediate knowledge. On the one hand was *worship* — acknowledgment of the otherness of an other — and on the other *knowing* — objects, nature. This distinction became a dichotomy of *worship* and *science.* This has made it difficult for us to understand our own action of knowing as a disguised form of worship. Nature is what moderns acknowledge as other, precisely as it is non-responsive. Our knowledge of it is not reciprocal, and thus not mediated, and the modern personality is both threatened and secured by its utterly non-personal quality.

Modernity, which does not acknowledge the many forms of being and otherness, makes a fatally simple contrast between scientific and fideistic knowledge, between scientific and religious language. It believes that worship — respect of some givens, acknowledgment of something other — is optional. We could refuse to concede it altogether, if we wished. The manyness of these givens and others is not acknowledged as a duty or task. Instead, only two imperatives are recognized: the cultivation of one's own subjectivity, and the acknowledgment of nature necessary to allow the cultivation of that subjectivity. Modernity has wiped away the many intermediate worships by which we could acknowledge the otherness of others and return to each its specific and particular difference. By acknowledging no specific and particular others or givens, we make ourselves indistinguishable from the totality, and so demonic.

The triune God is social. He is in himself all sociality and otherness. He is already one and complete, without us. He can also therefore make others other, and make their otherness resistant to assimilation by us. Their status as his creatures prevents them from being the object called into being by our knowing. Confession of this triune God is acknowledgment of his ability to make others other, and to make them complete without us and apart from us, and thus it is the possibility of acknowledging the particular claims of others. We must look for the origins of this Kantian distinction between ordinary language and religious language. We can do this by recovering a complex ontology, epistemology, and ethics by making them all subject to the discipline of eschatology.

The One *(hen kai pan)* claims to be prior and basic, the source and arbitrator of manyness. The less public that claim is, and the less it appears as a theological or political claim to rule (a *mon-archy*), the more determinative the One is. This One is most effectively total when it does not appear as one claim among others, in the miasma of many words that overlie and conceal what timelessly is. The question of the One is the question of power. Who has power so securely that they can prevent the question of power from coming to public expression? Such a power is exercised by the autonomous individual, the subject of the economy of modernity. The autonomous individual effects to prevent the action of others and to prevent this from becoming explicit. The autonomous individual can remain innocent about his action and never understand that he creates the captivity in which others are bound and in which he is bound with them.

We need to think again about the relationship of unity and action. Aristotle understood that thinking remains in the service of action. Out of every action arise considerations of how to do better and which actions are better than others simply because they involve greater virtuosity. The end of all action is public life.[10] Our peers judge our action, and everything we do is directed to improving our performance before this public. Our action and theirs together serve to increase the total sociality. All action aims to increase the market of public and therefore political life. Aristotle realizes that being must also mean action and that there are different sorts of action over different time-scales. An account of action requires an account of the reciprocal relationship of action, as well as the character and capabilities that enable it and derive from it. Action appears within a perichoretic hierarchy of action, good action, social action, and politics. Part of the purpose of truth statements is to improve our performance, so we can make more and better truth statements. All speech and thought are for the sake of *doing,* and doing *better,* which means a more social and public doing. What we do determines what we want to do; it gives us our

10. For the argument that sociality is the highest goal of all our action, see Aristotle, *Nicomachean Ethics* 1094a-96a. Martha C. Nussbaum, *The Therapy of Desire: Theory and Practice in Hellenistic Ethics* (Princeton: Princeton University Press, 1994), and Pierre Hadot, *Philosophy as a Way of Life* (Chicago: University of Chicago Press, 1995), represent therapy as private practice. Richard Bodéüs, *The Political Dimensions of Aristotle's Ethics* (Albany: State University of New York Press, 1993), and John R. Wallach, *The Platonic Political Art: A Study of Critical Reason and Democracy* (University Park: Pennsylvania State University Press, 2001), rightly argue that this private practice is in the service of public life.

character, which in turn determines our desire. Action occurs in this series: action[1] — character — desire — action[2]. Here we have an antidote to the ontology described by Plato. This ontology is less adept at conceptualizing change because it understands only that ideas belong to an upper realm of ideas and that beneath them is just one form of being — *nature*. It is therefore also an antidote to the economy of modernity, produced by this protology, in which the manyness of ideas is mere appearance, beneath which all is really the same, not many but one.

6.4. Christianity as Discipline

We can now say something about what the doctrine of God *does*. It instructs us in the better performance of the worship of the one God, and that worship is our share in his life and thus is our means to sociality. This exercise of the intellect is in the service of the growth of the Christian community elect to that doxological practice that witnesses to, and even begins to participate in, the real sociality of the Father and the Son. Our first duty is to confess that we are not God, that God is Creator and we are created: this is the first ontological difference that grounds all that is. But a second duty is equally important, for it will prevent this theological confession from turning into a dualism that separates the one creation of the one God into autonomous economies of upper and lower, in which humankind and God appear as equals that sometimes inhabit parallel universes without consequences for one another, at other times appear to be two evenly matched titans. The second confession is that this world is the world of God's creation, and present maintenance, and future redemption. All that we say about it must be driven and controlled by a pneumatology, itself controlled by Christology. So the confession of the Christian communion, and the theological talk that derives from it, is in the service of the formation of the one action, sociality, and body created by the Father and the Son. The discourse that distinguishes God from his creation must be disciplined by the discourse in which we understand God from his work (of creation, maintenance, and redemption), and vice versa. The pneumatology drives the descriptive christological statements that control the act of the church. One theological discourse must discipline another. Theology that does not challenge the priority of thought over action will accept the modern dichotomy of religious and nonreligious knowledge, "knowledge" and "faith," and be content meekly to occupy the sphere of private morality and spirituality that Kant reluctantly conceded to religion.

The purpose of action is politics, life lived in public together. Civic or political philosophy assumes, with Aristotle, that humankind is intrinsically social and that the achievement of more sophisticated sociality is the end and purpose of politics. It also provides a positive ethic. Modern moral philosophy, on the other hand, is the philosophy of individuals who contrast themselves with society, believing that other people threaten them. It provides a negative or formal ethic. Individuals such as these will demand freedom from society, a space that they may fill as they wish, without knowing what to wish for. Moral philosophy assumes that humankind is first natural and only subsequently and problematically social. Moral philosophy, as the philosophy of subjectivity, represents a giving up on life together, and thus a failure of public and political life. It does not understand politics as sociality, hospitality, and mutual formation, but as a technique for controlling the threat posed by other people. Kant believed in a self-imposed and self-interpreted discipline, and he ruled out the discipline imposed by others. He allowed public discourse no part in constituting our desires and character. Trinitarian theology understands that God is social in himself and that his creatures, who receive all their definition and discipline from him, will become social. According to the economy of modernity, on the other hand, we have to struggle alone to establish our *social being* on the basis of our *natural being,* because we are the functions of nature, this *deus absconditus,* that has abandoned us to sort out the problem of sociality in isolation.

The Enlightenment represented a giving up on political enlightenment and the public sphere. What took its place?[11] The public sphere was turned into the discourse of passions and natures by Shaftesbury, Hume, and Adam Smith.[12] The Stoic and Epicurean discourse of disengagement and

11. Ian Hunter, *Rival Enlightenments: Civil and Metaphysical Philosophy in Early Modern Germany* (Cambridge: Cambridge University Press, 2001), pp. 25-28.

12. See Jerome B. Schneewind, *The Invention of Autonomy: A History of Modern Moral Philosophy* (Cambridge: Cambridge University Press, 1998), pp. 171-83, 285-309; Isabel Rivers, *Reason, Grace and Sentiment: A Study of the Language of Religion and Ethics in England, 1660-1780,* Volume 2: *Shaftesbury to Hume* (Cambridge: Cambridge University Press, 2000), pp. 114-52; and Margaret J. Osler, *Atoms, Pneuma, and Tranquility: Epicurean and Stoic Themes in European Thought* (Cambridge: Cambridge University Press, 1991), for discussion of this move to interiority.

detachment became the mode of discourse of the public square. The language designed for withdrawal from public responsibility, and which disallowed comparison of accounts of what is good, paradoxically became the conceptuality in which people publicly reckoned what they owed one another. Economics became the mode of politics. Economics is a moral discourse, disguised as a science relating to nature. The Stoic and Epicurean vocabulary of which it consists was expressly intended to justify flight from the world and to disable formative public choice. It is, in Aristotle's sense, profoundly anti-moral. It purports to be a form of talk about nature, a pure physics, but is rather the self-assertion of the protological ontology, which understands the play of politics, passions, and all the phenomena of plurality as charade. I have argued that theology has to stay in discussion with Plato and Aristotle. Stoicism and Epicureanism represent a third and fourth discourse that Christian theology must also respond to. The Stoic and Epicurean *deus absconditus,* represented only by an empty space crossed by elements, or by a continuum of competing forces, does not interact with, or permit, any history or world. All four ancient — or, we should rather say, timeless — theologies (Platonism, Aristotelianism, Stoicism, and Epicureanism) must be challenged by the Christian doctrine of the triune God and by the Christian practice of praying for release from these rivals.

We must remind ourselves how this leaves the story of religion and secularization. The central claim of secularization is that religion is trying to tell us that there are two worlds, this world and the world above, but this religious claim is false. This is not so. Secular modernity is itself two worlds, one of nature and one of human action. It defines these so that they are set in opposition, and neither can establish itself or successfully rebut the other. The sphere of human action consists in dividing one world into two, but not then admitting that it is simultaneously combining these two worlds (or many worlds) into one — itself. Modernity understands only that it divides and separates, not that it unites, as it is itself united. It does not acknowledge that what it divides always merges together again, that it cannot make any separation or distinction last, so nothing it holds apart stays apart. What is divided comes together again, and it comes together to make that very separating creature, the human being. Modernity is not honest about either of these, preferring to keep them not only separate actions, but also separate economies that know nothing of each other. Human beings, the creatures of modernity, prefer to stay ignorant, in denial not only that they divide and create distinctions but also that they are themselves divided and created.

We have seen that we have not left behind the Platonic or other metaphysics. Our claim that we can summon the world to us as our object itself represents the top of the two-sphere cosmology that modernity claims to have left behind. The upper "sphere" now represented by *method,* the certainty of immediate modern knowledge, is the self-assertion of the individual, the person who exalts himself. This modern anthropology, which intends to be the science of all sciences, cannot allow otherness or plurality. Modernity believes that it has abolished heaven, but it has merely redefined it — as itself — by denying that there is anything outside itself. The two spheres — the theoretical, heavenly, and ideal, and the empirical, earthly, and practical — require each other, so that fundamentally the one knowledge is knowledge of the other. There are two sorts of reason, mediate and immediate. In the economy of modernity, only the latter is called reason. This "Reason," called so in contrast with "faith," is the issue of the self-assertion of the spectator. Spectators are not bound up in the world they look down upon, are not creatures of it, and do not minister to it. They are not of this world that they observe; they are above it. They can regard it with condescension and disdain. These worldly-wise, world-weary persons raise themselves above the complications and involvements of society and plurality. They extract themselves from this turmoil and ascend to a high place, in which none of those grubby forces can touch them. Those persons who are not involved usurp judgment.

The economy of modernity is the creation and the fantasy of persons who raise themselves above the rest. We make ourselves persons who will receive nothing, accept no definition, no authority. We are the human beings against all other human beings. But since God has stepped in to make himself known, and to protect the weak by making himself a party in this business, we are also the human beings against God.

6.4.1. Religion and Self-Promotion

Being is *doxa,* we said. Being is made up of appearances that accrue one on another to turn appearance to substance. Our whole being is sourced from our *striving,* and so from the assumption that we have to climb the ladder of being. We clamber over one another to get ahead. But we have misidentified our goal. It does not lie ahead of us. It is rather where Christ is crucified, far below us. Below us, where all non-being is, is our goal. Christ is available to us only there. We have to confess that we are not God, not autonomous. Only through this confession will we cease trying to oust all others, to place ourselves above them. But it is not as though we can stop ourselves from making such a claim. We have to be stopped. And we have been stopped. This was the conclusion of our discussion of the cross and resurrection.

The Western account of being separates *being* from *action* and *exertion*. We have said that all being is the effort and action of someone. It is not necessarily present and live action, or the action of any individual we can put a name to, but it is the result of concatenations of earlier acts that still ricochet around, the turbulence and cycles set up by earlier events. One result of this separation of being from exertion is that we do not understand that, simply by being what we are, we are making claims about what it is good to be. In being what we are, we intimate that others may like to be like us, and so we indicate a norm. We have returned to what we said about effort and exertion, about self-interest and motion. We may therefore say that we are indeed all examples and models. All *being* is a *showing*, and leading and exertion of power, by displaying an example of a life for emulation. We are guides, examples, and models of life. But the whole Western action consists in separating the being (nature) from the action (life), so the one can disown the other. Thus I can exert a lordship claim, while denying that I am doing this, and in this way exert that claim more effectively because anonymously. We have to understand that we are in a continuum of dominion, in which our action cannot help but subordinate others.

I said that the result of denying ourselves the conceptuality of ontological credit and debt is that we are unable to say that what we do changes what we are. In the two metaphysics of Western ontology, Aristotle accounts for bodies, while Stoicism accounts for processes and events. Common sense is basically Aristotelian. Science, noticeably the life sciences, has much more in common with Stoicism. In a Stoic metaphysic everything overlaps and is interpenetrated by everything else, so things are only very fuzzily identifiable. We have to operate both in the finite economy of discrete things and in the non-finite (infinite) economy of ceaseless change and process. Such a non-dualist account is always being argued for some scientific disciplines, so such a non-dualist account is not hard to find. It can be found in cognitive science, and it is accessible through works of popular science. Theology has to employ both cosmologies. Our too-Platonic cosmology must be corrected by such a non-dualist account of a continuum of action, of the sort represented by Stoic cosmology. This is what pneumatology provides. This pneumatology has been provided in this book by a range of forms of mediation that I have related to the indivisible work and working of God, combined with a theology of the word that has emphasized the ongoing speech and conversation of God. This is not to say that one must be replaced by the other, but just that we need both, each to correct the other. We need both a dualist and a non-dualist account in order to show that we take being from others, that we demote them by promoting ourselves, and that this constant effort of self-elevation is conceptualized by the concept of religion. We impose a discipline of self-control, "religion," on ourselves, the better to make our way beyond others. Thus religion represents both this discipline and the self-promotion that it conceals. Now we can say that the economy of modernity is a religion and that it can be identified and confronted as such only by Christian theology.

6.4.2. The Religion of Modernity

Next we have to examine modernity as an endeavor that costs effort. We said that the economy of modernity conceals action as a science. It pretends to be a description of a state of affairs, but it is not. It is merely something we *do*, the act by which we divide one entity to make two. To one of these new entities we attribute reality in one economy, while we attribute reality to the other entity in another economy. We do not allow that they can be real together in one conceptuality or that one vocabulary could extend to them both. The whole effort of the economy of modernity is the separation of the one economy of life into the two economies of inert nature and living human action. It separates the living from dead, though it is this very act that also renders it dead. It is an active work of wiping our memories and the means by which our past is determined to be past, and our accumulated, unfinished, unsettled action is removed from us.

The whole effort of economics is simply to separate one thing, the being of the human being, into these two discourses. It defers to nature here in this domain, the better to make unlimited claims about our utter freedom of action there in this other domain. Economics is nothing but this continuous work of separation, which succeeds to the extent that it is not understood for what it is. It is a deep piece of societal voodoo, the mechanism of atonement that keeps this society together. Business leaders, economists, and social scientists act as our priests. They divide up our being and carry it away into these two domains. They take what we cannot cope with and remove it from us. They distinguish the natural from the moral, the outer from the inner person. They are responsible for the enforcement of the inner and the outer, and they guard the sovereignty of these opposed dominions. This first cut creates endless variations and repetitions of itself. The economy of modernity, and all the human and social sciences that support it, is a massive effort of atonement that constitutes this secular society. It is led by the discipline of economics, itself an ethic masquerading as a form of physics. Modernity depends on this constant work of removal. This secular economy is the product of this process of repeatedly separating one economy into two and then joining these two economies into one, an act of division *(sacrifice)* and reconciliation *(at-onement)*.

The product of the modern economy is persons who assert themselves but cannot establish themselves. Individuals cannot secure their own existence or settle their position as the outcome and product of this economy. We need to return to theology, which understands that humankind is the work of God, and still a work in progress.

6.4.3. *The Purpose of Theological Statement*

I have said that the world claims to be one but that theology must show that it is many. But theology must also say that this manyness is no real plurality but amounts to just a single entity: the world held by, and indistinguishable from, the opponent of God that is addressed and opposed by the Word of God.[13] The rival word of the economy of modernity resists being named and brought to the surface. We are dealing, therefore, not merely with ideas and ideologies but with sets of movements with extremely long time-spans that determine the modality and effect of our action, by which our action serves to surrender our particularity to a single being and entity. This demon may be so distant that he does not appear to be a discrete figure, a nameable king or god, or so close that he is not separate from us but constitutes a single economy within which we are all absorbed.

---

13. I said in the Introduction that we must give an account in which we are not distinguishable from the world or it from us, and that theology must conceptualize this single entity that cannot sustain particularity or plurality as "the Opponent." The Word of God opposes this entity and distinguishes and releases us from it.

The modern anthropology is an ontology without an account of time. It releases humankind from the tension between this world and the world to come. It has made the transcendental city of *not yet* the basis for the present city of sure and certain knowledge of the world, alleging that human beings are already in the "not yet." Kant mistook anthropology for a *problem* and solved that problem. We should rather take anthropology as a *task*. Kant understood time as a problem and abolished it so that we live not between two times but in a two-aspect space, in which the space of sensation is set within the space of intellect, which must be presupposed. The upper realm of the Timaean cosmology has become the subjectivity, and thus the mastery, of the knower of the world.[14] The individual is a master, now, already. This individual, well represented by Kant, denies that the action of others constitutes his world. He intends his world to be an inert thing of nature, not a loud bustling place composed of many agents who make demands on him, contradict him, and insist that he is in one economy of response with them.[15] As long as this core claim of the priority of nature is not challenged, other disciplines subordinate themselves to the claim of economics to be the first science of being. An insufficiently trinitarian theology is always liable to become another vehicle for this protology, with the result that it becomes an ideology of interiority. If it does not break out of the sphere of interiority, it will remain unable to impact on the routines by which human beings give and receive from one another without ever becoming answerable to one another and becoming *personal*. These routines make up that economy of interaction and exchange conceptualized as *economics*. Economics makes this interaction a phenomenon of nature, a simplistic form of physics premised on an underlying timelessness, an equilibrium. Theology, by contrast, is an address that intends to make us answerable to one another, responsible for bringing one another into being, and making us what we are not yet. Theology

14. See T. K. Seung, *Kant's Platonic Revolution in Moral and Political Philosophy* (Baltimore: Johns Hopkins University Press, 1994). Douglas Farrow, *Ascension and Ecclesia* (Edinburgh: T&T Clark, 1999), p. 168, argues that Kant represents a philosophical chiliasm (Kant's own description of Lessing) in the tradition of Joachim of Fiore, a fully realized eschatology and anthropology (and thus one that is not eschatological at all) against which we saw Foucault protest.

15. We have discussed this economy of response in terms of Anselm's single fabric of being, of Janowski's response to Kant, and of the continuum of motion and emotion, which understands us as not only actors but sufferers of the continuum of movement.

is a mode of political hermeneutics, a practice of interrupting the simple statements the world makes about itself, by which it always seems to want to close itself down, and of providing complex statements that keep the world open. Theology is a work of intercession and advocacy, of calling on one another, and on God, to give the world more time. Theology is a mode of politics, and Christianity the best mode of politics, because the God of Jesus Christ is our ruler and under his rule we may flourish.

This requires several other claims. One is that Christians participate in the rule of the one ruler. Another is that political talk is inseparable from ethics talk, and ethics talk is inseparable from political talk.[16] A third and larger claim must be made, one that was once a commonplace of Platonic philosophy: that politics (the *polis*) and ethics (what to do) and psychology (talk of our mind, emotions, and soul, and therefore also our religious inclinations), and cosmology and theology all relate one to another. These claims represent a range of tasks for theology. We will start with the first.

Christianity has taken up some of the resources of political thought provided by classical republicanism. In this vanished tradition, the ruler was understood to do much more than rule: he was a teacher and model of the good life, and the law was a resource of positive description of the good life.

I have distinguished between ideology that can be named and ideologies so successful and normative that they have ceased to be ideologies and have become modes of our action too mundane to be dignified with a name. Such actions hover beneath the threshold of our intellectual attention and inveigle their way into us. They create self-reinforcing circles of action, so that they become the only thing we *can* do. We do not think them; we *do* them. If we cannot escape them, they may be said to have a demonic character, and then we can say that it is not we who do these actions, but they do us. They determine our action, while giving us the illusion of freedom. Without the conceptual means to distance ourselves from them, they are all we can do. It is the task of Christian theology to render these practices visible for the first time. Politics is therefore the bringing up to the surface, for publicly responsible discourse, all those nameless practices in which our modern normality consists. Politics is therefore not one domain among others, but the task of

---

16. Oliver O'Donovan, *The Desire of the Nations: Rediscovering the Roots of Political Theology* (Cambridge: Cambridge University Press, 1996), gives a historical sketch of the political framework as preparation for an ethics that is to follow. Here I am presenting politics and ethics together.

identifying the forces that operate on us, because we operate them on one another. We must drag the hidden and constrained up into the open discourse of politics and ethics. It is our task to name the powers. Then we can, for the first time, exercise our will, and either approve of these powers or repent of them. Only Christian theological statements about the victory of Christ can do this, the first task of politics. It can do this because it talks about our captivity and bondage, and it is able to do so because it witnesses to a captivity brought to an end. The end of this captive mind is the beginning of a free and public action — politics — in Christ.

We are therefore wrong to protest that we do not hold power unless we are elected to it. All of us already wield power over one another. Others emulate us, and our every action makes that action first acceptable, then compelling, and, over the long term, binding on others. The purpose of the Christian concept of sin is to make us drop our declaration of our innocently nonpolitical status. Theology has to show that it is no one other than ourselves who, by myriad everyday acts, create complexes of action, vocabulary, rules, and institutions that allow certain forms of behavior and inhibit others, and so enforce particular modes of personhood on one another. When these modes give rise to forms of agency not under authority, they exert a stolen but real power that enforces constrictive forms of life on some. Those crushed by them may properly identify such modes as false gods and ask for their release. They can even, in the name of Jesus Christ, address them as demons and have them driven out. Theology is therefore first interested in flushing out the rulers and authorities of this age from their cover in the mundane imperatives of modern society. It is not Caesar who is the enemy, for behind this or that political regime is an amorphous collective that refuses authority and resists being named. Each of us attempts to assert our individuality in order to dominate or escape one another. All this striving creates the figure of disobedient Adam, the sum of all our recalcitrance. This originates not in one individual leader rather than another, but in long generations and traditions and so in humanity as a whole. The purpose of all talk of rule is to show that we have exalted ourselves, that we have made ourselves the sort of individual who needs no others, who has raised himself above others, who has extracted himself from the fray, and who can now be an onlooker, detached and serene. This individual has been dethroned. Our attempts to extract ourselves from one another, to save ourselves from others, to make ourselves untouchable have been brought to an end. God has opposed and ended the attempt of each of us to escape our creatureliness and become divine. The purpose of the doctrine of God is to confess that we are not God and to put in our hands the means to ask him to make us human.

Theology is not *Christian* until it can give some account of the bound and involuntary situation of humankind. Satan must be named and thrown out before humanity becomes free enough even to hear the word of God. It is crucial to the health of the university for it to admit that discussion of the recalcitrance and deviousness of humankind is the context of our knowing. Christian theology must represent publicly the closedness of human knowing that is intrinsic to the real complexity of human motivation, a complexity that the concept of the individual disallows. So Christian theology gives us the tools by which to exercise a proper skepticism about the world and about humankind. It allows us to ask whether it is we moderns who are "ever hearing but never understanding, and ever seeing but never perceiving" (see Isa. 6:9-10; Mark 4:11-12). We have true knowledge of the world because a good God has made a creation that is good for us, not deceptive — "what may be known about God is plain to them since God has made it plain to them" (Rom. 1:19). But this requires a moment in which we are disciplined and warned; and when this warning is not heard, our thinking becomes futile, and our minds are darkened. We have not thought it worthwhile to retain the knowledge of God, and God left us to suffer the results. The oppressive, unchallenged assumption of modern theology is that we already have a free and mature mind and are already entirely capable of choice. It is not true, and it is not merciful to insist that it is.

We must emphasize the *intrinsically* political purpose of the doctrine of God. We need to show that it is not enough for theology to talk as though the human already had a will and freedom — the discourse of voluntarism. It must also talk about the absence of will and the captivity of will — the discourse of sloth, compulsion, and delusion. We must recover from earlier theology the resources to talk about a will and freedom that can come into being as a result of Christ's victory. We must learn from earlier generations how to name the powers and thus to proclaim faithfully a liberating gospel of the defeat of the usurper and the rule of the one God.

In order to bring the whole world into the domain of existing political discourse, there must therefore be at least three accounts. In one of them (1) we are victims; in another (2) we are masters, and, as the mode of our mastery, (3) we play the bystander. In this third account we abjure public and political responsibility to conceal ourselves behind complex ideological constructions about the constraints on us. We disguise ourselves as victims, the better to promote our claim to autonomy. But this is only an apparent autonomy. In it we are trying to carry off an unsustainable claim to be ourselves without other people. Our task is then to reintroduce political discourse where it has been squeezed out, and we do this by arguing from the first theologically. Theology is the politics that says that God is king, and thus that there is authority that is given, external to us. Recognition of this authority is the beginning of public well-being and the political life. God-talk is given to the Christian community so that this community will prevent the world from making hubristic anthropological claims. Theology is the control on the discourse of anthropology. It tells us that we do not yet know humankind, that humankind is not yet our object to know; rather, humankind is the possession, and work, and secret of God. Only a long, slow lesson from God will provide us with any information about humankind, the creature of God. We may come to know others only as they are entrusted to us, given to us on leasehold, and we are responsible to God for their well-being. When we fail to know others in this custodial and paideutic way, they are taken away from us and protected from us. Social science can only make an ideological claim that affects to create the creature it claims to know: it cannot recognize anything that is not a function of its own projection, and thus it is not able to know any creature at all. Christian theology says that God has made himself available to us so that we might appeal to him. Only in Christian speech is there a figure who is available to us as an object of knowledge because he gives himself to be known, while utterly unknown and uncomprehended by us, and who, in all our knowledge of him, remains the master. Only this theological discourse removes from us all our modern pretension not to be implicated in any form of authority over others, the better secretly to keep in play our claim to be master. Christianity is the discipline of persons brought under no other discipline than that of their Creator.

6.5. The King and His People

6.5.1. God as King and Judge

The Christian gospel announces that God is King, Jesus is Lord. Talk about God is our response to the declaration by the God of Israel of his kingship: he is our ruler, and the ruler of our rulers. That is to say that his rule over us is both mediated, by intermediary holders of power, and immediate. His word, and the word of his body that participates in it, warns the rulers and political authorities that their authority is held from God and will be assessed by him. He acts to protect those exposed to the domination or indifference of these many self-regarding masters. God declares war on those authorities that do not understand that they are themselves under discipline. They must publicly acknowledge the discipline imposed by God to protect those otherwise vulnerable. Theology obedient to this word must be done in the face of those political authorities, often against their resistance.[17] We have to go out to name those centers of authority that exercise a hidden and illegitimate power over us. These are then political-cosmological authorities — the spirit of this world, and rulers and authorities in the heavenly realms. These represent the cosmological consequences of the failure of Adam to take up the office of stewardship given to him and his resultant failure to keep the power and energies of the cosmos in their proper order. This cosmological language represents the consequences of the sloth of humanity that has as yet no will.[18]

God alone is king and judge. God liberates us from the temptation to be our own judges and masters. Because God holds these offices exclusively, we cannot seize and hold them ourselves.[19] God lifts from us the compul-

17. O'Donovan, *The Desire of the Nations*, p. 93, seems to contrast political and cosmological resistance ("Jesus' preference for addressing the demonic rather than the colonial oppressors . . . "), but the point is rather that many of these authorities are not yet visible in any realm of political discourse and must be named and called to account by public and therefore prophetic theological statement.

18. The writer of the letter to the Ephesians mentions "the ways of this world and the ruler of the kingdom of the air" (2:2) and "rulers and authorities in the heavenly realms" (3:10). Philo mentions a host of conceptual and political entities: *logoi, aretai, angeloi, daimones, psuchai, ideai, eikones, sphragides, paradeigmata.*

19. Oliver O'Donovan and Joan Lockwood O'Donovan, *Irenaeus to Grotius: A Sourcebook in Christian Political Thought* (Grand Rapids: Eerdmans, 1999), p. 14, quote Theophilus of Antioch making this point in *To Autolycus:* "Accordingly, I will pay honour to the emperor not by worshiping him but by praying for him. I worship God who is the real and true God, since I know that the emperor was made by him. You will say to me, 'Why do you not worship the emperor?' Because he was made not to be worshipped but to be honoured with legitimate honour. He is not God but a man appointed by God, not to be worshipped but to judge justly. For in a certain way he has been 'entrusted with a stewardship' (1 Cor. 9:17) from God. He himself has subordinates whom he does not permit to be called emperors, for 'emperor' is his name and it is not right for another to be given this title. Similarly worship must be given to God alone."

sion to exert an absolute and tyrannical rule on one another. That God alone is judge over us is the guarantee that there will be justice, both for us and for those who have been denied justice by us. Critics of the forensic atonement ask by what right God brings us to court to try us as sinners. We exercise this right against each other, and against God, in an all-against-all, competitive, open field. We have seen that we bring each other to court by appealing to one another to acknowledge our claim and vindicate us. In this assembly every agent puts himself forward, and every agent is there to judge between every other and to deny them all what he awards to himself. This assembly is a court in which each attempts to give judgment and vindicate his own right, appealing to all others to do so while simultaneously attempting to deny them the right to oppose his own claim.[20] We are in the assembly by the very action of our own self-promotion. It is this that makes the assembly a court in which our right and rule are tried: we put ourselves there by intending to exert a rule over all others.[21]

But such a statement, that God alone is judge, is not sufficient. God does not intend to be alone in exercising judgment and authority. He intends that we also come to learn this action and exercise it with him and under him. He intends that we come to find his action good, be informed by it, and come to share it. The end and purpose of his judging is that he brings us up into the office and work of judges. God gives us an action. It is an action that is intrinsically his and that will always remain his; yet he intends us to participate in it, so that it is also subordinately ours. This new action must be understood both as servanthood and as leadership. We must understand this not only as an action given, but also as an action only loaned to us, held by us only as long as we exercise it with him and under him. In the event that we do not grow into its proper use, he takes it away

20. This argument is made by Gillian Rose, *Dialectic of Nihilism: Post-Structuralism and Law* (Oxford: Blackwell, 1984), pp. 11-15.

21. The modern division and separation of powers distinguishes the law court from a (parliamentary) assembly, and both of these from the more obvious contest of the marketplace or battlefield. Isaiah 3:13-14: "The Lord takes his place in court; he rises to judge peoples. The Lord brings an indictment." We are in court because we are in an assembly in which all nations, regimes, and rulers assert themselves over all others, and over against the God of Israel. O'Donovan's *Christus Victor* theology shows that the medium is initially in our possession, but Christ commandeers it and transforms it into his medium — for us. As such it is a demonstratively non-modern theology: it does not allow an epistemology to function in ignorance of the doctrine of God.

from us again, and the shreds of what we learned remain only to baffle us and make us believe we know something when we know nothing.

6.5.2. The Rule of the People of God

God makes us participants in our own constitution. If we participate in it, we will be free in it. To this end we need a pneumatological account in which God devolves some of his virtuosity to us, making us share some of his competence. We are given the gifts of the Spirit — though since they remain the Spirit's, it would perhaps be better to say that the Spirit loans them to us. God intends to admit new members to the council and assembly of heaven.[22] This assembly will then govern a combined kingdom of heaven and earth, in which we will be, not divine, but for the first time properly *human*, creatures made holy. This assembly is gathered as an earthly ecclesia that inducts its members into the skill of judging and giving recognition. Part of the skill of judging is the skill of advocacy, the office of defense counsel, which puts the case for mercy. These trainee judges — the saints — must be taught the skills of entering a plea, interceding, *prayer*. They must learn to argue on behalf of those who are not yet holy that a little more time is needed, and to argue on behalf of the oppressed that their release come now, without delay. They must be able to say both "Have mercy on us — give us more time," and "Come Lord Jesus — give no more time to the oppressors." These advocates must be able to say which plea is at any time appropriate. The new Christian action is that of the members of the assembly that God gathers around himself.[23] This

22. See Patrick D. Miller, "Cosmology and World Order in the Old Testament: The Divine Council as a Cosmic-Political Symbol," in *Israelite Religion and Biblical Theology* (Sheffield: Sheffield Academic Press, 2000), pp. 425-40.

23. In Mark 6:7 the disciples are appointed the judges of the twelve tribes of Israel, and in Mark 11:17 (see Isa. 56:6-8) Israel is the judge of the earth who brings justice to the nations. Jeremy Thomson, "The Conflict-Resolving Church: Community and Authority in the Prophetic Ecclesiology of John Howard Yoder" (Ph.D. thesis, London University, 2000), pp. 113, 193-96, argues, in agreement with Yoder, that the church must regard these instruments of judgment and discipline as Caesar's and not employ them. In reply we can say that courts are not bound to be the wicked instruments of a wicked Caesar or Constantinianism. But even when they are this, we are told in Romans 13 that we are to take advantage of the discipline lashed out on us by God's (unrighteous) servant by understanding it as God's discipline for our benefit. It is no concern of ours that this servant will also receive his discipline from God for overstepping the mark.

training starts as the exercise of self-government of the church.[24] The people of the world will come to this assembly of saints for justice.

Christians are elected to serve and care for the world entrusted to them. They are to exercise oversight. They are to put the case to the Lord their God for mercy and justice and together pray to him to exercise the power of binding and loosing (Matt. 16:19; 18:19). Christians are held responsible for *the least of these* (Matt. 25) and are subject to judgment when they lose even one of them.[25] The whole Christian body is elected to this work.[26] But of course the Christian body is not yet obediently at work. Teaching and leadership must presently be limited to those appointed specifically to teach and prepare others. The only purpose of the appointment of some to particular offices in the church is to prepare the whole church to exercise this single office. When Christ is all in all, even the most modest members will be made able to play their part and receive their proper honor.[27] In the same way, authority in the church is in the service of the church's authority over the world. To exercise this authority is to participate in the Lord's work of releasing the world from all the alien authorities — other gods — that presently divide it and hold it captive. All Christians are members of this parliamentary and juridical assembly, which speaks the truth, teaches and enables truthful public speech, practices justice, and praises God for his justice. All are citizens in a commonwealth in which all will grow up to the fullness of Christ.

The ecclesia is the body responsible for the education and sanctification of this community and, through this community, of the world. It nur-

24. In *The Desire of the Nations*, O'Donovan argues that the church is (1) a gathering community, (2) a suffering community, (3) a glad community, and (4) a community that speaks the words of God. It is prophetic in that it addresses the world, and its speech includes prayer (petition) and laying on of hands.

25. Paul for example is able to say in Acts 18:6 that he is clear of his responsibility and that the blood of his listeners is therefore upon their own heads. He declares in 20:24-26 that he is "innocent of the blood of all men" because he has completed "the task the Lord Jesus has given" him.

26. "There are different kinds of service but the same Lord. To this end God has appointed first apostles, second prophets, third teachers, then workers of miracles" (1 Cor. 12:4-11, 28).

27. "But God has combined the members of the body and has given greater honor to the parts that lacked it" (1 Cor. 12:24). "The body that is sown is perishable [because it is a part], it is raised imperishable [because it is a part integrated into the whole]; . . . it is sown a natural body, it is raised a spiritual body" (1 Cor. 15:42, 44).

tures and is nurtured by a body of tradition from which it creates legislation and assembles as a law court that judges individual hard cases. Right-judging and right-doing are the proper actions of the new people. They involve coaching the saints in the action of right speech and public speech: they see that God judges rightly and they say so; they learn to praise God for the generosity and finesse of his practice of justice. The Christian community is being trained up to a range of offices that serve a single end. The singleness of this end, and the oneness of this assembly, offends the separation of powers that under the modern constitution are understood to be incompatible.[28]

Leadership of the project of the formation of a people is the proper work of the Christian community.[29] The church may identify and address

---

28. Bernd Wannenwetsch, "The Political Worship of the Church," *Modern Theology* 12 (1996): 278, argues that the church's worship of God is the overcoming of political antinomies, the most important of which is that between public and private, *polis* and *oikos*. Plato and Aristotle understood politics to be based upon the distinction of public and private: in the *polis* the free rich male citizen can find the fulfillment of his life, whereas the *oikos*, though necessary for the *polis*, is the realm of (unfree) labor and the maintenance of the means of life. "Thus the concept of politics is highly exclusive and parasitic, resting on the basis of the *oikos*, which is at the same time conceived and dismissed as a restricted area for lower human beings such as women, slaves, artists and so on" (p. 278). He argues that "The first important political impact of the new evolving Christian community was the de-totalising of politics" (p. 279). This brought to an end the exclusion of the *oikos* and realm of nature from the *polis*. "The first urban Christians described their common life not only in terms of family language (as was usual for religious communities) but also in terms of political language. . . . The Church's 'self-designation' as *ekklesia* associates the original Greek political meaning of the notion as the voting assembly of a polis. . . . Worship includes in full participation all the representatives of the debased *oikos*: women, slaves, children and so on" (p. 279). See also Reinhard Hütter, *Suffering Divine Things: Theology as Church Practice* (Grand Rapids: Eerdmans, 1999), pp. 147-70, especially pp. 163-64, "Difference from the Polis: Church as 'Polis' and 'Oikos.'" John Milbank, *Theology and Social Theory: Beyond Secular Reason* (Oxford: Blackwell, 1990), p. 432, asserts, "The church did not succeed in displacing politics" and as a result politics returned, "yet in a virulent form unknown to antiquity."

29. O'Donovan, *The Desire of the Nations*, p. 26, replies to the charge that such Christian leadership would be not only Christendom but Constantinianism, the exercise of an utterly illegitimate authority. In Wyclif and the Franciscan poverty tradition O'Donovan has found a non-Constantinian definition of authority and dominion. In this tradition "Human justice depends upon God's sanctifying of our relations to material possessions. Political right must spring directly from the charity to God and neighbour which the gospel imparts; *ius* must flow from the fountain-head of *iustitia*. Only the righteous (elect, forgiven, sanctified) can have a full title to 'dominion' — a word, which in the manner of the period, em-

leaders as leaders, regardless of the legitimacy with which they are understood to have come to such a position. They can address anyone as a leader, even though such persons may protest that they hold no formal position and cannot be held to account. Leaders must be held to this paideutic task of nurturing law and public discourse to educate this people. They must be criticized in particular when they do not give a lead. The church must, therefore, not give up on the state. It must model the leadership that the state must give to the people and model the openness of public political discourse. The church does not yearn to take away the task of ruling from the state, to do it better, but always to encourage leadership, on such a broad definition, to grow in confidence and competence.

6.6. The Two Economies

6.6.1. Pagan Practices

Next we must look for a theological response to the modern separation of powers. The Christian political tradition represents one side of a conversation. The gospel is in conversation and confrontation with pagan thought. In part, at least, modernity is pagan, so pagan thought must be the other half of the conversation. Or rather, not pagan thought, but pagan *practice,* the practices of captivity, sloth, and compulsion, must be the other half of the conversation. Pagan practice cannot be opened to us by pagan thought alone. Only the Scriptures can reveal pagan thought to us as *pagan*, as that which is present temptation to us, and indeed as our own present practice. The Bible is the Scriptures of the church, not of the West; the church is not the West, but only the leaven of the West.

The pagan practices most constitutive for modernity are represented by the political philosophy of the ancient world rediscovered in the sixteenth and seventeenth centuries, which Kant formalized into the modern political-and-epistemological separation of powers. This is the effective

---

braces the two notions of property and jurisdiction" (p. 16). Only the righteous can hold property, Wyclif argues. Thus they do not hold it, so much as hold it in trust, employ it for another. We can therefore say that any possession of authority and any right to exercise leadership are entirely a spiritual possession and right. This possession and right remain that of the Spirit, and he can withdraw them from his ministers. God can remove the authority extended to us, and he can do this without our noticing, to leave us with nothing.

"scripture" of the modern West. It has brought about the division and re-duction of public discourse into the techniques of our withdrawal into ever smaller spheres of selfhood. The West attempts to lay aside the tools by which its own version of its history can be challenged. We must ask whether, in response, God has withdrawn the Scriptures from the West, with the result that the Bible is quite closed to us, held closed by God. Yet the Christian work is, by use of the Bible as a diagnostic political instru-ment, to re-reveal to the West its intellectual sources and with them to question the practices that, by the endless process of division driven by the modern separation of powers, seek to stay invisible and normative. Now we can relate the political to the epistemological; we can link the defeat and dethronement of the usurper-judge to the commissioning of the crea-ture who participates in the justice-giving action of God. We can link the defeat and dethronement of the autonomous knower to a new licensing and empowerment of an obedient creaturely knowing.

Other than by the mediation of God, not only is knowledge of *God* not attainable, but knowledge of the *world of God's creation* is not knowable. It is his and not ours. It takes a long course of education even to come to real-ize the difficulty of acquiring knowledge of this world. There are plenty of resources for the conceptualization of this difficulty and of the purifica-tions required by this course of education.[30] Plato offers a course of educa-tion that aims to teach us that we do not know what moderns are sure they do know. He teaches that we must start to step out of such knowledge and divest ourselves of such worldly wisdom. The early part of the philosophical life teaches us to reexamine that of which we are too certain. The Socratic or Platonic education prescribes instrumental action that has to be adopted in order to begin to sense the barriers there are between us and true knowl-edge so that we are no longer under the dictatorship of a mere worldview.

The political philosophy of Plato expects all citizens to be taught their laws and constitution.[31] Athenians are free because they are under law.

---

30. See Seth Bernadete, *Plato's "Laws": The Discovery of Being* (Chicago: University of Chicago Press, 2000), pp. 42-53, for a recent exposition of the epistemology that belongs to Plato's political philosophy.

31. See Plato, *Meno* and *Laws*. We need, not democracy (for the *demos* is the mob), but nomocracy. "For a polity moulds its people; a goodly one moulds good men, the opposite bad. Therefore I must show that our ancestors were moulded in a good polity, thanks to which they and the present generation — amongst them these men who have died — are good men" (*Menexenus* 238c).

They do not suffer the alien authority of dictatorship because they obey this intrinsic authority. Philo of Alexandria points out that Jews already do this every seventh day. On the Sabbath they read, learn, and rehearse their constitution and law. Their law includes a definition of the full status of a human being very like the one Aristotle sets out in the *Nicomachean Ethics*. By learning their law they have become a people of great virtue, who exhibit the self-control that is the basis of all life in a *polis* and which the Greeks wish to emulate.[32] They know that the law intends first to *teach*. It is a bank of resources for description of the good, and only subsequently for the adjudication of what is good in each case. Without such a resource of description — and without the cultivation and care this resource requires — we have no means of saying what particular thing we want and will be satisfied by. In the classical republican tradition we find that generosity is the defining characteristic of the justice or righteousness of the great human being. The modern definition of justice is negative: it involves not getting in another person's way and making restitution when you do. The positive classical definition of justice involves giving the other person your wisdom, encouragement, and support. Such a benefactor must act with the same generosity as the gods, giving rulings, counsel, instruction, and justice. Justice-giving is a mercy.[33] He is not to leave his people idle and listless but must share out offices and give them work to do. All this extra-large definition of justice is part of the generosity of the person brought into being by the law and by vigorous public contest of the good.

6.6.2. *The City of God*

This brief discussion of paideia and Platonic political philosophy has prepared us for the argument of Augustine in *The City of God*. Augustine is responding to Cicero's defense of the possibility of responsible political life, the life of the republic.[34] Cicero believes that the *res publica*, public affairs,

32. See Philo, *Life of Moses* 2.2; 2.5; 2.187 on the philosopher-king who is a shepherd of his people (1.150). His subjects imitate him. The shepherd and horticultural analogies are commonplace in ancient political thought.

33. See, for example, Seneca, *De Clementia* 1.5.7, and *De Beneficiis* 3.18.1; 4.12.5.

34. See Malcolm Schofield, "Epilogue," in *The Cambridge History of Greek and Roman Political Thought*, ed. Christopher Rowe and Malcolm Schofield (Cambridge: Cambridge University Press, 2000), pp. 666-71; and O'Donovan and O'Donovan, *Irenaeus to Grotius*, pp. 161-63.

are the affairs of the people and that where there is no justice, the virtue that must underpin all fair dealing in society, there can be no law or justice; where there is no law, there is no common interest, no commonwealth, and a rabble, but no people. Cicero says that the tyrant is a model of the vice of injustice, of being above the law, lawless. Such a leader cannot be a model of justice. Under him there can be no just society or politics. The very existence of the community is made impossible.[35] Cicero argues that in its earliest days Rome met the criterion of agreement on justice. Augustine disagrees.[36] True justice did not flourish in Rome's heroic days because Rome worshiped many gods and thus many incompatible accounts of virtue and justice. So, following Cicero's argument, there was no community agreement on justice, and thus no justice. Only God's nation, the *polis* that rules and combines heaven and earth, counts as a people in Cicero's sense, for only in this heavenly city is there the agreement, and obedience to it, which underpins justice.[37] This, argues Augustine, makes the heavenly city a *better* community.

Augustine argues that the church is the exemplary nation and the model for all other nations.[38] We should not let "nation" be defined, as it has been in the modern period, by territoriality; instead, we must understand the concept of nation to refer to a particular regimen and form of life. So, for example, the nation and regimen of industrialists overlaps to some degree with that of financiers and with that of opinion-makers: each such mode of sociality is supported by sets of codes, practices, and disciplines. All members of each fraternity have an idea of what its members do and do not do. Inasmuch as modern political science does not understand that nations compete for intellectual resources in the form of definitions of what is desirable, it rules out discussion of what *is* worth doing. It has not appreciated that we are all driven to seek what is better, as present public discourse — "earthly glory" — believes it is better, and that everyone has some idea of what it is to be successful and, within the context of earthly glory, can usually tell a better performance from a poorer one. Augustine says that being a member of any nation or regime demands constant reappraisal of precisely which virtues are worth pursuing and which

---

35. Cicero, *De Re Publica* 3.43; Cicero, *On the Commonwealth and On the Laws,* ed. James E. G. Zetzel (Cambridge: Cambridge University Press, 1999), p. 75.

36. Augustine, *City of God* 19.21.

37. Augustine, *City of God* 19.24.

38. Augustine, *City of God* 19.17.

should be discarded, so that some of these virtues really are attained. His definition of a regime does not require that we already agree on what is good; nor does he insist, as Cicero and Kant do, that we must say that, because I think it is good for me, I must assert that it is good for everyone.[39] Augustine starts from the assumption that we all compete. We pursue glory. Then he refers to the retrospective discovery that heavenly glory is better than earthly glory, not least because it lasts longer. This may be hidden to everyone on earth because, on earth, the effort of competing for earthly glory does not allow us to see that there is a better nation — and in it superior glory — available to us in the kingdom that unites earth to heaven. Augustine's political philosophy relies on eschatology because this enables a more consistent pursuit of the logic of political philosophy.

Augustine contrasts two regimes and modes of being human. These are in themselves definitions of what it is to be human, and they are training regimes that intend to develop each of us to the full status of that mode. Augustine is contrasting two modes — a short-term mode and a long-term, or rather eternal, mode. There is nothing wrong with the short-term mode, other than that it is partial and eventually comes to an end. That there is an endless variety of short-term modes is a good thing. The eternal mode is full and perfect and does not come to an end. Indeed, it is this mode that supplies life to the short-term modes, did they but know it. Only those who participate in the eternal mode can see that all others are merely partial. With very great caution they can say that the partial forms can be seen, by the pure person only, as anticipations of, and witnesses to, the complete form. These (pagan) training regimes intend to improve our performance at acquiring a range of goods. They constitute many wonderful ways of failing to get started on the process of learning the (heavenly) mode. But only retrospectively can it be seen — by the new mind — that all (pagan) modes were poor modes of what God does perfectly for us, to which the gospel witnesses. At a conceptual level, at least, there is a recognition that Christianity and paganism — that is, all persons — are aiming at one thing. They are aiming at how to be a human being. Christianity, Augustine argues, shows that the way to be a human being is to be a son of the God of Jesus Christ. Christianity not only shows this but also brings it about through participation in the Spirit

39. Kant's categorical imperative (*Groundwork of the Metaphysics of Morals* 4.421: "Act only in such a way that you can at the same time will that your maxim should become a universal law") was first Cicero's, in *De Officiis* 3.26-27, 52.

who brings such sons into being. To this end Christianity commandeers and discards all other regimes. All kingdoms claim some small share of earth, but one kingdom, that of God, comprises the whole of earth and heaven in a single combined regime. Buy into this kingdom, and you will inherit the best of the rest anyway. No other nation knows what hope is, because the other nations have no means of conceiving of more than the best of humankind already is. Christianity, however, intends to take us way beyond what already is, to God. This, for Augustine, is political philosophy on theological definition. It is political philosophy done properly.

A people is a people because they have a unity. But they do not bestow this unity on themselves. Their unity comes from outside them, from God. If they are just a *demos* without law, then they are a rabble in which each seeks to make himself the one who is over all others. Not until this people are ruled by the theological monarchy of one God can there really be a *demos* — democracy and *koinonia*.[40] Christianity is the better way to do politics. It is a better performance, which marks all other ways as self-defeating by raising the definition of politics to life with God in this God's Spirit.

From Platonism we learn that absolutely nothing of the fullness of this world as the creation of God is available to us from the impressions of our senses. Without being tutored by the teacher we can only be oblivious to the fullness of this world and exist in an infinitely impoverished version of it. Plato said we have fallen into a deep crevasse in which we have only very poor refractions of a reality far above us.[41] Down here we suffer from a reality deficit. By a process of paideia some few of us can return to that reality, learn it, and come back to educate the rest of us in it. Christianity says that one man has been raised from the cave and has come back to us. He has come back as the Spirit — that is, in many gentle modes that I have described variously in terms of paideia, the law, the teacher, and the many other material modes that we discussed in Chapters 3 and 4. I argued that modernity had abolished the metaphysics of the good and the project of paideia but held onto criticism, which now functions as a vicious practice of disowning all resources of tradition and law.

So now we can say that what is significant about modernity is not that

---

40. See Augustine, *City of God* 19.14: "But in the household of the just man who 'lives by faith' and who is still on pilgrimage, far from that heavenly city, even those who give orders are the servants of those they appear to command."

41. See Plato, *Phaedo* 111c-114c; *Republic* books 6-7.

modern human beings have turned away from God, but that their turning away has been commandeered by God. It has been redetermined by God's action, so that even in their turning away the actions of human beings are taken and turned to their own eventual good. Just where human beings believe that they have succeeded in being most their own person and are on the point of turning demonic, their ambition is prevented. Modernity, and the assertion of the autonomy of humankind from God, is a way of being that suffers from a deficiency of reality. It is just not very real. It has been put into receivership, but the receiver is keeping it going by short-term loans of reality. It has become, despite itself, a vehicle for the project of God, the creation of human beings who freely cooperate in their own constitution. God has made modernity an instrument of his mercy — albeit that for the sake of their own safety this must be kept well hidden from all modern human beings.[42]

6.7. The Responsibility of Theology

We have set out the political character of the immediate epistemological claim of modernity. We have gathered resources to ask whether the turn from Christianity toward other options is accompanied by God's turning and hiding his face from us and so is the result not only of our failure but of a failure that God has inflicted on us. Christians must be able to pass this judgment of modernity onto modernity, or they will suffer the punishment due to modernity. But the church has failed to take up its role as watchman, and so the indivisible witness to the indivisible God has been unaccountably divided between the several jurisdictions set out under the modern separation of powers, which declares that religion is not politics. The Western church is itself now suffering this judgment that the church has failed to pronounce on the West.[43] The secularization thesis must be countered by the theological caution that the God of Jesus Christ does not intend for this generation to hear him and so does not say anything it can

---

42. We can therefore argue that the term "modernity" has meaning only in theological statement. O'Donovan, *The Desire of the Nations*, p. 57, argues that theology invented the concept of the state as a local area of paideutic performance, requiring leadership with which the church must stand in conversation and confrontation.

43. See Ephraim Radner, *The End of the Church: A Pneumatology of Christian Division in the West* (Grand Rapids: Eerdmans, 1998).

hear. We have begged not to be disturbed by God's interruptions, and he has conceded this request. We have hardened our hearts, with the consequence that he has hardened our hearts.

To restate the public and political purpose of the doctrine of God is not to recommend a particular political constitution. It is to insist that theological statement keeps several accounts in parallel and so remains properly complex. At the minimum it means that any description of the state of affairs is accompanied by an account of what God will do, a statement of hope, and this is accompanied by a call to repent. Which account has to be given now depends on the particular predicament of the world to which the church must respond with harder or softer judgment. We must say that the being that resists the Word of God is nothing but the product of our own action. The division of this being into the two economies of nature and will is the whole precept of modernity. Modernity claims that, once payment has been made in the first economy of nature, we are free to enter the second economy of absolute freedom. We concede what necessity demands and are then quite free. We have seen that real choice relies on the possibility of identifying some choices as non-choices and excluding them. This second economy of utter and indeterminate freedom has no memory and allows for no growth of character. Modernity believes that religious discourse is a voluntary and inexplicable binding of ourselves when we could and should be utterly free. It believes that acknowledgment of difference is an elective matter that we should avoid and that only religious people unaccountably take on. It believes that any form of self-restraint is an illegitimate failure to take advantage of freedom, rather than what it really is, a preference for greater freedoms over lesser, more repetitive ones.

Every member of the economy of modernity is engaged in paying worship to unfreedom — necessity — in order briefly to enter the economy of freedom understood to lie behind it. This division between two economies divides us again between each of the proliferating jurisdictions created by this dialectic of nature and absolute freedom. Where we have autonomous jurisdictions of economics, politics, culture, psychology, and the still deeper recesses of subjectivity, we have no responsibility for the formation of the subjectivity of the other. Under this balkanized jurisdiction we have only a general duty not to make any positive or paideutic claims, not to teach one another or attempt to get too close to one another. This regime makes choice the first and most binding imperative. But without a set of publicly arrived at skills and criteria for the prioritizing and formation of choices, such choice represents only a failure to stick by one's choice, a failure really to continue to choose it and be formed by it. We are free always to change our mind without consequence. This regime supposes that no choice forecloses on any other choice, and thus every choice is as easily reversed as made. This discourse of choice free from definition is opposed to that discourse within which we may hear and acknowledge any external address or obligation. When we have absolutized choice, we never have to hear any specific claims or receive any external discipline.

Plato insisted that some will rule over others. These others will then at least have the dignity of having a ruler to blame. His dominion, our subordination, and this hierarchy of being is the outcome of all our *doing*. But Kant wants to go much further than Plato and say that we may all be a ruler, all autonomous. Kant therefore represents the hubris and collapse of this hierarchy. Because it denies that there is any status differential, this arrangement now appears not as top-down but as everywhere alike. It is everywhere, and no longer *appears* anywhere, with the result that the hierarchy is hidden. We are entirely complicit in this arrangement. We cannot therefore say that we wish to be other than it; we cannot therefore shake our fist at it or plead to be released from it.

All the plurality and culture open to us in this economy represent a celebration of our absolute will and subjectivity, which leaves us without the means to acknowledge any other world not made by this will and subjectivity. Our autonomy and totality would be threatened by the existence of any other economies of being.[44] Moderns say there is no God, and no issue of "God." But this is because we ourselves are that god. Our enlightenment is only complicity to conceal the discourse of protest by which we could be dethroned, freed, and transformed from a demonic to a creaturely status. This is the reason for acknowledging the claims of other systems that represent other forms of being, other priorities, and thus other "gods." The economy of modernity has given up the apparatus by which we could name or recognize anything that could dethrone us and

---

44. Gerard Loughlin, "The Basis and Authority of Doctrine," in *Cambridge Companion to Christian Doctrine*, ed. Colin E. Gunton (Cambridge: Cambridge University Press, 1997), p. 42, argues that "It is a paradox of postmodern culture that its pluralism obscures a deep homogeneity: a universal reason no less socially constructed and rhetorically maintained than those supposedly overcome, yet more insidious and ferocious because of the condition of the very pleasures of postmodern pluralistic society. This 'reason' is the material law of the market-place, predicated upon the metaphysical concept of the Void."

distinguish us from the demonic totality claimed by the economy of our action.

The economy of modernity is the function of an anonymous high god who does not intend to save us from being the prey of the contending jurisdictions. The oneness of this One allows a merely apparent manyness, and so a merely apparent politics, that will eventually be taken away by the reversion to oneness. This manyness is only the play of the real underlying sameness. Recovery of the conceptual possibility that there may really be many gods, authorities, priorities, demands, creatures, and worlds is necessary to rid us of this totalitarian monism. It is the contribution of trinitarian theology to allow us to say that *one* is the exclusive characteristic of the Father and the Son, and that by the Spirit they make their creatures one, and one with themselves. The oneness and manyness of the trinitarian God is the guarantee of the possibility that sociality, public life, and politics constitute a real, and not merely a temporary and ultimately illusory, manyness.

We must therefore say both that the world is many and that it is one. It is one over and against us and holds us captive. And worse still, we are one with it and complicit in our captivity. By declaring that we are held in bonds, the Christian gospel holds out the hope that we can be distinguished from these bonds and that we will be made distinct both from the cosmos and from the claim to be its maker. I have asked whether our theology demolishes this dichotomy between religious and nonreligious discourse and whether it turns back to rid us of that distinction by showing the self-proclaimed world of freedom and secularity as religious, superstitious, and bound. I have suggested that theology requires that we say that there is no simple account of what modernity is or what the world is. Theology is a series of duties. Among them is the duty of preventing the world from coming to any peace until its redeemer comes and of replying to the world in compassion with whatever therapeutic statement that will serve as an antidote to each specific self-inflicted injury.

We have compared two events. In one, the opponent of the Word of God puts his hand on us, locking us into a circuitry in which we can only ever repeat his action. It is an event that this opponent does not succeed in sustaining. The second is the event in which God puts his hand on humankind and keeps it there, training and leading human beings into wider and more complex forms of action so that they can reply to God and freely be with him. God brings humankind into being by himself initiating humankind's responses. He plays Adam until Adam can, with God's assistance, play himself. This act does not merely go out from God but also freely returns to him in response, in a self-sustaining exchange. It creates a time of its own that cannot be interrupted by any other and so is eternal. The trinitarian community is the source of the community of Israel. It receives Israel again as a true performer of the life of the trinitarian community. The economy of the God of Israel therefore outlives the economy of the opponent. The former has eternal life; the latter does not. An account of the God of Israel must include an account of his opponents in order to be an account of their defeat. The rival gods — the world, our mundane practices, time, and modernity — must all feature in our account of the God who is for us.

Bibliography

Albertz, R. *A History of Israelite Religion in the Old Testament Period.* 2 volumes. Louisville: Westminster, 1994.

Alexander, T. D. "Messianic Ideology in Genesis." In *The Lord's Anointed: Interpretation of Old Testament Messianic Texts,* edited by Philip E. Satterthwaite, Richard S. Hess, and Gordon J. Wenham. Carlisle: Paternoster, 1995.

Alliez, Éric. *Capital Times: Tales from the Conquest of Time.* Minneapolis: University of Minnesota Press, 1996.

Allison, Dale C. "The Eye Is the Lamp of the Body." *New Testament Studies* 33 (1987): 61-83.

———. *The New Moses: A Matthean Typology.* Edinburgh: T&T Clark, 1993.

Anderson, Bernhard W. "Creation." *The Interpreter's Dictionary of the Bible,* volume 1, pp. 725-31. Nashville: Abingdon Press, 1986.

———. *From Creation to New Creation: Old Testament Perspectives.* Minneapolis: Fortress Press, 1994.

———, ed. *Creation in the Old Testament.* Philadelphia: Fortress, 1984.

Anderson, Gary A. "Sacrifice and Sacrificial Offerings." *Anchor Bible Dictionary,* volume 5, pp. 871-86. New York: Doubleday, 1992.

Anselm. *Cur Deus Homo.* In *Basic Writings.* La Salle, IL: Open Court, 1962.

Aristotle. *Nicomachean Ethics.* Translated by David Ross. Oxford: Oxford University Press, 1980.

Arnold, Clinton E. *Ephesians, Power and Magic: The Concept of Power in Ephesians in Light of Its Historical Setting.* Cambridge: Cambridge University Press, 1989.

Aune, David E. *Prophecy in Early Christianity and the Ancient Mediterranean World.* Grand Rapids: Eerdmans, 1983.

Augustine. *City of God.* Translated by H. Bettenson. Harmondsworth: Penguin, 1984.

Bailey, Daniel P. "Christ as *Kapporet.*" Ph.D. thesis, Cambridge University, 1999.

Balentine, Samuel E. *The Torah's Vision of Worship*. Minneapolis: Augsburg Fortress, 1999.

Barba, Eugenio. *The Secret Art of the Performer*. London: Routledge, 1991.

Barclay, John. *Jews in the Mediterranean Diaspora*. Edinburgh: T&T Clark, 1996.

Barker, Margaret. "Beyond the Veil of the Temple: The High Priestly Origins of the Apocalypses." *Scottish Journal of Theology* 51 (1998): 1-21.

————. *The Gate of Heaven: The History and Symbolism of the Temple in Jerusalem*. London: SPCK, 1991.

————. *The Revelation of Jesus Christ*. Edinburgh: T&T Clark, 2000.

————. *The Risen Lord: The Jesus of History as the Christ of Faith*. Edinburgh: T&T Clark, 1996.

Barr, James. *Biblical Faith and Natural Theology*. Oxford: Clarendon, 1993.

Barrett, C. K. *From First Adam to Last: A Study in Pauline Theology*. London: A. & C. Black, 1962.

Barth, Karl. *Church Dogmatics*. Edited by G. W. Bromiley and T. F. Torrance. Edinburgh: T. & T. Clark, 1956-75.

Barton, Stephen C. "New Testament Interpretation as Performance." *Scottish Journal of Theology* 52 (1999).

Bassler, Jouette M. *Pauline Theology: 1 Thessalonians, Philippians, Galatians, Philemon*. Minneapolis: Fortress Press, 1991.

Bauckham, Richard. *The Climax of Prophecy: Studies on the Book of Revelation*. Edinburgh: T&T Clark, 1993.

————. *Jude and the Relatives of Jesus in the Early Church*. Edinburgh: T&T Clark, 1990.

Bauerschmidt, Frederick C. "The Word Made Speculative?" *Modern Theology* 15 (1999): 417-32.

Bayer, Oswald. "The Conflict of Interpretations: Theology in the Conflict of Interpretations — Before the Text." *Modern Theology* 16 (2000): 495-502.

————. *Gott als Autor*. Tübingen: Mohr Siebeck, 1999.

Behr, John. *Asceticism and Anthropology in Irenaeus and Clement*. Oxford: Oxford University Press, 2000.

Beiser, Frederick C. *The Fate of Reason: German Philosophy from Kant to Fichte*. Cambridge, MA: Harvard University Press, 1997.

————. *The Sovereignty of Reason: The Defense of Rationality in the Early English Enlightenment*. Princeton: Princeton University Press, 1996.

Bell, Richard H. *No One Seeks for God: An Exegetical and Theological Study of Romans 1.18–3.20*. WUNT 106. Tübingen: Mohr, 1998.

————. *Provoked to Jealousy: The Origin and Purpose of the Jealousy Motif in Romans 9–11*. WUNT 63. Tübingen: Mohr, 1994.

Belleville, Linda L. *Reflections of Glory: Paul's Polemical Use of the Moses-Doxa Tradition in 2 Corinthians 3.1-18*. Sheffield: Sheffield Academic Press, 1991.

Bender, John, and David E. Wellbery. *Chronotypes: The Construction of Time.* Stanford: Stanford University Press, 1991.

Bermudez, José Luis, Anthony Marcel, and Naomi Eilan. *The Body and the Self.* Cambridge, MA: MIT, 1995.

Bernadete, Seth. *Plato's "Laws": The Discovery of Being.* Chicago: University of Chicago Press, 2000.

Billig, Michael. *Arguing and Thinking: A Rhetorical Approach to Social Psychology.* Cambridge: Cambridge University Press, 1987.

Binder, Donald D. *Into the Temple Courts: The Place of Synagogues in the Second Temple Period.* Atlanta: Society of Biblical Literature, 1999.

Bockmuehl, Markus. *Revelation and Mystery in Ancient Judaism and Pauline Christianity.* Grand Rapids: Eerdmans, 1997.

———. "'To Be or Not to Be': The Possible Futures of New Testament Scholarship." *Scottish Journal of Theology* 51 (1998): 271-306.

Bodéüs, Richard. *The Political Dimensions of Aristotle's Ethics.* Albany: State University of New York Press, 1993.

Bogue, Ronald. "Art and Territory." In *A Deleuzian Century?* edited by Ian Buchanan. Durham: Duke University Press, 1999.

Booth, Edward, O.P. *Aristotelian Aporetic Ontology in Islamic and Christian Thinkers.* Cambridge: Cambridge University Press, 1983.

Borgen, Peder. *Bread from Heaven: An Exegetical Study of the Concept of Manna in the Gospel of John and the Writing of Philo.* Leiden: Brill, 1965.

Bourdieu, Pierre. *Language and Symbolic Power.* Oxford: Polity, 1991.

Bowman, John. *The Fourth Gospel and the Jews: A Study in R. Akiba, Esther and the Gospel of John.* Pittsburgh: Pickwick, 1975.

Boyarin, Daniel. *A Radical Jew: Paul and the Politics of Identity.* Berkeley: University of California Press, 1994.

Braaten, Carl, and Robert W. Jenson. *Christian Dogmatics.* Philadelphia: Fortress, 1984.

Brett, Mark. *Biblical Criticism in Crisis: The Impact of the Canonical Approach on Old Testament Studies.* Cambridge: Cambridge University Press, 1991.

———. *Ethnicity and the Bible.* Leiden: Brill, 1996.

Brooks, Roger, and John J. Collins. *Hebrew Bible or Old Testament?* Notre Dame: Notre Dame University Press, 1990.

Brower, K. E., and Mark W. Elliott. *'The Reader Must Understand': Eschatology in Bible and Theology.* Leicester: Apollos, 1997.

Brown, Raymond E. *The Death of the Messiah from Gethsemane to the Grave: A Commentary on the Passion Narratives in the Four Gospels.* Anchor Bible. New York: Doubleday, 1994.

Brown, William P. *The Ethos of the Cosmos: The Genesis of Moral Imagination in the Bible.* Grand Rapids: Eerdmans, 1999.

Brueggemann, Walter. *Theology of the Old Testament: Testimony, Dispute, Advocacy.* Minneapolis: Augsburg Fortress, 1997.

Bruner, Jerome S. *Acts of Meaning.* Cambridge, MA: Harvard University Press, 1990.

Bryan, David. *Cosmos, Chaos and the Kosher Mentality: The Roots and Rationale of Zoomorphic Imagery in the Animal Apocalypse, the Testament of Naphtali and Daniel 7.* Sheffield: Sheffield Academic Press, 1995.

Buchanan, Ian. *A Deleuzian Century?* Durham: Duke University Press, 1999.

Buckley, Michael J., S.J. *At the Origins of Modern Atheism.* New Haven: Yale University Press, 1987.

Buell, Denise K. *Making Christians: Clement of Alexandria and the Rhetoric of Legitimacy.* Princeton: Princeton University Press, 1999.

Burkert, Walter. *Greek Religion: Archaic and Classical.* Oxford: Blackwell, 1985.

—————. *Homo Necans: The Anthropology of Ancient Greek Sacrificial Ritual and Myth.* Berkeley: University of California Press, 1983.

Burrell, David B. *Aquinas: God and Action.* London: Routledge & Kegan Paul, 1979.

Burtchaell, James T. *From Synagogue to Church: Public Services and Offices in the Earliest Christian Communities.* Cambridge: Cambridge University Press, 1992.

Caputo, John D. *The Prayers and Tears of Jacques Derrida: Religion without Religion.* Bloomington: Indiana University Press, 1997.

Carrithers, Michael, Steven Collins, and Steven Lukes. *The Category of the Person: Anthropology, Philosophy, History.* Cambridge: Cambridge University Press, 1985.

Carroll, John T., and Joel B. Green. *The Death of Jesus in Early Christianity.* Peabody, MA: Hendrickson, 1995.

Carroll, M. Daniel, David J. A. Clines, and Philip R. Davies, eds. *The Bible in Human Society: Essays in Honour of John Rogerson.* Sheffield: Sheffield Academic Press, 1995.

Carruthers, Mary J. *The Book of Memory: A Study of Memory in Medieval Culture.* Cambridge: Cambridge University Press, 1990.

Casey, Edward S. *The Fate of Place: A Philosophical History.* Berkeley: University of California Press, 1997.

Cavanaugh, William T. "The City — Beyond Secular Parodies." In *Radical Orthodoxy: A New Theology,* edited by John Milbank, Catherine Pickstock, and Graham Ward. London: Routledge, 1999.

Charry, Ellen T. *By the Renewing of Your Minds: The Pastoral Function of Christian Doctrine.* New York: Oxford University Press, 1997.

Childs, Brevard S. *Biblical Theology of the Old and New Testaments.* London: SCM Press, 1992.

—————. *Exodus: A Commentary.* London: SCM Press, 1974.

—————. *Introduction to the Old Testament as Scripture.* Philadelphia: Fortress, 1979.

—————. *Old Testament in a Canonical Context.* Minneapolis: Fortress, 1989.

Chilton, Bruce D. *A Feast of Meanings: Eucharistic Theologies from Jesus through Johannine Circles.* Leiden: Brill, 1994.

————. "The Hungry Knife: Towards a Sense of Sacrifice." In *The Bible in Human Society: Essays in Honour of John Rogerson.* Edited by M. Daniel Carroll, David J. A. Clines, and Philip R. Davies. Sheffield: Sheffield Academic Press, 1995.

————. *Pure Kingdom: Jesus' Vision of God.* London: SPCK, 1996.

————. *The Temple of Jesus: His Sacrificial Program within a Cultural History of Sacrifice.* University Park: Pennsylvania State University Press, 1992.

Chilton, Bruce D., and Craig A. Evans. *Studying the Historical Jesus: Evaluation of the State of Current Research.* Leiden: Brill, 1994.

Chilton, Bruce D., and Jacob Neusner. *Judaism in the New Testament: Practices and Beliefs.* London: Routledge, 1995.

Cicero. *On the Commonwealth and On the Laws.* Edited by James E. G. Zetzel. Cambridge: Cambridge University Press, 1999.

Cioffi, Frank. *Wittgenstein on Freud and Frazer.* Cambridge: Cambridge University Press, 1998.

Clark, Elizabeth A. *Reading and Renunciation: Asceticism and Scripture in Early Christianity.* Princeton: Princeton University Press, 1999.

Clements, R. E. *The World of Ancient Israel: Sociological, Anthropological, and Political Perspectives.* Cambridge: Cambridge University Press, 1989.

Collins, John J. *The Apocalyptic Imagination: An Interpretation of the Jewish Matrix of Christianity.* New York: Crossroad, 1984.

————. *Apocalyticism in the Dead Sea Scrolls.* London: Routledge, 1997.

Collins, Adela Yarbro. *Cosmology and Eschatology in Jewish and Christian Apocalypticism.* Leiden: Brill, 1996.

Connerton, Paul. *How Societies Remember.* Cambridge: Cambridge University Press, 1989.

Craigo-Snell, Shannon. "Command Performance: Rethinking Performance Interpretation in the Context of Divine Discourse." *Modern Theology* 16 (2000): 475-94.

Crenshaw, James L. *A Whirlpool of Torment: Israelite Traditions of God as Oppressive Presence.* Philadelphia: Fortress, 1984.

Crossan, John D. *The Historical Jesus: The Life of a Mediterranean Jewish Peasant.* Edinburgh: T&T Clark, 1991.

Dahl, Nils A. *The Crucified Messiah and Other Essays.* Minneapolis: Fortress, 1974.

Dalferth, Ingolf U. "Christ Died for Us." In *Sacrifice and Redemption: Durham Essays in Theology,* edited by S. W. Sykes. Cambridge: Cambridge University Press, 1991.

————. "Creation — Style of the World." *International Journal for Systematic Theology* 1 (1999).

————. *Der auferweckte Gekreuzigte: Zur Grammatik der Christologie.* Tübingen: Mohr Siebeck, 1994.

————. *Gedeutete Gegenwart: Zur Wahrnehmung Gottes in den Erfahrungen der Zeit.* Tübingen: Mohr Siebeck, 1997.

————. "Mythos, Ritual, Dogmatik: Strukturen der religiösen Text-Welt." *Evangelische Theologie* 47, no. 4 (1987): 272-91.

————. *Theology and Philosophy.* Oxford: Blackwell, 1988.

Damasio, Antonio R. *Descartes's Error: Emotion, Reason and the Human Brain.* London: Macmillan, 1996.

Davies, Philip R., and Bruce D. Chilton. "The Aqedah: A Revised Tradition History." *Catholic Biblical Quarterly* 40 (1978): 514-46.

Davies, W. D., and Dale C. Allison. *Matthew.* The International Critical Commentary, volume 1. Edinburgh: T&T Clark, 1988.

Dawson, J. David. "Figural Reading and the Fashioning of Christian Identity in Boyarin, Auerbach and Frei." *Modern Theology* 14 (1998): 181-212.

d'Costa, Gavin. *Christian Uniqueness Reconsidered: The Myth of a Pluralistic Theology of Religions.* Maryknoll, NY: Orbis, 1990.

Deacon, Terence W. *The Symbolic Species: The Co-evolution of Language and the Human Brain.* Harmondsworth: Penguin, 1997.

Dennett, Daniel C. *Consciousness Explained.* Harmondsworth: Penguin, 1991.

————. *Darwin's Dangerous Idea: Evolution and the Meanings of Life.* Harmondsworth: Penguin, 1995.

Derrida, Jacques. *Given Time (Donner le Temps, 1 Fausse Monnaie).* Chicago: University of Chicago Press, 1992.

Douglas, Mary. "The Eucharist: Its Continuity with the Bread Sacrifice of Leviticus." *Modern Theology* 15 (1999): 209-24.

————. *In the Wilderness: The Doctrine of Defilement in the Book of Numbers.* Sheffield: Sheffield Academic Press, 1993.

————. *Leviticus as Literature.* Oxford: Oxford University Press, 1999.

————. "The Pangolin Revisited: A New Approach to Animal Symbolism." In *Signifying Animals: Human Meaning in the Natural World,* edited by Roy G. Willis. London: Unwin Hyman, 1990.

————. *Purity and Danger: An Analysis of the Concepts of Pollution and Taboo.* London: Routledge & Kegan Paul, 1966.

Dunn, James D. G. "1 Corinthians 15.45 — Last Adam, Life-Giving Spirit." In *Christ and the Spirit in the New Testament,* edited by Barnabas Lindars and Stephen S. Smalley. London: Cambridge University Press, 1973.

————. *The Parting of the Ways between Christianity and Judaism and Their Significance for the Character of Christianity.* London: SCM, 1991.

————. *Theology of Paul the Apostle.* Edinburgh: T&T Clark, 1998.

Dupré, Louis. *Passage to Modernity: An Essay in the Hermeneutics of Nature and Culture.* New Haven: Yale University Press, 1993.

Eilberg-Schwartz, Howard. *The Savage in Judaism: An Anthropology of Israelite Religion and Ancient Judaism.* Bloomington: Indiana University Press, 1990.

Eisen, Arnold M. *Rethinking Modern Judaism: Ritual, Commandment, Community.* Chicago: University of Chicago Press, 1998.

Elster, Jon. *Alchemies of the Mind: Rationality and the Emotions.* Cambridge: Cambridge University Press, 1999.

———. *Political Psychology.* Cambridge: Cambridge University Press, 1993.

Evans, Craig A., and Bruce D. Chilton. *Jesus in Context: Temple Purity and Restoration.* Leiden: Brill, 1997.

Evans, Craig A., and Stanley E. Porter. *The Historical Jesus.* Sheffield: Sheffield Academic Press, 1995.

Evans, Craig A., and James A. Sanders. *Paul and the Scriptures of Israel.* Sheffield: JSOT Press, 1993.

Evans, Craig A., and W. R. Stegner. *The Gospels and the Scriptures of Israel.* Sheffield: Sheffield Academic Press, 1994.

Fardon, Richard. *Mary Douglas: An Intellectual Biography.* London: Routledge, 1998.

Farrow, Douglas. *Ascension and Ecclesia.* Edinburgh: T&T Clark, 1999.

Feenstra, Ronald J., and Cornelius Plantinga Jr., eds. *Trinity, Incarnation and Atonement: Philosophical and Theological Essays.* Notre Dame: Notre Dame University Press, 1989.

Feldman, E. *Biblical and Post-Biblical Defilement and Mourning: Law as Theology.* New York: Yeshiva University, 1977.

Feldman, Louis H. *Jew and Gentile in the Ancient World: Attitudes and Interactions from Alexander to Justinian.* Princeton: Princeton University Press, 1993.

Fernandez, James W. *Persuasions and Performances: The Play of Tropes in Culture.* Bloomington: Indiana University Press, 1986.

Fletcher-Louis, Crispin. "The Destruction of the Temple and Relativisation of the Old Covenant." In K. E. Brower and Mark W. Elliott, *"The Reader Must Understand": Eschatology in Bible and Theology.* Leicester: Apollos, 1997.

———. "Jesus Inspects His Priestly War-Party." In *The Old Testament in the New Testament: Essays in Honour of J. L. North,* edited by Steve Moyise. Sheffield: Sheffield Academic Press, 2000.

———. *Luke-Acts: Angels, Christology and Soteriology.* Wissenschaftliche Untersuchungen zum Neuen Testament 94. Tübingen: Mohr, 1997.

Ford, David F., and Daniel W. Hardy. *Jubilate: Theology in Praise.* London: Darton, Longman & Todd, 1984.

Ford, David F., and Frances M. Young. *Meaning and Truth in 2 Corinthians.* London: SPCK, 1987.

Forde, Gerhard. "The Work of Christ." In *Christian Dogmatics,* edited by Carl Braaten and Robert W. Jenson. Philadelphia: Fortress Press, 1984.

Forster, Michael N. *Hegel's Idea of a Phenomenology of Spirit.* Chicago: University of Chicago Press, 1998.

Foucault, Michel. *The Order of Things: The Archaeology of the Human Sciences.* London: Tavistock, 1970.

Fowl, Stephen E. *Engaging Scripture: A Model for Theological Interpretation.* London: Blackwell, 1998.

Frei, Hans W. *The Eclipse of Biblical Narrative: A Study in Eighteenth and Nineteenth Century Hermeneutics.* New Haven: Yale University Press, 1974.

Fretheim, Terence E. *The Suffering of God.* Philadelphia: Fortress, 1984.

Funkenstein, Amos. *Theology and the Scientific Imagination from the Middle Ages to the Seventeenth Century.* Princeton: Princeton University Press, 1986.

Gallagher, Shaun. *The Inordinance of Time.* Evanston: Northwestern University Press, 1998.

Garber, Daniel, and Michael Ayers. *The Cambridge History of Seventeenth-Century Philosophy.* Cambridge: Cambridge University Press, 1998.

Gell, Alfred. *The Anthropology of Time: Cultural Constructions of Temporal Maps and Images.* Oxford: Berg, 1992.

————. *Art and Agency: An Anthropological Theory.* Oxford: Clarendon, 1998.

Gellner, Ernest. *Culture, Identity and Politics.* Cambridge: Cambridge University Press, 1986.

Gese, Hartmut. *Essays on Biblical Theology.* Minneapolis: Augsburg, 1981.

Gestrich, Christof. "God Takes Our Place: A Religious-Philosophical Approach to the Concept of *Stellvertretung.*" *Modern Theology* 17 (2001): 313-34.

————. *The Return of Splendor: The Christian Doctrine of Sin and Forgiveness.* Grand Rapids: Eerdmans, 1997.

Geyer, Hans-Georg. "Solus Christus." In *Ja und Nein: Christliche Theologie im Angesicht Israels,* edited by Klaus Wengst and Gerhard Sass. Neukirchen-Vluyn: Neukirchener, 1998.

Gibson, J. J. *The Ecological Approach to Visual Perception.* Boston: Houghton Mifflin, 1986.

Girard, René. *Violence and the Sacred.* Baltimore: Johns Hopkins University Press, 1977.

Glendinning, Simon. *On Being with Others: Heidegger, Derrida, Wittgenstein.* London: Routledge, 1998.

Goffman, Erving. *Interaction Ritual: Essays on Face-to-Face Behaviour.* New York: Doubleday, Anchor Books, 1967.

————. *The Presentation of Self in Everyday Life.* New York: Doubleday, Anchor Books, 1959.

Goldberg, Harvey E. "Cambridge in the Land of Canaan: Descent, Alliance, Circumcision and Instruction in the Bible." *Journal of Ancient Near East Studies* 24 (1996): 9-34.

Goldingay, John. *Atonement Today.* London: SPCK, 1995.

Gorman, F. H., Jr. *The Ideology of Ritual: Space, Time, and Status in the Priestly Theology.* Sheffield: JSOT Press, 1990.

————. "Ritual Studies and Biblical Studies: Assessments of the Past, Prospects of the Future." *Semeia* 67 (1994): 13-36.

Gray, Marion. "Time for Jenson." Paper read to the Institute for Systematic Theology, King's College, London, 2002.

Green, Arthur. *Jewish Spirituality*. 2 volumes. London: Routledge & Kegan Paul, 1986.

Green, Garrett. *Theology, Hermeneutics and Imagination: The Crisis of Interpretation at the End of Modernity*. Cambridge: Cambridge University Press, 2000.

Green, Joel B. *The Death of Jesus: Tradition and Interpretation in the Passion Narrative*. Tübingen: Mohr, 1988.

Green, Ronald M. *Kierkegaard and Kant: The Hidden Debt*. Albany: State University of New York Press, 1992.

Griswold, Charles L., Jr. *Adam Smith and the Virtues of Enlightenment*. Cambridge: Cambridge University Press, 1999.

Gunton, Colin E. *The Actuality of Atonement: A Study of Metaphor, Rationality and the Christian Tradition*. Edinburgh: T&T Clark, 1988.

————. *The Cambridge Companion to Christian Doctrine*. Cambridge: Cambridge University Press, 1997.

————. *The One, the Three and the Many: God, Creation and the Culture of Modernity*. Cambridge: Cambridge University Press, 1993.

————. Review of H. Steindl, *Genugtuung: Biblisches Versöhnungsdenken — eine Quelle für Anselms Satisfaktionstheorie?* (Freiburg: Universitätsverlag, 1990), *Journal of Theological Studies* 43 (1992): 283-85.

————. "Sacrifice and the Sacrifices." In *Trinity, Incarnation and Atonement: Philosophical and Theological Essays*, edited by Ronald J. Feenstra and Cornelius Plantinga Jr. Notre Dame: Notre Dame University Press, 1989.

————. *Theology through the Theologians*. Edinburgh: T&T Clark, 1996.

————. *Trinity, Time, and Church: A Response to the Theology of Robert W. Jenson*. Grand Rapids: Eerdmans, 2000.

Hacker, P. M. S. *Insight and Illusion: Themes in the Philosophy of Wittgenstein*. Oxford: Clarendon, 1986.

Hadot, Pierre. *Philosophy as a Way of Life*. Translated by Michael Chase. Chicago: University of Chicago Press, 1995.

Hafemann, Scott J. "Paul and His Interpreters." In *Dictionary of Paul and His Letters*, edited by Gerald F. Hawthorne, Ralph P. Martin, and Daniel G. Reid. Leicester: Inter-Varsity Press, 1993.

————. *Paul, Moses and the History of Israel: The Letter/Spirit Contrast and the Argument from Scripture in 2 Corinthians*. Wissenschaftliche Untersuchungen zum Neuen Testament 81. Tübingen: Mohr, 1995.

————. *Suffering and the Spirit: 2 Corinthians 2:14-33*. Wissenschaftliche Untersuchungen zum Neuen Testament 19. Tübingen: Mohr, 1986.

Haran, Menachem. *Temples and Temple Services in Ancient Israel: An Inquiry into the*

Character of Cult Phenomena and the Historical Setting of the Priestly School. Oxford: Clarendon, 1978.

Hardy, Daniel W. "Christ and Creation." In *The Incarnation: Ecumenical Studies in the Nicene-Constantinopolitan Creed,* edited by T. F. Torrance. Edinburgh: Handsel Press, 1981.

Harré, Rom. "'Berkeleyan' Arguments and the Ontology of Cognitive Science." In *The Future of the Cognitive Revolution,* edited by David M. Johnson and Christina E. Erneling. New York: Oxford University Press, 1997.

Harries, Jill. *Law and Empire in Late Antiquity.* New York: Cambridge University Press, 1999.

Harvey, Anthony E. *Renewal through Suffering: A Study of 2 Corinthians.* Edinburgh: T&T Clark, 1996.

Hauerwas, Stanley. "The Truth about God: The Decalogue as Condition for Truthful Speech." In *Sanctify Them in the Truth.* Edinburgh: T&T Clark, 1998.

Hayes, John H., and J. Maxwell Miller. *Israelite and Judaean History.* London: SCM, 1977.

Hays, Richard B. *Echoes of Scripture in the Letters of Paul.* New Haven: Yale University Press, 1989.

————. *The Faith of Jesus Christ: The Narrative Substructure of Galatians 3:1–4:11.* Grand Rapids: Eerdmans, 2002.

————. *The Moral Vision of the New Testament: Community, Cross, New Creation.* Edinburgh: T&T Clark, 1996.

————. "*Pistis* and Pauline Christology: What Is at Stake?" In *Pauline Theology 4,* edited by David M. Hay and E. Elizabeth Johnson. Minneapolis: Fortress, 1997.

Haywood, C. T. R. "Sacrifice and World Order: Some Observations on ben Sira's Attitude to the Temple Service, Sacrifice and Redemption." In *Sacrifice and Redemption: Durham Essays in Theology,* edited by S. W. Sykes. Cambridge: Cambridge University Press, 1991.

————. *The Second Temple: A Non-Biblical Sourcebook.* London: Routledge, 1998.

Hegel, G. W. F. *Lectures on the Philosophy of Religion.* Volume 3: *The Consummate Religion.* Edited by Peter C. Hodgson. Berkeley: University of California Press, 1985.

Heidegger, Martin. "On the Essence and Concept of *Phusis* in Aristotle's *Physics* B, I." Translated by Thomas Sheehan in *Pathmarks,* edited by William McNeill. Cambridge: Cambridge University Press, 1998.

Hemming, Laurence P. "Nihilism, Heidegger and the Grounds of Redemption." In *Radical Orthodoxy: A New Theology,* edited by John Milbank, Catherine Pickstock, and Graham Ward. London: Routledge, 1999.

Hendriks-Jansen, Horst. *Catching Ourselves in the Act: Situated Activity, Interactive Emergence, Evolution and Human Thought.* Cambridge, MA: MIT, 1996.

Hengel, Martin. *Crucifixion in the Ancient World and the Folly of the Message of the Cross.* London: SCM Press, 1977.

————. *Studies in Early Christology.* Edinburgh: T&T Clark, 1995.

Heschel, Susannah. *Abraham Geiger and the Jewish Jesus.* Chicago: University of Chicago Press, 1998.

Hochstrasser, T. J. *Natural Law Theories in the Early Enlightenment.* Cambridge: Cambridge University Press, 2000.

Hoffman, Lawrence A. *Covenant of Blood: Circumcision and Gender in Rabbinic Judaism.* Chicago: University of Chicago Press, 1996.

Hofius, Otfried. "Gemeinschaft mit den Engeln im Gottesdienst der Kirche." *Zeitung für Theologie und Kirche* 89 (1992): 172-96.

Holland, Dorothy, and Naomi Quinn. *Cultural Models in Language and Thought.* Cambridge: Cambridge University Press, 1987.

Hollis, Martin. *Trust within Reason.* Cambridge: Cambridge University Press, 1998.

Hooker, Morna. *From Adam to Christ: Essays on Paul.* Cambridge: Cambridge University Press, 1990.

Horbury, William. *Jewish Messianism and the Cult of Christ.* London: SCM Press, 1998.

————. "Land, Sanctuary and Worship." In *Early Christian Thought in Its Jewish Context,* edited by John Barclay and John Sweet. Cambridge: Cambridge University Press, 1996.

Horbury, William, and Brian McNeil. *Suffering and Martyrdom in the New Testament.* Cambridge: Cambridge University Press, 1981.

Houston, Walter. *Purity and Monotheism: Clean and Unclean Animals in Biblical Law.* Sheffield: JSOT, 1993.

Hunter, Ian. *Rival Enlightenments: Civil and Metaphysical Philosophy in Early Modern Germany.* Cambridge: Cambridge University Press, 2001.

Hurst, L. D. *The Epistle to the Hebrews: Its Background of Thought.* Cambridge: Cambridge University Press, 1990.

Hurtado, Larry. *One God, One Lord.* Edinburgh: T&T Clark, 1988.

Hütter, Reinhard. *Suffering Divine Things: Theology as Church Practice.* Translated by Doug Stott. Grand Rapids: Eerdmans, 1999.

Ihde, Don. *Expanding Hermeneutics: Visualism in Science.* Evanston: Northwestern University Press, 1998.

Iser, Wolfgang. *The Range of Interpretation.* New York: Columbia University Press, 2000.

Israel, Jonathan I. *Radical Enlightenment: Philosophy and the Making of Modernity, 1650-1750.* Oxford: Oxford University Press, 2001.

James, Susan. *Passion and Action: The Emotions in Seventeenth-Century Philosophy.* Oxford: Clarendon, 1997.

Janowski, Bernd. "Die Tat kehrt zum Täter zurück: Offene Fragen in Umkreis des tunergehen-Zusammenhangs." In *Die Rettende Gerechtigkeit.* Neukirchen-Vluyn: Neukirchener, 1999.

————. "Er trug unsere Sunden: Jesaja 53 und die Dramatik der Stellvertretung." In

Gottes Gegenwart in Israel: Beiträge zur Theologie des Alten Testaments. Neukirchen-Vluyn: Neukirchener, 1993.

————. *Sühne als Heilsgeschehen.* Neukirchen-Vluyn: Neukirchener, 2000.

Janowski, Bernd, and Michael Welker. *Opfer: Theologische und kulturelle Kontexte.* Frankfurt am Main: Suhrkamp, 2000.

Jay, Martin. *Downcast Eyes: The Denigration of Vision in Twentieth-Century French Thought.* Berkeley: University of California Press, 1993.

Jay, Nancy. *Throughout Your Generations Forever: Sacrifice, Religion and Paternity.* Chicago: University of Chicago Press, 1992.

Jenson, Philip. *Graded Holiness: A Key to the Priestly Perception of the World.* Journal for the Study of the Old Testament — Supplement Series 106. Sheffield: JSOT Press, 1992.

Jenson, Robert W. *Essays in Theology of Culture.* Grand Rapids: Eerdmans, 1995.

————. "Justification as a Triune Event." *Modern Theology* 11 (1995): 421-27.

————. *Systematic Theology.* New York: Oxford University Press, 1997-99.

————. "You Wonder Where the Spirit Went." *Pro Ecclesia* 2, no. 3 (1993).

Jervis, L. Ann, and Peter Richardson, eds. *Gospel in Paul: Studies on Corinthians, Galatians, and Romans for Richard N. Longenecker.* Journal for the Study of the New Testament — Supplement Series 108. Sheffield: Sheffield Academic Press, 1994.

Johansen, Karsten Friis. *A History of Ancient Philosophy: From the Beginnings to Augustine.* London: Routledge, 1998.

Johnson, David M., and Christina E. Erneling, eds. *The Future of the Cognitive Revolution.* New York: Oxford University Press, 1997.

Johnson, Mark. *The Body in the Mind: The Bodily Basis of Meaning, Imagination, and Reason.* Chicago: University of Chicago Press, 1987.

Jüngel, Eberhard. *The Doctrine of the Trinity: God's Being Is in Becoming.* Edinburgh: Scottish Academic Press, 1976.

————. *God as the Mystery of the World.* Translated by Darrell L. Guder. Edinburgh: T&T Clark, 1983.

Kant, Immanuel. *Groundwork of the Metaphysic of Morals.* Edited by Mary Gregor. With an introduction by Christine M. Korsgaard. Cambridge: Cambridge University Press, 1997.

————. *Perpetual Peace and Other Essays.* Edited by T. Humphrey. Indianapolis: Hackett, 1983.

————. *Religion within the Boundaries of Mere Reason.* Translated and edited by Alan Wood and George di Giovanni. Cambridge: Cambridge University Press, 1998.

Keel, Othmar. *The Symbolism of the Biblical World: Ancient Near Eastern Iconography and the Book of Psalms.* Translated by Timothy J. Hallett. London: SPCK, 1978.

Keel, Othmar, and Christoph Uehlinger. *Gods, Goddesses and Images of God in Ancient Israel.* Edinburgh: T&T Clark, 1998.

Kerr, Fergus. *Theology after Wittgenstein.* London: SPCK, 1997.

Kierkegaard, Søren. *Fear and Trembling.* Edited by W. Lowrie. Princeton: Princeton University Press, 1941.

Kim, Seyoon. *The Origin of Paul's Gospel.* Tübingen: Mohr Siebeck, 1981.

————. *The "Son of Man" as the Son of God.* Tübingen: Mohr Siebeck, 1983.

Knight, Douglas H. "Jenson on Time." In *Trinity, Time, and Church: A Response to the Theology of Robert W. Jenson,* edited by C. E. Gunton. Grand Rapids: Eerdmans, 2000.

Kontopoulos, Kyriakos M. *The Logics of Social Structure.* Cambridge: Cambridge University Press, 1993.

Kovesi, Julius. *Moral Notions.* London: Routledge & Kegan Paul, 1967.

Kraftchick, Steven, Charles D. Myers Jr., and Ben C. Ollenburger, eds. *Biblical Theology: Problems and Perspectives, in Honor of J. Christiaan Beker.* Nashville: Abingdon, 1995.

Kraus, Wolfgang. *Das Volk Gottes. Zur Grundung des Ekklesiologie bei Paulus.* Wissenschaftliche Untersuchungen zum Neuen Testament 85. Tübingen: Mohr Siebeck, 1996.

————. *Der Tod Jesu als Heiligtumsweihe.* Neukirchen-Vluyn: Neukirchener, 1991.

Kugler, Robert. "Holiness, Purity, the Body and Society: The Evidence for Theological Conflict in Leviticus." *Journal for the Study of the Old Testament* 76 (1997): 3-27.

Kuper, Adam. *The Invention of Primitive Society: Transformations of an Illusion.* London: Routledge, 1988.

Kupp, David. *Matthew's Emmanuel: Divine Presence and God's People in the First Gospel.* Cambridge: Cambridge University Press, 1996.

LaCocque, André, and Paul Ricoeur. *Thinking Biblically: Exegetical and Hermeneutical Studies.* Chicago: University of Chicago Press, 1998.

Lakoff, George, and Mark Johnson. *Metaphors We Live By.* Chicago: University of Chicago Press, 1980.

Lash, Nicholas. "Not Exactly Politics or Power?" *Modern Theology* 8 (1992): 353-64.

————. "When Did the Theologians Lose Interest in Theology?" In *Theology and Dialogue: Essays in Conversation with George Lindbeck,* edited by Bruce D. Marshall. Notre Dame: University of Notre Dame Press, 1990.

————. "Where Does Holy Teaching Leave Philosophy? Questions on Milbank's Aquinas." *Modern Theology* 15 (1999): 433-44.

Leithart, Peter J. "The Gospel, Gregory VII and Modern Theology." *Modern Theology* 19, no. 1 (2003): 5-28.

Levenson, Jon D. *Creation and the Persistence of Evil: The Jewish Drama of Divine Omnipotence.* Second edition. Princeton: Princeton University Press, 1988.

————. *The Death and Resurrection of the Beloved Son: The Transformation of Child Sacrifice in Judaism and Christianity.* New Haven: Yale University Press, 1993.

————. "The Hebrew Bible, the OT and Historical Criticism." In *Reading in Commu-*

nion: Scripture and Ethics in Christian Life, edited by S. E. Fowl and L. G. Jones. Grand Rapids: Eerdmans, 1991.

———. "The Jerusalem Temple." In *Jewish Spirituality,* edited by Arthur Green. London: Routledge & Kegan Paul, 1986.

———. *Sinai and Zion: An Entry into the Jewish Bible.* Minneapolis: Winston, 1985.

———. "Theological Consensus or Historicist Evasion?" In *Hebrew Bible or Old Testament?* edited by Roger Brooks and John J. Collins. Notre Dame: Notre Dame University Press, 1990.

———. "The Universal Horizon of Biblical Particularism." In *Ethnicity and the Bible,* edited by Mark G. Brett. Leiden: Brill, 1996.

———. "Why Jews Are Not Interested in Biblical Theology." In *Judaic Perspectives on Ancient Israel,* edited by Jacob Neusner, Baruch A. Levine, and Ernest S. Frerichs. Minneapolis: Fortress Press, 1987.

Levin, David M. *Modernity and Hegemony of Vision.* Berkeley: University of California Press, 1993.

———. *Sites of Vision: The Discursive Construction of Sight in the History of Philosophy.* Cambridge, MA: MIT, 1997.

Lindars, Barnabas. *The Theology of the Letter to the Hebrews.* Cambridge: Cambridge University Press, 1991.

Lindars, Barnabas, and Stephen S. Smalley. *Christ and the Spirit in the New Testament.* London: Cambridge University Press, 1973.

Lindbeck, George. "Postcritical Canonical Interpretation." In *Theological Exegesis: Essays in Honor of Brevard S. Childs,* edited by Christopher Seitz and Kathryn Greene-McCreight. Grand Rapids: Eerdmans, 1999.

Lloyd, G. E. R. *Polarity and Analogy: Two Types of Argumentation in Early Greek Thought.* Cambridge: Cambridge University Press, 1966.

Longenecker, Bruce. *Eschatology and the Covenant: A Comparison of 4 Ezra and Romans 1–11.* Sheffield: JSOT Press, 1991.

Losonsky, Michael. *Enlightenment and Action from Descartes to Kant: Passionate Thought.* Cambridge: Cambridge University Press, 2001.

Loughlin, Gerard. "The Basis and Authority of Doctrine." In *Cambridge Companion to Christian Doctrine,* edited by Colin E. Gunton. Cambridge: Cambridge University Press, 1997.

Lucretius. *On the Nature of Things.* Translated by Martin F. Smith. London: Sphere, 1969.

Lyonnet, Stanislas, and Leopold Sabourin. *Sin, Redemption and Sacrifice: A Biblical and Patristic Study.* Rome: Biblical Institute Press, 1970.

Maccoby, Hyam. *Ritual and Morality: The Ritual Purity System and Its Place in Judaism.* Cambridge: Cambridge University Press, 1999.

MacIntyre, Alasdair. *After Virtue: A Study in Moral Theory.* Second edition. London: Duckworth, 1985.

————. *Three Rival Versions of Moral Enquiry: Encyclopaedia, Genealogy and Tradition.* London: Duckworth, 1990.

————. *Whose Justice? Which Rationality?* London: Duckworth, 1988.

MacKinnon, Donald. "'Substance' in Christology — A Crossbench View." In *Christ, Faith and History: Cambridge Studies in Christology,* edited by S. W. Sykes and J. P. Clayton. London: Cambridge University Press, 1972.

Malina, Bruce J. *The New Testament World: Insights from Cultural Anthropology.* London: SCM, 1983.

Marshall, Bruce D. "Christ and the Cultures." In *Cambridge Companion to Christian Doctrine,* edited by Colin E. Gunton. Cambridge: Cambridge University Press, 1997.

————, ed. *Theology and Dialogue: Essays in Conversation with George Lindbeck.* Notre Dame: University of Notre Dame Press, 1990.

Martin, Dale B. *The Corinthian Body.* New Haven: Yale University Press, 1995.

Martin, Raymond, and John Barresi. *Naturalization of the Soul: Self and Personal Identity in the Eighteenth Century.* London: Routledge, 2000.

McCabe, Herbert. *Law, Love and Language.* London: Sheed & Ward, 1979.

McFarland, Ian. "Christ, Spirit and Atonement." *International Journal of Systematic Theology* 3, no. 1 (2001): 83-93.

McLean, B. Hudson. "The Absence of an Atoning Sacrifice and Paul's Soteriology." *New Testament Studies* 38 (1992): 531-53.

————. *The Cursed Christ: Mediterranean Expulsion Rituals and Pauline Soteriology.* Sheffield: Sheffield Academic Press, 1996.

Milbank, John. "The End of Dialogue." In *Christian Uniqueness Reconsidered: The Myth of a Pluralistic Theology of Religions,* edited by Gavin D'Costa. New York: Orbis, 1990.

————. "Intensities." *Modern Theology* 15 (1999): 445-97.

————. "Sacred Triads: Augustine and the Indo-European Soul." *Modern Theology* 13 (1997): 451-74.

————. "Stories of Sacrifice." *Modern Theology* 12 (1996): 27-56.

————. "The Sublime in Kierkegaard." *Heythrop Journal* 37 (1996): 298-321.

————. *Theology and Social Theory: Beyond Secular Reason.* Oxford: Blackwell, 1990.

————. *The Word Made Strange: Theology, Language, Culture.* Oxford: Blackwell, 1997.

Milbank, John, Catherine Pickstock, Graham Ward, eds. *Radical Orthodoxy: A New Theology.* London: Routledge, 1999.

Milgrom, Jacob. "Impurity Is Miasma: A Response to Hyam Maccoby." *Journal of Biblical Literature* 119.4 (2000): 729-33.

————. *Leviticus.* Anchor Bible Commentaries. 3 volumes. New York: Doubleday, 1991.

Miller, Patrick D. *Israelite Religion and Biblical Theology.* Sheffield: Sheffield Academic Press, 2000.

Moberly, R. W. L. *The Bible, Theology and Faith: A Study of Abraham and Jesus.* Cambridge: Cambridge University Press, 2000.

―――. "Did the Serpent Get It Right?" *Journal of Theological Studies* NS 39, no. 1 (1988): 1-27.

―――. "Towards a Definition of the Shema." In *Theological Exegesis: Essays in Honor of Brevard S. Childs,* edited by Christopher Seitz and Kathryn Greene-McCreight. Grand Rapids: Eerdmans, 1999.

Moltmann, Jürgen. *The Crucified God: The Cross of Christ as the Foundation and Criticism of Christian Theology.* London: SCM, 1974.

Moxnes, Halvor. *Constructing Early Christian Families: Family as Social Reality and Metaphor.* London: Routledge, 1997.

Murphy, Roland E. "Old Testament/Tanakh — Canon and Interpretation." In *Hebrew Bible or Old Testament?* edited by Roger Brooks and John J. Collins. Notre Dame: Notre Dame University Press, 1990.

Murphy, W. Tim. *The Oldest Social Science? Configurations of Law and Modernity.* Oxford: Clarendon, 1997.

Murray, Robert. *The Cosmic Covenant: Biblical Themes of Justice, Peace and the Integrity of Creation.* London: Sheed & Ward, 1992.

Nadler, Steven. *Spinoza: A Life.* Cambridge: Cambridge University Press, 1999.

Neill, Stephen C., and N. T. Wright. *The Interpretation of the New Testament, 1861-1986.* Cambridge: Cambridge University Press, 1988.

Neusner, Jacob. "Judaism after the Destruction of the Temple." In *Israelite and Judaean History,* edited by John H. Hayes and J. Maxwell Miller. London: SCM, 1977.

―――. "Judaism and Christianity in the First Century: How Shall We Perceive Their Relationship?" In *Essays on Jewish and Christian Literature and History,* edited by Philip R. Davies and Richard T. White. Sheffield: JSOT Press, 1990.

―――. *The Transformation of Judaism: From Philosophy to Religion.* Urbana: University of Illinois Press, 1992.

Neusner, Jacob, and Bruce D. Chilton. *Judaism in the New Testament.* London: Routledge, 1995.

Newman, Carey C. *Jesus and the Restoration of Israel: A Critical Appreciation of N. T. Wright's 'Jesus and the Victory of God.'* Carlisle: Paternoster, 1999.

Nussbaum, Martha C. *The Fragility of Goodness.* Cambridge: Cambridge University Press, 1986.

―――. *The Therapy of Desire: Theory and Practice in Hellenistic Ethics.* Princeton: Princeton University Press, 1994.

Ochs, Peter. "Rabbinic Pragmatism." In *Theology and Dialogue: Essays in Conversation with George Lindbeck,* edited by Bruce D. Marshall. Notre Dame: University of Notre Dame Press, 1990.

O'Donovan, Oliver. *The Desire of the Nations: Rediscovering the Roots of Political Theology.* Cambridge: Cambridge University Press, 1996.

O'Donovan, Oliver, and Joan Lockwood O'Donovan. *From Irenaeus to Grotius: A Sourcebook in Christian Political Thought.* Grand Rapids: Eerdmans, 1999.

Olafson, Frederick A. *What Is a Human Being? A Heideggerian View.* Cambridge: Cambridge University Press, 1995.

Olson, Alan M. *Hegel and the Spirit: Philosophy and Pneumatology.* Princeton: Princeton University Press, 1992.

Onians, R. B. *The Origins of European Thought about the Body, the Mind, the Soul, the World, Time and Fate.* Cambridge: Cambridge University Press, 1951.

Osler, Margaret J. *Atoms, Pneuma, and Tranquility: Epicurean and Stoic Themes in European Thought.* Cambridge: Cambridge University Press, 1991.

Padel, Ruth. *In and Out of the Mind: Greek Images of the Tragic Self.* Princeton: Princeton University Press, 1992.

Pannenberg, Wolfhart. *Anthropology in Theological Perspective.* Edinburgh: T&T Clark, 1985.

————. *Jesus — God and Man.* London: SCM, 1968.

————. *Metaphysics and the Idea of God.* Edinburgh: T&T Clark, 1990.

————. *Systematic Theology.* 3 volumes. Edinburgh: T&T Clark, 1991-94.

Park, David. *The Fire within the Eye: A Historical Essay on the Nature and Meaning of Light.* Princeton: Princeton University Press, 1997.

Patterson, Sue. *Realist Christian Theology in a Postmodern Age.* Cambridge: Cambridge University Press, 1999.

Pelikan, Jaroslav. *Christianity and Classical Culture: The Metamorphosis of Natural Theology in the Christian Encounter with Hellenism.* New Haven: Yale University Press, 1993.

Perdue, Leo G. *The Collapse of History: Reconstructing Old Testament Theology.* Minneapolis: Fortress Press, 1994.

Perkins, R. L. *Kierkegaard's* Fear and Trembling: *Critical Appraisals.* Birmingham: Alabama University Press, 1981.

Person, Raymond F. "The Ancient Israelite Scribe as Performer." *Journal of Biblical Literature* 117, no. 4 (1998): 601-9.

Philo. *The Works of Philo.* Translated by C. D. Yonge. Peabody, MA: Hendrickson, 1993.

Pickstock, Catherine. *After Writing: On the Liturgical Consummation of Philosophy.* Oxford: Blackwell, 1998.

————. "Music: Soul, City and Cosmos after Augustine." In *Radical Orthodoxy: A New Theology,* edited by John Milbank, Catherine Pickstock, Graham Ward. London: Routledge, 1999.

Plato. *Complete Works.* Edited by John M. Cooper. Indianapolis: Hackett, 1997.

Polanyi, Michael. *Personal Knowledge: Towards a Post-Critical Philosophy.* London: Routledge and Kegan Paul, 1958.

Popkin, Richard H. *The History of Scepticism from Erasmus to Spinoza.* Berkeley and Los Angeles: University of California Press, 1979.

Preuss, Horst Dietrich. *Old Testament Theology.* 2 volumes. Edinburgh: T&T Clark, 1995-96.

Rad, Gerhard von. *Genesis.* London: SCM, 1961.

———. *Old Testament Theology.* London: SCM, 1975.

Reiser, Marius. *Jesus and Judgement: The Eschatological Proclamation in Its Jewish Context.* Minneapolis: Fortress Press, 1997.

Riesner, Rainer. "Jesus as Preacher and Teacher." In *Jesus and the Oral Gospel Tradition,* edited by Henry Wansbrough. Sheffield: JSOT Press, 1991.

Rist, John M. *The Mind of Aristotle: A Study in Philosophical Growth.* Toronto: University of Toronto Press, 1989.

Ritschl, Dietrich. *The Logic of Theology: A Brief Account of the Relationship between Basic Concepts in Theology.* London: SCM Press, 1986.

Rivers, Isabel. *Reason, Grace and Sentiment: A Study of the Language of Religion and Ethics in England, 1660-1780.* Volume 2: *Shaftesbury to Hume.* Cambridge: Cambridge University Press, 2000.

Rogers, Eugene F., Jr. "Supplementing Barth on Jews and Gender." *Modern Theology* 14 (1998).

Rorty, Richard. *Philosophy and the Mirror of Nature.* Princeton: Princeton University Press, 1979.

Rorty, Richard, J. B. Schneewind, and Quentin Skinner, eds. *Philosophy in History: Essays on the Historiography of Philosophy.* Cambridge: Cambridge University Press, 1984.

Rose, Gillian. *The Broken Middle: Out of Our Ancient Society.* Oxford: Blackwell, 1992.

———. *Dialectic of Nihilism: Post-Structuralism and Law.* Oxford: Blackwell, 1984.

———. *Hegel Contra Sociology.* London: Athlone, 1981.

———. *Judaism and Modernity: Philosophical Essays.* Oxford: Blackwell, 1993.

———. *Mourning Becomes the Law: Philosophy and Representation.* Cambridge: Cambridge University Press, 1996.

Rousselle, Aline. *Porneia: On Desire and the Body in Antiquity.* Oxford: Blackwell, 1988.

Rowe, Christopher, and Malcolm Schofield. *The Cambridge History of Greek and Roman Political Thought.* Cambridge: Cambridge University Press, 2000.

Rowland, Christopher. *Open Heaven: A Study of Apocalyptic in Judaism and Early Christianity.* London: SPCK, 1982.

Samuelson, Norbert. "The Death and Revival of Jewish Philosophy." *Journal of the American Academy of Religion* 70, no. 1 (2002).

Sanders, E. P. *Judaism: Practice and Belief, 63 BCE–66 CE.* London: SCM, 1992.

———. *Paul and Palestinian Judaism: A Comparison of Patterns of Religion.* London: SCM, 1977.

Sanders, J. "Hebrew Bible or Old Testament?" in *Hebrew Bible or Old Testament?* edited by Roger Brooks and John J. Collins. Notre Dame: Notre Dame University Press, 1990.

Sanders, James A. *Sacred Story to Sacred Text: Canon as Paradigm.* Philadelphia: Fortress Press, 1987.

Sanders, John T. "Affordances: An Ecological Approach to First Philosophy." In *Perspectives on Embodiment: The Intersections of Nature and Culture,* edited by Gail Weiss and Honi F. Haber. London: Routledge, 1999.

Satterthwaite, Philip E., Richard S. Hess, and Gordon J. Wenham, eds. *The Lord's Anointed: Interpretation of Old Testament Messianic Texts.* Carlisle: Paternoster, 1995.

Scarry, Elaine. *The Body in Pain: The Making and Unmaking of the World.* Oxford: Oxford University Press, 1985.

Schechner, Richard, and Willa Appel. *By Means of Performance: Intercultural Studies of Theatre and Ritual.* Cambridge: Cambridge University Press, 1990.

Schmid, H. H. "Creation, Righteousness and Salvation." In *Creation in the Old Testament,* edited by Bernhard W. Anderson. Philadelphia: Fortress, 1984.

Schmitt, Charles B., gen. ed. *The Cambridge History of Renaissance Philosophy.* Cambridge: Cambridge University Press, 1988.

Schneewind, Jerome B. "The Divine Corporation and the History of Ethics." In *Philosophy in History: Essays on the Historiography of Philosophy,* edited by Richard Rorty, J. B. Schneewind, and Quentin Skinner. Cambridge: Cambridge University Press, 1984.

————. *The Invention of Autonomy: A History of Modern Moral Philosophy.* Cambridge: Cambridge University Press, 1998.

Scott, James M. *Adoption as Sons of God.* Tübingen: Mohr, 1992.

————. *Exile: Old Testament, Jewish and Christian Conceptions.* Leiden: Brill, 1997.

Searle, John R. *Expression and Meaning: Studies in the Theory of Speech Acts.* Cambridge: Cambridge University Press, 1979.

Segal, Alan F. "He who did not spare his own son. . . ." In *From Jesus to Paul,* edited by J. C. Hurd. Waterloo, Ont.: Wilfrid Laurier University Press, 1984.

————. "Paul's Thinking about Resurrection in Its Jewish Context." *New Testament Studies* 44 (1998): 400-419.

————. *Paul the Convert: The Apostolate and Apostasy of Saul the Pharisee.* New Haven: Yale University Press, 1990.

Seitz, Christopher R. "Christological Interpretation of Texts and Trinitarian Claims to Truth: An Engagement with Francis Watson's *Text and Truth.*" *Scottish Journal of Theology* 52 (1999): 209-26.

————. *Figured Out: Typology and Providence in Christian Scripture.* Louisville: Westminster John Knox, 2001.

————. *Word without End: The Old Testament as Abiding Theological Witness.* Grand Rapids: Eerdmans, 1998.

Seitz, Christopher R., and Kathryn Greene-McCreight, eds. *Theological Exegesis: Essays in Honor of Brevard S. Childs.* Grand Rapids: Eerdmans, 1999.

Seneca. *Moral and Political Essays.* Edited by John M. Cooper and J. F. Procopé. Cambridge: Cambridge University Press, 1995.

Seung, T. K. *Kant's Platonic Revolution in Moral and Political Philosophy.* Baltimore: Johns Hopkins University Press, 1994.

Shore, Bradd. *Culture in Mind: Cognition, Culture and the Problem of Meaning.* New York: Oxford University Press, 1996.

Shuger, Deborah K. *The Renaissance Bible: Scholarship, Sacrifice and Subjectivity.* Berkeley: University of California Press, 1994.

Skinner, Quentin. *The Foundations of Modern Political Thought.* Cambridge: Cambridge University Press, 1978.

———. *The Return of Grand Theory in the Human Sciences.* Cambridge: Cambridge University Press, 1985.

Smart, Ninian, John Clayton, Patrick Sherry, and Steven T. Katz, eds. *Nineteenth Century Religious Thought in the West.* Cambridge: Cambridge University Press, 1985.

Smith, Christopher P. *The Hermeneutics of Original Argument: Demonstration, Dialectic, Rhetoric.* Evanston: Northwestern University Press, 1998.

Sorabji, Richard. *Emotion and Peace of Mind: From Stoic Agitation to Christian Temptation.* Oxford: Oxford University Press, 2000.

Soulen, Kendall. *The God of Israel and Christian Theology.* Minneapolis: Fortress Press, 1996.

———. "Karl Barth and the Future of the God of Israel." *Pro Ecclesia* 6, no. 4 (1997): 413-28.

———. "YHWH the Triune God." *Modern Theology* 15 (1999): 25-54.

Southern, Richard W. *Saint Anselm: A Portrait in a Landscape.* Cambridge: Cambridge University Press, 1990.

Spencer, Paul. *Society and the Dance: The Social Anthropology of Process and Performance.* Cambridge: Cambridge University Press, 1985.

Stern, David. "Practices, Practical Holism, and Background Practices." In *Heidegger, Coping, and Cognitive Science: Essays in Honor of Hubert L. Dreyfus,* volume 2, edited by Mark Wrathall and Jeff Malpas. Cambridge, MA: MIT Press, 2000.

Stock, Brian. *Augustine the Reader: Meditation, Self-Knowledge and the Ethics of Interpretation.* Cambridge, MA: Harvard University Press, 1996.

Stowers, Stanley K. *Rereading of Romans: Justice, Jews, and Gentiles.* New Haven: Yale University Press, 1994.

Strauss, Leo. *Philosophy and Law: Essays Towards Understanding Maimonides and His Predecessors.* Philadelphia: The Jewish Publication Society, 1987.

———. *Spinoza's Critique of Religion.* Chicago: University of Chicago Press, 1997.

Strenski, Ivan. "Between Theories and Speciality: Sacrifice in the 90's." *Religious Studies Review* 22 (1996): 10-20.

———. *Durkheim and the Jews of France.* Chicago: University of Chicago Press, 1997.

————. "Reading Sacrifice: Politics, Theology and History in Hubert and Mauss' 'Sacrifice.'" In *Religion in Relation*. London: Macmillan, 1993.

Stuckenbruck, Loren T. "Johann Philipp Gabler and the Delineation of Biblical Theology." *Scottish Journal of Theology* 52 (1999): 139-57.

Stuhlmacher, Peter. *Biblische Theologie des Neuen Testaments*. 2 volumes. Göttingen: Vandenhoeck & Ruprecht, 1992-99.

Sutton, John. *Philosophy and Memory Traces: Descartes to Connectionism*. Cambridge: Cambridge University Press, 1998.

Sykes, Stephen W. *Sacrifice and Redemption: Durham Essays in Theology*. Cambridge: Cambridge University Press, 1991.

Tambiah, Stanley J. *Culture, Thought and Social Action: An Anthropological Perspective*. Cambridge, MA: Harvard University Press, 1985.

————. *Magic, Science, Religion, and the Scope of Rationality*. Cambridge: Cambridge University Press, 1990.

Taylor, Charles. *Human Agency and Language*. Cambridge: Cambridge University Press, 1985.

————. *Sources of the Self: The Making of Modern Identity*. Cambridge: Cambridge University Press, 1989.

————. "What Is Wrong with Foundationalism? Knowledge, Agency and World." In *Heidegger, Coping, and Cognitive Science: Essays in Honor of Hubert L. Dreyfus*, volume 2, edited by Mark Wrathall and Jeff Malpas. Cambridge, MA: MIT Press, 2000.

Thiselton, Anthony C. *Interpreting God and the Postmodern Self on Meaning, Manipulation and Promise*. Edinburgh: T&T Clark, 1995.

Thomson, Jeremy H. "The Conflict-Resolving Church: Community and Authority in the Prophetic Ecclesiology of John Howard Yoder." Ph.D. thesis, London University, 2000.

Torrance, Alan J. *Persons in Communion: Trinitarian Description and Human Participation*. Edinburgh: T&T Clark, 1996.

Torrance, Thomas F. "Karl Barth and the Latin Heresy." *Scottish Journal of Theology* 39 (1986).

————. *Space, Time, and Incarnation*. Edinburgh: T&T Clark, 1969.

Tully, James. *An Approach to Political Philosophy: Locke in Contexts*. Cambridge: Cambridge University Press, 1993.

Turner, Victor. *Dramas, Fields and Metaphors: Symbolic Action in Human Society*. Ithaca, NY: Cornell University Press, 1974.

Vanhoozer, Kevin. *Is There a Meaning in This Text? The Bible, the Reader and the Morality of Literary Knowledge*. Leicester: Apollos, 1998.

Varela, Francisco J., Evan Thompson, and Eleanor Rosch. *The Embodied Mind: Cognitive Science and Human Experience*. Cambridge, MA: MIT Press, 1991.

Vaux, Roland de. *Ancient Israel: Its Life and Institutions*. London: Darton, Longman & Todd, 1961.

Wallach, John R. *The Platonic Political Art: A Study of Critical Reason and Democracy*. University Park: Pennsylvania State University Press, 2001.

Wannenwetsch, Bernd. "The Political Worship of the Church: A Critical and Empowering Practice." *Modern Theology* 12 (1996): 269-99.

Watson, Francis. *Text and Truth: Redefining Biblical Theology*. Edinburgh: T&T Clark, 1997.

———. *Text, Church and World: Biblical Interpretation in Theological Perspective*. Edinburgh: T&T Clark, 1994.

Weber, Max. *The Protestant Ethic and the Spirit of Capitalism*. Translated by Talcott Parsons. New York: Scribner, 1958.

Webster, John. "The Dogmatic Location of the Canon." *Neue Zeitschrift für Systematische Theologie und Religionsphilosophie* 43 (2001): 17-43.

———. "Hermeneutics in Modern Theology." *Scottish Journal of Theology* 51 (1998): 307-41.

Weinandy, Thomas G., OFM, Cap. *Does God Suffer?* Edinburgh: T&T Clark, 2000.

———. *The Father's Spirit of Sonship*. Edinburgh: T&T Clark, 1995.

Weiss, Gail, and Honi F. Haber. *Perspectives on Embodiment: The Intersections of Nature and Culture*. London: Routledge, 1999.

Welker, Michael. *God the Spirit*. Minneapolis: Fortress Press, 1994.

Whitekettle, R. "Leviticus 15.18 Reconsidered: Chiasm, Spatial Structure and the Body." *Journal for the Study of the Old Testament* 49 (1991): 131-45.

Whitsett, Christopher. "Son of God, Seed of David: Paul's Messianic Exegesis in Romans [1]:3-4." *Journal of Biblical Literature* 119, no. 4 (2000): 661-81.

Williams, Robert R. *Hegel's Ethics of Recognition*. Berkeley: University of California Press, 1997.

Williams, Stephen N. *Revelation and Reconciliation: A Window on Modernity*. Cambridge: Cambridge University Press, 1995.

Willis, Roy G. *Signifying Animals: Human Meaning in the Natural World*. London: Unwin Hyman, 1990.

Wrathall, Mark, and Jeff Malpas, eds. *Heidegger, Coping, and Cognitive Science: Essays in Honor of Hubert L. Dreyfus*, volume 2. Cambridge, MA: MIT Press, 2000.

Wright, N. T. *The Climax of the Covenant: Christ and the Law in Pauline Theology*. Edinburgh: T&T Clark, 1991.

———. "Gospel and Theology in Galatians." In *Gospel in Paul: Studies on Corinthians, Galatians and Romans for Richard N. Longenecker,* edited by L. Ann Jervis and Peter Richardson. Sheffield: Sheffield Academic Press, 1994.

———. *Jesus and the Victory of God*. London: SPCK, 1996.

———. *The New Testament and the People of God*. London: SPCK, 1992.

———. *The Resurrection of the Son of God*. London: SPCK, 2003.

Wyschogrod, Michael. *The Body of Faith: God in the People of Israel.* San Francisco: Harper & Row, 1989.

———. "A Jewish Perspective on the Incarnation." *Modern Theology* 12 (1996): 194-209.

———. "Sin and Atonement in Judaism." In *The Human Condition in the Jewish and Christian Traditions,* edited by Frederick E. Greenspahn. Hoboken, NJ: Ktav, 1986.

Yeago, David S. "Jesus of Nazareth and Cosmic Redemption: The Relevance of St. Maximus the Confessor." *Modern Theology* 12 (1996): 163-93.

Yoder, John Howard. *For the Nations: Essays Public and Evangelical.* Grand Rapids: Eerdmans, 1997.

———. *The Priestly Kingdom: Social Ethics as Gospel.* Notre Dame: Notre Dame University Press, 1984.

Young, Frances M. *The Art of Performance: Towards a Theology of Holy Scripture.* London: Darton, Longman & Todd, 1990.

———. *Biblical Exegesis and the Formation of Christian Culture.* Cambridge: Cambridge University Press, 1997.

———. *Sacrifice and the Death of Christ.* London: SPCK, 1975.

———. "Understanding Romans in the Light of 2 Corinthians." *Scottish Journal of Theology* 48 (1991).

Zammito, John H. *The Genesis of Kant's Critique of Judgement.* Chicago: University of Chicago Press, 1992.

Zizioulas, John D. *Being as Communion: Studies in Personhood and the Church.* London: Darton, Longman & Todd, 1985.

———. *Eucharist, Bishop, Church: The Unity of the Church in the Divine Eucharist and the Bishop during the First Three Centuries.* Brookline, MA: Holy Cross Orthodox Press, 2001.

———. "The Father as Cause: A Response to Alan Torrance." Paper given at King's College, London, 1998.

———. "Human Capacity and Incapacity: A Theological Exploration of Personhood." *Scottish Journal of Theology* 28 (1975).

———. "Preserving God's Creation: Three Lectures on Theology and Ecology." *King's Theological Review* 12 (1989): 1-5, 41-45; 13 (1990): 1-5.

———. "Towards an Eschatological Ontology." Paper given at King's College, London, 1999.

Index

Abraham, 77, 79n.34, 79n.36, 88-89, 111-15, 123, 140, 214

Adam, 13-16, 78, 108-10, 116-17, 139-41, 240, 258. *See also* Humanity

Affordance, 49, 183, 220. *See also* Habitus

Agency, 2, 4, 7, 16-17, 34, 36, 43, 53, 96, 122, 182, 212, 240

Analogy, 41, 55, 148-50, 192-93, 220

Animals, 44, 49, 122-23, 143-48, 155-57, 161-62, 218

Anselm, 18, 23-24, 121

Apocalyptic, 86, 100, 107, 129, 148, 159, 162, 166-68. *See also* Microcosm; Ritual; Temple; Vision

Aquinas, 44n.8, 190-91, 193

Aristotle, 9-10, 45-46, 178n.12, 183, 188n.31, 189, 232, 250

Articulation, 36-37, 41, 126, 139, 176n.7, 184, 201, 213, 221

Assembly, 27-28, 215-16, 244-47

Atonement, 61, 81-82, 120-23, 125-26, 130, 142-43, 145, 153, 155, 156, 158, 169, 171, 197, 236-37, 244

Audience, 28, 53-57, 89-90, 99, 107, 122, 146, 166. *See also* Assembly; Courtroom

Augustine, 14, 21, 32n.44, 40, 184, 195, 250-53

Baptism, 32, 68, 75, 120, 127, 133, 135-36, 159, 161-62, 169-70, 209

Barth, Karl, 64-66, 142

Bayer, Oswald, 180n.18, 207

Becoming, 4, 34, 149n.53, 166, 169

Being, 5-11, 13, 22-23, 183-84, 189, 193, 198, 202-3, 209, 217-20, 224-25, 230-32, 234-37, 238

Biblical studies, 67, 70, 74-75, 84, 90-91, 92, 95, 102-3, 140-41, 158, 160, 168-70, 179-81, 192, 211

Blood, 55, 78-79, 82, 119-20, 129-30, 143, 155, 160, 162, 196n.54, 246n.25

Bockmuehl, Markus, 94n.86, 99n.91, 99n.92, 99n.93

Body (bodiliness, embodiment), 12, 22, 32-33, 37, 41-46, 58-59, 141, 184-85, 201, 205, 216, 218, 220, 246

Brueggemann, Walter, 93-94, 103n.101

Burkert, Walter, 55n.39, 112n.129

Charry, Ellen, 187n.29, 191n.39

Childs, Brevard, 93, 115n.138

Chilton, Bruce, 98n.88, 104, 145n.45, 159n.89

Church, 1, 17, 27, 29, 32n.44, 51-52, 67, 106n.114, 175, 178-79, 182n.21, 194, 201n.63, 215, 246-48, 251, 254-55

Circumcision, 127-28, 135, 159-62

Commentary, 36-38, 99, 114, 177, 180, 183n.24, 185n.27, 186, 209, 212, 215, 216

Continuum, 22, 52, 184, 200-202, 204, 233

Conversation, 1, 21, 27-30, 41, 47, 52-54, 100, 105-7, 143, 177, 181, 188, 218, 248

Cosmos, cosmology, 97-98, 140-41, 149-51, 160-62, 166-68, 194, 201, 206, 225-28, 230, 235-37, 239, 243. *See also* Microcosm

Cost, 25, 125-26, 199

Courtroom, 19-20, 23-24, 55, 57, 142, 166, 174, 244, 247

Covenant, 54, 65, 68, 81, 86, 93, 148, 158, 164-65, 197

Creation, doctrine of, 38-39, 97-98, 102, 149-50, 162, 197-99, 204, 207, 223n.7, 231, 249

Cross (crucifixion), 15, 87, 128-37, 128-31, 140, 151n.61, 164n.100, 171, 216

Currency, 25, 83, 130. *See also* Cost; Economy; Mediation

Dalferth, Ingolf, 83, 120n.153

Death, 15, 117, 127-28, 134-35, 137, 154, 215

Douglas, Mary, 127n.4, 130n.10, 148n.50, 152, 157-58

Drama, 57-58, 100, 107, 218

Dualism, 11, 42, 161, 194, 201, 203-4, 218, 226-27, 231, 235

Dunn, James, 63, 78n.39, 109n.123

Economy, 2-3, 6-8, 20-23, 25-26, 30, 33-35, 37-38, 51-52, 78, 80, 83n.57, 97, 100, 121, 125, 130, 139, 198-99, 217, 221-23, 235-38. *See also* Continuum; Medium

Elect, election, 4, 17, 21, 61, 64-69, 87, 91, 94-96, 114-15, 118, 123-24, 141, 181, 208-9, 246

Enlightenment, 174, 181-84, 205, 232, 256. *See also* Immediacy; Vision

Eschaton, eschatology, 14-15, 17, 22, 34, 37-38, 51, 61, 77-78, 95-97, 103, 105, 113, 139, 162, 222, 229

Exegesis, 70-72, 99, 179-80, 212

Fall, 11-13, 109-10, 116-17, 126-27, 173, 188, 193-94

Farrow, Douglas, 67, 75n.33, 106-7, 238

Fire, 147-49, 158, 162-65, 166-68

Forgiveness, 24, 122, 197-98

Fowl, Stephen, 88, 90n.73, 90n.75

Freedom, 13-14, 16, 34, 36, 62, 97, 102, 110-11, 113, 174n.1, 174n.3, 186, 232, 236, 239, 241, 255

Funkenstein, Amos, 179n.15, 188n.31, 196

Gentiles, 35, 67-70, 75, 82, 85-87, 91, 93, 97-98, 101, 107, 114, 118-19, 122, 126-30, 132-33, 145, 157, 168, 195, 199, 208-9, 212

Gestrich, Christof, 109, 116n.139, 121n.156

Girard, René, 71, 83n.57, 199n.59, 201

God, 16-17, 27-34, 62-63, 68-70, 100, 106-7, 127, 197-99, 212, 229, 231, 242-44

Gunton, Colin E., 24, 130, 142-44

Habitus, 42-44, 221

Hafemann, Scott, 70, 133n.17

Harré, Rom, 47-48

Hays, Richard B., 78n.39, 84n.57, 89, 90n.75, 93n.84, 164-65

Hegel, G. W. F., 116n.139, 131n.11, 181n.19, 182n.20, 187n.30, 203n.67

Hengel, Martin, 105-6, 128n.7, 135n.22

Hermeneutics, 42, 55-57, 82, 84, 88-90, 107, 170-71, 199, 209, 211-12, 214, 218-19, 220n.3, 221-22, 239

History, 15, 21, 51, 61, 65-66, 88, 90-91, 96, 102, 106, 109, 116, 139, 173, 180n.18, 181, 184, 188-89, 193-95, 197, 206, 208-9, 222, 225, 233, 249. *See also* Supersession; Time

Holy Spirit, 29-31, 65-66, 105-7, 125, 139, 161-62, 168, 221-22, 245. *See also* Pneumatology

Holy, holiness, 142, 152-54, 158

Hospitality, 21, 23, 97-98, 156, 159. *See also* Creation, doctrine of

House, household, 39-40, 93, 97, 156, 210. *See also* Economy; Mediation; Medium

Humanity, 1-2, 4-5, 8-9, 12, 14, 19, 30-31, 51, 61, 73, 78, 97, 109, 116, 115-16, 122-23, 241

Hütter, Reinhard, 51-52, 175n.4, 247n.28

Individual, 4, 6-8, 19, 22, 53, 71, 75, 80-81, 84, 108-10, 115, 173, 201-2, 210, 230, 232, 234, 238, 240

Irenaeus, Saint, 13-14, 66, 106, 116-17

Israel, 21, 32, 38, 68, 87, 96-98, 126-27, 138, 140-47, 149-71, 186, 194-96, 199-200, 207-9, 212, 216, 218, 242. *See also* Jesus Christ; Jews; Judaism

Janowski, Bernd, 83, 121n.154, 121n.156

Jenson, Robert W., 21n.27, 31n.42, 51, 65-66, 182-83

Jerusalem (Zion), 87, 99, 118-19, 147, 149, 168

Jesus Christ, 28-32, 64-67, 71, 75, 86-88, 105-7, 127-31, 134-37, 139, 170-71, 214-16

Jews (Jewish), 21, 63-64, 70, 73, 85-86, 91-96, 156, 160, 250

Judaism, 63, 71, 85-86, 94, 160, 200n.60

Kant, Immanuel, 18, 19, 22, 25-26, 80, 109, 116, 179, 200n.60

Law, 24, 26n.40, 37, 55-56, 71, 89, 91, 99, 101, 110, 113, 119-21, 127, 147, 151n.61, 152, 155, 174-76, 179, 186, 194-99, 205, 207-9, 212-13, 216, 239, 248-53. *See also* Old Testament; Scripture; Torah

Leadership, 62, 134, 150, 174, 178, 185, 209, 219, 244, 246-48, 254n.42. *See also* Law

Learning, 35-43, 68, 75, 99, 122-23, 151, 184, 200, 250

Levenson, Jon, 91, 113-14, 127n.4, 149n.56, 149n.58, 179, 180n.17

Light, 148-49, 162-68. *See also* Fire; Vision

Liturgy, 98, 99-102, 158-59, 212, 215, 218

Loughlin, Gerard, 180n.18, 189-92, 256n.44

Maccoby, Hyam, 155-56

MacIntyre, Alasdair, 185n.27, 188

Man. *See* Adam; Humanity

McCabe, Herbert, 44-46

Mediation, 21, 25, 65n.7, 96, 160, 170, 173, 184-85, 188, 191-94, 206, 214, 224, 227, 236, 249. *See also* Medium

Medium, 23, 25, 28, 30, 33, 56, 67-68, 82, 122-25, 130, 132n.14, 135, 144-45, 149, 159, 181, 186, 194, 197-98, 200, 244n.21. *See also* Mediation

Metaphor, 49-50, 61, 143, 170, 206, 209. *See also* Hermeneutics

Metaphysics, 6, 23, 163, 169, 200, 203-6, 227, 234-35, 253

Microcosm, 115, 133, 149-50, 158, 201, 218, 222

Milbank, John, 113n.130, 178n.12, 190-92, 198n.58, 199n.59, 206, 247n.28

Milgrom, Jacob, 77n.37, 119, 120n.150

Moberly, R. W. L., 111n.125, 115n.138, 118n.145, 118n.146

Modernity, 2-3, 176, 181-83, 185-86, 189, 203, 206, 218, 224-29, 236-37, 248, 254-57

Murder, 111-12, 115, 118-19, 126-27, 155

Narrative, 89, 100, 209. *See also* Story

Neusner, Jacob, 63n.3, 98n.89, 104, 154n.72, 159n.88

Nussbaum, Martha, 45-46, 174n.1, 230n.10

O'Donovan, Oliver, 97n.87, 129n.8, 132n.15, 175n.4, 176, 197n.56, 239n.16, 243n.17, 246n.24, 247n.29, 254n.42

Old Testament, 32, 70, 141, 214. *See also* Law

Ontology, 10-11, 22, 26, 50, 200, 205, 227-29

Paideia, 19, 35, 40, 84, 122, 174, 187, 194, 197, 199, 217, 250, 253. *See also* Learning

Pannenberg, Wolfhart, 22, 44n.9, 49n.28, 51, 116n.139, 135n.22, 137n.26

Paul, the Apostle, 64n.4, 70-71, 76n.36, 85-86, 95, 105, 128, 132, 133n.17, 160-61, 166

Performance, 36-38, 42, 56-57, 99, 101-2, 123, 126, 133, 152n.63, 169-71, 175-77, 182, 184, 186-87, 192, 205, 215, 221, 230-31, 251-54

Person, 5-11, 22, 34, 46, 48, 53, 62, 80, 84, 90, 201, 215, 223n.7

Place, 48, 50-52, 84-85, 122, 148n.50, 219

Plato, 11, 225-28, 234, 247n.28, 249, 253, 256

Plurality, 34, 49, 54-56, 94, 182, 215, 218, 227, 237

Pneumatology, 32, 69, 72n.27, 125, 141, 160-62, 203-4, 231, 236, 245. *See also* Holy Spirit

Practical knowledge, 58, 117, 181, 183, 188, 192, 225-40, 249-50

Practices, 48-49, 114, 119, 123, 169, 181, 189, 191-92, 194, 205, 213, 222, 239, 248-49, 251

Priest, priesthood, 15-18, 100, 110, 120, 145, 150-51, 155-56, 178n.13, 237

Reconciliation, 84, 122, 136, 142, 237

Redemption, 25, 65-66, 83n.57, 130, 157. *See also* Economy

Religion, 176-79, 202, 206, 231-33, 236, 254-57

Representation, 22-23, 80-84, 122. *See also* Atonement; Substitution

Resurrection, 131-32, 136-39, 151, 161-62, 215-16

Ritual, 38, 55, 99-101, 119, 152, 155, 184n.25

Rogers, Eugene, 64-65, 72n.27

Rose, Gillian, 176n.7, 207n.75, 207n.76, 244n.20

Rules, 38, 42, 48n.22, 56, 215-17, 240. *See also* Law

Sabbath, 96, 103-7, 139, 147, 150, 250

Sacrifice, 56, 79-84, 98, 108, 111-15, 118-24, 142-48, 195, 199, 210

Sanctification, 4, 142, 212, 246

Sanders, E. P., 80-81, 84

Scott, James, 75, 89n.72

Scripture, 32, 38, 61, 63, 70, 72, 88-95, 99-100, 159, 168-69, 180-81, 186, 190, 192, 207-9, 211-16, 219-22, 248-49

Secularization, 109-10, 116, 170, 173, 177-78, 189, 193, 206, 227, 233, 237, 254, 257

Segal, Alan, 73-74

Seitz, Christopher, 86n.60, 89n.69, 92n.82, 93n.83, 221n.5

Servant, 62, 74-75, 88, 97, 100, 108, 123, 133, 137-38, 244, 245n.23

Sin, 12, 15, 19, 37-38, 126-27, 153, 199, 202, 212, 240

Soulen, Kendall, 65-66

State, 172-75, 177-79, 185, 188, 248

Story, 29, 54, 88-90, 100, 209, 229, 233

Substitution, 19, 80-84, 121-23, 197

Suffering, 71, 74, 95, 130, 132-33, 140, 161, 202, 254. *See also* Cross

Supersession, 62, 63n.1, 65-66, 73, 93-95, 109, 165. *See also* History; Time

Symbol, 55, 84, 89, 143. *See also* Hermeneutics

Temple, 99, 119, 147-49, 155-58, 167-68, 218. *See also* House, household

Time, 18, 20-22, 52-53, 96, 138-39, 142, 147, 171, 173, 181, 193, 196-97, 202-3, 206-7, 215-16, 218, 220-21, 228, 238-39, 245

Torah, 68, 85, 92, 99n.92, 102, 159. *See also* Law; Old Testament
Torrance, T. F., 135n.23
Trinity (the doctrine of), 16, 27-30, 34, 62-66, 79, 96, 215, 257

Vision, 162-67, 182-84, 225, 228

Wannenwetsch, Bernd, 51-52, 178n.13, 201n.63, 247n.28
Watson, Francis, 63, 71n.26, 93n.83, 219n.2

Webster, John, 90n.76, 219n.2
Witness, 19, 32, 55, 69, 70, 92-93, 96-97, 100, 118, 127, 139-45, 151, 159, 180, 193, 195, 211, 214-15, 221, 252, 254
Worship, 99-101, 107. *See also* Liturgy
Wright, N. T., 85-87, 90n.74, 90n.75, 163
Wyschogrod, Michael, 72-73

Zizioulas, John, 8-17, 20, 131n.12, 120n.153